THE
RED BARON
COMBAT WING

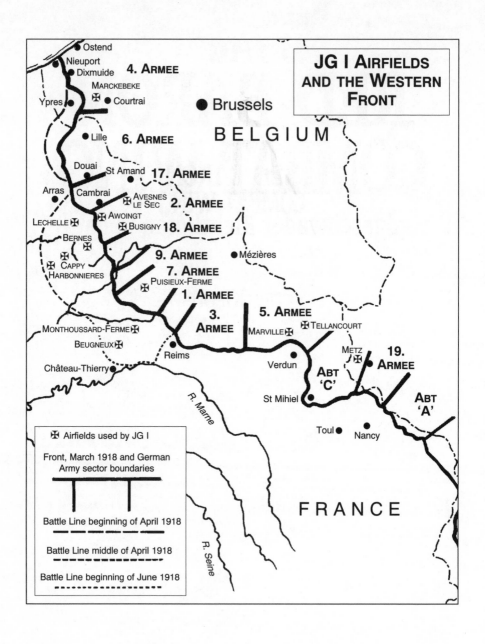

JG I AIRFIELDS AND THE WESTERN FRONT

Ostend
Nieuport
Dixmuide
4. ARMEE
MARCKEBEKE
Ypres ✠ Courtrai
Brussels
BELGIUM
Lille
6. ARMEE
Douai
St Amand 17. ARMEE
Arras Cambrai
AVESNES
LE SEC ✠ 2. ARMEE
LECHELLE ✠ ✠ AWOINGT
BERNES ✠ BUSIGNY 18. ARMEE
✠
CAPPY 9. ARMEE Mézières
✠ HARBONNIERES 7. ARMEE
✠ PUISIEUX-FERME
1. ARMEE
3. 5. ARMEE
MONTHOUSSARD-FERME ✠ ARMEE
MARVILLE ✠ TELLANCOURT
BEUGNEUX ✠
Reims METZ ✠ 19.
ARMEE
Château-Thierry Verdun ABT
'C' ABT
St Mihiel 'A'
Toul Nancy
R. Marne

FRANCE

R. Seine

✠ Airfields used by JG I

Front, March 1918 and German
Army sector boundaries

Battle Line beginning of April 1918

Battle Line middle of April 1918

Battle Line beginning of June 1918

THE
RED BARON
COMBAT WING

Jagdgeschwader Richthofen in Battle

Peter Kilduff

ARMS AND
ARMOUR

Arms and Armour Press
A Cassell Imprint
Wellington House, 125 Strand, London WC2R 0BB

Distributed in the USA by Sterling Publishing Co. Inc.,
387 Park Avenue South, New York, NY 10016-8810.

British Library Cataloguing-in-Publication Data:
a catalogue record for this book is available from the
British Library

ISBN 1-85409-266-9

Designed and edited by DAG Publications Ltd.
Designed by David Gibbons; edited by Michael Boxall;
cartography by A. A. Evans; printed and bound
in Great Britain.

Contents

This book is dedicated to
the memory of A. Edward Ferko (1927–1996),
a leading researcher and scholar in German aviation
history of the First World War, a good friend,
and a generous helper.

Introduction

' ... the one pure unsullied good [that] men can hope to attain, is heroism ...
The power of good is shown not by triumphantly conquering evil, but by
continuing to resist ... A heroic death, like a martyr's death, is not a defeat,
but a triumph ...'[1]

THIS OBSERVATION BY A NOTED CLASSICIST HELPS TO CLARIFY THE CULTURAL
values that reinforced the attitudes and actions of German airmen in the First
World War. They had many outstanding and inspirational leaders and some of
the best aircraft available, but for the most part they were struggling against
great odds. Some perverse element in their nature kept these young air warriors
at their grim task, knowing that they faced death in every flight. Their watch-
word was like that of a tragic figure from Virgil: 'Quem metui, moritura' (What
had I to fear, since I was to die anyway?)[2] In seeming to rise above the fear of
death, and almost to embrace it, early German combat airmen became modern
incarnations of the legendary Teutonic heroes.

Certainly this was the case with regard to the best-known German fighter
pilot of the period, Manfred Freiherr (Baron) von Richthofen, who lived and died
in the classic heroic tradition. Renowned as 'the Red Baron', he shot down 80
enemy aircraft, a feat unmatched by any other pilot in the First World War, and
his reputation for outstanding combat leadership earned him medals and honour
as a national hero during his lifetime. He was remembered in death when the
fighter air wing he commanded – Jagdgeschwader I – was named after him. Since
then his fame has lived on; the Richthofen-Geschwader designation has remained
a constant and proud element of German military aviation up to the present time.

Jagdgeschwader I was established on 26 June 1917 as the first élite formation of fighter units specifically charged by Air Chief of Staff Hermann von der
Lieth-Thomsen with 'securing air superiority in critically important combat
sectors'.[3] JG I's success was built on aerial combat techniques and strategies
developed by the early fighter aces Max Immelmann and Oswald Boelcke. Those
techniques were refined by Boelcke's most famous pupil, Manfred von
Richthofen, the first commander of JG I.

Although the Second Reich forged by Otto von Bismarck and the Hohenzollern monarchy had existed only since 1 January 1871, the German people

7

had long sought unity through a shared base of mythology and culture. From this common link, literature and music were used to support national goals as Imperial Germany prepared for a major war against what were to prove daunting odds.

Within this context Manfred von Richthofen, his comrades and successors became 20th-century counterparts of mythic Teutonic figures. Their successes were portrayed in the popular German press as acts of epic bravery in the new battlefield of the air. The First World War was hardly a month old when a national news service reported the third German combat flight over Paris and its effect on the populace and the government:

'After a German airman bombarded the electrical power plant early yesterday, in the evening another pilot flew over the city and dropped bombs on the rue de Hanovre, rue d'Amsterdam, the St-Lazare railway station, the Boulevard Montmartre and elsewhere. Five persons were killed. The pilot also dropped a letter demanding surrender, as the Germans were just outside Paris. The [French] War Minister ordered development of a squadron of armoured, machine-gun-equipped aeroplanes to hunt down the German airmen ...'[4]

The courage and daring of German airmen were, by implication, fused to a cultural root that ran from the lore of the 13th-century *Nibelungenlied* to the works of Richard Wagner which drew on the same mythology in powerful music and dramatic staging.

By the time of Manfred von Richthofen's birth, on 2 May 1892, Wagner's four-opera cycle *The Ring of the Nibelungen* had become entrenched in contemporary German culture. As German writer-cum-national-conscience Thomas Mann observed: 'The works of Wagner were installed as a national concern, as an official apanage of the [Hohenzollern] empire.'[5]

The composer died in 1883, but his works and their appeal to the national spirit inspired the generation of Germans which prepared the young men who were to fight in the First World War. When the imagery of German mythology was used as a lens to clarify international politics, the message was not lost on those military men. In 1908 the last Hohenzollern emperor (Kaiser), Wilhelm II, supported the Austro–Hungarian annexation of Bosnia and Herzegovina by 'pledging a "Nibelungen oath of fidelity" to Austria and declaring that he stood behind his ally "in shining armour"'.[6] The mythic allusion was used again at the beginning of the First World War, when 'the "troth of the Nibelungs" had to be honoured and Austria saved, if only because Germany had no other ally'.[7]

So a young man such as Manfred von Richthofen, commissioned into an Uhlan regiment, could see himself as a lance-armed knight on horseback, bound for daring missions. When war broke out in August 1914, however, he served without distinction in Russia and then headed westwards, still filled with visions of glory. Within a short time the horse-soldiers' mobility in France was restricted by seemingly endless miles of trenches that demarcated the Western Front from the North Sea to the Swiss border.

After ten months of inglorious service, in May 1915 the 23-year-old cavalry officer realised his dream of doing more for his country when he was permitted to transfer to the German air service (*Fliegertruppe*). Freed from the trenches, Richthofen became a warrior of the air. Ahead of him lay fulfilment in the heroic values espoused in the views of Wagner's one-time disciple Friedrich Nietzsche, which included: ' ... to die is best; the next best, however, is to die in battle, and sacrifice a great soul'.[8]

Acceptance of that philosophy is seen in Richthofen's account of the last aerial combat of a close friend and fellow nobleman, Count Erich von Holck, over Verdun. Like Richthofen, Holck had been a cavalry officer,[9] accustomed to exposing himself to danger. In the same spirit, on 1 May 1916, Richthofen bucked a headwind to try to help Holck, only to witness a 'whole swarm of Frenchmen ... on him. With a bullet through his head, [Holck] fell from an altitude of 3,000 metres – a beautiful death.'[10]

Thirteen months later a tubercular and self-destructive flying comrade, Georg Zeumer, who had been in the infantry,[11] was killed aged 27 in an air fight against an overwhelming British force that he could have avoided. As in the case of Holck, Richthofen again saw in Zeumer's fatal clash fulfilment worthy of a Germanic hero: 'Perhaps it was best for him, for he knew the end of his life was just ahead of him ... It would have been terrible if he had been tormented to death slowly. So this was a beautiful hero's death.'[12]

In Richard Wagner's rendering of Germanic mythology, the gods used mortals as pawns and meddled in earthly affairs. There is a parallel in the relationship between Manfred von Richthofen (who, like the warrior Siegfried, seemed to tempt fate in search of a hero's death) and Kaiser Wilhelm II (who, like the god Wotan, held powers of life and death). Hence it was pure theatre when the monarch invited Richthofen to lunch on 2 May 1917 and asked an aide: 'Have I not forbidden him to fly?' as if to protect the air warrior as a national treasure, a living monument to heroism. It was left to the aide to explain for everyone's benefit: 'Majesty, in the interests of the whole situation, we cannot do that. We need Richthofen as an example and as a Wing Commander [*Geschwader-Kommandeur*], we need him as a combat pilot ...'[13]

Almost two months later Manfred von Richthofen was appointed to lead the four-squadron group that became Germany's first dedicated fighter wing. As a fighter pilot and combat leader, he remained an outstanding example of bravery and success until the late morning of Sunday, 21 April 1918. Then, with the last great German offensive losing momentum and victory less and less likely for the Central Powers, 'the Red Baron' led his men and machines into battle over the valley of the River Somme. Again like Siegfried, who was also on a final hunt, Richthofen let down his guard and was struck down from behind. Spared Siegfried's lingering death, Richthofen died instantly from a single shot through the heart. A favourable wind brought his blood-red Fokker Dr.I triplane to rest in a beet field within British lines.[14]

Having played his role in the German pageant of modern aerial combat, Manfred von Richthofen was elevated to the status of fallen hero – noble in deed, as well as by birth. While his adversaries prepared a funeral with the honours due a worthy foe, German Air Force (*Luftstreitkräfte*) Commanding General Ernst von Hoeppner issued a Nietzsche-like tribute to begin the process of enshrining Richthofen in the pantheon of Germanic heroes: 'We will not direct our gaze on what he could have been; rather, from what he was we will derive [a] living force, [a] force that stays alert in permanent memorial to his deeds.'[15]

Two weeks later members of Germany's royal family and military élite honoured Richthofen with a memorial service in Berlin. At an altar where other great national heroes had been eulogised and sent on the final journey, armed sentinels wearing black leather helmets and flying coats flanked a centrepiece composed of Richthofen's medals, crossed machine-guns and a broken propeller. It was a spectacle of which master showman Richard Wagner would have been proud – except that Brahms' funereal 'Ein deutsches Requiem' gave the ceremony a more traditional Christian feeling.[16]

The rest of the modern myth was played out during the remaining seven months of the war. Like Wotan's warriors, Richthofen's comrades eventually retired from the fields of battle with honour. Believing that they had not been defeated in the air, they inspired the next generation of combat airmen. Manfred von Richthofen's younger brother, Lothar, and his cousin, Wolfram, added lustre to the family name. Other members of Jagdgeschwader Richthofen – such as its last commander, Hermann Göring – gained combat and leadership experience to carry into the next world war.

The story of Richthofen's successors of the next generation is a worthy topic for another book. This volume is devoted to the development of German fighter aviation and the deployment of the first Jagdgeschwader. Like their leader, Manfred von Richthofen, the pilots of JG I had escaped from the frustration and despair of the trenches to seek a mythical glory in the sky. Their stories and deeds are the heart of this book, and appendices at the end of the volume are offered to add the perspective of relevant organisational and operational developments. For the sake of consistency, all time references have been converted to military time within the German lines unless otherwise noted. And to demonstrate the broad representation of army units that made up the German Air Force, regimental affiliations are end-noted for many of the airmen mentioned in the text.

*   *   *

This book derives from three previous works by the author: *The Red Baron* (1969), a translation of the 1933 edition of Manfred von Richthofen's memoirs; *Germany's First Air Force* (1991), an overview of early German military air operations; and *Richthofen – Beyond the Legend of the Red Baron* (1993), a biography of the legendary air fighter. Research for these works and information gathered since they were published inspired the creation of this work, to examine the combat organisation that shaped Manfred von Richthofen and was influenced by him.

Nations have always sacrificed the best of their young men in the crucible of war. In preparing this book, this writer could not resist the temptation to point out whenever possible – if even to excess – the full names and ages of air warriors who fought during the era of the 'the Red Baron'. It is too late to sermonise on the subject, but the young ages of combatants and casualties, as well as their individual identifications, are aspects of warfare that need to be restated and considered if mankind is to have any hope of ending the self-destruction of its youth and developing other more rational and humane forms of conflict resolution.

Over and above all the archival material, books and other sources of information, the author was fortunate to know and enjoy the friendship of a number of surviving First World War aviation personnel from both sides of the lines. The experiences and insights they shared have put a human face on what could be a numbing recitation of terrible events. Gone now, but deserving of remembrance are: Wing Commander Ronald Adam, OBE; Gottfried Freiherr von Banfield; Oscar Bechtle; Douglas Campbell; Major a.D. Carl Degelow; Major Carl A. Dixon; Generalingenieur der Luftwaffe a.D. Wolfram Eisenlohr; Generaloberst a.D. Alfred Keller; Dipl.-Ing John Knauer; Major Clayton Knight, OBE; Dr.-Ing. Oskar Kuppinger; Major Cecil Montgomery-Moore, DFC; Oberstleutnant der Reserve a.D. Hanns-Gerd Rabe; and Oberst a.D. Paul Strähle.

Other writers, researchers and friends who have been helpful in the creation of this book include: F. W. Bailey; Dr. Friedrich R. Bechtle; the late Dr. Gustav Bock; Oberstleutnant Dipl.-Ing. Uwe Peter Böhm; Charles H. Donald and the unique material from his extensive archives; the late A. E. Ferko with his keen understanding of German aviation history; Dr. Achim Fuchs; Peter M. Grosz with his encyclopaedic knowledge of German aircraft; Volker Harms-Ziegler; Georg Hermann; Uwe Houdelet; Dr. Volker Koos; Dr. Zdzislaw Kremens; Klaus Littwin; the late Russell Manning; Otto Michaelis; Dr.-Ing. Niedermeyer; the late Heinz J. Nowarra; Neal W. O'Connor and his extensive studies of German military honours and awards; Prof.-Dr. Maria Passaro; Fritzcarl Prestien; Oberbürgermeister a.D. Prof.-Dr. Franz J. Rothenbiller; Michael Schmeelke; the Revd. Carl Heinrich A. Schmutzler; Roland Schneider; Noel C. Shirley; Thorbjørn (Tony) Svensen; Stewart K. Taylor with his vast knowledge of Canadian aviators; the late Erich Tornuss and his early study of German fighter pilots; Leo van de Pas and his research into the German nobility; Lothair Vanoverbeke and his extensive study of aviation history in Belgium; Greg VanWyngarden; Prof.-Dr. Martha Kaarsberg Wallach; George H. Williams; Dr. Jürgen Willisch; and Eckert von Winterfeld.

Much valuable help has been received from staff members of the following institutions: Bayerisches Hauptstaatsarchiv; Bundesarchiv Militärarchiv in Freiburg; Generallandesarchiv Karlsruhe; Hauptstaatsarchiv Stuttgart; Luftwaffenmuseum der Bundeswehr in Berlin-Gatow; Institut für Stadtgeschichte in Frankfurt am Main; Militärhistorisches Museum der Bundeswehr in Dresden; Public Record Office at Kew, London; Sächsisches Hauptarchiv Dresden; Service Historique de l'Armée de l'Air in Vincennes; Stadt Pasewalk Museum, U.S.A.; National Archives in Washington, D.C., and Wehrgeschichtliches Museum in Rastatt.

Special thanks go to a brave trio who read the manuscript in early stages: Dr. Stuart Barnett, Dena Harwin and Karl Kilduff. An extra *Siegerkranz* goes to Lieutenant Colonel John Moncure, US Army (Retd.), whose dissertation has become the excellent book *Forging the King's Sword: Military Education Between Tradition and Modernization – The Case of the Royal Prussian Cadet Corps 1871–1918*. His comments, observations, questions and resources were very helpful in bringing this work to a satisfactory conclusion.

This volume is the fourth I have produced for Arms and Armour Press, and I offer sincere appreciation to its director, Rod Dymott, for his continued confidence and encouragement in these projects. David Gibbons of DAG Publications Ltd. has, once again, created a marvel of layout and typography which makes me glad to be working with him.

Once again I express gratitude to a cadre of non-aviation friends who supported my research and writing in unseen but important ways. They are, in alphabetical order: Karl L. Eckert, who listens patiently to ramblings about these long-ago events; Dr. S. Martin Harwin, who has done his usual marvellous job in preparing photographs; and Gary Warner, who helps me derive maximum benefit from the computer into which I entrust the text that results from my research into, and understanding of, the people, equipment and events of early military aviation.

Finally, a special note to two important women in my life: my wife, Judy Baumer Kilduff, who keeps the daily routine going – household, kids and cats – during my many solitary hours of research and writing; and my mother, the late Beatrice Leake Kilduff, who wanted to be a writer and in many ways helped assure that I had the opportunity to pursue this craft.

Peter Kilduff

New Britain, Connecticut

June 1997

Notes

1   Hamilton, E., *Mythology*, p. 301.
2   Virgil, *Aenid*, IV, p. 604.
3   Quoted in Bodenschatz, K., *Jagd in Flanderns Himmel*, p.14.
4   Quoted in 'Deutsche Flieger über Paris' in Wolff'schen Telegr.-Bureau, *Amtliche Kriegs-Depeschen*, vol. I, 2 September 1914, p. 66.
5   Mann, T., *Essays of Three Decades*, p. 89; as an example of Wagner's influence within Germany, it is noted that music from *The Ring* inspired a popular piece, 'The Nibelungen March', which included clearly identifiable Wagnerian tunes. Appropriately, the march was adopted by the Bavarian 7. Infanterie-Regiment, garrisoned in Bayreuth, the home, since its inauguration, of the annual Wagner music festival.
6   Goodspeed, D., *Ludendorff*, p. 4.
7   Ibid., p. 124.
8   Nietzsche, F., *The Philosophy of Nietzsche*, p. 75.
9   Commissioned into Dragoner-Regiment König Carl I. von Rumänien (1. Hannoversches) Nr. 9 (Ref: *Ehrenrangliste des ehemaligen deutschen Heeres*, vol. I, p. 415)
10 Richthofen, M. von, *Der rote Kampfflieger*, p. 94.
11 Commissioned into 6. Infanterie-Regiment Nr. 105 König Wilhelm II. von Württemberg (Ref: *Ehrenrangliste*, op. cit., vol. II, p. 898).
12 Richthofen, M. von, *Ein Heldenleben*, pp. 196–7.
13 Quoted in Lampel, P., 'Als Gast beim Rittmeister Frhr. v. Richthofen', in Neumann (ed.), *In der Luft unbesiegt*, p. 219.
14 Kilduff, P. *Richthofen – Beyond the Legend*, p. 204.
15 *Nachrichtenblatt*, 2. Jahrgang, Nr. 9, 25 April 1918, p. 128-A.
16 Kilduff, op. cit., pp. 210–11.

CHAPTER 1

Thunder Under the Sun

A CLEAR, BRIGHT BLUE SKY GRACED THE FLANDERS FRONT ON MONDAY, 18 March 1918.[1] At Andigny, a scene of pastoral beauty was shattered by harsh commands of drill sergeants and the uneven cadence of thousands of feet trampling down the tall grass. In a broad, open field outside the village, just 20 kilometres behind the German 2. Armee (2nd Army) front, troops of the 238. Infanterie-Division were being prepared for the spring offensive set to begin in three days' time.

Just before 1100 hours the training exercise was interrupted by a steady rumbling noise that grew ever louder. The soldiers looked up and saw a block of dots approaching from the south-west.

A member of the training corps recalled seeing 30 to 40 aircraft 'at 4,000 to 5,000 metres, flying very neatly in a great rectangle in the direction of Le Cateau [north of Andigny]. They came ever closer to us and the air vibrated lightly from the ... many engines. With their field glasses, our officers soon determined that they were British aircraft ...'[2]

Turning to the north, the soldiers spotted a wedge-shaped formation of German aircraft and watched it approach, steadily and without deviating from its course. Then the German triangle sliced into the invading force.

'In a moment the neat British rectangle was torn apart and suddenly everything was in disarray like a swarm of gnats. We heard the first rattling of machine-gun fire and then we saw a multitude of small groups [of aircraft] roaring around after one another and firing. Most of the aircraft came lower and lower, and we were able to follow them all more precisely. Suddenly an Englishman pulled away from the swarm and dived westwards towards the ground, towards our village.'[3]

From out of the confused mass, a wingless fuselage hurtled earthwards, trailing a ribbon of black smoke. It erupted into bright yellow and red flames before crashing into the ground. Seconds later the wings came tumbling down, the British tri-coloured cockades flashing at every twisting turn.

As the dog-fight descended to about 1,000 metres' altitude, a greenish-brown aircraft bearing the same cockades swooped down over Wassigny, just east of Andigny. There now came a departure from the warriors' stern code of never surrendering and the taking of no prisoners. Directly above the recruits of 238. Infanterie Division a small, dull-coloured single-seat biplane emerged from the swarms of twisting, swerving and clattering aircraft, and glided in quietly with the engine shut off.

'A German machine circled over him like a bird of prey', a witness recalled. 'The Englishman set his aircraft on the ground about 150 metres from us. He climbed out and we brought him into the village. He was a Canadian whose aircraft had been shot in the propeller. The German airman landed right near the enemy machine, climbed out and cut the [serial] number from the [fuselage] of his opponent. At the same time, he made us aware of a red [Fokker triplane] that was circling only a hundred metres above us and at which everyone waved. It was Rittmeister [Cavalry Captain] Manfred von Richthofen.'[4]

Portrait of a dog-fight

The intense aerial combat witnessed by the soldiers at Andigny was a consequence of the ever-increasing Allied efforts to penetrate the German line. Inevitably the forthcoming offensive had been signalled by much vehicular and other noise at night, and troop movements by day, so the German strategists anticipated enemy efforts to reconnoitre and disrupt their preparations. Despite careful planning on both sides, this day's large-scale dog-fight became a swirl of events in which much was claimed, but little achieved within the loosely defined boundaries of the air war arena.

Aerial combat on such a large scale was exceptional for the First World War, but the fight on 18 March 1918 was typical in the composition of machines and men involved. On the British side, a force of two-seat reconnaissance and bombing aircraft performing important tactical roles in support of ground-war objectives. Opposing them was a well co-ordinated air wing of single-seat fighters whose sole intent was to destroy the camera- and bomb-bearing aircraft. British fighter escorts were deployed to sweep aside the interceptors, but were attacked by such an overwhelming fighter force, led by Germany's most formidable air fighter, that they could not prevail. There was more than enough courage and talent on both sides, as a group of men ranging in age from 18 to 30 engaged one another with a fury that mixed primeval passion with the latest machines of war.

Flight Commander Charles P. O. Bartlett, a bomber pilot with No. 5 Squadron, RNAS, was, at 29, among the 'old men' in the fight. On the previous evening he recorded in his diary: 'Tomorrow we are to attempt to clear the enemy right out of the sky. We are to be over Busigny exactly 1¼ hours after take-off, at which time there will be twelve [Sopwith F.1] Camels at 15,000

[feet] and eighteen S.E.5as at 16,000 [feet] in the vicinity waiting to deal with anything and everything that comes up. Let us hope it comes off all right.'[5]

The main British effort was assigned to 22nd (Army) Wing, including the two-seat Airco D.H.4 bombers of No. 5 Naval Squadron, which recently had been pressing the area hard. Indeed, this mission was the third consecutive day that No. 5 Naval's aircraft were directed against Busigny, home of two German reconnaissance squadrons, two close air support units,[6] and other attractive targets. The lumbering D.H.4s were joined by the Wing's smaller, faster Sopwith F.1 Camel and S.E.5a single-seat fighter units Nos. 54 and 84 Squadrons, RFC, respectively, together with Bristol F.2B two-seat fighters from 13th (Army) Wing's No. 11 Squadron.[7]

Movements of large aircraft formations on the other side of the Front were monitored by German air defence posts in the forward lines. Shortly before 1030 hours that day, they notified German fighter units that noise levels indicated a large formation of RFC aircraft heading toward the Front. From their airfield at Avesnes-le-Sec, some 25 kilometres north-north-west of Busigny, Albatros D.V biplane and Fokker Dr.I triplane fighters of Jagdgeschwader I took off under the command of Manfred von Richthofen.

Just over six weeks short of his 26th birthday, Richthofen was Germany's most successful fighter pilot and a highly experienced air combat leader. On this mission he headed one of the largest German fighter forces of the war: 30 aircraft in close formation. As he began to climb above 5,000 metres in the bright blue sky, his aircraft was immediately recognisable; a Fokker Dr.I triplane with the blood-red top wing, cowl and tail[8] that earned him the nickname 'the Red Baron'. Jagdstaffel 6's ten aircraft, identified by their black and white striped markings, were staggered about 500 metres off to his left. Jasta 11's fighters, proudly bearing red noses and tails from Richthofen's earlier days as their Staffel leader, flew directly behind him. The bright yellow-nosed aircraft of Jasta 10 were off to his right-hand side. The array of their unit colours made it clear why JG I's adversaries referred to them as the 'flying circus'.[9]

In his combat report Richthofen wrote: 'I encountered the first two-seater group in the vicinity of Le Catelet (15 kilometres north of St-Quentin) at about 5,500 metres' altitude. Together with Leutnant [Siegfried] Gussmann of Jasta 11, I fired at the last of the opponents, a Bristol Fighter. He lost his wings. Leutnant Gussmann brought him crashing down at Joncourt.[10]

'After that, I gathered my 30 aircraft, climbed to 5,300 metres and followed two British groups that had broken through toward Le Cateau. When the opponent attempted to turn away and head back toward the Front,

I attacked him in the vicinity of Le Cateau. I got to the enemy first and, together with Leutnant [Erich] Loewenhardt, shot down the enemy nearest us, a Bristol Fighter [sic].[11] I saw the Englishman go straight down and burst apart in the air.

'Meanwhile, my Staffel was embroiled in a bitter dog-fight with enemy single-seat formations, which up to now had been flying at greater altitude and suddenly swooped down. At the same time, individual Staffeln of Jagdgruppe 2, among them Jagdstaffel 5, rushed over [to the scene] and joined in the battle. An enormous dog-fight broke out. Stopping the group formation was now out of the question. Everyone dived on the closest flying opponent. A chaotic muddle of individual combats was the result. Often one could not distinguish friend and enemy from one another. The air was interlaced with the white streaks of phosphorous ammunition; in their midst one saw aircraft shot down in flames or plunging out of control toward the ground.

'I went after a Sopwith Camel with pennants [fluttering from the struts][12] and forced it to land alongside the road between Molain and Vaux-Andigny. The occupant was a Canadian, the leader of one of the two single-seater formations. Altogether, the enemy suffered the loss of fifteen aircraft,[13] nine of which were shot down by my Staffeln. We had to mourn the loss of only one aircraft of Jagdstaffel 10.'[14]

The Camel forced down by Richthofen was piloted by 28-year-old Second Lieutenant William G. Ivamy, a deputy flight commander with No. 54 Squadron, and was recorded as the celebrated ace's 66th victory. Ivamy, a resident of British Columbia when he enlisted in the army in 1915, was uninjured in this encounter and was taken prisoner.[15]

The Richthofen air wing's sole loss that day was a newcomer to Jasta 10, 23-year-old Flieger [Private] Rudolf Ihde, who had been shot down over Andigny.[16] This overall engagement was virtually a dress rehearsal for the offensive to come, as aircraft from nearby fighter groups – Jagdgruppe 2 (Jastas 5 and 46), Jagdgruppe 9 (Jastas 3, 37, 54 and 56) and Jagdgruppe 10 (Bavarian Jastas 16 and 34)[17] – accompanied JG I to intercept the large British formation.

No. 54 Squadron's Second Lieutenant Eric A. Richardson scored the unit's only victory that day when he went after a Fokker triplane five miles east of Busigny. Flying at 15,000 feet, he reported that 'after manoeuvring for several minutes ... [I] got into a favourable position and got in a long burst at a range of 50 feet. The triplane nose-dived and burst into flames.'[18]

At the same time, a squadron mate of Richardson's, Second Lieutenant N. M. Drysdale, reported 'firing a long burst at close range ... [at an Albatros D.V, which] turned over on his back and went down in a vertical nose-dive, apparently out of control.'[19] Drysdale's claim was not confirmed, but it is likely that Richardson's victim was 24-year-old Unteroffizier [Corporal] Gustav Ecke of Jasta 54, who crashed to his death near Busigny.[20]

Other victories were claimed by S.E.5s of No. 84 Squadron about half an hour later. Near St-Souplet, Second Lieutenant William H. Brown attacked a Fokker triplane which, he reported, 'turned over and started spinning, but came out again about 3,000 feet below. I then turned my attention on a V-strutter [Albatros] and fired a long burst into it at a range of about 50 feet. He turned over on his back and started a series of spins and dives, absolutely out of control. I lost sight of him as I discovered a triplane firing at me ... [at] about 10,000 feet ... from a stalling position. I immediately dived at him ... firing with both guns as I dived ... and, when I got close, I fired a long burst at him from a short range. He immediately started spinning and, after doing a few turns [he] went into a vertical dive. He continued to dive until he hit the ground.'[21] A short distance away, American-born Lieutenant Jens F. Larson attacked an Albatros and a Fokker triplane. He reported that the triplane 'fell onto its back, floated a short distance, and went into a slow spin'.[22]

Brown was credited with sending an Albatros 'down out of control' (OOC) and with causing the crash of the Fokker. Larson's report shows an 'OOC' for the triplane he encountered. Contained within these accounts are the deaths of Flieger Rudolf Ihde of Jasta 10, who crashed near Andigny, and 21-year-old Leutnant der Reserve [Second Lieutenant, Reserves] Franz Riedle of Jasta 16b, who was found dead in his aircraft 3 kilometres away.[23]

It is virtually impossible to determine 'who got who' in the course of such a mad, destructive swirl of events. The confusion is just as apparent in JG I's war diary, which credited all the fight's nine aerial victories to its pilots.

JG I Victory Claims

Just minutes after Richthofen watched Siegfried Gussmann destroy a Bristol F.2B, Oberleutnant [First Lieutenant] Wilhelm Reinhard, commanding officer of Jasta 6, reported shooting down an F.2B near St-Souplet, some 17 kilometres away. There is no corresponding F.2B loss for this claim,[24] which was recorded as Reinhard's ninth 'kill'.[25] As in Gussmann's account, Reinhard reported that the aircraft had 'burst apart in the air and its burning remnants crashed onto the desolate landscape'.[26]

Wilhelm Reinhard, who had turned 27 a few days earlier, was a devoted student of Richthofen's and had earned his combat command by scoring his first five victories in five weeks of flying with Jasta 11.[27] He fought valiantly during this present battle, but his claim conflicts with that of Jasta 10's Erich Loewenhardt, who reported shooting down a two-seater in the same area five minutes later under nearly identical conditions. Loewenhardt was credited with his 13th aerial victory. The identity of the victor remains unclear, but there is no doubt about who was in the other two-seater brought down in that fight. The bodies of Flight Sub-Lieutenant Lionel B. Ransford, aged 18, and Air Mechanic I George Smith, DSM, aged 27, were retrieved and buried at St-Souplet.[28]

One of Reinhard's Jasta 6 protégés, 21-year-old Leutnant Hans Kirschstein, achieved the first of his 27 victories by forcing a Sopwith Camel to land near Vaux-Andigny.[29] The lucky pilot was Captain F. L. Luxmoore of No. 54 Squadron, whose aircraft was reported 'last seen in combat two miles east of Busigny under control' and who was later confirmed as being a prisoner of war.[30]

At 1115 hours, Leutnant Hans Joachim Wolff, aged 22, achieved his first victory when he shot down in flames an S.E.5a; it crashed and disintegrated near Escaufourt.[31] Another Richthofen acolyte, this Jasta 11 pilot was the namesake (but no relative) of Oberleutnant Kurt Wolff, a 33-victory ace who too had developed into a major fighter ace under the Rittmeister's tutelage. In the fighting over Busigny No. 84 Squadron lost two S.E.5s and their pilots,[32] one of whom also bore a name renowned in aerial combat: Second Lieutenant John A. McCudden, MC, the 20-year-old brother of the celebrated ace, Major James T. B. McCudden, VC. The younger McCudden had been flying combat missions for six months and had eight confirmed victories to his credit[33] when it appears that Wolff gained the upper hand in this fight. Second Lieutenant McCudden was buried at St-Souplet next day.[34]

Five minutes after Wolff's victory, one of his more experienced Jasta 11 mates, Vizefeldwebel [Sergeant-Major] Edgar Scholtz, chased a Sopwith Camel eastward and shot it down at la Vallée-Mulâtre, not far from Molain. The Sopwith was credited as the 19-year-old pilot's fourth victory.[35]

Farther west, at Awoingt, another future prominent fighter ace claimed his first triumph. Leutnant der Reserve Fritz Friedrichs, aged 23, reported shooting down a Sopwith Camel, but did not receive official credit for it. No. 54 Squadron lost five aircraft that day[36] and some of these losses were credited to German airmen from other fighter units that joined with JG I for this fight.[37] Fritz Friedrichs, whose left leg had been so severely wounded when he was in the infantry that he had been designated as unfit for army service,[38] would return to fight another day as a member of Imperial Germany's first fighter air wing. Personal tenacity compelled him to swing his game leg into his aircraft, and the example of Manfred von Richthofen inspired Friedrichs and many of his comrades to become well-known, highly decorated air fighters.

The effectiveness of JG I that day was summed up by one of the infantrymen who witnessed the fight: 'At a greater distance from us, meanwhile, still other machines crashed [and] we could not really tell if friend or enemy was destroyed there. But there was something that, to our great joy, we could tell without question: the immense formation had turned back; one after the other, dispersed across the whole sky, they turned back. On the horizon, a lone German airman turned one loop after another, surely at the joy of such a victory.'[39]

'Very Nice in Theory'

After confiding to his diary the devastation he had witnessed during the raid against Busigny, Flight Commander Bartlett of No. 5 Squadron, RNAS, could see the trend towards ever more massive aerial combats when he wrote:

'This must have been the greatest aerial battle of the war so far, a total of nearly 100 aircraft engaged ... Undoubtedly the Germans accepted yesterday's challenge and concentrated their forces, including Richthofen's startlingly coloured 'Circus', with the idea of annihilating us, but they suffered more than we did despite the enormous tactical advantage of fighting many miles behind their own lines. Many of them were really full-out and put up a good show, particularly the Fokker Triplanes. The Colonel [Lieutenant-Colonel F. V. Holt, DSO, Officer Commanding, 22nd (Army) Wing] came over after lunch and discussed tomorrow's show, his idea being finally to smash up these big enemy formations in one huge aerial battle. He proposes putting up some 60 fighters, we ourselves being used as bait once more – though I really don't think any bait is needed ... Very nice in theory – let's hope it will work.'[40]

Massed air power in the final battles on the Western Front was the ultimate tactical use of the military aircraft at that time. What began as a bold move for the German forces, part of the war's last great offensive, set the stage for Allied supremacy in the air to complement their overwhelming triumphs on the ground and at sea. But, despite the eventual loss of the war, the use of co-ordinated formations of fighter aircraft under an internationally-famous and charismatic leader also created a new level of German hero: *der Jagdflieger*, the aerial hunter. That image inspired the next generation of German airmen, the Messerschmitt and Focke-Wulf pilots of the Luftwaffe, who flew and fought over Europe and North Africa. When the name or spirit of the most celebrated *Jagdflieger* – Manfred von Richthofen – is mentioned, the dog-fight of 18 March 1918 stands out as one of the great triumphs for him and the air wing he trained and led into battle.

Notes

1 Weather report in RFC *Communiqué* No. 131, 20 March 1918, p. 7.
2 Quoted in Bodenschatz, K., *Jagd in Flanderns*, p. 68.
3 Ibid., p. 69.
4 Ibid., pp. 69–70.
5 Bartlett, C., *Bomber Pilot*, p. 142.
6 Flieger-Abteilungen (A) 239 and 269, and Schlachtstaffeln 17 and 22 (Ref: Jones, H. A., *War in the Air*, vol. IV, map, p. 364).
7 Ibid., pp. 449–50.
8 This description of Fokker Dr.I 152/17 comes from Richthofen's report of the combat (Ref: Bodenschatz, op. cit., p. 171).
9 VanWyngarden, G., *Von Richthofen's Flying Circus*, gives an excellent exposition of the colours and markings of JG I.
10 Possibly, Bristol F.2B C.4844 of No. 11 Squadron, Capt Alan P. Maclean, aged 22, and Lt Frederick H. Cantlon, MC, aged 24 (both KiA).
11 Sources list Loewenhardt's 13th victory as a 'D.H.4/Bréguet' shot down south of Le Cateau at 1110 hours (Ref: Franks, N., et al., *Above the Lines*, p. 159). It is very likely that this aircraft was D.H.4 A.7663 of No. 5 Squadron, RNAS, Ft-Sub-Lt Lionel B. Ransford, aged 18, and AMI George Smith, DSM, aged 27, both KiA (Ref: Hobson, C., *Airmen Died*, pp. 12, 14).
12 Sopwith F.1 Camel B.5243 of No. 54 Squadron, RFC (Ref: RFC *Western Front Casualty List*).
13 This figure is at odds with RFC *Western Front Casualty List*, which notes that only nine RFC/RNAS aircraft were lost during this mission.
14 Quoted in Bodenschatz, K., 'Das Jagdgeschwader Frhr. v. Richthofen Nr. 1 im Verbande der 2. Armee' in Neumann (ed.), *In der Luft unbesiegt*, pp. 226–7.
15 Gibbons, F., *Red Knight*, pp. 326–8.
16 *Kommandeur der Flieger der 2. Armee Wochenbericht* for 14–20 March 1918.
17 Bodenschatz, K., *Jagd in Flanderns* , p. 172.
18 No. 54 Squadron Combat Report of 2/Lt E. A. Richardson in Sopwith F.1 Camel C.6703.
19 No. 54 Squadron Combat Report of 2/Lt N. M. Drysdale in Sopwith F.1 Camel B.5241.
20 *Kofl 2. Armee*, op. cit.
21 No. 84 Squadron Combat Report No. 117 of 2/Lt W. H. Brown in S.E.5a C.9623.
22 No. 84 Squadron Combat Report No. 114, 18 March 1918, of Lt J. F. Larson in S.E.5a C.1077.
23 *Kofl 2. Armee*, op. cit.
24 Hobson, op. cit., pp. 225, 270.
25 Bodenschatz, op. cit., pp. 67, 171–2.
26 Ibid., p. 67.
27 Franks, et al., op. cit., p. 186.
28 Hobson, op. cit., pp. 12, 14.
29 Ibid., pp. 142–3.
30 Sopwith F.1 Camel B.6720 (Ref: RFC *Western Front Casualty List*).
31 Bodenschatz, op. cit., pp. 67, 172.
32 S.E.5a B.172, 2/Lt John A. McCudden, MC, aged 20, and S.E.5a B.169, 2/Lt Horace A. Payne, aged 22, both KiA (Ref: Hobson, op. cit., pp. 68, 81).
33 Shores, C., et al., *Above the Trenches*, pp. 267–8.
34 Hobson, op. cit., p. 68.
35 *Kofl 2. Armee*, op.cit.
36 In addition to 2/Lt Ivamy and Capt Luxmoore, previously noted, also shot down from No. 54

Squadron were: Sopwith F.1 Camel C.1566, 2/Lt Glen Russell, aged 30 (KiA), buried at Awoingt; Sopwith F.1 Camel C.1576, 2/Lt E. B. Lee (PoW); and Sopwith F.1 Camel B.5421, Lt Norman Clark, aged 23, (KiA), buried at Awoingt (Ref: RFC *Western Front Casualty List*).

37 *Kofl 2. Armee*, ibid., credits: Gefreiter August Schwind, Jasta 54, with his first victory, an S.E.5a at St-Martin at 1110 hours; Vfw Robert Heibert, Jasta 46, his sixth, an S.E.5a at Honnechy at 1110; Ltn Heinrich Geigl, Jasta 16b, his seventh, a D.H.4 at Wassigny at 1115; Vfw Benedikt Jehle, Jasta 16b, his first, a Sopwith Camel over Busigny airfield at 1120; and Ltn Fritz Oppenhorst, Jasta 5, his second, a Sopwith Camel south of Awoingt.

38 Zuerl, W., *Pour-le-Mérite-Flieger*, p. 507.

39 Quoted in Bodenschatz, op. cit., p. 69.

40 Bartlett, op. cit., pp. 143–4.

CHAPTER 2

Eagles Rising

SHOOTING DOWN THE ENEMY – THE COMBAT TRIUMPH NEEDED TO QUALIFY as a warrior of the air – was not just a matter of the pilot of one aircraft drawing close to another and opening fire; it was rather more complex than that. Manfred von Richthofen had learned from his mentor, Oswald Boelcke, that basic tactics were necessary to ensure success in attacking or repelling enemy aircraft, whether individually or in a group.

Generalleutnant (Lieutenant-General) Ernst von Hoeppner, the career cavalry officer and strategist who re-organised German army aviation into a true air force, recognised the value of single-seat fighter aircraft and Boelcke's seminal role in deploying them effectively when he wrote: 'The real [air] fighting power of the army – single-seat combat aircraft – was for practical purposes not retained when used with the Flieger-Abteilungen [flight sections], to which they were assigned; but rather, when they were drawn together in groups of ten to twelve Fokkers.

'But [in the early days] they lacked the strong organisation ... [for] effective use in a tactical situation. Their deployment was left too much to the inclination of individual commanders. The number of machine-guns in the air at any given moment did not guarantee success; they also had to be in the right position at the right time. Chiefly, it is due to Boelcke's sense of duty and enterprise that we were not overwhelmed by the numerical superiority of enemy flyers at the time. His Fokker always proved to be superior to all enemy aircraft ...'[1]

Oswald Boelcke

As was the case with Richthofen, Boelcke did not set out to become a military flyer. After he transferred from a ground unit to the Fliegertruppe (air force), however, he put all his skill and effort into aviation and became a leading developer of early combat tactics.

Born in the Saxon town of Giebichenstein, near Halle an der Saale, on 19 May 1891, Boelcke contracted whooping cough as a child and built up his physical strength by a vigorous devotion to sports.[2] In March 1911, Oswald followed his elder brother Wilhelm into military service and was accepted as an officer cadet (Fahnenjunker) with a field communications unit[3] at Koblenz. After completing his formal military education in Metz a year later, he was commissioned as a Leutnant in the Regular Army.

At that time the German kingdoms offered their own commissions to native sons, but Boelcke, whose three elder siblings had been born in Argentina during his father's overseas teaching service,[4] felt no bond with the Saxon state in which he was born. Consequently he accepted a Prussian commission, a distinction that became apparent later when the Kingdom of Saxony heaped honours on other airmen but ignored Oswald Boelcke.

During army manoeuvres in 1912 near the aviation training unit Flieger-Ersatz-Abteilung 3 at Darmstadt, Boelcke made friends with several pilots there and became interested in flying. By now his brother was already in training to become an observer and, once again following Wilhelm's lead, Oswald applied for a transfer.

The German government augmented the relatively few military aviation centres at the time by assigning prospective aviators to civilian training facilities. In June 1914, while the leaders of Europe pondered the implications of the assassination of the heir to the Austro–Hungarian throne, 22-year-old Oswald Boelcke began a six-weeks' basic pilot training course at the Halberstadt Aeroplane Works' flying school. He passed his examinations and, on 1 August, the day Germany declared war on Russia, he was en route to the aviation training unit at Darmstadt.

There he concentrated on navigation, paying little attention to the quickening pace of the war that had just begun. Below him, the main roads and railways were filled with traffic, carrying men and equipment toward the emerging battle front in France. Two weeks later he was fully qualified.

Boelcke was posted to Trier, where aviation units were being organised for the 4. Armee commanded by Generaloberst [Colonel General] Duke Albrecht of Württemberg.[5] On 1 September his first battle orders directed him to fly to Sedan. Along the way he landed at La Ferté-sur-Chiers, 60 kilometres short of his destination, to 'visit' his brother, newly promoted to Hauptmann (Captain) at Feldflieger-Abteilung 13. Wilhelm arranged for Oswald to remain temporarily with his unit and together the brothers reconnoitred the Argonne and Champagne regions.[6] They flew so often that other crews complained that they 'monopolised' an Albatros two-seat biplane as if it were their personal property.[7] Their effectiveness in combat flying was recognised when, on 12 October 1914, Oswald Boelcke was presented with the Iron Cross 2nd Class, an outstanding award at this early stage of the war. The black, silver-edged cast-iron, cross-*patée* design of the badge linked modern Germans to the medieval knights of the Teutonic Order.[8] Twelve days later, Wilhelm received the Iron Cross 1st Class.

It took another three months for Oswald to catch up with his brother in attaining the higher award of the Iron Cross.[9] Reaching that milestone was the first in several competitive relationships Boelcke pursued in his flying career. On 25 April 1915, he reported to the airfield at Döberitz, west of Berlin, where Feldflieger-Abteilung 62 was being established under the command of 30-year-old Hauptmann Hermann Kastner, a pre-war aviator.[10] Among the other pilots and observers assigned to the new unit was Fähnrich (Officer Cadet) Max Immelmann, who had served with Feldflieger-Abteilung 10 in France.

Max Immelmann

The careers of Oswald Boelcke and Max Immelmann are closely linked and reflecting on the career of one invites a commentary on the other. Upon graduation from the cadet corps in his home town of Dresden in 1911, Immelmann began his military service in the rail transport unit Eisenbahn-Regiment Nr. 2 in anticipation of gaining a commission in the Royal Saxon Army. In March 1912 he left the army to study mechanical engineering at the Technical College in Dresden, the Saxon capital.

When the war began he returned to the army as a Reserve officer candidate and was assigned to Eisenbahn-Regiment Nr. 1 at Schöneberg, near Berlin. As the unit had a long list of candidates, but no vacancies for new officers, Immelmann had to find another army unit in order to receive his commission. Eventually he responded to an Inspectorate of Aviation notice of 10 August 1914 offering pilot training to qualified personnel.[11] Because of his technical background, Immelmann was accepted and assigned to Flieger-Ersatz-Abteilung 2 at Adlershof outside Berlin. At the Military Flying School at Johannisthal he qualified as a two-seater pilot and on 4 March 1915 was posted to Armee Flugpark 3, an aviation supply depot near Rethel in France.

During the war, German pilots typically finished their formal training at a flying school in Germany and were posted to a depot for orientation flights over the Front. They were then sent to an air unit to complete a series of combat flights with the objective of earning the Pilot's Badge as proof of their qualifications.

After five weeks at Rethel, Immelmann was assigned to Feldflieger-Abteilung 10 at Vrizy. Generally, he and his observer, Leutnant Bissmeyer, flew reconnaissance missions in an unarmed LVG B.I two-seat biplane over the Champagne sector. They were also assigned to range the guns of Artillerie-Regiment Nr. 99, which proved to be a much more hazardous duty.[12] The pilot had to remain over the Front, while his companion noted where the shells hit. Then the observer placed his notes on firing corrections into message canisters and dropped them at the battery's headquarters. The crew went back and forth over the lines and, even though they were at 2,200 metres' altitude, which was relatively high for that time, they came under constant fire from enemy gunners. With a steady hand on the controls, Immelmann remained dedicated to his task, and his good performance may be the reason why after only thirteen days he was transferred to a combat unit being formed at Döberitz.

The Synchronised Machine-Gun

While Feldflieger-Abteilung 62 was being organised, Boelcke and Immelmann had the opportunity to see and admire a variety of new aircraft arriving at Döberitz, including several A-Type unarmed two-seat monoplanes.[13] One in particular, the Fokker A.I (M.8) mid-wing monoplane, was much more manoeuvrable than the LVG B.I two-seat biplanes they were flying. Unbeknown to them, a restricted hangar at Döberitz hid a secret which, when married with the single-seat Fokker A.III, would enable them to become Germany's first great fighter pilots and air combat tacticians.

Shortly before Boelcke and Immelmann arrived there, German ground fire had brought down a Morane-Saulnier Type L parasol monoplane,[14] the first operational front-engine combat aircraft with a functional fixed forward-firing gun.[15] The celebrated pre-war French pilot Lieutenant Roland Garros of Escadrille MS 23 had scored three victories with this single-seat aircraft after his mechanic, Jules Hue, had bolted hardened-steel Vee-shaped deflector rails to the propeller blades; any bullet that would have struck a passing blade shot off at an angle or was sliced in half.[16] Garros tried to protect this secret by destroying the wreckage, but he was stopped by his captors and the machine was sent to the test facility at Döberitz. The crude device was turned over to the Dutch-born aircraft designer Anthony Fokker, then 24 years old, to develop a synchronisation system that would allow bullets to pass through the propeller arc. Within a week Fokker's engineers produced a functional mechanical interrupter gear. When it was applied to a Fokker M.5K,[17] the Eindecker (armed defensive monoplane) series was born, and the machine-gun equipped monoplane changed the nature of aerial warfare.

Packed into lorries and cars, the components of Feldflieger-Abteilung 62 departed Döberitz on Ascension Day, Thursday, 13 May 1915. On the Saturday Hauptmann Kastner and his six pilots, five observers, maintenance and other staff, and aircraft arrived at Pont Faverger outside Douai. The site of a major railhead, the area needed special protection against enemy bombers.

Two weeks later Anthony Fokker came to Douai to demonstrate two of his new E.I aircraft. He was accompanied by Leutnant Otto Parschau, a 24-year-old former infantry officer and pre-war pilot[18] who had already flown front-line missions with Feldflieger-Abteilungen 22 and 42, as well as with the early combat unit with the odd and ineffective cover name Brieftauben-Abteilung Ostende (Carrier Pigeon Section at Ostend). Parschau put in a masterful performance with the fast little monoplane and left Kastner's best pilots – Boelcke and Immelmann – eagerly awaiting their own Eindeckers.

First Eindecker Triumph

On 1 July, Leutnant Kurt Wintgens scored the first Fokker E.I victory. Wintgens, aged 20 and a one-time field communications officer,[19] had trained at the Fokker facility in Schwerin and was thoroughly familiar with the Flying Dutchman's products. He was temporarily attached to the Bavarian unit Feldflieger-Abteilung 6b at Bühl-Saarburg when he shot down a Morane-Saulnier Type L two-seater east of Lunéville.[20]

Although this was probably the first E.I victory, Wintgens' success was not officially credited, because the fight ended over French territory and there was no independent confirmation of the victory. Indeed Wintgens had violated orders by pursuing the Morane as far as he did. In keeping with the German strategy of largely defensive use of combat aircraft, Eindecker pilots were forbidden to cross the battle lines for fear that Fokker's interrupter gear might fall into Allied hands.

On 4 July Leutnant Oswald Boelcke was piloting one of the first Albatros armed aircraft,[21] when he surprised a Morane-Saulnier two-seat parasol monoplane over the German lines near Douai. After 25 minutes of manoeuvring, Boelcke got into position to enable his observer, Leutnant Heinz-Hellmuth von Wühlisch,[22] to open fire on the French reconnaissance aircraft. In a letter home Boelcke described the scene: 'Shortly before the [final] dive, the enemy observer made a movement with his hand as if he wanted to say: "Just let us go [down], we are defeated and we surrender." But in such a case who can trust an opponent in the air! After that he went into a glide, [and] I went after him immediately. My observer gave the opponent another 30 to 40 shots, [and] then suddenly the aircraft disappeared.'[23]

German troops found the wreckage of the French aircraft and its dead crew.[24] For the victors the rewards were the Iron Cross 1st Class to 22-year-old Leutnant von Wühlisch and, for Boelcke, the promise of the Fokker Eindecker assigned to the unit. When it arrived, in mid-July, Boelcke's old Albatros went to Max Immelmann.

Oswald Boelcke went up in his new aerial weapon[25] at every opportunity. There were significant differences between flying an Albatros equipped with a stationary engine and a Fokker with a rotary engine that spun like a big gyro-scope, creating considerable torque. Boelcke mastered the Eindecker quickly and taught its fine points to Immelmann, who was eager to engage enemy aircraft.

The unit received a second Fokker E.I and Boelcke flew it on 1 August and intercepted an early morning flight of British bombers heading for Arras. The marauding B.E.2c biplanes – notably stable aircraft, but with poor manoeuvra-bility – were no match for the new Fokkers.[26] Boelcke took off first and, having learned that simply firing at a fleeing enemy is not sufficient to bring him down, he gained altitude and made the swift, hawk-like dive that became the hallmark of Fokker Eindecker tactics. No sooner had he opened fire, however, when his gun jammed.

Immelmann, following the other Fokker E.I,[27] saw Boelcke's problem and pulled up above the British bomber. Usually configured as a two-seat aircraft, this B.E.2c had no observer aboard and was therefore unprotected from the rear. Immelmann dived on it, opened fire and sent it down south-west of Douai. Like many fighter pilots during this early stage of the war, Immelmann was so taken with his success that he followed his victim down and landed nearby. The pilot, Second Lieutenant William Reid, a Canadian member of No. 2 Squadron, RFC,[28] had been wounded in the left arm during the fight and offered no resistance. Immelmann approached his adversary and, using a very basic command of English, announced proudly: 'Ah, you are Englishman? You are my prisoner.'[29]

Next day, Abteilung leader Hermann Kastner pinned the Iron Cross 1st Class to Max Immelmann's tunic, making him Oswald Boelcke's equal in victories and awards.

Boelcke's Second Victory

Boelcke worked at his air fighting skills with determination. His second victory – and his first in an Eindecker – came on 19 August when he shot down a Bristol two-seater. He later wrote about his opponent: 'As he noticed that I was shooting at him, he turned back promptly. I went after him with a vengeance and continued to press him. In the course of that he must have been hit, for suddenly he turned away and disappeared down below.'[30]

Feldflieger-Abteilung 62 exchanged one of its early Eindeckers for a Fokker E.II[31] and the new machine was assigned to Boelcke. Before he could score again, however, on 26 August Immelmann shot down an enemy biplane that had slipped in behind Boelcke. As such a feat was so new, the Kingdom of Saxony honoured him with its Knight's Cross of the Order of Albert 2nd Class with Swords.

On 18 September Boelcke shot down a Morane, his third victory. As the rivalry continued, Feldflieger-Abteilung 62 received improved Fokker aircraft, and Boelcke and Immelmann developed tactics for future fighter pilots. One of these, the so-called 'Immelmann Turn', was attributed to the Saxon airman. The writer 'Vigilant' described it: 'Pulling the stick well back he made his Fokker's nose rear up as if he wanted to loop the loop; then he turned sideways over the vertical and came out in the opposite direction. It was a simple method of gaining height quickly at the same time as he reversed direction, but no one had ever thought of it before, and it took the British airmen by surprise.'[32]

Max Immelmann's 25th birthday, on 21 September 1915, was a splendid day for him. In the morning he shot down a B.E.2c for his third confirmed victory.[33] A little later he was informed that he had been awarded Saxony's highest decoration for bravery, the Knight's Cross of the Military Order of St. Henry. He went to Lille to receive the award from Prince Ernst Heinrich, the 20-year-old third son of King Friedrich August III of Saxony.[34]

Boelcke's New Assignment

The massive French assault on the Champagne Front on 23 September led to a swift re-ordering of Western Front resources; other Armees sent selected units and personnel to bolster 3. Armee. As part of that process, Boelcke was transferred from Douai to Metz, where a second Brieftauben-Abteilung had been established by elements of the BAO on 17 August.[35] To develop its capabilities to the utmost, command of Brieftauben-Abteilung Metz had been given to the former BAO chief, 34-year-old Hauptmann Hermann Gustav Kastner, who was succeeded in Ostend by another pre-war aviator, Hauptmann Ernst Freiherr von Gersdorff[36] who, at the age of 37, was relatively old for a combat pilot.

Boelcke's proven skill with the Eindecker brought strength to the new BAM. On 25 September, three days after his arrival at Metz, he shot down one of ten French aircraft that were attacking the main railway station at Metz. Kaiser Wilhelm II was having breakfast that morning at a nearby castle under an 'aerial umbrella' of all other available German aircraft; hence, Boelcke went after the French formation on his own and pressed on until one aircraft went down behind the French lines near Pont-à-Mousson. A forward German artillery unit commander watched the fight through binoculars and confirmed Boelcke's fourth victory.[37]

Boelcke's triumph over the Voisin bomber was reported in newspapers throughout Germany[38] and his status as a national hero was such that, a few days later, he was recognised while travelling by train to a new location on the 3. Armee Front. A BAO pilot of about his own age, wearing a cavalry officer's smartly cut uniform, approached him in the dining-car and blurted out: 'Tell me honestly, how do you really do it?'[39] Boelcke was greatly amused at the bold question of a man obviously very keen to become a fighter pilot.

He explained that his combat style was a matter of closing up behind his target, aiming carefully and firing at the right moment. The other pilot thought there had to be 'a trick' to such success and continued to press him. Boelcke was impressed, and discussed questions of technique during the remainder of the journey. He also remembered the pilot's name: Manfred von Richthofen.

Immelmann scored his fourth victory on 10 October 1915. Six days later Boelcke achieved his fifth. His sixth victory, on 30 October, was followed two days later by a telegram from General Erich von Falkenhayn, Chief of the General Staff, informing him that, in recognition of his 'magnificent achievements against enemy airmen', he had been awarded the Knight's Cross of the Royal House Order of Hohenzollern with Swords.[40] Oswald Boelcke became the first airman to receive Prussia's second highest bravery award. After Immelmann's sixth victory, on 7 November, he too received the Hohenzollern award.

In November Boelcke was invited to the Fokker Aeroplane Factory in Schwerin to test-fly the latest Eindecker: the more heavily armed Fokker E.IV.[41] It was more powerful than previous models, but the engine's additional weight and increased gyroscopic effect made it less manoeuvrable than its predecessors. A lengthened wingspan compensated somewhat for the increased engine power and made the E.IV more stable and, initially, Boelcke approved of the latest Eindecker.

Hail the Hero

While Oswald Boelcke was helping to develop new aircraft, Max Immelmann was doing what he could to meet the national need of heroes. Trim, good-looking and with strict personal habits – he was a vegetarian and neither drank nor smoked[42] – Immelmann was a good role model to inspire clean living among German youth.

On 14 November he was invited to Lille by Crown Prince Rupprecht of Bavaria, Commanding General of the 6. Armee. The young pilot was a special guest at a function for King Friedrich August III and Prince Ernst Heinrich of Saxony, but soon became the centre of attention, as the monarch boasted that a Saxon was one of the first two airmen to receive the coveted Hohenzollern award.

Next day Immelmann joined the entourage that reviewed the Saxon unit Feldflieger-Abteilung 24 commanded by Hauptmann Meinhard Rosenmüller. Immelmann flew in so that he could later proceed directly back to Douai. Upon landing, however, he found photographers and cinematographers busily recording his arrival. The cameramen followed and covered his discussions with Hauptmann Rosenmüller and the king, as well as his inspection of the unit's ten aircraft and, a prize of war, Immelmann's fourth victim, a B.E.2.[43]

Then, King Friedrich August used his own camera to photograph Immelmann standing by the British aircraft. This event was also captured on film, as was the pilot's subsequent demonstration flight and its dramatic conclusion of 80 rounds fired into the air with the synchronised machine-gun. Finally the monarch presented Immelmann with a Meissen plate specially created by the Royal Porcelain Factory, depicting a German Taube monoplane defeating an Allied biplane. Within weeks these scenes were shown in cinemas throughout Germany.

The new national hero reflected credit on his benefactor with a modest comment on the distinctive Meissen plate: 'Certainly such a gift is a much more personal object than an Orden [high decoration].'[44] King Friedrich August beamed with pride.

New Combat Units Formed

Since his appointment as Chef der Feldflugwesens (Chief of Field Aviation) of the German Army, Major Hermann von der Lieth-Thomsen, had instituted a number of organisational changes. A protégé of General Erich Ludendorff's, von der Lieth-Thomsen had the high-level support needed to make the changes effective. He provided the Armee-Oberkommandos (High Commands of the individual Armees) with aviation staff officers to facilitate communications and operations and began diversifying various air units.[45]

Late in 1915 Thomsen began grouping Eindeckers into operational sub-units within the Armee areas and Oswald Boelcke was returned to Feldflieger-Abteilung 62. He was warmly greeted by Max Immelmann and a new Eindecker pilot, Leutnant Albert Oesterreicher, a pre-war airman.[46] Boelcke arrived on 12 December in a new Fokker E.IV, which Immelmann was eager to try. With its more powerful engine, the E.IV promised stunning performance: climbing to 3,000 metres in fifteen minutes and a top speed of up to 170 kmh.[47] On his first flight the following day, however, Immelmann had scarcely attained 50 metres' altitude when the engine failed. The E.IV crashed in a heap and, although uninjured, Immelmann had to be extricated from the wreckage.

Christmas Eve 1915 was a happier time. The high point of Feldflieger-Abteilung 62's celebration took place in the officers' mess. Hauptmann Kastner opened a parcel from Major von der Lieth-Thomsen, who had sent each man a 1-litre silver goblet inscribed 'Dem Sieger im Luftkampf' ('To the Victor in Aerial

Combat') and showing one eagle defeating another in the air. Named the *Ehren-becher* (Cup of Honour), this distinction was eventually awarded to every pilot, observer and aerial gunner on the occasion of attaining his first victory. As word of the award spread, the *Ehrenbecher* became one more incentive to encourage German airmen to seek out and destroy enemy aircraft.

The First Aviation Pour le Mérites

Up to this point, no airmen had received the Kingdom of Prussia's highest award for bravery, the *Orden Pour le Mérite*.[48] As air fighting gained more attention, the Orders Chancery in Berlin determined that eight victories would qualify an officer for the high honour. On 12 January 1916, after Boelcke and Immelmann had each attained the necessary score, they became the first aviation recipients. Eventually, the Order's handsome badge, a Maltese Cross of deep blue enamel with gold trim, worn at the neck, became Germany's *de facto* highest bravery decoration for commissioned officers. While other German states also awarded high military merit honours in the grade of Commander's Cross, worn as a necklet, the *Pour le Mérite* – nicknamed 'the blue Max' – is by far the best-known award of the period. The honours accorded to Boelcke and Immelmann became a powerful inducement to like-minded combat pilots and shooting down eight enemy aircraft became an important goal.

The growing success of the Eindeckers forced British and French air commanders to make drastic changes in their operations. Britain's air units were notified: 'Until the Royal Flying Corps is in possession of a machine as good as or better than the German Fokker it seems that a change in the tactics employed becomes necessary ... In the meantime, it must be laid down as a hard and fast rule that a machine proceeding on reconnaissance must be escorted by at least three other fighting machines. These machines must fly in close formation and a reconnaissance should not be continued if any of the machines become detached.'[49]

By sending up more aircraft on individual missions, the Allied forces thereby reduced the number of missions that could be flown with existing aircraft. In response, the Fliegertruppe became even more defensive in nature, faced with greater numbers of enemy aircraft trying to penetrate German lines at any one time. The answer seemed to be more barrier flights (*Sperreflüge*) intended to maintain a tight aerial perimeter over German lines, as if the air could be secured as readily as ground positions were wired, mined and made otherwise inaccessible.

Compounding this perverse strategy, Fliegertruppe leaders were mesmerised by their short-term successes and continued to rely on Fokker improvements. Further victories by Eindecker pilots reinforced the contention and, of course, led to increased numbers and importance of awards and incentives.

Boelcke's First Command

Under Major von der Lieth-Thomsen, the Fliegertruppe responded to changing times with developments of its own. The Brieftauben-Abteilungen (Carrier Pigeon Units) cast off the feeble attempt to disguise their purpose and evolved into Combat Wings of the Supreme High Command (Kampfgeschwader der Obersten-Heeresleitung), each comprising six Combat Sections (Kampfstaffeln) for bombing and close support missions. The Wings – known by the acronym Kagohl – were followed by newly created Kagohls 2, 3 and 4. The Flieger-Abteilungen retained reconnaissance and artillery-ranging duties. Separate Combat Single-seater Detachments (Kampfeinsitzer-Kommandos) – abbreviated to KEKs – were charged with interdicting enemy aircraft.

In preparation for the forthcoming spring offensive against tenacious French forces at Verdun, Hauptmann Wilhelm Haehnelt, Officer in Charge of Aviation for the 5. Armee (Stabsoffizier der Flieger der 5. Armee), set up two Eindecker units[50] at forward bases to thwart enemy aircraft attempting to gather intelligence about the pre-offensive build-up: KEK Nord east of the Meuse at Avillers and KEK Süd, west of the Meuse at Bantheville. On 11 March 1916 Oswald Boelcke received permission to set up KEK Sivry, north of Verdun.[51] The unit was allotted two Fokkers, flown by Boelcke and Leutnant Werner Notzke, a former artillery officer[52] who was detached from Flieger-Abteilung (A) 203 for this assignment.

The savagery of the ground fighting was matched by the aerial combatants, as noted in Boelcke's description of his 11th victory, scored on 13 March: 'At about 1:00 o'clock in the afternoon I saw a French squadron near Toter Mann [Dead Man's Hill][53] flying over the Front in the direction of Dun-sur-Meuse. I selected one of them and dived at it, it was a Voisin biplane, which was turning to the right. As I was very high over him, I came down fast and fired at him vigorously before he grasped the situation. He turned in his tracks immediately, to get back to the Front. I attacked him vigorously again and again, then he tumbled over to the right and disappeared beneath my wing.'

'I believed that he crashed, turned about again to keep him in sight and saw to my astonishment that the opponent had straightened out again. I went after him repeatedly, [and] then beheld something quite extraordinary. The observer had scrambled out of the thing and sat on the bottom left wing, looked up at me in terror and [tried to] wave me off with his hand.

'The whole picture looked very pitiful and for a moment I hesitated to fire at him. He was indeed completely unarmed. I had shot the thing's steering controls to pieces and the machine was crashing; to regain control of it, the observer had scrambled out and had sat on the wing to restore equilibrium.

'I fired some more shots at the pilot to bring down the opponent completely. Then I was interrupted by a second Frenchman, who had come to his comrade's aid. As I had only a few rounds left and was already down above the trenches, I flew away quickly. After my departure the enemy aircraft glided a short distance, but then finally crashed from a low altitude. It lay before one of our outposts, east of the village of Malancourt. From our Front one could see clearly where it lay.'[54]

Boelcke's promotion to Oberleutnant, on 23 March, was early and came with a personally signed letter from Kaiser Wilhelm II, congratulating him on attaining his 12th victory a few days earlier.[55] Boelcke appreciated the honours, but knew that his first priority was his work. On the day of his promotion, he warned in a special report to von der Lieth-Thomsen that the existing Eindecker design was at its limit and not equal to the French Nieuport 17 then entering service.[56]

More Awards for Immelmann

Following his 12th victory, on 30 March, Max Immelmann also received a personal letter from the Kaiser. King Friedrich August III of Saxony was not to be outdone by the Prussians and had his son, 23-year-old Crown Prince Georg, elevate Immelmann within Saxony's highest bravery order by awarding him the grade of Commander 2nd Class of the Military Order of St. Henry. He was the only airman to be so honoured.[57] 'For me as a Saxon, the Commander's Cross is a higher award than the *Pour le Mérite*,' Immelmann said.[58] To demonstrate the point, he wore the Saxon honour in the most prominent position at the base of his collar, with Prussia's highest bravery order nudged off to the side.

Many successful First World War air fighters had good 'political' skills and a sense of their value to the nation. Max Immelmann, for instance, was a fairly regular guest of Saxon and Bavarian royalty when they entertained in Lille, and he used the occasions to advance his career. The example he set was not lost on the fighter pilots who came after him, including Manfred von Richthofen.

Without a doubt, Immelmann and Boelcke had set the standard for success in the Fliegertruppe. But the standards would change in the months ahead.

Notes

1   Hoeppner, E., von. *Deutschlands Krieg*, pp. 52–3.
2   Boelcke, O., *Feldberichte*, p. 10.
3   Telegraphen-Bataillon Nr. 3.

4 Boelcke, op. cit., p. 9.

5 Nowarra, H., *Eisernes Kreuz*, p. 33.

6 Supf, P. *Deutschen Fluggeschichte*, vol. II, p. 342.

7 Albatros B.II 176/14 (Ref: Robertson, B. (ed.). *Air Aces*, p. 169).

8 O'Connor, N., *Aviation Awards*, vol. II, p. 7.

9 27 January 1915.

10 Deutsche Luftfahrt Verband licence No. 216 on 24 May 1912 (Ref: Supf, P., *Deutschen Fluggeschichte*, vol. I, p. 568). Hptm Hermann Kastner is not to be confused with Hptm Gustav Kastner (who in 1924 changed his family name to Kastner-Kirdorf), another prominent early German military aviator.

11 Immelmann, F., *Adler von Lille*, p. 42.

12 Ibid., p. 66.

13 Neumann, G., *Luftstreitkräfte*, p. 82.

14 Nowarra, op. cit., p. 35.

15 Bruce, J., *Morane Saulnier Type L*, p. 3.

16 Ibid.

17 Werknummer 216; Bruce, J., *Fokker Monoplanes*, p. 5.

18 Parschau was commissioned into 2. Ermländisches Infanterie-Regiment Nr. 151 in 1911 and received DLV licence No. 455, 4 July 1913 (Ref: Supf, *Fluggeschichte*, vol. II, p. 664).

19 With Telegraphen-Bataillon Nr. 2.

20 Nowarra, op. cit.

21 Ibid.; Albatros C.I 162/15.

22 Heinz-Hellmuth von Wühlisch was commissioned into Husaren-Regiment Fürst Blücher von Wahlstatt (Pommersches) Nr. 5 and then transferred to the Fliegertruppe. He remained in military service after the war and attained the rank of Generalleutnant in the Luftwaffe on 1 April 1942. Following the German surrender on 8 May 1945 he was held in a PoW camp. His death in Ellecom, Holland on 20 September 1947, ten days before his 55th birthday, was reported as a suicide (Ref: Hildebrand, K., *Die Generale*, vol. III, pp. 547–8).

23 Boelcke, op. cit., p. 38.

24 Lieutenants Maurice Tétu and Jean-Marie François comte de Rochefoucault of Escadrille MS 15; Aschenborn, 'Als Beobachter Boelckes im Westen', in von Eberhardt, W. (ed.), *Unsere Luftstreitkräfte*, p. 217, dates this fight as 1 July 1915; but Boelcke's war letter of Tuesday 6 July, notes that the victory occurred on the preceding Sunday, 4 July. The official French casualty list (No. 6590) lists 4 July.

25 Fokker E.I 3/15, powered by a 9-cylinder 80hp Oberursel U.O. rotary engine and armed with a light-weight, air-cooled Parabellum 7.9mm IMG.08/15 machine-gun.

26 Whitford, R., *Fighter Design*, p. 340.

27 Fokker E.I 13/15 (Ref: Immelmann, op.cit., p. 103–4).

28 Wise, S., *Canadian Airmen*, pp. 345, 351.

29 Ibid., p. 104.

30 Boelcke, op. cit., p. 43.

31 Fokker E.II 37/15, equipped with a 9-cylinder 100hp Oberursel U.I engine.

32 'Vigilant', *German War Birds*, p. 56.

33 B.E.2c 2004 of No. 10 Squadron, Lt Stanley W. Caws, aged 36, (KiA) and Lt W. H. Sugden-Wilson (WiA/PoW) (Ref: Franks, N. 'Max Immelmann's Victories', in *Cross & Cockade*, 1980, p. 40).

34 Immelmann, op. cit., pp. 116, 125, 165.

35 Von Hoeppner, op. cit., p. 40.

36 Commissioned into Lauenburgisches Jäger-Bataillon Nr. 9, Gersdorff received DLV licence No. 356, 24 January 1913 (Ref: Supf, op. cit., p. 663).

37 Boelcke, op. cit., pp. 48–51.

38 In 'Fortsetzung der französisch–englischen Offensive' in Wolff'schen Telegr.-Bureau, *Amtliche Kriegsdepeschen*, vol. III, p. 918.

39 Richthofen, M. von, *Rote Kampfflieger*, p. 80.

40 O'Connor, op. cit., p. 137.

41 The prototype was armed with two IMG.08/15 machine-guns and powered by a 160hp twin-row 14-cylinder Oberursel U.III rotary engine.

42 Immelmann, op. cit., p. 16.

43 Franks, et al., op. cit.; B.E.2c 2003 of No. 16 Squadron, RFC was forced down north-west of Lille on 10 October 1915, 2/Lt John Gay, aged 22 (KiA) and Lt D. Leeson (WiA/PoW).

44 Immelmann, op. cit., pp. 132–4.

45 Trained as a ground officer, Hermann von der Lieth-Thomsen is best known for his role in the development of German military aviation. He was promoted to Major on 20 March 1911, to Ober-stleutnant on 22 March 1916 and to Oberst on 18 August 1918. He was awarded the *Pour le Mérite* on 8 April 1917. Often referred to simply as Thomsen, he was recalled to active duty as a General-major in the Luftwaffe on 1 November 1935 and rose to the rank of General der Flieger prior to his death at the age of 75 on 5 August 1942 (Ref: Hildebrand, K., op.cit., vol. II, pp. 296–7).

46 DLV licence No. 515, 15 September 1913 (Ref: Supf, op. cit.).

47 Immelmann, op. cit., p. 138.

48 O'Connor, op. cit., p. 62.

49 Quoted in Jones, H. A., *War in the Air*, vol II, pp. 156–7.

50 Supf, op. cit., p. 308.

51 Cuneo, J., *Winged Mars*, vol II, p. 212.

52 Commissioned into Feldartillerie-Regiment General-Feldzeugmeister (1. Brandenburgisches) Nr. 3.

53 'Le Mort Homme', barely 2 kilometres from Hill 304, the site of fierce fighting during the Battle of Verdun.

54 Boelcke, op. cit., pp. 64–5.

55 Supf, op. cit., p. 346 notes this date of promotion in conjunction with Boelcke's twelfth victory. Immelmann, op. cit., p. 160 gives the date as 18 February 1916, following Boelcke's ninth victory, noting that Boelcke had received his commission in 1910, which was not the case. Boelcke received it in 1912, making it likely that the March date applied to his promotion to Oberleutnant.

56 Bericht Boelckes über 160er E-Flugzeuge (to the Chief of Field Aviation), 23 March 1916.

57 O'Connor, op. cit., vol. III, p. 25.

58 Immelmann, op. cit., p. 164.

CHAPTER 3

Race for Glory

THE RISING NUMBER OF AIR COMBAT SUCCESSES ONLY BUOYED CONFIDENCE among the Eindecker pilots. The feeling was bolstered by news of a third aviation recipient of the *Pour le Mérite*, Leutnant Hans-Joachim Buddecke,[1] on 14 April 1916. Buddecke, a 25-year-old pilot assigned to the German Military Mission to Turkey, had earned the sobriquet '*El Schahin*' (The Hunting Falcon) for his successful attacks against lightly armed, boxkite-like Farman biplanes and other Allied observation aircraft over Turkish lines.

Reality began to set in when, on 21 April, just seven weeks past his 21st birthday, Leutnant Werner Notzke[2] was killed in a crash at Oswald Boelcke's Kampfeinsitzer-Kommando (KEK) at Sivry. Notzke's replacement was Rittmeister Erich Count von Holck, a former flying partner of Manfred von Richthofen's. After serving with Richthofen in Russia, the ever aggressive Holck had graduated from two-seaters to an Eindecker assigned to Notzke's parent unit, Flieger-Abteilung (A) 203.

Just over a week later, on 1 May, Holck was killed while attacking a flight of two-engined Caudron bombers near Verdun. He had shot down one of the lattice-tail bombers and then seemed to have a jam in his machine-gun. As Holck attempted to fly back to his own lines, the Caudrons went after him.[3] Richthofen, then an Eindecker pilot with Kampfstaffel 8 of Kagohl 2, saw the fight from a distance and went as fast as he could into the prevailing wind, but was unable to reach the scene in time to help. He knew that Holck had been hit because he saw his friend go down in a dead man's spiral.

Next day, Manfred von Richthofen's 23rd birthday, he attended Count von Holck's funeral at Sivry. His friend's death at the age of 30 was surely on Richthofen's mind a few weeks later, when he was home on leave. At one point he turned to his mother and said: 'I do not believe we will win this war ... You have no idea at all how strong our opponent is.'[4]

From Freifrau [Baroness] Kunigunde von Richthofen's recollection of the event,[5] in that moment her son determined to become a superior combat pilot; as if some Teutonic epiphany made clear to him that he had to take a more active role in the air war regardless of the outcome.

Richthofen recognised that the air war was changing. On the Western Front in the late spring of 1916, Allied squadrons were receiving new aircraft that were about to strip away the Fokker Eindecker's superiority. The French Nieu-port XI *Bébé* biplane, powered by an 80hp Gnôme Monosoupape rotary engine and fitted with a single Mk I Lewis 0.303in machine-gun mounted on the top wing, was replaced by the Nieuport 17 with the more powerful 110hp Le Rhône rotary engine and a synchronised machine-gun on the cowl, in addition to the gun on the top wing. Nieuport variants were also used by British squadrons, together with the first Royal Flying Corps fighter aircraft with a synchronised machine-gun, the Bristol Scout D, which, in fact, appeared before the Fokker Eindecker.[6] One of the new RFC pilots in the area, 19-year-old Second Lieutenant Albert Ball of No. 11 Squadron, demonstrated the Bristol Scout D's effectiveness on 15 May 1916, when he forced down an Albatros two-seater from Kampf-staffel 17 of Kagohl 3.[7] The following day Ball scored the first of 44 aerial victo-ries that would make him a leading British fighter ace before the air-fighting talents of Manfred von Richthofen were recognised.[8]

The Fokkers Press On

Oswald Boelcke had not received as many honours as Max Immelmann, but he was promoted rapidly in the Fliegertruppe and given greater responsibilities. He achieved his 17th and 18th victories on Saturday, 20 May, and the following Wednesday, four days before his 25th birthday, he was promoted to Hauptmann [Captain].[9] By early June Boelcke was leading three Fokkers designated as his own battle section, Kampfgruppe Boelcke, at Sivry and was responsible for air defence in the Meuse Valley.[10]

Individual Armee commanders continued to group Eindeckers within their areas. These concentrations – designated Abwehr-Kommandos (Defence Detach-ments), Kampfeinsitzerstaffeln (Combat Single-seater Sections), Einsitzerab-wehr-Kommandos (Single-seater Defence Detachments), Fliegerabwehr-Kommandos (Aviation Defence Detachments), et al.[11] – were all flying single-seat fighters to destroy enemy aircraft, if even on a largely defensive basis and with aircraft that had passed their prime.

During one such mission on 31 May Max Immelmann was nearly killed. He, Leutnant Max Mulzer and Unteroffizier (Corporal) Wolfgang Heinemann flew to an area between Bapaume and Cambrai to intercept seven 'Vikkers', as the Germans commonly called British two-seat rear-engine 'pusher' aircraft following encounters with Vickers F.B.4s in 1914.

Just as Immelmann opened fire, his Fokker E.IV began shaking violently. He cut the ignition and the aircraft settled down as the engine revolutions decreased. When the rotary engine stopped spinning, he saw that half the propeller was gone. A malfunction in the synchronisation gear must have caused the machine-gun to shoot off part of his own propeller. Mulzer finished off the two-seater which his leader had attacked, while Immelmann glided homeward, his Fokker seriously overstressed, but with all controls working sufficiently to enable him to make a safe return.[12]

Despite Immelmann's problem, the RFC report described the encounter as a classic Eindecker assault: 'The III Army reconnaissance, consisting of five F.E.2b's and two Martinsydes, was attacked by three Fokkers when over ... Cambrai. The enemy were first seen diving at our machines from the rear, with the sun at their backs. Our machines ... retaliated as occasion offered, by either [the observer's] firing over the top of the [wings] or else by [the pilot's] partially turning and bringing the front gun into play. 2/Lt [Lindsay C.] Powell, in one of our F.E.s, was shot through the head and instantly killed while firing his gun. The machine was safely brought back and landed at its aerodrome.[13]

'Soon after the fight began, one of the Fokkers was seen to turn half a loop, side-slip badly and nose-dive. It was last seen nose-diving, having apparently been hit by the fire from an F.E. The two remaining Fokkers pursued our reconnaissance, one breaking off the fight or else being compelled to descend before reaching the lines, while the third one followed until within the zone of the advanced German A.A. guns. Several of our machines were badly hit during this encounter.'[14]

Preparing for the Battle of the Somme

General der Infanterie Erich von Falkenhayn, Chief of the German General Staff, envisaged the Battle of Verdun as a protracted affair that would 'bleed' the French army until it capitulated.[15] As part of an overall counter-strategy and to relieve pressure on Verdun, preparations were under way for a British–French assault against German positions along the Somme River.[16] The attack was set to begin on 1 July 1916.

German forces adjacent to the Somme Valley also responded to the build-up. In the 6. Armee area Feldflieger-Abteilung 62 was transferred from Douai to the Eastern Front on 12 June. Two days earlier, Kampfeinsitzer-Kommando III led by Oberleutnant Max Immelmann was detached from it and assigned to operate with the Bavarian unit Feldflieger-Abteilung 5b,[17] which counted among its members 22-year-old Leutnant Max Mulzer, who was on his way to becoming an ace and Pour le Mérite recipient.[18] The units were under the overall command of 39-year-old Major Friedrich Stempel, the 6. Armee's Staff Officer for Aviation.[19]

Stempel, one of the founders of Bavaria's independent pre-war military air arm, devised the command structure of the single-seater units[20] and credited

Immelmann with helping to refine fighter tactics, noting: 'He visited me almost every evening to report the experiences of his many air fights. We formulated the conclusions to be drawn from them for the other combat pilots of 6. Armee and [issued them] in the form of definite instructions and orders. He made his methods of attack so convincingly clear to us by means of simple sketches that they soon became the common property of the airmen of the 6. Armee ...'[21]

Black Sunday

Low clouds in the morning offered little promise for Sunday, 18 June 1916. By late afternoon, however, the sky was clear and, when alerted to enemy aircraft approaching south-west from Arras, four Eindeckers took off to intercept them.

Just before 1700 hours, the Germans caught up with a flight of what they called '*Gitterschwanz*' [lattice-tail] biplanes. Despite the frail-sounding name, the rear-engined two-seat F.E.2bs were formidable opponents; each had a flexible Mk I Lewis 0.303in machine-gun in the pilot's cockpit and a second Lewis gun on a telescopic mounting between the cockpits to enable the observer to fire backwards over the top wing. Immelmann had defeated F.E.2bs before, however, using the Fokker E.IV's more powerful engine to make swift dives and quickly regain the advantage of height.

Once again Immelmann reached altitude quickly and pressed the attack until he had mortally wounded the pilot. The aircraft came down south of Arras, and a German anti-balloon battery at Grévillers confirmed it as the ace's 16th victory.[22]

After dinner, the Staffel intercepted a flight of enemy aircraft heading for Lens. Immelmann's Fokker E.IV[23] had taken several hits during the earlier fight and so he flew the second mission in an E.III. In the darkening sky he pursued what would be his 17th triumph. He was catching up with Oswald Boelcke, whose score then stood at eighteen.[24] The opposing pilot, 17-year-old Second Lieutenant John R. B. Savage,[25] used his four months' front-line experience to elude the German pilot who seemed to anticipate his every move. Fixed on his objective, Immelmann closed in without noticing another F.E.2b and crew intent on drawing him away from their young comrade. Suddenly, Max Immelmann's aircraft plunged to the ground.

According to a Royal Flying Corps report: 'An F.E. of No. 25 Squadron, pilot 2/Lt [G. R.] McCubbin, observer Cpl [J. H.] Waller, when patrolling over Annay at about 9 p.m. attacked three Fokkers seen behind the lines. One of the latter went off. The remaining two made for Lens towards another F.E. of No. 25 Squadron, pilot 2/Lt Savage, observer A/M Robinson, which they attacked. Lt

McCubbin followed and joined in the fight, diving on to one of the attacking Fokkers [Immelmann's] which turned away and dived perpendicularly towards the ground. It was seen to crash by the 22nd A.A. battery. Then Lt McCubbin turned again [and] the other F.E. and Fokker had disappeared. The second F.E., 2/Lt Savage, is missing and is reported to have landed [within] the enemy's lines without crashing.'[26]

Despite the grim tenacity of aerial combat, the opposing forces often exchanged information about downed airmen. Accordingly, a German message dropped over British lines clarified the fate of the missing aircraft:

'To the Royal Flying Corps. F.E. No. 4909 of No. 25 Squadron was shot down by a Fokker on the afternoon [sic] of 18-6-16 at Lens. Pilot, Lt. Savage, was killed and buried in the military cemetery at Sallaumines. Observer, 2/AM [N. U.] Robinson, slightly wounded in the head [and] taken prisoner. [signed] Flying squadron in sector opposite Béthune.'[27]

Immelmann's fate was another matter. Leutnant Erwin Böhme, a future flying comrade of Richthofen's, wrote home that Immelmann had been 'a bundle of nerves lately – someone should have forced him to really relax for a long time; admittedly, it is hard to find the exact limits [of endurance]. Further-more, Immelmann did not fall in aerial combat, but, on the contrary, crashed as a result of the stupid chance occurrence that a piece of his propeller flew off and ripped open a wing.'[28]

'Our Brave and Chivalrous Opponent'

From the earliest days of warfare, the mortal remains of heroes have been honoured by friend and foe alike. Max Immelmann became Germany's first national hero of the air to perish in combat and his funeral set the standard for final honours and displays of chivalrous conduct by his opponents.

Immelmann crashed near the town of Sallaumines. He seemed to be just another dead airman to the first soldiers on the scene, but after removing his body from the wreckage, they could see that he had been an important person by the blue and gold *Pour le Mérite* badge at his collar. His identity was inferred by the 'M.I.' monogram on the back of his Iron Cross 1st Class badge. His body was positively identified at the Bavarian War Hospital in Douai, where it was taken, probably to be embalmed; the remains of many officers – and certainly those of prominent persons – were sent back to Germany for burial.

On Thursday, 22 June, the northern French city of Douai was the site of a ceremony as magnificent as a scene from a Wagnerian opera. Oberleutnant Max Immelmann was given a farewell worthy of a Teutonic hero being sent to Valhalla.

Nature provided a backdrop of sombre, low-hanging clouds, as his body lay in state in the open courtyard of the Bavarian War Hospital. The simple oak coffin was ringed by tall obelisks emitting pitch-black smoke of mourning. Then, to the beat of muffled drums, the long funeral cortège made its way to the railway station. The coffin was borne on a gun-carriage flanked by Feld-flieger-Abteilung 5b enlisted men carrying memorial wreaths. Behind the gun-carriage, Leutnant Max Mulzer carried Immelmann's *Ordenskissen* [a black felt pillow on which rested all the dead man's awards]. In accordance with protocol, the *Pour le Mérite* medal, damaged in the ace's last fight, was placed above all the other awards, but his Commander's Cross of the Military Order of St. Henry was positioned prominently in the centre.

Mulzer was followed by Franz Immelmann, a younger brother who was also a pilot. The formal military contingent was led by two of the dead airman's royal acquaintances, Crown Prince Georg of Saxony and Crown Prince Rupprecht of Bavaria. They were joined by other royal figures, generals, Haupt-mann Oswald Boelcke and other airmen from throughout the area, high-ranking officers, soldiers, nurses and even a delegation of French citizens.

Five Eindeckers streaming long black pennants flew over the procession. At the railway station, as the coffin was lifted on to a flower-decked flatcar, one Fokker dived down and dropped a black wreath – the final tribute from Immel-mann's comrades. Then the train departed for Dresden, where an official state funeral was held, with the national anthem – *Deutschland über alles* – played at the slow tempo of a dirge.

On the Sunday, during graveside services at the *Johannisfriedhof* [St. John's Cemetery] in Tolkewitz, then a suburb of Dresden, an Army Zeppelin airship flew over and dropped two bouquets of roses, one with black, white and red ribbons of the national colours, the other with white and green ribbons emblematic of Saxony.

News of Immelmann's death spread on both sides of the lines. Late the following Saturday evening, 1 July, a British monoplane flew over the Germans' airfield at Bertincourt and dropped an object by parachute;[29] not a simple message canister, but a huge laurel-wreath wrapped with a black mourning ribbon, a band with the German national colours and a Union Flag. Another ribbon bore the inscription 'To the memory of Lieutenant Immelmann, our brave and chivalrous opponent from the British Royal Flying Corps' and was accompanied by a hand-written note: 'We have come over to drop this wreath as a tribute of the respect that the British Flying Corps held for Lieut. Immel-mann. We consider it an honour to have been detailed for this special work. Lt. Immelmann was respected by all British airmen, one and all agreeing that he was a thorough sportsman.' The note was signed by Lieutenant Allister H. Hiller, pilot, and Lieutenant Howard O. Long, observer, members of No. 3 Squadron, RFC. [30]

Major Friedrich Stempel, the 6. Armee's air chief, convened a board of inquiry to determine the cause of Immelmann's fatal crash. Stempel had been preparing Immelmann to take charge of a larger unit of specialised offensive/defensive aircraft. As part of a command mentoring process, Stempel had Immelmann working closely with pre-war aviator Oberleutnant Fritz Moosmaier,[31] the 33-year-old commander of Feldflieger-Abteilung 5b. Ironically the proposed new unit's first Halberstadt biplane fighter arrived on the day Immelmann's body left Douai.[32] Before proceeding with the new organisational development Major Stempel needed to know what had caused the death of such a talented air combat leader, but the lack of clear evidence prevented the board from arriving at a satisfactory conclusion.

Whatever the cause of Max Immelmann's death, it was an ominous sign for other Eindecker pilots to whom Immelmann and Boelcke had become their premier heroes. Certainly, the unexplained loss of a top fighter pilot in a Fokker did not bode well for that company, which had Boelcke testing the 120hp Mercedes stationary-engine-powered D.I biplane, a proposed successor to the E-series.

To make matters worse, the following day another prominent pilot was lost in a Fokker Eindecker. Hauptmann Ernst Freiherr von Gersdorff, commander of Kagohl 1, was shot down over Neuburg in the German-occupied province of Lorraine, not far from Verdun. During the next six weeks other Eindecker pilots would be overwhelmed by superior Allied aircraft flown by a corps of devoted combat pilots, including Albert Ball and Lanoe G. Hawker.

The 'Fokker scourge' was at an end. To keep German combat pilot morale from eroding further and to prevent the loss of another famous pilot, Oswald Boelcke was removed from flight status on the direct order of Kaiser Wilhelm II, and was sent to the Balkans on an 'inspection tour' of German units and their local allies.

More Eindecker Heroes Emerge

Meanwhile, other Eindecker pilots seemed to know no fear as they relentlessly pursued Allied airmen and their increasingly improving aircraft. In Boelcke's absence, new air heroes emerged. After attaining eight victories in six weeks, the coveted *Orden Pour le Mérite* went to: 21-year-old Leutnant Kurt Wintgens of Feldflieger-Abteilung 67, Leutnant Max Mulzer (aged 22) of Feldflieger-Abteilung 5b, Leutnant Otto Parschau (aged 25) of Abwehr-Kommando Nord,

Leutnant Walter Höhndorf (aged 23) of Feldflieger-Abteilung 67, Oberleutnant Ernst Freiherr von Althaus (aged 25) of Feldflieger-Abteilung 23, and Leutnant Wilhelm Frankl (aged 22) of Feldflieger-Abteilung 23.[33]

But the creation of new Eindecker heroes on the Western Front did not halt the continued deterioration of the air situation. Eleven days after receiving the *Pour le Mérite*, Leutnant Otto Parschau was on a lone 'hunting' patrol over Bapaume when he engaged six British and French aircraft. Parschau waged a brave fight and shot down an opponent, but one enemy round grazed his head and another hit him in the abdomen. He made it back behind German lines, but died of his wounds at Grévillers.[34]

Boelcke Returns

Oswald Boelcke's admirer and patron, Oberstleutnant [Lieutenant-Colonel] von der Lieth-Thomsen, developed plans to reorganise the Fliegertruppe. In creating *Jagdstaffeln* [literally 'hunting flights'] for the co-ordinated tactical support of each Armee, he selected Boelcke, the highest scoring ace at the time, to lead Jagdstaffel 2, and Hauptmann Martin Zander, a pre-war aviator who had shot down one enemy aircraft while leading Kampfeinsitzer-Kommando Nord, to command Jagdstaffel 1.[35]

After receiving his orders,[36] Boelcke had a brief meeting on 12 August with General Alexander von Linsingen, commander of the Süd-Armee, which had pushed up from the Carpathian Mountains to Kovel (now in Ukraine), and then the ace relaxed for a short time with his brother Wilhelm at Kagohl 2.

Prior to his departure from Kovel on 15 August,[37] Oswald Boelcke invited two of his brother's pilots to join his new unit. One of them, Leutnant Erwin Böhme, a former rifleman[38] and twelve years Boelcke's senior, was eager to join the new élite unit. He wrote to his prospective bride: 'The famous Boelcke ... is actually assembling at the Somme [Front] a single-seater Jagdstaffel, for which he may select those who appear to him to be the best people in the Fliegertruppe. I went to sleep that evening with the thought: Pity that you are such an old boy and not fifteen years younger! Fighter flights in a sleek single-seater – that would be your downfall.

'Imagine my surprise when, in the morning, Boelcke suddenly came up to me and simply asked: "Do you want to go to the Somme with me?" I have never let out a more joyous *Ja* in my life. Of all bad habits, I have only the slightest tendency toward vanity, but I am really proud of this display of confidence. In addition to myself, Boelcke has recruited from here a young Uhlan Leutnant [Manfred] von Richthofen, a splendid fellow, who has already proven himself at Verdun and here as a daring and reliable airman.'[39]

A New Era Begins

While the new Jagdstaffeln were being formed, the German military structure underwent dramatic change. Generalfeldmarschall Paul Ludwig von Beneckendorf und von Hindenburg, the 69-year-old renowned commander of the Eastern Front, succeeded General der Infanterie Erich von Falkenhayn as Chief of the General Staff. Falkenhayn was blamed for the unsuccessful Verdun offensive and on 29 August was relieved of his command; he retired at the age of 55. The change in command benefited the Fliegertruppe because younger leaders were more air-minded. Oberstleutnant von der Lieth-Thomsen, 49, was a protégé of Erich Ludendorff's, who had been promoted to General der Infanterie and appointed Quartermaster General, as well as Hindenburg's chief of staff.

German military area commanders, encouraged to seek new solutions to their problems, recognised that the free-ranging combat single-seater units on the Western Front were tactically ineffective and were receptive to Thomsen's changes.

The New Jagdstaffeln

Boelcke's new unit was formally established on 10 August 1916[40] as Royal Prussian Jagdstaffel 2 (abbreviated as Jasta 2). The Prussian distinction was made because the Kingdoms of Bavaria, Saxony and Württemberg also had a small number of aviation units, comprised mostly (but not entirely) of their own subjects.[41]

During the next two weeks, Jasta 2 welcomed pilots from other units throughout the Fliegertruppe. Not all the newly assigned pilots made it, however. Leutnant Joachim von Arnim was flying his last patrol with Kampfstaffel 14 of Kagohl 3 on the morning of 28 August when he was shot down and killed south-east of Bapaume. The 22-year-old former cavalry officer[42] was most likely the 13th victim of Second Lieutenant Albert Ball,[43] now a Nieuport fighter pilot with No. 60 Squadron and fast becoming a major figure in air battles over the Western Front.

On 1 September Leutnant Manfred von Richthofen arrived, together with the 25-year-old Westphalian Leutnant Hans Reimann, with whom he had once shared the use of a Fokker Eindecker in Kampfstaffel 8. They were joined by the Saxon-born acting officer (*Offizierstellvertreter*) Leopold Reimann, aged 23 (and unrelated to Richthofen's erstwhile partner). Later that day, Hauptmann Boelcke arrived from the local air depot in a new rotary-engined biplane.[44]

Over the Somme Front

On the ground, the Battle of the Somme was a furious effort to break the stalemate that had locked the belligerents into siege-type warfare that denied a clear victory to either side. In the air, however, it was a time of conquest and glory. Oswald Boelcke doubled his score of victories and watched his most successful student begin a series of 'kills' that would eventually number twice the master's record.

That pilot, Manfred von Richthofen, recalled: 'In my entire life I have never known a more beautiful hunting ground than during ... the Battle of the Somme. In the morning, when we got up, the first Englishman came over and the last disappeared only long after the sun had gone down. "An El Dorado for fighter pilots," Boelcke once said. That was the time when Boelcke's victories climbed from 20 to 40 within two months. We beginners did not have the experience that our master had at that time, and were quite satisfied when we did not get a sound thrashing ourselves. But it was wonderful! Not a flight without a fight. Often, there were great air battles of 40 to 60 Englishmen against, unfortunately, not always so many Germans. They did it with quantity and we did it with quality ...

'There were splendid times at our Jagdstaffel. The spirit of the leader spread to his pupils. We could blindly trust his leadership. There was no possibility that anyone would be abandoned. The thought never occurred to us. And so, snappily and briskly, we made a clean sweep of our enemies.'[45]

Notes

1 A graduate of the Prussian Cadet Corps, Buddecke was commissioned into Leibgarde-Infanterie-Regiment (1. Grossherzoglich Hessisches) Nr. 115 (Ref: Zuerl, W., *Pour le Mérite-Flieger*, p. 113).

2 Commissioned into Feldartillerie-Regiment General-Feldzeugmeister (1. Brandenburgisches) Nr. 3.

3 Richthofen, M. von, *Rote Kampfflieger*, p. 94.

4 Quoted in Richthofen, K. von, *Kriegstagebuch*, p. 56.

5 Ibid., p. 57.

6 Bruce, J., *British Aeroplanes*, p. 118.

7 Bowyer, C., *Albert Ball*, p. 54.

8 Ball had nineteen confirmed victories (Ref: Ibid., p. 183) when Richthofen achieved his first on 17 September 1916.

9 Supf, P., *Fluggeschichte*, vol. II, p. 346.

10 *AOK 5. Armee Berichte*, Anlage 21, Verteilung der Fliegerverbände der 5. Armee Anfang Juni 1916, p. 2.

11 Ferko, A. E., 'Origin of First Jagdstaffeln', in '*Cross & Cockade*', 1965, pp. 341–6.

12 Immelmann, F., *Adler von Lille*, pp. 173–5.

13 F.E.2b 5235 of No. 23 Squadron, RFC, was flown back by Lt E. F. Allen who was unhurt; Lt Lindsay C. Powell was aged 21 (Ref: Hobson, *Airmen Died*, pp. 84, 231).

14 RFC *Communiqué No. 38*, 4 June 1916, p. 2.

15 Falls, C., 'Western Front 1915–1917: Stalemate', in Esposito, *Concise History*, p. 86.

16 Ibid., pp. 88–9.

17 *AOK 6. Armee Bericht*, Nr. 54749 Besondere Anordnungen,12 June 1916, p. 1.

18 O'Connor, N., *Aviation Awards*, vol. I, p. 25.

19 Immelmann, op. cit., p. 84 contends that at this time KEK III became 'the first self-standing Kampfeinsitzerstaffel'. Stofl 6. Armee reports of the time continued to refer to operations of both KEK III and Feldfl.-Abt 5b.

20 Supf, op. cit., p. 308.
21 Quoted in Immelmann, op. cit., p. 176.
22 Ibid., pp. 178–9; F.E.2b 6940 of No. 25 Squadron, 2/Lt Charles S. Rogers, aged 24 (KiA) and Sgt H. Taylor (WiA/PoW); (Ref: Hobson, op. cit., pp. 88, 232).
23 Probably Fokker E.IV 127/16.
24 Franks, N., et al. *Above the Lines*, p. 76.
25 Ibid., p. 41.
26 RFC *Communiqué No. 39*, 21 June 1916, p. 4.
27 RFC/RAF *Western Front Casualty List*.
28 Böhme, E., *Briefe eines deutschen Kampffliegers*, pp. 30-1.
29 Welkoborsky, N., *Vom Fliegen*, p. 108.
30 Kempe, R., *Immelmann*, pp. 62–5; the original English text appears in Welkoborsky, op. cit., pp. 96–7. Lt H. O. Long was an active member of No. 3 Squadron, RFC, and was mentioned five times in the RFC Communiqués. On 16 July he and Capt A. J. Evans were brought down in Morane-Saulnier Parasol Type PA.197 and taken prisoner (Ref: *Western Front Casualty List*).
31 DLV licence No 631, 19 December 1913 (Ref: Supf, op. cit., p. 666); born on 11 June 1883, Moosmaier received his *Flugzeugführer-Abzeichen* 30 years and six days later.
32 Immelmann, op. cit., p. 178.
33 O'Connor, op. cit., p. 219; it should be noted that the units listed had sub-units which evolved as *Jagdstaffeln* (see Appendix 2). They were: Kampfeinsitzerstaffel Douai under Feldflieger-Abteilung 5b, part of Kampfeinsitzerstaffel Vaux under Feldflieger-Abteilung 23, and part of Kampfeinsitzerstaffel Vaux under Feldflieger-Abteilung 67.
34 Zuerl, op. cit., p. 359; Ltn Otto Parschau's last fight, on 21 July 1916 over Bapaume, may well have been with a Morane Parasol of No. 3 Squadron, two F.E.2bs of No. 22 Squadron and three Airco D.H.2s of No. 24 Squadron; however, no British losses were acknowledged (Ref: RFC *Communiqué No. 44*, 24 July 1916, pp. 3–4).
35 Ferko, A. E., *Fliegertruppe 1914–1918*, p. 6.
36 Miller, T. and Puglisi, W., 'Jasta B', in '*Cross & Cockade*', 1968, p. 314.
37 Boelcke, op. cit., p. 106.
38 Commissioned into the Garde-Jäger-Bataillon in Potsdam.
39 Böhme, op. cit., pp. 43–4.
40 Kriegsministerium (organisation manual), Teil 10 Abschnitt B, *Fliegerformationen*, p. 234.
41 Ritter, H., *Luftkrieg*, pp. 166–7.
42 With 2. Husaren-Regiment Nr. 19 Kronprinz Wilhelm des Deutschen Reiches (Ref: Zickerick, W. 'Verlustliste', in von Eberhardt (ed.), *Unsere Luftstreitkräfte*, p. 6).
43 Bowyer, op. cit., pp. 74, 183. This source indicates that Ltn von Arnim was a member of 'Flieger-Abteilung 207, Kampfstaffel 3, based at Bertincourt'. AOK 1 report *Anlage zu Ic/A./IId Nr 4341/634* of the same time period shows Bertincourt hosting only Kagohl 3 Staffeln 13 and 14, Fl.-Abt. (A) 210, and Jastas 1 and 2. Kasta 14 combat reports in the author's archives record Ltn von Arnim's earlier flights with that unit. Fl.-Abt (A) 207 operated on 5. Armee's Front.
44 Fokker D.III 352/16.
45 Richthofen, M. von, op. cit., pp. 107–8.

CHAPTER 4

Twist of Fate

OSWALD BOELCKE'S THREE-MONTHS' ABSENCE FROM THE FRONT HAD NOT dulled his air fighting skill, which he demonstrated on the afternoon of 2 September 1916. Blossoming puffs of black smoke drew his attention to a greenish-brown B.E.2c two-seat bomber over Bapaume. The German anti-aircraft battery commanders stopped firing as soon as they spotted a German aircraft and, left to his work, Boelcke dived on the bomber and fired both machine-guns in the hope of scoring a quick victory.

His quarry managed to slip away, but an Airco D.H.2 single-seat pusher biplane escort came after Boelcke. The master soon drew his would-be attacker away from the others and, as he later wrote: 'I did not let him get away, [and] he did not get off any more shots. On the way down he made violent convulsive swings, all quite involuntarily, as he told us later, because his elevator control wires had been shot away. He came down north-east of Thiepval. The pilot jumped out of the burning machine[1] and beat on his hands and feet, which were also burning. [Then] I flew home to get fresh ammunition so that I could go out again ...'[2]

The pilot, Captain R. E. Wilson, was taken prisoner and Boelcke recorded his 20th victory. Next day he drove to the prisoner holding area and, casually trading on his prestige – very identifiable by the *Pour le Mérite* at his neck – had Wilson released into his temporary custody. Back at Bertincourt both men enjoyed a rare and pleasant occasion to sit and chat over a cup of coffee. Boelcke walked with Wilson around the airfield, pointing out items of interest as if the Briton were a normal visitor. Later that morning, having had his first and perhaps only experience of German hospitality, Wilson was transported back to the PoW compound.[3]

Then it was back to business for Boelcke. During the next two weeks, he kept Jagdstaffel 2's score high by shooting down six more British aircraft. Behind the lines, he had his pilots practise close formation flying and in mock dogfights showed them how to penetrate enemy formations. When he felt that his young hunters were ready, he took them along on combat sorties.

Leutnant Erwin Böhme described the mission of Monday, 11 September: ' ... our new machines will arrive at the end of this week. So I have pushed to be allowed to use temporarily a cast-off Halberstadt, [while] Boelcke has his old Fokker [D.II] ... Yesterday I flew with Boelcke for the first time. This morning we had several encounters with great swarms of Englishmen, who are now quite unbelievably daring – when we are all together [as a unit] we are cautious of them.

'Boelcke has already dispatched his 22nd.[4] He is quite a splendid fellow, not only as a flyer, but also esteemed as a human being – not a trace of personal ambition and braggadocio, always completely devoted to duty, and with enviably strong nerves.'[5]

The Albatros Era Begins

The Fokker D-Types, with their steel tube frames and 160hp Oberursel U.III rotary engines, proved unworthy successors to the once formidable Eindeckers that had gained aerial superiority for the Germans, and in short order they were replaced by the new single-seat biplane series developed by the Albatros Flugzeugwerke, which had built its reputation on strong, reliable two-seat B-Type and C-Type biplane reconnaissance aircraft.

The Albatros D.I's eminently reliable water-cooled Mercedes 160hp stationary engine made it faster and more manoeuvrable than the Fokker and the 120hp Halberstadt D-Types then in service.[6] The Albatros' sleek appearance – marked by its streamlined, plywood-covered semi-monocoque fuselage – led to its being nick-named the *Haifisch* [shark]. Its twin machine-guns, as opposed to the singles on the Fokker and the Halberstadt, gave the sleek fighter killing power akin to its voracious namesake.

Erwin Böhme wrote: 'Our new machines ... are far improved over the single-seaters we flew at Verdun. Their climb rate and manoeuvrability are astonishing; it is as if they were living, feeling beings that understand what their master wishes. With them, one can dare and achieve everything.'[7]

A significant event in aerial combat history is contained within the terse Royal Flying Corps account of a sortie on Sunday, 17 September 1916: 'A bombing raid carried out by machines of the 3rd Brigade was heavily engaged by about 20 hostile machines on its return from Marcoing Station ... Four [F.E.2b] machines of No. 11 Squadron and two [B.E.2cs] of No. 12 Squadron, which took part in the raid, did not return.'[8]

At about 1100 hours, Boelcke and five comrades were flying in close formation towards the British lines. At about the same time, fourteen RFC aircraft were heading for Marcoing railway station, south-south-east of Cambrai. Boelcke spotted them crossing the lines and led his flight eastwards to intercept them.

The British aircraft reached their target first and were dropping more bombs on the blazing station when the Jasta 2 fighters arrived and plunged into the formation of bombers and their escorts,[9] splitting them into isolated targets. Boelcke did not fire at first; he paused to watch and, if need be, protect a new man who might be too intent on his quarry to notice an enemy fighter on his tail.

Richthofen closed in on an F.E.2b whose pilot took evasive action while the observer kept up a constant fire from the rear machine-gun. The British aircraft veered off into an evasive zig-zag pattern. Moments later, when it seemed that the F.E. crew had eluded him, Richthofen suddenly appeared behind them and began firing into the engine compartment until it shut down.

The F.E.2b came down on the German airfield at Flesquières,[10] and Richthofen followed and landed near his victim. He approached the wreckage as soldiers removed the dying pilot and dead observer.[11] This time Richthofen stood by and watched silently; in the future, his hunter's instincts would prevail and he would cut the serial number from the fuselage or rudder fabric and take other trophies.

Back at Bertincourt here was much to celebrate. Jasta 2 had recorded the first confirmed victories for Richthofen and for Böhme, who had shot down a Sopwith two-seater.[12] Leutnant der Reserve Hans Reimann had achieved his second 'kill', an F.E.2b[13] from the flight that Richthofen had attacked, and Staffel leader Boelcke recorded his 27th, this too an F.E.2b.[14] The day's successes had been remarkable. Flying unfamiliar aircraft which had arrived only the previous evening, Jasta 2 had outfought seasoned opponents. This achievement gave Boelcke's new unit immediate prestige[15] and it was celebrated that evening.

Ordinarily, Army ground officers would get together in the *Kasino* [officers' club], the non-commissioned officers would have their party in another facility and other ranks held their festivities in the General Mess. But, as the newest branch of the service, the Fliegertruppe established new traditions. Officers and enlisted pilots flew and fought together, and had much in common with one another, as well as with the enlisted ground crews who maintained the aircraft, so an open display of camaraderie was in the best interest of everyone.

Boelcke crowned the evening by presenting the Iron Cross 1st Class to Böhme, personally pinning the Teutonic battle symbol to the new pilot's tunic. Richthofen had already received this award and it was too soon for his *Ehren-becher* to have arrived; but later that evening, he marked his achievement in his own way. He wrote to a jeweller in Berlin, ordering a plain silver cup, two inches high by one inch wide. The inscription was to read: '1. Vickers 2. 17.9.16', to mark his first victory, achieved against a 'Vickers' -type two-seater on 17 September 1916. He was to continue ordering these cups until, after his 60th victory in September 1917, the jeweller was no longer able to produce them because of the shortage of silver.[16]

Boelcke scored his 28th victory two days later, 19 September, when he led his Albatros against a flight of F.E.2bs, escorted by Morane-Saulnier 'Bullet' monoplane fighters. He shot down one of the Moranes[17] over Grévillers Wood. Shortly afterwards, General der Infanterie Fritz von Below, commander of 1. Armee, singled out Boelcke's and Jasta 2's performance in the daily reports:

'On 17 September, twelve enemy airmen were shot down in the 1. Armee area. Of these, ten fell victim to the bold attacks of our pilots and two to the well-aimed fire of our anti-aircraft guns ... During the period from 1 to 19 September, 50 enemy aircraft were shot down in combat, of which nine were by Hauptmann Boelcke, who has in total knocked down 28 aircraft.'[18]

Three days later, Leutnant der Reserve Winand Grafe went up, looking for his first victory. This 22-year-old pilot from the Ruhr probably never saw the lone Nieuport that dived out of the clouds and opened fire from beneath him with its wing-mounted Lewis machine-gun. Grafe's aircraft went into a steep dive and crashed just east of Bapaume. It is likely that he was the 23rd victim of Lieutenant Albert Ball of No. 60 Squadron.[19]

Jasta 2's first combat loss was a sobering experience for the new unit, but Oswald Boelcke was determined not to let it affect morale. Next morning, taking off despite a ground mist, he led five comrades towards their hunting-ground over Bapaume. There they attacked six Martinsyde G.100 'Elephant' single-seaters. The big, ungainly two-bay biplanes were aptly named; they were better bomb-carriers than combat machines.[20]

Manfred von Richthofen shot down a G.100 over Beugny for his second victory.[21] Moments later, Erwin Böhme and Hans Reimann each hit an intruder.[22] Reimann turned towards his intended fifth victim, another Martinsyde,[23] and suddenly was knocked out of the sky when the pilot of the bomber deliberately rammed him. He went down out of control and crashed at Noreuil, just north of Beugny, and was killed. The Martinsyde was badly damaged, but got away and its pilot survived.

Aces Down

The Jagdflieger seemed to be bound to one another by a blood knot that manifested itself in various ways. Hans Reimann's death was followed quickly by the loss of two other early Eindecker pilots: Boelcke's first competitor, Kurt Wintgens, on 25 September and Immelmann's Bavarian comrade, Max Mulzer, on 26 September.

According to a German account, Wintgens and fellow *Pour le Mérite* holder Walter Höhndorf were escorting a reconnaissance unit over the lines when they were surprised by two Martinsydes that dived out of the sun.[24] Wintgens' fuel tank was pierced by machine-gun fire, his Fokker caught fire and, as parachutes had not been issued at this date, he crashed to his death. When the 19-victory ace was buried at St-Quentin next day, his *Ordenskissen* was carried by Leutnant Höhndorf, who had less than a year of life left to him.

Max Mulzer, who had carried Immelmann's awards, died on the day that Wintgens was buried. He was test flying a new Albatros D.I from the 6. Armee's air depot at Valenciennes and suddenly the aircraft went out of control and crashed. Mulzer's black velvet awards pillow bore the *Pour le Mérite*, which he had received on 8 July 1916 after achieving the then required eight victories. More importantly for the Bavarian airman was that, on 6 September, he had become the first fighter pilot to receive his kingdom's highest award for bravery, the Knight's Cross of the Military Max Joseph Order. The award also conferred personal nobility on the recipient and for twenty days he had been known as Leutnant Max Ritter (knight) von Mulzer.[25]

On 27 September, Boelcke and four comrades went up near Bapaume, each intent on avenging the death of their popular comrade Hans Reimann. Just west of their airfield they caught a patrol of six Martinsyde G.100s and Boelcke shot down one of them north of Ervillers; it was credited as his 29th victory.[26]

The Staffel leader then got on the tail of another Martinsyde and fired at it repeatedly. 'I was astonished at the opponent's tenacity,' Boelcke wrote. 'I must have long since really finished him off, but he flew on in the same way, around in a big circle. Finally it became apparent. I said to myself the fellow is long since dead and the machine is held on course by the rubber cords on the steering mechanism being in the right-hand position. Therefore I flew right up next to him and saw the occupant slumped over to the right, lying dead in the fuselage. In order to know later which of my victories this one was, I noted the [rudder serial] number – 7495 – pulled away from him and then took on the next one.'[27]

Although both Boelcke and Reimann had attacked the Martinsyde, neither had actually shot it down and, consequently, neither pilot received credit for it. Eventually the 'ghost aircraft' came down within the German lines, where the pilot's body was recovered and buried.[28]

Jasta 2 scored again on 30 September. Under a bright autumn sun, British ground forces were recovering the Pozières Ridge and the Ancre Valley, reinforced by the Royal Flying Corps. Pushing ahead briskly, aircraft of Nos. 12 and 13 Squadrons bombed Jasta 2's airfield at Lagnicourt-Marcel. They were escorted by Nieuport and Morane fighters of No. 60 Squadron and F.E.s of No. 11 Squadron. The bombers paid for their success when Richthofen pounced on an F.E.2b over the town of Frémicourt and sent it down in flames. It was credited as his third victory.[29]

The following day, Sunday, 1 October 1916, was no day of rest. There was heavy fighting for Eaucourt l'Abbaye, south-west of Bapaume, as British and Canadian ground forces advanced against German positions with continual help from artillery spotting aircraft.[30] Boelcke attacked a 'B.E. biplane' over the village and brought it down near Flers; it was recorded as his 30th victory.[31]

At the end of a week of bad weather, on the morning of 7 October, Boelcke and Richthofen claimed further successes. The Master opened fire on his 31st victim, a Nieuport two-seater. He must have hit the fuel tank because the Nieuport exploded in a cloud of flame and fragments east of Morval.[32]

Minutes later and just over 10 kilometres to the east, Boelcke's pupil caught up with a B.E.12 single-seater and shot it down for his fourth victory.[33] Richthofen obtained the serial number patch of fabric from the crash site and sent it home to Schweidnitz, later to be displayed in a family museum. German authorities confirmed having examined the B.E.12 wreckage and identifying the pilot and his squadron, but less care seems to have been taken with the Englishman's corpse, which has no known grave.[34]

The Air Service is Reorganised

A period of foul weather hindered flight operations on the Somme Front. During a reorganisation of German forces at that time, on 8 October the Fliegertruppe was transformed from a loose structure to a unified command. Generalleutnant Ernst von Hoeppner, a cavalry veteran,[35] was appointed Commanding General of the Luftstreitkräfte (Air Force). Later he wrote that a prime objective was to change 'the scope of what had been under Chief of Field Aviation von der Lieth-Thomsen for aviation, captive balloons, Army airships and the Army Weather Service, as well as the anti-aircraft and home defence units'.[36]

Under Hoeppner, the fifteen Jagdstaffeln were expanded to 37 in time for the spring offensive of 1917.[37] Pilots continued to fly individual patrols, seeking targets of opportunity, but greater emphasis was placed on developing strategies and tactics for masses of aircraft and even entire air units.

Within this operational area, the progress of several fellow Regular Army officers reinforced in Richthofen the opportunities that the Luftstreitkräfte offered to dedicated, ambitious pilots. Oberleutnant Hans Berr,[38] at age 26 two years older and a flyer months longer than Richthofen, became commanding officer of Jasta 5 at Gonnelieu. Richthofen's former pilot, Oberleutnant Paul

Hennig von Osterroht,[39] then 29 and soon to be promoted Hauptmann, was commanding Rumaucourt-based Kampfstaffel S 1, a forerunner of the two-seat low-level attack aircraft units that were to be introduced in the following year's spring offensive. And Richthofen's former superior from Kampfstaffel 8, 29-year-old Hauptmann Victor Carganico,[40] was now leading the Bavarian unit Feld-flieger-Abteilung 3b out of Raillencourt.[41]

During a break in the bad weather on 10 October, Boelcke led repeated attacks against RFC aircraft attempting to bomb German airfields and other targets along a north-easterly course from Longueval to Jasta 2's airfield at Lagnicourt. Within three hours the Staffel claimed the destruction of five enemy aircraft. In combat, when a fighter pilot must be intent on his target while keeping a sharp look-out to avoid becoming one himself, the situation is confused. So two or more pilots may have claimed the same victory and, lacking the gunsight cameras installed in fighter aircraft during the Second World War, the awarding process was imperfect, to say the least.

The morning's successes began at 0950 hours when Erwin Böhme scored his second victory, a D.H.2[42] shot down over British-held Longueval. At 1100 hours Offizierstellvetreter Max Müller's first victory was an F.E.2b which he brought down over Bancourt.[43] At 1200 hours Leutnant der Reserve Hans Imelmann, a recent arrival from Kampfeinsitzer-Kommando Metz and no relation to the renowned Saxon ace, also achieved his first victory, a Sopwith 1½ Strutter[44] over Lagnicourt. At the same time, Manfred von Richthofen claimed a 'Vikkers' over the village of Ytres, a few kilometres east of Léchelle, but credit was given to a two-seater crew.[45] That was the first and last time that Richthofen lost a contested claim; in the future, he would fly as close as possible to his opponent, leaving no question as to the victor's identity. Also at noon, Boelcke was credited with knocking down an F.E.2b over le Sars,[46] his 32nd victory.

Following several days of wind, rain and low clouds, when the weather broke on the afternoon of 16 October, Jasta 2 headed south-west for its hunting-grounds in the vicinity of Bapaume, an important rail centre. German ground commanders reported heavy artillery shelling being directed by aircraft and Boelcke led his flight to the most active area. At 1405 hours, Leopold Reimann attacked an artillery-spotting B.E.2 over Warlencourt.[47] After a protracted fight during which the RFC observer was wounded, the two-seater[48] went down south-west of Thiepval; it was recorded as Reimann's third victory. At 1430 hours Boelcke achieved his 33rd victory when he attacked a B.E.2d that was directing artillery along the front line and shot it down east of Hébuterne.[49] At 1700 hours Leutnants Manfred von Richthofen and Jürgen Sandel, a new arrival from Flieger-Abteilung 39, attacked a formation of single-seat B.E.12s over

Ruyaulcourt and shot down two of them over Ytres. No doubt mindful of his earlier disappointment near Ytres, Richthofen stayed with his quarry this time and received credit for his fifth victory, but Sandel's claim was disallowed, despite the fact that both RFC aircraft fell within German lines and no other pilot claimed credit for shooting it down.[50] Boelcke capped the day's triumphs at 1745 hours, when he shot down an Airco D.H.2[51] north-east of Beaulencourt; it was credited as his 34th victory.

Good Hunting

Boelcke and a more senior comrade, 27-year-old Oberleutnant Stephan Kirmaier, took the 'old man' of Jasta 2, Leutnant Erwin Böhme, up for a hunt on Tuesday, 17 October.[52] Boelcke scored his 35th victory and Kirmaier also shot down a two-seater, which was confirmed as his fourth victory. Only 'old' Böhme was scoreless that day, but he did not complain. He remained full of admiration for his leader, as indicated in a letter home: 'I assure you, I admire Boelcke not only as my boss, on the contrary – as remarkable as it is that I am 37 and he is just 25 years old – I look up to him as a man and I am proud that a friendly relationship has grown between us.'[53]

Boelcke's score mounted: No. 36 on 20 October, and Nos. 37 and 38 two days later. His string of victories was interrupted when elements of French Fourth and Sixth Armies advanced against le Transloy, south of Bapaume, under cover of fog on the morning of 23 October. Bad weather for the next two days enabled RFC units to continue to direct artillery in the area, relatively unhampered by German fighters. During a break in the weather on the morning of the 25th, Jasta 2 attacked the artillery spotters and achieved the day's only German victories in the area,[54] all within a three-hour period.

Manfred von Richthofen opened the score-sheet by bringing down a B.E.12 single-seater north of Bapaume at 0935 hours.[55] This, his sixth victory, was also his third consecutive B.E.12, which was regarded as so 'clumsy and incapable' against German fighters that Major-General Hugh M. Trenchard, Commander of the RFC in France, felt compelled to order that no more B.E.12s be sent to the Front.[56] Boelcke's 39th victory, a B.E.2,[57] went down between Miraumont and Puisieux at 1210 hours.

Despite blustery weather, on the afternoon of 26 October, Boelcke got behind a B.E.2,[58] just south-west of Serre, and killed the observer with a burst of machine-gun fire during his first pass. He returned and killed the pilot and then watched the aircraft go down and crash and burn within the forward British lines. Boelcke withdrew only when he was attacked by an Airco D.H.2.[59] It was the master fighter pilot's 40th and last victory. Hans Imelmann forced down a Nieuport single-seat fighter[60] that had shot at Boelcke; it was credited as his third victory.

Boelcke's Last Fight

Rain and heavy wind all day caused most flight operations to be cancelled on Friday, 27 October, offering welcome relief to airmen on both sides. The following afternoon, what promised to be a time of rest for Jasta 2 changed. Just after 1600 hours, Staffel members were roused to readiness by a report of enemy air activity during an infantry attack. Boelcke led a flight to Flers and began attacking British single-seat fighters.

According to a British account: ' ... six Halberstadters and small Aviatiks attacked [Lieutenant Arthur G.] Knight and [Lieutenant Alfred E.] McKay, No. 24 Squadron, in the vicinity of Pozières. During the fight the enemy were reinforced by six more machines. At the end of about five minutes of strenuous fighting two of the German machines collided. Bits were seen to fall off, and one of the hostile aircraft glided away to the east, apparently under control, but was lost to sight. The fight continued for another fifteen minutes, when all the enemy machines withdrew, and the de Havillands [Airco D.H.2s] returned undamaged.'[61]

In the frenzy of the fight, Oswald Boelcke and Erwin Böhme were chasing Knight's Airco D.H.2 when another D.H.2. pursued by Manfred von Richthofen crossed in front of them. Instinctively the other two Albatros pilots took evasive action, but, obstructed by their top wings, lost sight of each other for an instant. Just as Böhme pulled up, his undercarriage was grazed by Boelcke's upper wing. That slight bump loosened the wing, which collapsed and sent Boelcke into a steep dive to his death.[62]

No blame for Boelcke's death was assigned to any member of the Jasta 2 flight, but Böhme assumed a great measure of guilt for the rest of his brief life. Richthofen, on the other hand, made no concession regarding the interference he caused by his pursuit of a potential victory. In a letter home he admitted only that his mentor's death 'affected all of us very deeply – as if a favourite brother had been taken from us'.[63]

A special RFC flight crossed the German lines and dropped a wreath by parachute near the airfield at Lagnicourt. It bore the inscription: 'To the memory of Captain Boelcke, our brave and chivalrous foe. From the British Royal Flying Corps.'[64]

Hauptmann Oswald Boelcke died at the pinnacle of achievement. At 25 he was the same age as Immelmann, but had more than doubled his Saxon rival's score. Boelcke had become Germany's highest scoring fighter ace and, accordingly, his body was taken to Germany for a hero's funeral. The Staffel's representative was Manfred von Richthofen, who was accorded the honour of carrying Boelcke's black velvet *Ordenskissen* during the ceremony at Cambrai. Then 24, Richthofen would go on to double Boelcke's score in the next eighteen months. Having missed the funeral train to Boelcke's adopted home town of Dessau and having to return to flying duties at Lagnicourt, Richthofen paid a warrior's tribute to his fallen mentor by scoring a victory on 3 November.

Pursuing the Pour le Mérite

Meanwhile, on 30 October 1916, Oberleutnant Stephan Kirmaier became Jasta 2's new commander. He was a seasoned combat pilot,[65] having scored two victories with Kampfeinsitzer-Kommando Jametz and five more with Jasta 2. He was the Staffel's senior officer, after Boelcke, and its next highest scoring fighter pilot. Like his predecessor, Kirmaier allowed no aerial stunts, but concentrated on the twin tasks of becoming an aggressive fighter pilot and a fitting successor to Boelcke.[66]

Following his eighth victory, a B.E.2 which he attacked over le Sars on the afternoon of 1 November,[67] 27-year-old Kirmaier should have been recommended for the *Pour le Mérite*. He was a rising star among the Jagdflieger and set a good example for his men, but he would have to do even more in order to qualify for the much-coveted blue Maltese cross.

Meanwhile, Kirmaier's ambitious subordinate, Manfred von Richthofen, achieved his seventh victory on 3 November.[68] Six days later, Kirmaier was credited with his ninth after he drove down a single-seat B.E.2 near Mory.[69] An hour later on that morning of 9 November, Richthofen stayed right behind the Staffel leader in the rankings by shooting down a single-seat B.E.2, which was recorded as his eighth victory.[70]

On 11 November, the award of the *Pour le Mérite* was announced for Leutnants der Reserve Gustav Leffers of Jasta 1 and Albert Dossenbach of Feldflieger-Abteilung 22. An army report also noted that both Leutnant Manfred von Richthofen of Jasta 2 and Oberleutnant Hans Berr of Jasta 5 had been awarded the Knight's Cross of the Royal Order of the House of Hohenzollern with Swords.[71] Even though Berr had attained his ninth victory two days before Dossenbach, he had not yet received the Hohenzollern award, which Dossenbach had been awarded on 21 October. With few exceptions this high award from the Kaiser's own royal house became a required intermediate award between the Iron Cross 1st Class and the *Pour le Mérite*.[72]

After receiving the Hohenzollern award, Richthofen went on leave, returning in time to celebrate Kirmaier's tenth victory on 16 November 1916. During a day marked by 'low clouds, strong winds and showers',[73] Kirmaier claimed his eleventh and last victory at about 0900 hours on 20 November.[74] Striving to match his leader's performance, Richthofen scored his ninth victory 40 minutes later.[75]

On 22 November, Kirmaier sought to raise the score even higher as he led the Staffel over British lines, west of Bapaume. Leutnant Erwin Böhme wrote: 'Our British clientele is somewhat intimidated – we must seek them out farther and farther on the other side. Five of us were under way and were attacked by two big squadrons at the same time over there. Each of us had to handle several opponents. I saw Kirmaier as he hotly pursued a Vickers two-seater, but [he] had several behind him ...'[76]

A Morane-Saulnier parasol monoplane[77] suddenly appeared in front of Böhme; he fired and sent it crashing down into Delville Wood, east of Longueval, as his sixth confirmed victory.[78] Four Jasta 2 Albatroses returned to Lagnicourt that afternoon – minus Staffel leader Kirmaier who had been shot down over Lesboeufs, north-west of Morval, by one or more Airco D.H.2s.[79] Generally, the *Pour le Mérite* was not awarded posthumously[80] and so consideration of Kirmaier for the high honour would have been withdrawn.

The Rise of Richthofen

On an interim basis, Jasta 2 was nominally commanded by Oberleutnant Karl Bodenschatz, the Staffel's chief administrative officer. Like Stephan Kirmaier before him, Manfred von Richthofen was the highest-scoring flying officer in the unit and he became the *de facto* leader in the air. He was the boldest, most aggressive pilot in the unit and displayed natural leadership qualities that commanded respect. The following day, he avenged Kirmaier's death and proved his worth by defeating the RFC's most highly decorated fighter pilot.

At about 1500 hours on Thursday, 23 November, Jasta 2 pilots encountered Airco D.H.2s of No. 24 Squadron. According to one British account, the squadron commander, Major Lanoe G. Hawker, VC, DSO, joined by Captain John O. Andrews and Lieutenant (later Air Marshal Sir) Robert Saundby, 'engaged two hostile machines near Bapaume and drove them East. They then saw two strong hostile patrols approaching high up. The [D.H.2] patrol was about to retire when Major Hawker dived and continued the pursuit of the first hostile machines. The de Havillands were at once attacked by the two strong hostile patrols, one of the enemy's machines diving on to the tail of Major Hawker's de Havilland ...'[81]

The first Albatros was driven off by Captain Andrews, who was then attacked from the rear and forced to break off the combat. The Albatros seen in the pursuit was piloted by Richthofen, who went after Hawker and, after a protracted fight, shot him down about 250 metres east of Luisenhof Ferme, an abandoned farm along the road to Flers, south of Bapaume.

The D.H.2 piloted by Major Hawker, a 9-victory ace and first 'air fighting' recipient of Great Britain's highest bravery award, the Victoria Cross,[82] became the 11th confirmed victim of Manfred von Richthofen. Hawker had been killed by one shot in the back of the head. He was buried where he fell, in an unmarked grave, with only the broken D.H.2 as a final monument.[83]

Jasta 2's next commanding officer, 30-year-old Oberleutnant Franz Josef Walz, was a pre-war military pilot[84] with both air combat and command experience. As a two-seater pilot in command of Kampfstaffel 2 of Kagohl 1, he had shot down six enemy aircraft within four months. More recently he had been in charge of establishing Jagdstaffel 19.[85]

When he arrived on 29 November 1916, Walz was expected to be a leader of Boelcke's calibre, but he scored only one victory during six months with Jasta 2 and, unfortunately for him, the lack of personal performance overshadowed his other qualities.[86]

At the time, Luftstreitkräfte Commanding General Ernst von Hoeppner was visiting front-line aviation units. During a dinner in his honour at Jasta 2, Erwin Böhme recalled, Hoeppner had been 'ordered from "on high" to convey some flattering comments to our Staffel, which was a welcome starting point for us, [and] to help influence all manner of wishes which would otherwise be held up in official channels; for example, regarding faster aircraft, more automobiles, etc. A special joy for the old gentleman was the décor of our officers' mess: on the ceiling, two big chandeliers made of captured British propellers and similar items.'[87]

Following General von Hoeppner's visit, an Imperial decree was issued, renaming Jagdstaffel 2 as Jagdstaffel Boelcke.[88] Within two weeks, on 20 December, Manfred von Richthofen brought some completion to the Boelcke saga when he shot down the RFC pilot whom his mentor and Erwin Böhme had been chasing at the time of their fatal collision. Richthofen was flying the same Albatros D.II in which he had defeated Major Hawker – the man he called 'the British Boelcke'[89] – when, at 1130 hours, he closed in on an Airco D.H.2 pusher biplane fighter and shot it down between Monchy le Preux and Adinfer Wood.

Like Hawker before him, this D.H.2 pilot – 21-year-old Captain Arthur G. Knight, DSO, MC – was experienced in aerial warfare, but was outclassed by an equally skilled adversary flying a superior aircraft. The 8-victory ace[90] and Hawker squadron-mate was recorded as Richthofen's 13th victory.

On 7 January 1917, Jasta Boelcke received its first Albatros D.IIIs. Although the new aircraft were powered by the same 160hp Mercedes engine used in the

D.IIs, they had wing and other design changes that gave them greater speed and faster rate of climb, while retaining great manoeuvrability.[91]

Richthofen Commands Jagdstaffel 11

Manfred von Richthofen was assigned one of the new Albatros D.IIIs, but did not get to use it in combat with Jasta Boelcke. A week later, on 14 January, he was appointed commanding officer of Royal Prussian Jagdstaffel 11, on the 6. Armee Front.[92] Jasta 11 was one of six new fighter units established on 28 September 1916,[93] as part of the concentration of single-seater combat aircraft. Under its first commander, 27-year-old Oberleutnant Rudolf Lang, the Staffel had been the least distinguished of the three fighter units attached to 6. Armee. Richthofen would change that.

Air chief Friedrich Stempel's early efforts to organise and deploy Kampfein-sitzer-Kommandos to provide air support for 6. Armee were refined by his successor, Hauptmann Otto Zimmer-Vorhaus. On 25 September 1916, Zimmer-Vorhaus assembled all the Prussian 'Fokker' (fighter) pilots under his command into Jagdstaffel Linck at Phalempin,[94] north of Douai. The unit was commanded by Oberleutnant Ludwig Karl Linck, a former cavalry officer[95] whom Zimmer-Vorhaus knew to be an aggressive pilot from their time together in Feldflieger-Abteilung 18. Three days later, as part of the Ministry of War's general directive, Linck's unit was redesignated Jasta 10[96] and, for a short time, its leader lived up to expectations. On 10 October he achieved the Staffel's first triumph by forcing a 'British Vikkers to land at Vitry, south-west of Douai'.[97]

Linck's career ended on Sunday, 22 October 1916, three days after his 27th birthday. He was shot down and killed over Provin, less than 10 kilometres west of his own airfield.[98] Ten days later, the luckless and demoralised Jasta 10 was transferred to Stenay, near the Meuse, and did not score again until January.

Until Jasta 12 arrived in mid-December 1916, the 6. Armee had only the lacklustre Jasta 11 for offensive patrols. A brief mention of the unit's protracted aerial battle with 27 enemy aircraft on 23 November indicated no German success.[99] By the time Manfred von Richthofen took command of Jasta 11, the nearby two-seater unit Feldflieger-Abteilung 18 had a higher victory score than his unit. On 7 January 1917, Abteilung 18's Leutnant Lübbert and Leutnant der Reserve Zühl were credited with forcing an F.E.2b to land within its own lines; the event having been witnessed by a nearby anti-aircraft unit.[100] Richthofen made note of the pilot's name, Friedrich-Wilhelm Lübbert, and eventually had him transferred to Jasta 11. Like Boelcke before him, Richthofen cultivated aggressive protégés who could become successful air fighters.

After two months of waiting, during which time his score doubled to sixteen, Manfred von Richthofen was awarded the *Pour le Mérite* on 12 January 1917.[101] Eight days later he arrived at Jasta 11's airfield at La Brayelle, just north-west of Douai, and set a new tone in air combat leadership. Here one of his first acts was to make a dramatic change in Jasta 11's appearance. The new Albatros D.III he had brought with him from Jasta B was decorated in the basic colour scheme then used – natural wood finish fuselage and olive-green and brown (or lilac-mauve) upper wing surfaces – and this was replaced by something radically different. Realising that it was virtually impossible to camouflage an aircraft in the air, he had his Albatros painted in a 'glaring red' to ensure that it would be immediately identifiable.[102]

Richthofen's pilots were concerned that the new paint scheme would make their leader a singular target, so he directed that *all* aircraft of his Staffel be painted mostly red, with each pilot adding additional markings in other colours. This system had the practical effect of enabling unit pilots to recognise one another in the air; for example, Leutnant Karl-Emil Schäfer had his elevator, rudder and most of the rear fuselage painted black, Leutnant Carl Allmenröder preferred white, and the one-time railway transportation officer Leutnant Kurt Wolff,[103] green.[104]

Jasta 11's First Fights

It was bright and clear on Tuesday, 23 January, when Richthofen led six of his pilots to the trenches near Lens for their first patrol. His flight arrived at the Front at the moment when two German reconnaissance aircraft were succumbing to attacks by RFC single-seat pusher fighters. After the wings of one of the large two-seaters had broken away and the fuselage plummeted to the ground, the British pilot attacked the second and sent it down.[105]

Richthofen charged head-on at one fighter, an F.E.8 'pusher', which dived away. He then chased another F.E.8 and stayed with it until it began to smoulder. At about 500 metres' altitude, the British pilot jumped or fell from his burning aircraft, which plunged to the ground leaving a pillar of thick smoke behind it.[106] The F.E.8 was logged as Richthofen's 17th victory[107] and his first in an Albatros D.III.

At noon next day he went up to monitor the performance of Sergeant Hans Howe, whose earlier service with Feldflieger-Abteilung 5b and Jasta 10 were good credentials for a new Staffel leader seeking to form a cadre of first-class fighter pilots. Richthofen spotted a flight of F.E.2bs on a photographic reconnaissance west of Vimy Ridge, less than 20 kilometres from Douai, and signalled to Howe to follow him. The sun directly behind the pair of Albatros made them nearly invisible to their intended victims. Richthofen and Howe dived on the leading aircraft. The F.E.2b crew put up a hard fight and, even after Richthofen hit the fuel tank and the big two-seater had to go down, the observer fired relentlessly at the red Albatros to deny it a complete kill. The big 'pusher'[108] came down near German trenches and the observer pulled the pilot from the wreckage and succeeded in setting fire to it while German soldiers were running towards it in the hope of securing it for intelligence value or as a trophy.

While requesting credit for his 18th victory, Richthofen reported that a crack in one of his lower wings required him to land quickly after the fight. The weakness may have been caused by the F.E.2b observer's machine-gun fire, but other recent losses of Albatros D.IIIs caused by wing failure made the latest occurrence a cause for concern. Shortly after this, all Albatros D.IIIs were sent to the Armee air depots for modifications: the undercarriage was strengthened, auxiliary braces were added to the lower section of the vee-interplane struts, and changes were made to the radiator to alleviate cooling problems.[109]

Until the Albatros were returned Richthofen flew a Halberstadt D.II, one of the early single-seat biplane successors to the Fokker Eindecker series, and scored one victory with the older fighter on 1 February 1917. That day it was Leutnant Carl Allmenröder's turn to be tutored by the leader. Carl, who had left his medical studies to join the artillery[110] with his elder brother Wilhelm in 1914, had joined his brother as a pilot with Flieger-Abteilung (A) 227, and the two of them transferred to Jasta 11 in November 1916.[111] Both became successful Richthofen protégés.

On this cold afternoon Richthofen saw a British two-seater ranging artillery against German troops near Vimy. He and Carl Allmenröder went after it and approached to within 50 metres of the target – to the point where Richthofen could not miss – and then opened fire. The two-seater did not return fire, but made a steep right-hand turn as if seeking to escape; it then went down out of control and crashed within German forward lines south-west of Thélus.[112] Immediately after the crew had left the wrecked B.E.2d, it was destroyed by shellfire from a Canadian battery.

Following confirmation of his 19th victory, Richthofen went on a short leave to visit his family in Schweidnitz, a town near his birth place, Breslau. During his absence two of his pupils added to the unit's success. On 5 February Vizefeldwebel Sebastian Festner and Anton Baierlein claimed a pair of B.E.2s north of Arras.[113] The fight ended over British lines and only Festner's claim was confirmed, but the demonstration was clear enough: Jasta 11 was inspired by its leader and took the initiative to look for opportunities even in his absence.

The same day, Leutnant Karl-Emil Schäfer reported to the Staffel for duty. Schäfer, a former infantry officer and proficient rifleman,[114] popularly known as 'Emil', had been badly wounded early in the war. When he realised that his effectiveness on the ground was impaired (he ended up with his left leg slightly shorter than his right)[115] he joined the Fliegertruppe. He scored his first victory while serving as a two-seater pilot with Kampfstaffel 11, and then the bold 25-year-old Rhinelander sent a telegram to Jagdstaffel 11 and asked if they could use him. Schäfer showed the spirit that Richthofen wanted and soon received orders to join the red aircraft Staffel.

After returning from leave, on the morning of 14 February Richthofen flew his newly repaired Albatros D.III to Pronville, where he visited friends at Jasta 2. On his way back, at about 1300 hours, he spotted a two-seater ranging artillery over the Lens–Hulluch road. He was not entirely sure that his aircraft was ready for combat, but, never one to pass up an opportunity, he approached to within 50 metres of the RFC aircraft and opened fire. The two-seater crashed into forward-area German trenches and was recorded as the ace's 20th victory.[116]

Later that afternoon Richthofen and his men returned to the area and in deteriorating weather attacked another flight of artillery-spotters. He went after a B.E.2 and claimed to have sent it down within British lines south-west of Mazingarbe. Although there was no corroborative statement and physical evidence to reinforce the claim, his standing was such that he was credited with his 21st victory.[117]

By now Richthofen had decided that Sergeant Hans Howe did not have the requisite qualities needed by a successful Staffel; since his arrival on 17 January 1917 he had not scored a single victory, and on 17 February he was posted out. Richthofen tended to give new men a relatively short time in which to prove themselves, and would settle for nothing less than cool-headed and resourceful pilots who shared his own devotion to duty.

A case in point is when Richthofen was made aware of the *second* report published in the 6. Armee area noting the bravery and daring of Leutnant Friedrich-Wilhelm Lübbert of Feldflieger-Abteilung 18, a unit from which many protégés would come. On 28 January 1917, according to the report, Lübbert and his observer, Oberleutnant Hans Helmuth von Boddien, both former mounted soldiers,[118] set out to destroy the bridge across the River Authie, 20 kilometres south of Etaples. They planned to land and blow up the bridge, but were frustrated by the presence of a large enemy force. So they flew over the target at 30 metres' altitude and dropped explosives which destroyed the railway line across the bridge. They then shot up two vehicles, setting fire to one of them.[119]

By year's end both men had been assigned to Jasta 11, which was fast becoming the most desired assignment for fighter pilots who felt that they had the ability to triumph in combat and who wanted advancement, recognition and the prestige of working with 'the new Boelcke'.

Notes

1   Airco D.H.2 7895 of No. 32 Squadron, Capt R. E. Wilson (PoW).
2   Boelcke, O., *Feldberichte*, pp. 111–12.
3   Ibid.
4   D.H.2 7842 of No. 24 Squadron on 9 September 1916 over Thiepval, pilot Lt Neville P. Manfield, aged 22 (KiA).
5   Böhme, E., *Briefe eines deutschen Kampffliegers*, pp. 51–2.
6   Grosz, P., 'Agile Albatros', in *Air Enthusiast* No. 1, p. 37.
7   Böhme, op. cit., p. 54.
8   RFC *Communiqué* No. 54, 24 September 1916, p. 3.
9   Jones, H. A., *War in the Air*, vol. II, pp. 282–3.
10 Being used then by Feldflieger-Abteilungen 22 and 41.
11 RFC *Western Front Casualty List* reports F.E.2b 7018, No. 11 Squadron, 'Left aerodrome at 9.10 a.m. Two F.E.s seen to go down under control west of Marcoing. Information received from 2/Lt. [A. L.] Pinkerton [of No. 11 Squadron, taken prisoner a day earlier] that both Morris and Rees were killed. Information from a private source that 2/Lt. Morris died at Cambrai hospital on Sept. 17th.' 2/Lt Lionel B. F. Morris was 19 years old and Capt Thomas Rees was 21 (Ref: Hobson, C., *Airmen Died*, pp. 75, 86, 234).
12 Sopwith 1½ Strutter A.1913 of No. 70 Squadron, 2/Lt Oswald Nixon (KiA) and Lt R. Wood (WiA/PoW) (Ref: Hobson, p. 234).
13 F.E.2b 4844 of No. 11 Squadron, 2/Lt T. P. L. Molloy and Sgt G. J. Morton (both PoW).
14 F.E.2b 7019 of No. 11 Squadron, Capt D. Gray and Lt L. B. Helder (both PoW).
15 Jones, op. cit., pp. 283ff.
16 Gibbons, F., *Red Knight*, p. 80.
17 Jones, op. cit., p. 284. According to RFC *Combat Casualty List* entry of that date, Morane-Saulnier Type N A.204 of No. 60 Squadron was observed 'with a hostile machine on his tail. Last seen going down in a spinning nose-dive at Achiet-le-Grand [less than 4 kilometres south-east of Grévillers]. One wing came off the machine.' Capt Hugh C. Tower, aged 30 (KiA).
18 *1. Armee Tagesbefehl* Nr. 17, 21 September 1916.
19 Shores, C., et al., *Above the Trenches*, p. 60.
20 Bruce, J., *British Aeroplanes*, p. 305.
21 Martinsyde G.100 7481 of No. 27 Squadron, Sgt Herbert Bellerby, aged 28 (KiA).
22 Both of No. 27 Squadron: Martinsyde 7475, 2/Lt Eric J. Roberts, and Martinsyde 7480, 2/Lt Oliver C. Godfrey, aged 28 (both KiA).
23 Martinsyde G.100 A.1565 piloted by Lt (later Air Marshal Sir) Leslie F. Forbes was badly damaged but got away and reached Bertangles airfield, the home of No. 24 Squadron at that time (Ref: Bowyer, C., *Flying Elephants*, pp. 40–1).
24 French ace Lt Albert Heurtaux of Escadrille Spa 3 claimed Wintgens as his eighth victory (Ref: Robertson, B. *Air Aces*, p. 70).
25 O'Connor, N., *Aviation Awards*, vol. I, pp. 9, 33.
26 Martinsyde G.100 A.1568 of No. 27 Squadron, 2/Lt Henry A. Taylor, aged 18 (KiA).
27 Boelcke, op. cit., pp. 117–18; Martinsyde G.100 7495 of No. 27 Squadron, 2/Lt Stephen Dendrino, aged 27 (KiA).
28 According to RFC *Western Front Casualty List*, 2/Lt Stephen Dendrino of No. 27 Squadron, 'left aerodrome 9.20 a.m. [and was] officially reported to have died whilst prisoner of war 27/9/16'. He was buried at Neuville-Vitasse, France (Ref: Hobson, op. cit., p. 40).

29 F.E.2b 6973 of No. 11 Squadron, Lt Ernest C. Lansdale, aged 21, and Sgt Albert Clarkson, aged 22 (both KiA).

30 Jones, op. cit., pp. 297–9.

31 *Stofl 1. Armee Wochenbericht*, Teil 3, 9 October 1916; no comparable RFC or French loss was recorded.

32 Ibid.; possibly a Nieuport N.XIIbis attached to the Farman unit Escadrille F.24, which reported Capt Cealle and Sous-Lt Fewius as 'missing in action' while on a reconnaissance patrol (Ref: *Etat Nominatif*, 16 November 1916, p. 2); there were no RFC Nieuport losses that day and the Morval area came under French control at the end of September 1916 (Ref: Jones, op. cit., pp. 300ff).

33 Ibid.; B.E.12 6618 of No. 21 Squadron, 2/Lt William C. Fenwick, aged 19 (KiA).

34 Hobson, op. cit., p. 45.

35 Neumann, G., *Deutschen Luftstreitkräfte*, p. 5; Zuerl, W., *Mérite-Flieger*, p. 227 gives 75. Reserve-Division.

36 Hoeppner, E. von, *Deutschlands Krieg*, p. 82.

37 Kriegsministerium, Teil 10 Abschnitt B, *Flieger-Formationen*, pp. 234–9.

38 Commissioned into Jäger-Regiment zu Pferde Nr. 4 in Graudenz.

39 Commissioned into Deutsch Ordens Infanterie-Regiment Nr. 152.

40 An early member of Flieger-Bataillon Nr. 4, Carganico remained active in aviation after the war, was re-activated in the Luftwaffe in 1934 and rose to the rank of Generalmajor. He was shot and killed while in the custody of Soviet troops on 27 May 1945 (Ref: Hildebrand, *Die Generale*, vol. I, pp. 144–5).

41 *Stofl 1. Armee*, op. cit., Teil 7 lists the various command and airfield assignments.

42 D.H.2 A.2540 of No. 24 Squadron, 2/Lt Norman Middlebrook (PoW), which was 'seen at 9.40 [a.m.] diving away from a hostile machine over le Transloy [north-east of Longueval]. The hostile machine was driven off and the de Havilland flattened out and was last seen flying west' (Ref: RFC *Western Front Casualty List*).

43 Despite the confirmation, no comparable RFC loss is recorded.

44 RFC *War Diary* entry for this date, confirmed by Hobson, op. cit., pp. 64, 235, the Sopwith two-seater was most likely A.382 of No. 70 Squadron, 2/Lt Francis M. Lawledge, aged 38 (KiA) and Lt J. B. Lawton (PoW).

45 Evans, W., 'Richthofen Victory List', in *Over the Front*, 1992, p. 131; aircraft claimed was probably F.E.2b 4292 of No. 25 Squadron, 2/Lt Moreton Hayne, aged 18 (KiA) and Lt Arthur H. M. Copeland (PoW), which was awarded to Vzfw Fritz Kosmahl and Oblt Neubürger of Feldfl.-Abt 22.

46 Despite official German confirmation, this is another 'elusive' victory; No. 11 Squadron lost F.E.2b 6992 that *afternoon* at a location north-east of Bapaume; le Sars is south-west of Bapaume. Further, the No. 11 Squadron loss had one particularly grim aspect – one of the two men jumped out of the burning aircraft – which Boelcke would have noted in his own short memoir, which contains no mention of this day's events.

47 Jones, op. cit., p. 303.

48 Very likely B.E.2e 5818 of No. 34 Squadron, observer 2/Lt C. K. M. Douglas (WiA), which made it back to British lines despite extensive damage (Ref: Jones, op. cit., p. 303)

49 B.E.2d 6745 of No. 15 Squadron, Sgt Frederick Barton and Lt Edward M. Carre, aged 22 (both KiA and buried at Hébuterne) (Ref: Hobson, op. cit., pp. 22, 31). 'Last [radio-telegraph] signal received at 1.20 p.m. Machine brought down in combat with five German aeroplanes and fell into cut wire entanglement in front of first line of trenches [at position] K.10. Machine shelled to pieces by enemy' (Ref: RFC *Western Front Casualty List*).

50 The aircraft, both from No. 19 Squadron, were B.E.12s 6620, flown by Capt Cecil R. Tidswell, aged 35, and 6580, flown by 2/Lt John Thompson, DCM, aged 22 (both KiA). It is likely that Richthofen was responsible for B.E.12 6580 because the fabric patch bearing that serial number was displayed in the Richthofen Museum at his home in Schweidnitz.

51 D.H.2 A.2542 of No. 24 Squadron, 2/Lt Patrick A. Langan-Byrne, DSO, aged 21 (KiA). RFC *Western Front Casualty List* states: 'The patrol of four [D.H.2s] was suddenly attacked north of le Transloy by 12 fast scouts. Lt [Langan-] Byrne's machine was seen to fall out of control, followed by a hostile machine. A.A. report that they saw these machines fall for a long way, but state the de Havilland

recovered about 6,000 feet and disappeared in the mist northeast, apparently pursuing the hostile aeroplane.' The ten-victory Irish ace has no known grave, but is listed on the Arras Memorial (Ref: Hobson, op. cit., p. 64, 235). Hobson and Shores, op. cit., list this casualty as occurring on 17 October; RFC *Communiqué* No. 58, 22 October 1916, p. 2, and the *Casualty List* report 16 October.

52 Boelcke mistakenly gave this day as 16 October 1916 (Ref: Boelcke, op. cit., p. 121), but other sources confirm that the action took place a day later.

53 Böhme, op. cit., p. 64.

54 Jones, op. cit., p. 310.

55 B.E.12 6629 of No. 21 Squadron, 2/Lt Arthur J. Fisher, aged 21 (KiA). RFC *Western Front Casualty List* reported: 'Left aerodrome at 7.45 a.m. A B.E.12 was reported by 11th A.A. Battery to be seen diving down 15,000 yards N.E. of Maricourt, apparently under control pursued by a German biplane. Letter from 5th Aus.Divn ... states the grave of 2/Lt. A. J. Fisher has been located ... [and] is marked with the regulation German wooden cross giving particulars.'

56 Jones, op. cit., p. 313.

57 B.E.2c 2524 of No. 4 Squadron, 2/Lt Stanley N. Williams and 2/Lt Geoffrey R. Bolitho, aged 23 (both KiA).

58 B.E.2c 6235 of No. 7 Squadron, 2/Lt Forrest G. Parsons and 2/Lt George A. Palfreyman, aged 23 (both KiA).

59 Boelcke, op. cit, p. 123. According to the British report: 'An attack made by a patrol of No. 60 Squadron dispersed a German formation. As a result of the engagement, two of our Nieuports had forced landings in our lines and a third is missing. The German formation, consisting of six machines, attacked and brought down a B.E.2c over Serre. Capt. [Ernest L.] Foot, No. 60 Squadron, dived at the leader [Boelcke], but was too late to assist the B.E.2c. Capt. Foot's Nieuport was considerably shot about, his gun mounting was put out of action, and he just succeeded in re-crossing the lines. He landed with his machine on fire. A patrol of No. 32 Squadron appears to have joined in this fight, and one of the enemy's machines [which was] brought down by [2/Lt F. H.] Coleman crashed to the ground close to the B.E.2c.' (Ref: RFC *Communiqué* No. 59, 28 October 1916, p. 3).

60 Nieuport Scout A.162, Capt Ernest L. Foot.

61 RFC *Communiqué* No. 60, 5 November 1916, p. 1.

62 Böhme, op. cit., pp. 69–70.

63 Quoted in Richthofen, K. von, *Kriegstagebuch*, p. 86.

64 Jones, op. cit., pp. 312ff.

65 Commissioned into the Bavarian 8. Infanterie-Regiment Grossherzog Friedrich II. von Baden.

66 Bolle, C., 'Jagdstaffel Boelcke' in Neumann, G., *In der Luft*, p. 41.

67 *Stofl 1. Armee*, ibid., Teil 3, 6 November 1916; B.E.2e 5006 of No. 9 Squadron, 2/Lt Stanley W. Mann, aged 21 (KiA), and 2/Lt Arthur E. Wynn, aged 20 (DoW) 'was reported to have been brought down near Rocquigny about 2.30 p.m. by hostile machines. It spiralled down under control and afterwards [was] observed intact on the ground.' (Ref: RFC *Western Front Casualty List*).

68 *Stofl 1. Armee*, ibid., Teil 4, 14 November 1916; F.E.2b 7010 of No. 18 Squadron, Sgt Cuthbert G. Baldwin, aged 28, and 2/Lt George A. Bentham, aged 21 (both KiA).

69 Ibid., Teil 4, 5 December 1916; B.E.2c 2502 of No. 12 Squadron, Lt G. F. Knight (PoW).

70 Ibid., Teil 4, 21 November 1916.; B.E.2c 2506 of No. 12 Squadron, 2/Lt Ian G. Cameron, aged 19 (KiA).

71 Ibid., Teil 8, 14 November 1916.

72 O'Connor, N., *Aviation Awards*, vol. II, pp. 132, 140, 142.

73 RFC *War Diary* entry for 20 November 1916.

74 *Stofl 1. Armee*, ibid., Teil 4, 5 December 1916; no comparable loss was recorded by the RFC.

75 Ibid.; B.E.2c 2767 of No. 15 Squadron, 2/Lt James C. Lees and Lt Thomas H. Clarke (both PoW).

76 Böhme, op. cit., p. 83.

77 Type P79 A.248 of No. 3 Squadron, 2/Lt E. P. Roberts and Capt G. L. Watson (both WiA).

78 Stofl 1. Armee, ibid., Teil 4, 5 December 1916.

79 Shores, C., et al., *Above the Trenches*, p. 125 credits Oblt Kirmaier's demise to 2/Lt Kelvin Crawford and Capt John O. Andrews of No. 24 Squadron; RFC *Communiqué* No. 63, 26 November 1916, p. 1,

mentions only Capt Andrews as having 'destroyed a hostile machine, which crashed on our side of the lines near Les Boeufs [Lesboeufs].'

80 O'Connor, op. cit., p. 91.

81 RFC *Communiqué* No. 64, 2 December 1916, p. 1; RFC *Combat Casualty List* entry for that day states: 'Left aerodrome 1.0 p.m. With two other de Havillands engaged 8 hostile machines over Achiet. Not seen after this encounter.'

82 Bowyer, C., *For Valour*, p. 40.

83 Ibid., p. 44.

84 Walz entered service in the 8. Infanterie-Regiment Grossherzog Friedrich II. von Baden, as did Kirmaier.

85 Zuerl, op. cit., pp. 467–8.

86 Walz was promoted to Hauptmann on 20 January 1917. Subsequently, he commanded Jasta 34b and Fl.-Abt. 304b and received the *Pour le Mérite* for his outstanding leadership. He remained in aviation between the wars and returned to active duty in the Luftwaffe in 1934. Rapidly promoted, he attained the rank of Generalleutnant on 1 April 1941. He was taken prisoner in Poland in May 1945 and died in captivity there on 18 December 1945. (Ref: Hildebrand, *Die Generale*, vol. III, pp. 470–1).

87 Böhme, op. cit., pp. 83–4.

88 *Kofl 1. Armee Wochenbericht*, Teil 8, 26 December 1916.

89 Richthofen, M. von, *Rote Kampfflieger*, p. 117.

90 Shores, et al., op. cit., pp. 226–7.

91 Grosz, op. cit., pp. 40–1.

92 *Kofl 6. Armee Wochenbericht* Nr. 22400, Teil 1, 23 January 1917.

93 Under Kriegsministerium *Befehl Nr 269. 10.16.A.7.L* of that date; the other units were Jagdstaffeln 10, 12, 13, 14 and 15 (Ref: Kriegsministerium, op. cit., pp. 234–5).

94 *Stofl 6.*, Nr. 19003, Teil 9, 2 October 1916; the same report notes that the Bavarians had their *Fokkerflieger* attached to one of their units, Feldfl.-Abt. 5b.

95 Commissioned into 2. Leib-Husaren-Regiment Königin Victoria von Preussen Nr. 2.

96 *Stofl 6.*, Nr. 19226, Teil 2, 9 October 1916; also see Appendix 2.

97 *Stofl 6.*, Nr. 19476, Teil 7, 16 October 1916. F.E.2b 4292 of No. 25 Squadron, 2/Lt Moreton Hayne, aged 18 (KiA), and Lt A. H. Copeland (WiA/PoW).

98 1st Brigade, RFC reported 22 air combats in this area and confirmed six enemy aircraft shot down over Pont-à-Vendin, Seclin and other locations reasonably close to Provin (Ref: RFC *Communiqué* No. 59, 28 October 1916, p. 2).

99 *Stofl 6.*, Nr. 20759, Teil 10, 28 November 1916.

100 *Kofl 6. Armee*, Nr. 22180, Teil 9, 16 January 1917.

101 Ibid., Nr. 22400, Teil 10, 23 January 1917.

102 Richthofen, M. von, *Rote Kampfflieger*, p. 120.

103 Commissioned into Eisenbahn-Bataillon Nr. 4.

104 Richthofen, M. von, *Heldenleben*, pp. 205–6.

105 The first two-seater shot down was probably one from Fl.-Abt. (A) 240, which lost the crew of Offstlvtr Wilhelm Mohs and Ltn.d.R Wilhelm Riehl over La Bassée; the second aircraft was very probably from Fl.-Abt. 13, which reported the loss of Offstlvtr Eduard Wesselewski and Ltn Wilhelm Schwarz at Avion, south of Lens (Ref: *Kofl 6. Armee*, Nr 22639, Teil 12, 30 January 1917).

106 Gibbons, op. cit., pp. 111–12.

107 *Kofl 6. Armee*, Nr. 22639, Teil 12, 30 January 1917; F.E.8 6388 of No. 40 Squadron, 2/Lt John Hay, aged 28 (KiA).

108 Ibid.; F.E.2b 6997 of No. 25 Squadron, Capt Oscar Greig, aged 27 (WiA/PoW) and 2/Lt John E. MacLenan, aged 20 (PoW).

109 Grosz, op. cit., pp. 41–2.

110 Ostfriesisches Feldartillerie-Regiment Nr. 62; his first name is often spelled 'Karl', but in his home town he was recorded as 'Carl'.

111 Schnitzler, E., *Carl Allmenröder*, p. 7.

112 Kofl 6., Nr. 22934, Teil 10, 9 February 1917; B.E.2d 6742 of No. 16 Squadron, Lt Percival W. Murray,

aged 20, and Lt Duncan J. McRae, aged 24 (both DoW). RFC *Western Front Casualty List* notes: 'Centre Group 3rd Can.Div.Art. reported one of our machines shot down and landed ... at 3.10 pm, as result of a fight between 3 British and 4 machines. [RFC] machine destroyed by shellfire 20 minutes later.'

113 *Kofl 6.*, op.cit.

114 First with Hannoversches Jäger-Bataillon Nr. 10 at Gosslar and then a Reserve component of West-fälisches Jäger-Bataillon Nr. 7 at Bückeburg.

115 Zuerl, op. cit., p. 406.

116 *Kofl 6.*, Nr. 23225 Teil 10, 15 February 1917; B.E.2d 6231 of No. 2 Squadron, 2/Lts Cyril D. Bennett, aged 19 (WiA/PoW) and Herbert A. Croft (KiA).

117 *Kofl 6.*, ibid.; possibly B.E.2c 2543 of No. 2 Squadron, Capt George C. Bailey, DSO, aged 26 (WiA) and 2/Lt George W. B. Hampton, aged 31, (KiA).

118 Lübbert came from Dragoner-Regiment König Carl I. von Rumänien (1. Hannoversches) Nr. 9, and von Boddien from Kürassier-Regiment Königen (Pommersches) Nr. 2.

119 *Kofl 6.*, op.cit., Nr. 22639, Teil 14.

CHAPTER 5
Springtime Successes

IN MID-FEBRUARY 1917, JAGDSTAFFEL 11 COMBAT FLIGHTS BECAME MORE numerous as air units of British First and Third Armies probed German lines in preparation for the coming spring offensive. Indeed, because the newly organised Jasta 30 had not yet received its aircraft, Jasta 11 was the only fighter unit in the 6. Armee area at the time and logged almost four times more sorties (84) and flight hours (86) than any other unit in that sector.[1]

There were few victories, but Manfred von Richthofen used these interdiction flights as training exercises for his new pilots. He taught them his tactics, based on what he had learned from Oswald Boelcke. Richthofen knew that novices at the Front were, like children, not yet fully formed in the art of survival. With practice, skill and luck in their early flights, they would mature and perhaps even thrive in the crucible of combat. As he told an officer from the General Staff: 'I have never had anything to do with '*Kanonen*' [aces], that is, with combat-proven, experienced airmen. Only with beginners. I do not always receive [the calibre of men] I request; it is not the way it is generally imagined. My gentlemen always come fresh out of flying school. I clearly emphasise that, first, they must be under my leadership, here in my Staffel ...

'The most important elements of flying, in my view, are skill in taking off and landing, and the personal courage with which a man goes after the enemy. To me, it is a thousand times better to have a daring fellow who might have difficulty making a left turn, but who goes hell bent for leather after the enemy, than the most elegant Johannisthal[2] airshow airman whom I cannot bring over the Front. We need daredevils, not aerial acrobats!'[3]

Citing the lessons of his own experience, Richthofen continued: 'I once flew with a gentleman who tore through dashing turns and made an absolutely marvellous impression. But in aerial combat, it seemed to me that he did not go after the enemy so smartly. And once when I was working with him, paying special attention to him – he was gone. I was in a damned tight spot and shot down an enemy, but got away by a hair. When I returned home, he reported to me that the moment the fight began he became so ill that he had to break off immediately. You could tell that when you looked at him. Aerial combat requires a special kind of nerve. [I said to him:] "Then I ask that you disappear immediately. I cannot use people who leave their comrades in the lurch. And when you feel sick, then you damned well better tell us at once." There are, of course, always people who try to delay things and think: no one will take any notice of it.'[4]

The fighting spirit that Richthofen wanted was displayed on 16 February by Leutnant Carl Allmenröder who spotted a B.E.2 with a new crew that was 'learning the country behind the lines'.[5] Determined not to let the two-seater get away, Allmenröder pursued it tenaciously and shot it down within German lines, east of Arras. The B.E.2 was recorded as the first[6] of his 30 confirmed victories.

Later in the month unfavourable weather hampered flight operations on both sides. When the RFC came out in significant numbers on Sunday, 4 March, Jasta 11 was ready for them. The unit was deployed in two Flights (*Schwärme*). Flight II carried out the morning patrol without incident. Close to midday, it was the other flight's turn to go hunting. Emil Schäfer recalled: '… Flight I was ready to take off and Richthofen wanted to go with it, but because of a small defect in his aircraft he had to stay behind. So I led the way. We were hardly at the Front when a British formation appeared, heading for Loos. We hit it over Lens, where at the same time it was attacked by three Germans from the Boelcke Staffel, as I learned later.

'My first opponent pulled away from me in a long dive. Before I could follow him, I saw Allmenröder being pressed by two Englishmen and I moved to give him room. In so doing, a Vickers [*sic*] single-seater[7] got right on my heels. I made a half-loop and went into a spin; two comrades who saw it thought I had been shot down, as did the Vickers pilot, who then left me alone. I got out of that scrape in such a way that I had a quiet overview and then … went after a Sopwith two-seater, which after taking about 100 rounds began to burn. It side-slipped, went over on its back and fluttered earthward in burning pieces, at which point I could not resist letting out a roaring "Hurrah!" As one of my rigging wires had been shot through, I took the shortest way home.'[8]

Within the hour, Richthofen was in the air and interrupted a B.E.2 on a photo-reconnaissance mission north of Lens. After a brief exchange of fire, the two-seater began to smoke and head for the ground. Even though it landed within forward British lines, the aircraft was credited as Richthofen's 22nd victory.[9]

That afternoon, Jasta 11 attacked a flight of Sopwith 1½ Strutters over Acheville, east of Vimy. Perhaps sensing that his morning had not been complete, Richthofen went after one two-seater and kept firing at it until one of its wings broke off and the fuselage fell to the ground and was smashed to bits. German soldiers in the area buried the bodies of the two crewmen and the aircraft's machine-guns were sent to Jasta 11 as souvenirs of Richthofen's 23rd victory.[10] They also recovered papers from one of the Sopwith wrecks which indicated that the aircraft was from No. 43 Squadron, which was operating from an airfield at Savy,[11] some 40 kilometres west of Jasta 11's airfield; German intelligence officers gathered such bits of information so as to provide area commanders with as much knowledge of their opponents as possible.

In the late morning of 6 March, Emil Schäfer shot down two Sopwith two-seaters near Lens. During this fight, however, Eduard Lübbert received a flesh-wound in the shoulder and was forced to withdraw.[12] Lübbert had been shot up on almost every fight, once coming back with 64 holes in his aircraft, without ever having scored. He was nick-named '*Kugelfang*' (bullet catcher).[13]

From the RFC side, Captain Harold H. Balfour of No. 43 Squadron reported seeing one of his squadron's crews going down in flames.[14] In the same encounter Balfour and his observer, Second Lieutenant A. Roberts, claimed to have driven down 'a hostile machine out of control near Givenchy',[15] south of Lens. Also in this fight, Second Lieutenant C. P. Thornton and Lieutenant Henry D. Blackburn[16] claimed 'a Halberstadt Scout in flames south of Lens'.[17] Likewise, F.E.8 pilot Lieutenant Edwin L. Benbow claimed 'a hostile machine, which fell in flames near Givenchy'.[18]

Eduard Lübbert was the only recorded German air casualty in the sector that day, yet it appears that his withdrawal was logged as Balfour's and Roberts' first victory, as well as Benbow's sixth (and last) victory.[19] Lübbert was not seriously wounded and landed his undamaged aircraft so successfully that, later that day, Richthofen was transported to the site and flew it back to La Brayelle.[20]

As part of the swirling sprawl of aerial combat, the Sopwiths and F.E.8s drifted away and were succeeded by a pair of B.E.s on a photo-reconnaissance mission. Leutnant Kurt Wolff dropped behind a two-seater and attacked it. Lieutenant A. V. Burlton and Second Lieutenant F. H. Baguley in the second aircraft[21] went after Wolff, and reported that the German aircraft 'seemed to go down out of control ... [while the other B.E.] ... flew very low towards Givenchy, where it was lost sight of'.[22] In fact, Wolff emerged unscathed and his target had become his first victory.[23]

During the afternoon patrol Richthofen and Allmenröder returned to the area and spotted two more B.E.s on a low-level artillery-spotting mission. Richthofen dived on one of them and opened fire. The two-seater's wings came off and it crashed near Souchez. Richthofen was credited with his 24th victory.[24]

Richthofen Forced Down

Low cloud, fog and snow-storms along the Front on 7 and 8 March severely limited flying. A slight break in the weather on Friday, the 9th, enabled Richthofen to get back in the air. The mission turned out differently from what he had anticipated, as recorded by the RFC:

'An offensive patrol of nine F.E.8s of No. 40 Squadron, whilst patrolling over Oppy [12 kilometres south-west of Douai] in the morning were unusually heavily fired on by anti-aircraft guns for about five minutes. The A.A. fire suddenly stopped and about eight hostile scouts dived on the formation from above the clouds. One F.E.8 was brought down and three others had their machine-guns hit, putting them out of action ... The remaining five F.E.8s continued to fight with the H.A. until three had been shot down and another one had its aileron [wire] cut, but managed to get back to an aerodrome. The last one succeeded in reaching our lines, but caught fire just before landing. The pilot [Second Lieutenant Rupert E. Neve], who was wounded in the chest and stomach, jumped from the machine. This fight lasted half-an-hour, and one H.A. is known to have been destroyed.'[25]

Manfred von Richthofen was flying one of the two 'hostile aircraft' reported as having been forced out of the fight. He was so focused on his target that he did not see Second Lieutenant H. C. Todd in another F.E.8 come within striking range. Richthofen was at his favourite point – 50 metres away from his victim – and just beginning to fire when Todd's bullets penetrated the Albatros' fuel tank. Todd, who could have ended Richthofen's life there and then, reported that he 'dived on H.A. tail, firing at close range and [then] H.A. retired east-wards'.[26] The F.E.8 returned to the formation to help fend off other German fighters.

Richthofen himself had not been hit by the F.E.8's bullets, but the fuel leak soon filled his cockpit with fumes. One spark could have blown him and the aircraft to bits. He cut the engine and headed for the ground, leaving behind him a ribbon of white vapour that invited disaster. Fortunately for him, none of his adversaries followed him down. He made a smooth landing in a small meadow alongside a main road.[27]

A German officer nearby saw Richthofen land and offered him a ride to Hénin-Liétard, about 5 kilometres away. From there he was fetched home by car and was soon aloft, heading back to the Front.

After Richthofen's departure, the fight continued northward over Meurchin. Moments later, Emil Schäfer shot down two F.E.8s, scoring his seventh and eighth victories, but his Albatros was badly damaged in the encounter and he was forced to make an emergency landing. Meanwhile, Carl Allmenröder and Kurt Wolff continued the fight and were credited with bringing down one F.E.8 apiece, marking a second victory for each man.[28]

At noon Richthofen was back in the air, searching for the F.E.8s when, over Roclincourt, he spotted a single-seat 'pusher' and went after it. The aircraft was an Airco D.H.2, which the ace sent down in flames for his 25th victory.[29]

The fight had been a noteworthy success for the Staffel and its new aircraft. Indeed, it inspired an account in the German press that took liberties with the numbers of aircraft involved and seemed more the product of the Albatros Aircraft Works' publicity office than that of a working journalist. Despite its hyperbole, the news article is accurate in portraying the effect that new German fighters had on older, out-moded RFC aircraft of that time:

'The indefatigable progress of our aviation has never been so clearly prominent as it is now ... The British airmen themselves frankly concede the superiority of the new German aircraft. On the 9th of March, British flying officers were shot down by the German Jagdstaffel 11 ...

'Apparently, the whole squadron was cut to pieces. The F.E. single-seaters are hopelessly inferior against the new Albatros single-seaters, which appeared here recently ... [A] prisoner, Second-Lieutenant G. J. [sic] Haseler of the 40th Squadron, emphasised vividly the superiority of the German air weapon. During their last fight there were nine British single-seat fighters against four Germans, but from the beginning the battle looked to be hopeless. Second-Lieutenant D. B. [sic] Hills of the 40th Squadron, a pilot who has been at the Front for four months, said: "Two months ago the squadron could have flown over the German lines for hours without being attacked or bothered. Since the appearance of the Albatros fighters, the balance has shifted ... The F.E. possesses entirely insufficient climbing ability against this opponent."'[30]

That evening, while Jasta 11 celebrated its great triumph, Manfred von Richthofen reflected on one of the day's other events. The officer who drove him to Hénin-Liétard had mistaken him for the observer of a two-seater and asked him where his 'driver' was. Richthofen responded coolly: 'I drive alone.'

Apparently, Richthofen's host thought that all pilots ('drivers') were enlisted men and became a bit more reserved towards his passenger. Richthofen paused at the officer's quarters for a few moments, responding to questions often asked of airmen:

'Have you ever shot down an aircraft?'

'Oh yes, now and then.'

'Is that so? Have you shot down two?'

'No [the pilot replied mischievously], twenty-four.'

Taking his guest to be a person who stretches the truth, the officer smiled and repeated his question, explaining what he meant by 'shot down'.

As they talked, Richthofen made himself comfortable by opening his scruffy-looking leather flying-jacket and heavy scarf. He apologised for wearing only a vest and not a uniform jacket beneath it. This comment drew his host's eye to the blue enamelled Maltese cross at Richthofen's collar – the *Pour le Mérite*.

'What did you say your name is? the officer asked, now greatly embarrassed.
'Richthofen.'

Suddenly the officer realised whom he was entertaining and his entire
demeanour changed.[31] Richthofen delighted in telling the story and did so at
length in his memoir *Der Rote Kampfflieger*. For Richthofen to have landed at
about 1030 hours and been back in the air for victory No. 25 at noon, however,
the actual episode must have been briefer than described.[32]

Another Richthofen Joins Jasta 11

Manfred von Richthofen's growing success in training former two-seater pilots
to become good fighter pilots was put to the test when his younger brother
Lothar was transferred from Kagohl 5 to Jasta 11. The Staffel leader's brother
had the necessary experience – initial wartime service in the cavalry,[33] followed
by combat flights as an observer in Kampfstaffel 23 and then pilot training –
but, surely, his assignment to Jasta 11 was made at the direction of senior officers in Berlin who understood the publicity and morale value of having two
heroic brothers, flying and fighting side by side.[34]

From his arrival on 10 March 1917, however, Lothar von Richthofen received
no special treatment. Indeed, he felt constant pressure to produce results within
a short time. For whatever they might offer as good-luck charms, Lothar
received a hand-me-down Albatros D.III with which Manfred had shot down ten
enemy aircraft and a pair of old flying-gloves that had been worn in many
dogfights.[35] Lothar proved worthy of the gifts by using them to score his first
ten victories during the next two months.[36]

With Lothar close by, learning his lessons as would any newcomer to Jasta
11, Manfred achieved his 26th to 31st victories in a fortnight. The day before his
30th victory, 23 March, he was promoted to Oberleutnant, six months ahead of
other officers with the same date of commission.[37] The rewards of a successful
air fighting career were abundant and would only get better.

It was a rewarding experience for Manfred five days later, when Lothar
forced down a two-seat 'pusher' biplane south of Lens. The aircraft came
down within German lines and was easily confirmed as Lothar's first triumph
in the air.[38]

Also that day, Jasta 11 joined a new element within 6. Armee. As part of the
Air Force's re-organisation and expansion, the Officers in Charge of Aviation
(*Kommandeur der Flieger*) of each Armee had under them several group aviation
commanders to co-ordinate air activities with counterparts on the anti-aircraft
and observation balloon staffs.[39] Each air group leader (*Gruppenführer der Flieger*
or *Grufl*) became responsible for the most effective deployment of air units

within an Armee.[40] Thus, on 28 March 1917, 6. Armee air units were divided between Grufl 2 (XII. Reservekorps), Grufl 3 (VI. Reservekorps) and Grufl 12 (I. Bayerische Reservekorps).[41] Jastas 3 and 11 became units of Grufl 12, commanded by Hauptmann Edmund Rutz,[42] and assigned to the Vimy area which was recording the heaviest activity within this Armee's Front.

A Staffel Comrade Falls

An orderly withdrawal to the *Siegfried Stellungen* (Siegfried Positions, known to the Allies as the Hindenburg Line), beginning in mid-March, placed the 6. Armee behind strong defensive positions while it re-organised its forces. Their British adversaries, using less adequate aeroplanes to disrupt German communications, conserved forces for the offensive while continuing to face Jagdstaffeln with technically improved aircraft.[43] As a further complication the month of April was unusually stormy, with many snowfalls.[44]

Jasta 11's victory score increased dramatically as RFC units were required to probe their adversaries' defences more deeply. The German units had only to wait in their own airspace for their foes and were aided by a strong westerly wind. On the late morning of 30 March, Lieutenant William A. Bishop was at the controls of one of six Nieuports of No. 60 Squadron on offensive patrol from Arras to Douai when they fell into a Jasta 11 trap.

While attacking what seemed to be a lone target, Bishop wrote: 'I must have been plunging fully 150mph at the German with the black crosses on his wings, when suddenly out of the clouds, and seemingly right under my nose, a second enemy machine appeared. I realised now that we were in for serious fighting, that we had run into an ambuscade, for it was a great trick of the Germans at this time to lurk behind patches of clouds to obtain the advantage of a surprise attack ...'[45]

Bishop, who had scored his first victory five days earlier, fought his way out of the ambush, eluded German anti-aircraft fire and made his way home safely. Next day he achieved the second of his 72 victories overall.[46] Bishop's 22-year-old squadron-mate Lieutenant William P. Garnett was not so fortunate; at 1145 hours over Gavrelle, less than 15 kilometres from Douai, he was shot down and killed by Leutnant Kurt Wolff, also aged 22, who was credited with his fourth victory.[47]

During the Staffel's afternoon patrol, they encountered a flight from No. 40 Squadron, which had recently changed from F.E.8 pusher biplanes to more conventional and superior 'tractor' engined Nieuport 17s. At 1415 hours, Leutnant Carl Allmenröder shot down one of the Nieuports[48] over Fresnoy, also close to Douai.

But his victory was not without cost. At the same time, according to a British account: 'Capt. [R.] Gregory of No. 40 Squadron observed and dived at two hostile machines near Bailleul, one of which he drove down apparently badly damaged.'[49] It is probable that Captain Gregory shot down and killed 23-year-old Leutnant Eduard Lübbert, the brave but unsuccessful 'bullet catcher'.[50] Lübbert, who had come from the same cavalry unit as Richthofen's old friend Count Erich von Holck,[51] suffered the same fate as the courageous nobleman and became Jasta 11's first combat casualty.

Next day Leutnant Kurt Wolff recorded his fifth victory and closed the book for the month of March when he brought down an F.E.2b at Gavrelle; one crewman was dead, the other taken prisoner.[52] Wolff's career was clearly on the rise. By the end of the following month he would have 27 victories to his credit.

Bloody April

Despite their tactical disadvantages on the ground, British forces had numerical superiority when the air offensive of the Battle of Arras began on 4 April 1917. That action was intended to draw German aircraft away from the immediate battle area so that RFC reconnaissance and bombing aircraft would be free to perform their missions.[53] At the outset, British First and Third Armies had 25 air squadrons, consisting of 365 serviceable aircraft, a third of which were single-seat fighters. The German 6. Armee mustered 195 aircraft, nearly half of which, including two-seater *Schutzstaffeln* (protection aircraft), had front-line aggressor roles.

The Germans soon demonstrated that numerical inferiority was more than compensated by generally better aircraft and by the fact that they were usually fighting over their own lines.[54] Consequently, April 1917 became a peak period for Manfred von Richthofen, who added 21 enemy aircraft to his personal score, surpassed the record set by his mentor Oswald Boelcke and became the war's highest-scoring fighter pilot. It also became the worst month so far for Britain's air forces, which in that four weeks lost one-third of their front-line airmen: 912 pilots and observers in 50 Squadrons.[55] This period became known in RFC history as 'Bloody April'.

One exceptional aircraft coming into the RFC inventory then was the single-seat Sopwith Scout. With its strong familial resemblance to the larger two-seat Sopwith 1½ Strutter, the new fighter soon acquired the popular name 'Pup', as if it were the offspring of the earlier aircraft.[56] By all accounts it was a frisky and tough adversary. Manfred von Richthofen's 16th victim on 4 January 1917 had been a Sopwith Pup from the Royal Naval Air Service,[57] which first deployed the aircraft. Although he defeated the nimble Sopwith, Richthofen acknowledged its superiority to the early Albatros then in use and admitted that, in his case, the Pup was outgunned by the Germans' numerical advantage.[58]

Much luckier in his encounter with Jasta 11 was Sopwith Pup pilot Lieutenant Patrick Gordon Taylor of No. 66 Squadron. On the afternoon of 5 April he was at 10,000 feet on a lone patrol towards Cambrai, he wrote later, when suddenly 'against the brown earth of the trenches I saw some tiny, coloured specks. There was a flock of five or six, their colours glinting prettily in the sunlight as they dipped and circled like tiny butterflies in the warm air.

'They seemed so small for a moment [that] I couldn't believe they were aircraft. Then I recognised them as the coloured Albatri [sic] of the Circus from Douai, putting on a fine show strafing our trenches. I could see them dive and flick on up in a climbing turn, circling and going in again.'[59]

Enjoying the advantage of surprise, Taylor went into a steep dive. As he approached the group of Albatroses, he selected a red aircraft with a chequered design on the fuselage; its pilot was intent on ground-strafing and didn't realise that he was in trouble until Taylor opened fire. The Albatros dived for the ground and, before Taylor could follow, another German fighter was behind him, firing away.

'Again the instant evasion,' Taylor recalled. 'I was suddenly conscious of the shark-like creatures closing in on me ... I held full throttle and tried to climb away, but it was futile. Whatever I did the [Germans] just soared above me. I continued to take evasive action, using my gun whenever I could make ... They had me cold. I couldn't reach them to attack and couldn't climb away to escape. The instant I flew straight they would nail me.'[60]

Taylor executed a partial barrel roll, straightened out and dived for the ground in hopes of escaping the swarm of Albatros. He gained precious seconds by his unexpected manoeuvre and by the time the Jasta 11 fighter had got on his tail again, he was snaking along at a perilously low altitude. His trick worked and his pursuer gave up and rejoined his comrades.

Failing to shoot down Patrick Gordon Taylor was a small loss to Jasta 11, which had an otherwise noteworthy day. That morning, despite fog and then wind, five Albatros attacked six of the new Bristol F.2A two-seat fighters of No. 48 Squadron who were out on an offensive patrol. Jasta 11 accounted for four of them.[61]

At about 1100 hours, Oberleutnant Manfred von Richthofen shot down two F.2As south-east of Douai[62] and Leutnant Georg Simon got one over Auchy.[63] The Bristol Fighters' newly issued machine-guns failed to work properly[64] and, although the RFC flight received credit for driving down three German aircraft near Douai,[65] no corresponding German losses were recorded. As part of that fight, Vizefeldwebel Sebastian Festner scored his fourth victory when he brought down an F.2A near Méricourt. The pilot of the aircraft was Captain William Leefe Robinson, VC, the first airman to earn Great Britain's highest award for valour, the Victoria Cross, over British soil for shooting down the Schütte-Lanz airship SL 11 in 1916.[66] He and his observer, Second Lieutenant E. D. Warburton, were uninjured and taken prisoner.

In Washington, D.C. next day – Good Friday – American President Woodrow Wilson announced the declaration of war between the USA and the Central Powers. It would be another year before American ground and air forces would arrive in Europe, offering an infusion of men and *matériel* to help defeat Germany and Austria–Hungary. That prospect was far from the minds of Jasta 11 pilots who were enjoying the most successful period of their careers.

On Holy Saturday, 7 April, Manfred von Richthofen received another reward for his proficiency. He was promoted to *Rittmeister* [Cavalry Captain] and marked the occasion with a flight in a new aircraft,[67] together with four comrades, and by scoring his 37th victory. The Jasta 11 flight ventured over British lines south of Arras and at about 1745 hours pounced on six Nieuport 17s. In addition to the advantage of surprise, each Albatros pilot was armed with two synchronised machine-guns when going after the single-gun, less manoeuvrable Nieuports. Richthofen's victim crashed in flames near Mercatel.[68] British troops found the pilot's burned body and buried it in a shellhole near the wreckage; later, a cross was erected at the site by his squadron.[69]

Late that evening and early the next morning, F.E.2bs of No. 100 Squadron forged through clouds and rain to bomb Douai airfield. Leutnant der Reserve Hans Klein of Jasta 4, who became a successful Staffel leader under Richthofen, went up after the marauders in the early light of dawn. The 26-year-old pilot shot down an F.E.2b just outside Douai, thereby scoring the third of his total of 22 victories.[70]

In the weeks prior to the offensive, significant numbers of air units had been transferred to 6. Armee from other areas; on 21 March alone, fourteen units – including Jastas 3, 27 and 28w – were moved.[71] Clear skies on Easter Sunday, 8 April, invited aircraft from both sides to come out in force. Jasta 11 rose to the occasion in more senses than one, as did the unit with which it shared facilities at Douai, Jasta 4, commanded by the ninth *Pour le Mérite* recipient,[72] 23-year-old Leutnant Wilhelm Frankl. Jasta 11's Easter 'bag' was five confirmed victories – including Richthofen's 38th and 39th,[73] Schäfer's 13th, and the eighth for Festner[74] and Wolff – as against one for Jasta 4.

While Jasta 11 was preparing for the afternoon patrol, Jasta 4 continued operations over Arras. At about 1330 Frankl, the only Jewish *Pour le Mérite* airman,[75] scored his 20th and last victory.[76] As his Staffel drew eastwards, Frankl was shot down and killed over Vitry. He fell within his own lines and was buried in the Vitry–Sailly German military cemetery.[77]

Also that Easter afternoon, four new Airco D.H.4 two-seat bombers of No. 55 Squadron tried to decapitate the 6. Armee's leadership by hitting Crown Prince Rupprecht's headquarters at Château Hardenpont near Mons,[78] far to the east of Douai. The D.H.4s made it to the target area and dropped their bombs, but took a south-westerly course back through a gauntlet of ground and air fire. At about 1445 hours a couple of the two-seaters fell to the guns of Jasta 11: one, recorded as Leutnant Schäfer's 13th victory, came down over Epinoy, about 17 kilometres south of Douai; a few kilometres to the east, Leutnant Wolff's eighth victory was a D.H.4 which he brought down at Blécourt.[79] One D.H.4 eluded Jasta 11 only to be hit by German anti-aircraft fire and crash south of Amiens.[80] Only one RFC aircraft returned from the mission to Mons.[81]

Leading by Example

The rising success of Schäfer, Wolff and Festner was a tribute to their training under Richthofen and adherence to his tactics: they singled out their targets, pursued them, manoeuvred into advantageous positions and then systematically destroyed them. Nothing fancy; just good flying and straight shooting.

Leutnant Erwin Böhme flew over from the Fighter Pilot School at Valenciennes to convey personal Easter greetings to his former comrade Richthofen. In a letter home that evening Böhme described the spirit that Richthofen engendered in his pupils:

'It is astonishing the heights to which he has brought his Staffel in such a short time. He has gathered around him really good people who would walk through fire for him ... Richthofen himself is the picture of fitness; one notices that, although he goes up five times on many days, there is no trace of fatigue about him. What I like is that he is so completely without pretension, a refined but quite natural man ... It would be good if he were soon placed at the head of all fighter aviation. After Boelcke, he would be just the right man.'[82]

The Battle of Arras

The British assault against the 6. and 17. Armee Fronts on 9 April was intended to be a single massive diversion. A French offensive on the Aisne would come a week later. The British drive had ample air cover, but for most of the opening day the RFC were hindered by low-level snow and drizzle and strong winds at higher altitudes. The scant German air opposition was noted in the 6. Armee's weekly report, which confirmed one victory that evening, a two-seater shot down over Aix-Noulette, west of Lens, by Leutnant Emil Schäfer – his 14th 'kill'.[83]

Strong wind and snow the following day did not keep RFC units from supporting the ground advance. Again there was virtually no German air resistance; but on Wednesday, 11 April, 6. Armee air units were back with a vengeance: Jasta 11 recorded seven victories and Leutnant Hans Klein of Jasta 4 logged two – all without loss. Just after 0900 hours Sebastian Festner and Emil Schäfer each shot down a B.E.2 during intense fighting over British-held Fampoux, east of Arras.[84] At the same time, Kurt Wolff and Lothar von Richthofen shot down a couple of Bristol F.2A two-seat fighters over Mouville Ferme, south of Arras.[85] Fifteen minutes later Wolff joined Manfred von Richthofen in attacking a low-flying two-seat infantry support aircraft over Willerval. The Staffel leader fired the decisive shots and the two-seater crashed into a shellhole in the forward lines and sheared off its wings. It was recorded as his 40th victory.[86] This achievement had a special meaning for Manfred von Richthofen; he was now Germany's most successful living fighter pilot.

More snow on 12 April was reason enough for Jasta 11 to leave patrol duties to the newly arrived black-painted Albatros of Jasta 12. In good weather on the 13th, however, Jasta 11 claimed fourteen of the day's eighteen British aircraft brought down along 6. Armee's Front. Again the Staffel suffered no losses.

While Jasta 11 pilots were preparing for the morning patrol that day, a visiting German journalist reported: 'Richthofen had already put on his [flight] gear and carefully scrutinised the heavens with his naked eye. All of a sudden ... quickly he turned to a bell hanging nearby and sounded the alarm. In an instant ... each pilot hurried to his own [aircraft], climbed into the seat, [as] the propellers thundered, [and] one after another the small fast [Albatros] aircraft ran along a stretch of the ground, lifted up and quickly climbed up into the blue ... '[87]

The Staffel's objective was a formation of six Royal Aircraft Factory R.E.8 two-seat aircraft reconnoitring the railway line from Quiéry-la-Motte to Etaing, within visual range of Jasta 11's airfield. Photo-reconnaissance requires steady, precise flying and, when the promised fighter escorts failed to rendezvous, four R.E.8s closed ranks to protect the two camera-carrying aircraft. The R.E.8 type was intended to succeed the B.E.2 series that had suffered high losses; in fact, it suffered from many of the same drawbacks. Like its predecessor, the R.E.8's inherent stability, while desirable in an observation aircraft, made it hopeless in a dogfight,[88] when manoeuvrability is needed for self-defence. The point was proven when Jasta 11 attacked the formation and, as 6. Armee Headquarters reported, the six RFC reconnaissance aircraft were 'completely annihilated'.[89] Indeed, five of the six aircrews were killed in that fight and have no known graves; they are remembered only on the Arras Memorial to the Missing.[90]

Manfred von Richthofen led the attack and his target was recorded as his 41st victory. Other 'kills' credited were: Kurt Wolff's tenth, Sebastian Festner's ninth, Lothar von Richthofen's fourth and fifth. Hans Klein of Jasta 4 shot down an R.E.8, thereby achieving his sixth.[91] From that auspicious beginning, Richthofen went on to score two more victories that day (Nos. 42 and 43).[92] Emil Schäfer claimed three shot down, but only one – his 17th victory – was officially confirmed.[93]

A careful accounting of the air triumphs was made, as visiting journalist Dr. Georg Wegener reported: 'While the ground crews were busy working on the machines, repairing recent damage, [Richthofen] wanted to trace the course of the aerial battle by accurately determining the crash-site locations. He knew that Vizefeldwebel Festner would carry out the mission precisely and dispatched him to the scene by motorcycle. Then [with the information in hand], he went to the telephone, to make his report.'[94]

Bavarian-born Sebastian Festner was another former Feldflieger-Abteilung 18 pilot selected by Richthofen. He proved to be a most worthy choice. Including his double victory of 13 April, he had shot down ten enemy aircraft in six weeks. Festner's success was acclaimed throughout Germany when his photograph was used in the series of nationally popular postcards produced by Wilhelm Sanke in Berlin. Indeed, his postcard was followed by one on which he appeared in a group scene with Manfred and Lothar von Richthofen, Emil Schäfer and Kurt Wolff; the five pilots had shot down 82 enemy aircraft in April.[95] Clearly Festner was a rising star in Jasta 11.

On the 14th the Staffel shot down eight of their adversaries. Manfred's own tally rose to 44[96] that day and he became a source of both pride and concern to the Luftstreitkräfte. He and Jasta 11 had become valuable symbols of German air superiority and the 'high ups' did not want to lose them to one of the RFC's dedicated bombing units which, despite great odds, continued to hit important targets. Bad weather on 15 April gave the High Command an excuse to move Jasta 11 from La Brayelle to an airfield at Roucourt, south-east of Douai.

Jasta 11 Prevails

The first patrol from the new airfield, on 16 April, brought the success to which Richthofen's men had become accustomed. Four enemy aircraft down –

including Manfred's 45th victory[97] and Lothar's eighth[98] – with only minor damage to Sebastian Festner's engine on the debit side.

Although it was obscure at the time, a clue to Britain's efforts to regain air superiority appeared in a brief reference in the mid-April weekly report of the Officer in Charge of Aviation for the 6. Armee: 'Enemy triplane sighted over *Gruppe* Loos [area].'[99] The aircraft observed was another creation of the Sopwith Aviation Company, a newly arrived triplane assigned to one of the four Royal Naval Air Service squadrons which had been attached to the RFC.[100] With their arrival in early April, the latest Sopwith single-seat fighters began to build a record of air combat success which would affect Jasta 11.

The Sopwith Triplanes had arrived at a critical time. Field Marshal Sir Douglas Haig's offensive at Arras had stalled. Several days of bad weather offered his forces a much-needed respite, but clearing skies on the afternoon of 21 April required the RFC to resume a full schedule of activity.[101] During the morning patrol, Jasta 11 attacked a formation of B.E.2 bombers escorted by Nieuport fighters. The Staffel claimed five victories within twenty minutes: two for Schäfer (only one confirmed), two for Wolff and one for Lothar von Richthofen.[102]

Air activity increased next day, as the RFC made a dedicated effort to bring down German observation balloons. German fighters were over the Front in strength to repel them.[103] In the course of this fighting, Jasta 11 logged another four victories: Manfred's 46th, Wolff's 19th and 20th, and Schäfer's 22nd. Wolff's 20th 'kill', a Morane Parasol, was also noted as Jasta 11's 100th victory in three months.[104]

The entire German Army aviation organisation was informed of this milestone and urged to emulate Jasta 11's success. The Air Force Commanding General's weekly report noted that 'from 23 January until 22 April 1917 Jagdstaffel 11 has shot down 100 enemy aircraft' and that 'this singularly unrivalled success' was due to 'a small band of brave pilots ... trained and led into battle by an outstanding leader, Rittmeister Freiherr von Richthofen, who alone has contributed 39 of these 100 aircraft'.[105]

There was no celebration that evening, however, because Leutnant Emil Schäfer was reported as missing. He had been last seen within the triangular area Monchy–Tilloy–Feuchy, east of Arras, attacking what he later described as a low-flying ground-support aircraft.[106] Attempting to regain altitude over Monchy, he was hit by British ground fire and forced down between the lines.

Schäfer abandoned his aircraft and headed for what he hoped would be friendly territory. At length he heard soldiers in a dug-out, chatting in a strange language. Further listening from his hiding-place in the darkness, however, convinced him they were Germans, speaking in the Bavarian dialect. Schäfer identified himself to the soldiers and they guided him through a maze of artillery and machine-gun fire to the village of Sailly-en-Ostrevent. From there he was brought back to the airfield at Roucourt in the early hours of the 23rd.[107]

After a catnap, Schäfer was back in action. Richthofen noted in his memoirs: 'Anyone else would have renounced the pleasure of flying fighter aircraft for the next 24 hours. But on the afternoon of the same day my Schäfer attacked a low-flying B.E. [two-seater] over Monchy.' This story sounds good, but no other source – including his own short memoir – claims a Schäfer victory on 23 April 1917.[108] The only Jasta 11 victories on that day were confirmed for Manfred and Lothar von Richthofen. North-east of Arras they attacked a pair of B.E.s and, even though both fell inside British lines, Manfred was credited with his 47th and Lothar with his tenth.[109]

The cost of the day's success was paid by the first pilot with whom Manfred von Richthofen had flown, 29-year-old Hauptmann Paul Henning von Oster-roht.[110] Having scored his tenth victory at noon, he led Jasta 12 on a late after-noon patrol over Cambrai. He was shot down at about 1800 hours over the front-line in the vicinity of Ecoust-St-Mein,[111] west of Cambrai. Osterroht's body was never recovered.

At this time Manfred von Richthofen was preparing to go on leave. He had been invited to dine with Kaiser Wilhelm at the Supreme Headquarters, then in the spa city of Bad Kreuznach, but first he had to select a worthy Staffel leader to cover his first absence from the unit.

Emil Schäfer was out of consideration, as he had already been appointed to lead Jasta 28w and was finishing his tour with Richthofen's Staffel. Manfred knew that his old friend Erwin Böhme would gladly give up his training duties at the Fighter Pilot School and so he flew to Valenciennes to offer him the command experience that would help gain a Staffel of his own.

Böhme was, of course, thrilled by the offer,[112] but he doubted whether even Richthofen's influence could free him to return to the Front. Combat pilots with Böhme's experience were needed to help develop the large numbers of fighter pilots required for new Staffeln yet to be created. Böhme proved to be correct and he remained at Valenciennes until July, while Richthofen continued to look for other men who had the leadership and combat experience needed to continue Jasta 11's progress.

Meanwhile Manfred's estimation of Schäfer rose even further. On 25 April the young man from Krefeld scored his 22nd and 23rd victories – and saved Lothar from certain death. During the morning patrol north of Arras, Lothar had been outmanoeuvred by an F.E.2b and was taking hits when Schäfer slipped in behind the 'Fee' and shot it down.[113]

Vizefeldwebel Sebastian Festner was not so lucky. Nine weeks short of his 23rd birthday, the 12-victory ace was shot down and killed by anti-aircraft fire over Gavrelle. His Albatros D.III fell within British lines and, though wrecked, was assigned the captured aircraft identification number G 26.[114] Festner had earned, but did not live long enough to wear, the Cross of a Member with Swords (*Kreuz der Inhaber mit Schwertern*) of the Royal Order of the House of Hohenzollern. This decoration was Prussia's second highest bravery award for enlisted men, but the Cross of a Member was so seldom bestowed – only sixteen during the war, of which ten went to non-commissioned officer pilots – that it was the rarest distinction to come from the Kaiser's royal house.[115]

An Honour Declined

Manfred von Richthofen was not mentioned in the air combat list on Thursday, 26 April, a cloudy day that resulted in three victories over the always vulnerable B.E.2s: Kurt Wolff's 21st, Lothar von Richthofen's 11th and Carl Allmenröder's eighth.[116] For the elder Richthofen, it was a day that reflected his leadership achievements. He was notified that Kaiser Wilhelm had ordered Jasta 11 to be called Jagdstaffel Richthofen.[117] Jasta 2 was the only other air unit to be honoured by being named after its commander. In this case, however, the new distinction was used for only three weeks, from 4 to 18 May, after which it reverted to being called Jasta 11. Richthofen never explained why he declined the high honour. He compared himself with his mentor in many other instances, such as when he equalled Boelcke's victory score, but perhaps Richthofen's admiration was such that he still considered Germany's first great ace as incomparable in such a sensitive area as having his name added to the unit nomenclature.

News was also received that Emil Schäfer, who had departed that day to take command of Jasta 28w at Douai, and Kurt Wolff had been awarded the Knight's Cross of the Royal Order of the House of Hohenzollern.[118] Apparently that high award had been late in catching up with Schäfer, as he received the *Pour le Mérite* on the same day that the House Order was conferred.[119] He was, therefore, a highly decorated, high-scoring fighter ace and Richthofen protégé when he arrived at Royal Württemberg Jagdstaffel 28 – only to succeed Oberleutnant Rudolf Lang, the officer Richthofen had replaced as commanding officer of Jasta 11 four months earlier. Again, the emphasis was on performance. While Lang was in command, Jasta 28w had logged only two victories, the first of which was the sixth victory of the emerging ace, Offizierstellvertreter Max Müller. Following the loss of his second Jasta command, Lang was transferred to a training unit in Bavaria. Emil Schäfer and the pilots he developed and motivated had brought Jasta 28w's score up to 22 by the time the 25-year-old Staffel leader was killed in action six weeks later.

German airmen in 6. Armee's area had been warned about the growing numbers of Sopwith Triplanes, which were said to 'surpass the Albatros D.III in manoeuvrability and above all in climbing ability'.[120] Any potential danger from the new fighters did not deter Jasta 11 on the evening of the 27th, when they intercepted F.E.2bs of No. 11 Squadron and B.E.s of No. 2 Squadron east of Arras. Lothar von Richthofen shot down his 12th victim, Kurt Wolff his 22nd and Carl Allmenröder his ninth.[121]

The numbers continued to climb; next morning Manfred claimed his 48th victory.[122] Later that day, Kurt Wolff added the 23rd and 24th to his list.[123]

Richthofen's 50th.

Manfred von Richthofen was determined to attain 50 victories before his meeting with the Kaiser. On 29 April 1917 he exceeded his expectations and shot down four aircraft.

During a midday patrol, he and five comrades were attacked by a trio of SPAD S.7 fighters from No. 19 Squadron. The squared-off and bulky-looking SPADs were tough opponents and this trio went right after their red Albatros adversaries. The SPAD pilots were outgunned, however, and were brought down. Manfred's victim was the first to fall. The red Albatros poured a stream of machine-gun bullets into the SPAD until its wings fell away from the fuselage, which, as the ace later noted, 'went roaring down like a stone on fire'.[124] Manfred's 49th victim crashed near Lécluse; Wolff's 25th came down just west of Douai; and Lothar's 13th made a forced landing near Sailly.[125]

That afternoon Manfred von Richthofen shot down his 50th enemy aircraft, an F.E.2b, south-west of Inchy. Moments later, Kurt Wolff scored his 26th. Some three hours later, on an evening patrol, Manfred claimed two more. No. 51 was a B.E.2 two-seater which was ranging artillery fire within German lines.[126] Lothar claimed an accompanying B.E.2 and received credit for his 14th victory.[127]

A little while later, Jasta 11 had re-grouped and was heading northwards towards Lens when they passed below eleven Sopwith Triplanes of No. 8 Squadron, RNAS, and a Nieuport 17 of No. 60 Squadron, RFC.[128] The British fighters pounced. During this fight, Richthofen shot down one of the vaunted Triplanes for his 52nd victory.[129]

The good day's work was an occasion for the Staffel to host a grand celebration that evening. Among the guests was Manfred's best friend from his combat service on horseback in 1914, Oberleutnant Erich-Rüdiger von Wedel, who by chance was in the area. The Uhlan must have been impressed by the deeds and life-style of the aerial knights, for soon he transferred to the aviation service. Within a year – and surely due to Manfred's intercession – Wedel was added to Jasta 11's roster.

Manfred von Richthofen spent the last day of April preparing for his leave. His brother was appointed interim Staffel-leader, even though Kurt Wolff, the next highest-scoring pilot after Manfred, seemed to be the logical successor. Lothar's appointment was probably decided at a higher command level, with the view that there was more morale value in having 'the other' Richthofen in command of Jasta 11.

Already feeling the pressure of his impending duties, on the morning of 30 April, Lothar led the Staffel's first patrol of the day. He was glad of the opportunity to demonstrate his worth on his own, without his elder brother looking after him.

Usually Jasta 11 operated alone, under the Staffel leader's personal command. On this day, however, Lothar's flight was ordered to patrol an area west of Douai with fighters from Jastas 3, 4 and 33 as part of a 20-aircraft formation specially organised by 38-year-old Hauptmann Maximillian Sorg, 6. Armee's officer in charge of aviation.[130] The formation was a prototypical use of massed fighter aircraft that would be refined when Manfred von Richthofen assumed command of the first *Jagdgeschwader* [Fighter Air Wing] less than three months later.

At 0715 hours, just after the flight crossed British lines, Lothar von Richthofen shot down his 15th enemy aircraft, a B.E.2 which fell in flames at Méricourt.[131] Barely half an hour later the massive German formation found opportunity over their own lines, near Izel. They attacked seven F.E.2s and their three Sopwith Triplane escorts. Lothar remained in the forefront and shot down his 16th victim, one of the F.E.2s, which crashed at Izel.[132] By the time of the day's last fight, at 1850 hours, each of the other Jastas had recorded a victory.[133]

That day's achievements brought a fitting close to Jasta 11's most successful month. But the new Sopwith Triplanes, SPADs and other RFC aircraft were shifting the balance of air superiority once more.

Notes

1   *Kofl 6. Armee Wochenbericht* Nr. 23225, Teil 4, 15 February 1917.
2   Johannisthal was the site of an airfield outside Berlin where many pre-war air shows were held.
3.   Quoted in Lampel, P., 'Als Gast beim Rittmeister Frhr. v. Richthofen', in Neumann (ed.), *In der Luft*, p. 220.

4 Ibid., p. 221.

5 RFC *Western Front Casualty Report*, 16 February1917.

6 *Kofl 6. Armee*, Nr. 23460, Teil 8, 22 February 1917; B.E.2c 4179 of No. 16 Squadron, 2/Lts Ernest W. Lindley, aged 20, and Leslie V. Munn, aged 22 (both KiA).

7 Probably a Royal Aircraft Factory F.E.8 of No. 40 Squadron, which was operating in that area.

8 Schäfer, K., *Jäger zum Flieger*, pp. 81–2. *Kofl 6. Armee*, Nr. 24030, Teil 9, 8 March 1917; most probably Sopwith 1½ Strutter A.1109 of No. 43 Squadron last seen over Lens at 1055 hours (British time) under attack by five hostile aircraft; 2/Lts Philip L. Wood and Alan H. Fenton, aged 23 (both KiA).

9 Ibid.; most probably B.E.2d 5785 of No. 2 Squadron, Lt James B. E. Crosbee, aged 20, and Sgt John E. Prance, aged 32 (WiA).

10 Ibid.; Sopwith A.1108 of No. 43 Squadron, 2/Lt Herbert J. Green, aged 19, and 2/Lt Alexander W. Reid, aged 20 (both KiA).

11 *Kofl 6. Armee*, Nr. 23460, op. cit., Teil 10.

12 Ibid., Teil 9.

13 Richthofen, M. von, *Rote Kampfflieger*, p. 131.

14 Most probably Schäfer's third victory, which was later confirmed as Sopwith A.978, Lt Stanley J. Pepler, aged 27, and Maj James D. Stuart, aged 22 (both KiA). A German message dropped over British lines reported: ' ... on the Sixth a Sopwith was brought down burning. We could only find a tailor's reference label ... for Lieut. Pepler. Another one [Sopwith?] came down and went smash' (Ref: RFC *Western Front Casualty List*). The second aircraft mentioned may have been the other Sopwith claimed by Schäfer.

15 RFC *Communiqué* No. 78, 11 March 1917, p. 2.

16 Crew of Sopwith A.961.

17 RFC *Communiqué*, Ibid.

18 Ibid.; Benbow's aircraft was F.E.8 A.4871.

19 Shores, C., et al., *Above the Trenches*, pp. 59, 73.

20 Ferko, A. E., *Richthofen*, pp. 17–19.

21 B.E.2e A.2785 of No. 16 Squadron.

22 No. 16 Squadron Combat Report of Lt A. V. Burlton and 2/Lt F. H. Baguley in B.E.2e A.2785.

23 *Kofl 6. Armee*, op. cit.; B.E.2d 5856 of No. 16 Squadron, 2/Lts George M. Underwood, aged 19, and Albert E. Watts (both KiA).

24 Ibid.; B.E.2e of No. 16 Squadron, 2/Lt Gerald M. Gosset-Bibby, aged 19, and Lt Geoffrey J. O. Brichta, aged 32 (both KiA).

25 RFC *War Diary* entry on this date.

26 No. 40 Squadron combat Report of 2/Lt H. C. Todd in F.E.8 6428.

27 Richthofen, M. von, op. cit., pp. 127–8.

28 *Kofl 6. Armee*, Nr. 24340, Teil 7, 16 March 1917; according to serial number information from German sources: F.E.8 A.6456, 2/Lt T. Shepard (PoW), was brought down near Annay by Ltn Wolff; F.E.8 A.6397, 2/Lt W. B. Hills (PoW), near Faschoda by Ltn Schäfer; and F.E.8 A.4874, 2/Lt G. F. Heseler (PoW), near Pont-à-Vendin by Ltn Schäfer. It is likely that Ltn Allmenröder's victim was F.E.8 A.6399, 2/Lt Rupert E. Neve, aged 23 (WiA), whose aircraft caught fire upon landing within British lines.

29 Ibid.; D.H.2 A.2571 of No. 29 Squadron, Lt Arthur J. Pearson, MC, aged 29 (KiA).

30 Quoted from 'Unsere siegreichen Jagdflieger', in *Kriegs-Echo*, Nr. 138, 30 March 1917, p. 411.

31 Richthofen, M. von, op. cit., pp. 129–30.

32 Another point that does not fit an extended time frame for this anecdote is Richthofen's recollection of Ltn Eduard Lübbert's having been shot down on 9 March, when in fact that incident had occurred three days earlier.

33 Dragoner-Regiment von Bredow (1. Schlesisches) Nr. 4.

34 'Vigilant', *Red Knight*, pp. 164–5.

35 Richthofen, M. von, *Heldenleben*, pp. 221–2.

36 Franks, N., et al., *Above the Lines*, p. 187.

37 Richthofen, M. von, op. cit., p. 195.

38 Kofl 6. Armee, Nr. 25000, Teil 10, 30 March 1917; F.E.2b 7715 of No. 25 Squadron, 2/Lt Norman L. Knight (WiA/PoW) and 2/Lt Alfred G. Severs, aged 23 (KiA).

39 Hoeppner, E. von, Deutschlands Krieg, p. 91.

40 Air Ministry, Handbook of German Military and Naval Aviation, p. 43.

41 Kofl 6. Armee, op. cit., Teil 1.

42 A veteran of Bavarian 8. Infanterie-Regiment Grossherzog Friedrich II. von Baden, together with Karl Bodenschatz, Stefan Kirmaier and Franz Josef Walz, all mentioned earlier in this book.

43 Jones, H. A., War in the Air, vol. III, p. 323.

44 RFC War Diary daily weather reports, April 1917; 'Vigilant', op. cit., pp. 134ff.

45 Bishop, W., Winged Warfare, p. 58.

46 Shores, op. cit., pp. 77–8.

47 Kofl 6. Armee, ibid., Teil 10; Nieuport 17 A.273.

48 Ibid.; Nieuport 17 A.6780 of No. 40 Squadron, Lt Douglas M. F. Sinclair (KiA).

49 RFC Communiqué No. 81, 1 April 1917, p. 2.

50 Kofl 6. Armee, op. cit., Teil 11; the combat report of Capt R. Gregory notes that while flying Nieuport 17 A.6680, at 1415 hours he attacked two aircraft identified as 'Halberstadts' south of Vimy and he sent one 'side-slipping into a cloud near Bailleul'; the time and location are a perfect match for the loss of Ltn Lübbert, whose Albatros may have been mistaken for a Halberstadt. He came down near Gavrelle, less than 3 kilometres from Bailleul.

51 Dragoner-Regiment König Carl I. von Rumänien (1. Hannoversches) Nr. 9; see also Introduction, pp. 9ff.

52 Kofl 6. Armee, Nr. 25500, Teil 10, 7 April 1917; F.E.2b 7691 of No. 11 Squadron, 2/Lt L. A. T. Strange (PoW) and 2/Lt William G. T. Clifton, aged 23 (KiA).

53 Jones, H. A,, op. cit., p. 334.

54 Ibid.

55 Morris, A., Bloody April, p. 15.

56 Bruce, J., British Aeroplanes, p. 552.

57 Sopwith Scout N.5193 of No. 8 Squadron, RNAS, Fl/Lt Alan S. Todd, aged 31 (KiA).

58 Bruce, op. cit., p. 554; German pilots saw the new fighter up close when Sopwith Pup A.633 of No. 54 Squadron made a forced landing at Longavesnes after a fight with Jasta 3 on 4 March 1917 (Ref: Kogenluft, Nachrichtenblatt der Luftstreitkräfte, Nr 4566 B, 29 March 1917, p. 6); the pilot, Capt Allan Lees, was uninjured and taken prisoner.

59 Taylor, G., Sopwith Scout 7309, p. 71.

60 Ibid., p. 72.

61 Kofl 6. Armee, op. cit., Teil 10.

62 Ibid.; F.2A A.3340, 2/Lt Arthur N. Leckler, aged 27 (WiA/PoW) and Lt Herbert D. K. George, aged 19 (KiA), and F.2A A.3343, Lts Alfred T. Adams, aged 20 (PoW), and Donald J. Stewart (WiA/PoW).

63 Ibid.; F.2A A.3320, Lt A. H. Cooper and 2/Lt A. Boldison (both WiA/PoW).

64 Bowyer, C., For Valour, p. 77.

65 RFC Communiqué No. 82, 8 April 1917, p. 2.

66 Bowyer, op. cit., pp. 66, 75–7.

67 Albatros D.III 789/17.

68 Kofl 6. Armee, Nr. 50150, Teil 10, 13 April 1917, p. 3; Nieuport 17 A.6645 of No. 60 Squadron, 2/Lt George O. Smart, aged 31 (KiA).

69 RFC Western Front Casualty List; despite this contention, 2/Lt Smart has no known grave (Ref: Hobson, C., Airmen Died, 1995, p. 93).

70 Ibid.; F.E.2b 7669 of No. 100 Squadron, 2/Lt L. Butler and 2/AM R. Robb (both PoW).

71 Kofl 6. Armee, Nr. 24620, Teil 1.

72 O'Connor, N., Aviation Awards, vol. II, p. 221.

73 Kofl 6. Armee, Nr. 50150; Richthofen victory No. 38 was Sopwith 1½ Strutter A.2406 of No. 43 Squadron, 2/Lt John S. Heagerty, aged 20 (WiA/PoW), and Lt Leonard Heath Cantle, aged 20 (KiA); No. 39 was B.E.2e A.2815 of No. 16 Squadron, 2/Lts Keith I. Mackenzie, aged 18, and Guy Everingham, aged 22 (both KiA).

74 Ibid.; Nieuport 17 A.311 of No. 60 Squadron, 2/Lt Hamilton E. Hervey (PoW).

75 Theilhaber, F., *Jüdische Flieger*, p. 87; Wilhelm Frankl is noted only once in Zuerl's otherwise complete *Pour-le-Mérite-Flieger*, which, in compliance with Nazi racial hatred of the time, gave no credit to this brave and highly accomplished German fighter pilot.

76 *Kofl 6. Armee*, op. cit.; Nieuport A.6773 of No. 60 Squadron, Capt Maurice B. Knowles (PoW).

77 Haehnelt, W., *Ehrenliste*, p. 21.

78 Jones, H. A., op. cit., p. 342.

79 *Kofl 6. Armee*,op. cit.; D.H.4 A.2140, Lts R. A. Logan and F. R. Henry (MiA); and D. H. 4 A.2141, Lt Bernard Evans, aged 29, and 2/Lt Basil W. White, aged 19 (both KiA).

80 D.H.4 A.2160 made it back to British lines, but its crew – Lt Alfred J. Hamar and 2/Lt John A. Myburgh, aged 19 – later died of wounds (Ref: Hobson, op. cit., pp. 52, 76).

81 Jones, op. cit.

82 Böhme, E., *Briefe eines deutschen Kampffliegers*, p. 101.

83 *Kofl 6. Armee*, op. cit.; B.E.2d 5742 of No. 4 Squadron, Lts Johannes H. Brink (DoW) and R. E. Heath (WiA).

84 Ibid.; one of the aircraft was B.E.2d 5848, Lts E. E. Gunner (WiA) and C. Curtiss.

85 Ibid.; No. 48 Squadron reported the loss of three aircraft: F.2A A.3318, 2/Lts Robert E. Adeney, aged 19, and Leslie G. Lovell (both KiA); F.2A A.3323; 2/Lts G. N. Brockhurst (WiA/PoW) and C. B. Boughton (PoW); and F.2A A.3388, Capt T. M. Tidmarsh and 2/Lt C. B. Holland (both PoW).

86 Ibid.; most probably B.E.2c 2501 of No. 13 Squadron, Lt Edward C. E. Derwin, aged 23, and 2/AM (Gnr) H. Pierson (both WiA).

87 Wegener, G., 'Jagdstaffel Richthofen (Aus der *Kölnischen Zeitung*)' in *Ein Heldenleben*, op. cit., pp. 302–3.

88 Bruce, op. cit., p. 428.

89 *Kofl 6. Armee*, Nr. 50369, Teil 3, 10, 20 April 1917.

90 Ibid.; No. 59 Squadron aircraft and crews brought down were: A.3225, 2/Lts Arthur H. Tanfield and Andrew Ormerod, aged 27 (both KiA); A.3190, Capt James M. Stuart, aged 20, and Lt Maurice H. Wood (both KiA); A.4191, Lts Herbert G. M. Horne and William J. Chalk, aged 27 (both KiA); A.3199, Lts. A. Watson and E. R. Law (both WiA/PoW); A.3216, Capt George B. Hodgson and Lt Charles H. Morris, aged 25 (both KiA); and A.3203, Lts Philip B. Boyd, aged 24, and Philip O. Ray, aged 23 (both KiA) (Ref: Hobson, op. cit., pp. 98, 78, 97, 109, 57, 31, 56, 75, 26, 85).

91 Ibid.

92 Ibid.; F.E.2b A.831 of No. 11 Squadron, Sgt James A. Cunniffe, aged 21, and 2/AM W. J. Batten (both WiA); and F.E.2b 4997 of No. 25 Squadron, 2/Lt Allan H. Bates, aged 20, and Sgt William A. Barnes, aged 31 (both KiA).

93 Schäfer, op. cit., p. 117; *Kofl 6. Armee*, op. cit., Teil 10 offers this curious comment: 'Ltn Schäfer, J.St 11, in the previous weekly report [period] shot down two enemy aircraft on the other side of the lines for which, however, no confirmation can be produced due to the combat actions then prevailing.' There was no official explanation as to why Richthofen's claims of victories over British lines were recognised. The one victory credited to Schäfer was F.E.2b A.6372 of No. 25 Squadron, Capt Lancelot L. Richardson, aged 20, and 2/Lt Douglas C. Wollen (both KiA).

94 Wegener, op. cit., p. 307.

95 O'Connor, op. cit., p. 32.

96 *Kofl 6. Armee*, op. cit.;Nieuport 17 A.6796 of No. 60 Squadron, Lt William O. Russell, aged 24 (PoW).

97 Ibid.; B.E.2e 3156 of No. 13 Squadron, Lt Alphonso Pascoe (WiA) and 2/Lt Frederick S. Andrews, aged 28 (DoW).

98 Ibid.; one of the Nieuport 17s of No. 60 Squadron shot down by Jasta 11 in a morning fight over Fampoux-Biache: Nieuport B.1501, 2/Lt David N. Robertson, aged 23 (KiA); Nieuport A.6769, 2/Lt Richard E. Kimbell, aged 19 (KiA); Nieuport B.1509, Lt John M. Elliott, aged 19, (KiA); and Nieuport B.1507, Lt Trevor Langwill, aged 26 (KiA).

99 Ibid., Teil 3; Gruppe Loos was served by the nine air units of Gruppenführer der Flieger 15, including Jasta 30 (Ref: *Kofl 6. Armee Verzeichnis der Feldpoststationen der Fliegerverbände* Nr 25940, 14 April 1917).

100 Bruce, op. cit., p. 566.

101 Jones, op. cit., p. 356.

102 *Kofl 6. Armee*, Nr. 50570, Teil 11, 28 April 1917; the German claim is not corroborated by the RFC *Western Front Casualty List*, which shows only these losses: Nieuport A.6797 of No. 29 Squadron, 2/Lt Ferrebee Sadler, aged 21 (KiA); Nieuport A.6755 of No. 29 Squadron, 2/Lt Cecil V. de B. Rogers (KiA); and B.E.2g 2766 of No. 16 Squadron, Capt E. J. D. Routh (WiA).

103 Jones, op. cit., pp. 356–7.

104 *Kofl 6. Armee*, op. cit.; aircraft brought down include: F.E.2b A.820 of No. 11 Squadron, Lts C. A. Parker and James C. B. Hesketh, aged 28 (KiA); F.E.2b A.5501 of No. 11 Squadron, Sgt T. K. Hollis (WiA) and Lt Bernard J. Tolhurst, aged 23 (KiA); Morane Parasol A.6727 of No. 3 Squadron, 2/Lt Frank L. Carter, aged 21, and Cpl Albert S. Morgan, aged 29 (both KiA).

105 Kogenluft, *Nachrichtenblatt*, Nr. 10, 3 May 1917, p. 3.

106 Schäfer, op. cit., pp. 109–10, 117; Although this victory was credited as Schäfer's 22nd, British records show no corresponding casualty in this area at this time. Jones, op. cit., p. 359 identifies Schäfer's adversary as 'a B.E. of No. 12 Squadron',' but indicates no RFC loss in the encounter.

107 Ibid, pp. 109–10.

108 Richthofen, M. von, op. cit., p. 143; perhaps this was the aircraft that Schäfer attacked the evening before, which was also over Monchy, behind British lines (Ref: *Kofl 6. Armee*, op. cit.).

109 *Kofl 6. Armee*, op. cit.; Manfred von Richthofen probably accounted for No. 16 Squadron's B.E.2e A.3168, 2/Lt Eric A. Welch, aged 23, and Sgt Alfred G. Tollervey, aged 21 (both KiA); Lothar von Richthofen probably shot down the same unit's B.E.2g A.2876, 2/Lts Charles M. Crow, aged 20 (KiA) and E. T. Turner (WiA).

110 Perthes, J., *Ehrentafel der Kriegsopfer*, p. 175; commissioned into Deutsch Ordens-Infanterie-Regiment Nr. 152, Osterroht qualified for German civilian pilot's licence No. 305 on 9 October 1912 (Ref: Supf, P., *Deutschen Fluggeschichte*, vol. I, p. 570).

111 *Kofl 6. Armee*, op. cit., Teil 12.

112 Böhme, op. cit., pp. 106–7.

113 *Kofl 6. Armee*, op. cit., Teil 11.

114 Albatros D.III 2251/16; Puglisi, W., 'German Aircraft Down', Part 1, in *Cross & Cockade*, 1969, p. 155; Zickerick, W., *Verlustliste* in von Eberhardt, p.21, recorded Festner's death as 23 April 1917; but Puglisi's rendering of British records and *Kofl 6. Armee*, ibid., Teil 12, agree on 25 April. Kofl 6 reported that Festner was killed in aerial combat (possibly with an aircraft of No. 43 Squadron).

115 O'Connor, op. cit., pp. 146–7, 151.

116 *Kofl 6. Armee*, op. cit.; B.E.2g 2806 of No. 5 Squadron, Lts Humphrey B. T. Hope, aged 20, and Lawrence E. Allan (both KiA); B.E.2g 2826 of No. 16 Squadron, Lts William S. Spence and William A. Campbell (both KiA); and B.E.2g A.2859 of No. 16 Squadron, 2/Lt W. K. Mercer (WiA).

117 *Kofl 6. Armee*, Nr. 50790, Teil 14, 4 May 1917.

118 *Kofl 6. Armee*, Nr. 50570, Teil 13.

119 O'Connor, op. cit., p. 140.

120 *Kofl 6. Armee*, op. cit., Teil 3.

121 *Kofl 6. Armee*, op. cit., Teil 11; comparable RFC losses for the Richthofen and Wolff claims were: F.E.2b 4850 of No. 11 Squadron, 2/Lt J. A. Cairns and 2/AM E. G. Perry (both PoW); F.E.2b 7698 of No. 11 Squadron, 2/Lt P. Robinson (WiA) and 2/AM H. Tilley.

122 Ibid.; B.E.2e 7221 of No. 13 Squadron, Lt Reginald W. Follitt, aged 26 (DoW), and 2/Lt Frederick J. Kirkham, aged 22 (WiA/PoW).

123 Ibid.

124 Richthofen, M. von, op. cit., p. 145.

125 *Kofl 6. Armee*, op. cit.

126 Ibid.; most probably this was B.E.2e 2738, 2/Lt David E. Davies, aged 25, and Lt George H. Rathbone, aged 21 (both KiA), which took off at 1645 hours (British time).

127 Ibid; this was probably B.E.2e 7092, 2/Lts John H. Westlake, aged 19, (DoW) and Cyril J. Pile (WiA).

128 Jones, op. cit., p. 368.

129 Ibid.

130 Ibid., pp. 368–9.

131 *Kofl 6. Armee*, op. cit.

132 Ibid.; most probably one of two F.E.2ds of No. 57 Squadron: A.6402, Lt P. I. Bowers and 2/Lt S. T. Willis, and A.6352, 2/Lts E. D. Jennings and J. R. Lingard; according to RFC *Western Front Casualty List*, all four men were unwounded and became PoW.

133 Ibid.

CHAPTER 6

The Tide Turns

ON TUESDAY, 1 MAY 1917, MANFRED VON RICHTHOFEN DEPARTED FROM Jagdstaffel 11 with a feeling of great satisfaction. Although he had been ordered to take leave after his victory score stood at 41, Germany's leading ace had stayed at the Front until he had shot down his 52nd enemy aircraft. Now he felt that he could visit Kaiser Wilhelm as the undisputed premier air warrior of the time.

Manfred passed leadership of the Staffel to his brother Lothar with a simple hand-shake and a smile. Then he settled in the rear cockpit of an Albatros two-seater flown by Leutnant der Reserve Konstantin Krefft, Jasta 11's technical officer, and set out for his meeting with the Supreme War Lord. Richthofen had great trust in Krefft, a man only five months older than himself and a product of the emerging technological age.

A native of Westphalia (Prussia), Krefft had been attending Nuremberg Technical College when the war began. Because he was living in Bavaria, he had applied for training in that kingdom's air service. He served with distinction in two units for which Richthofen had the highest regard – Feldflieger-Abteilungen 5b and 18 – and was a founding member of Jagdstaffel 11.[1] Under Richthofen's tutelage, Krefft developed into a skilled fighter pilot and had already shot down two enemy aircraft. He had the fighting spirit that his leader wanted and the ability to grasp the complex subjects taught by the various engine and aircraft producers; at Richthofen's urging, he became the Staffel's expert in technical matters. Although his score did not increase beyond his initial successes, with such a man overseeing technical matters, Manfred von Richthofen felt confident the Staffel would continue to be the aerial killing machine it had been in April. Indeed, the unit fought hard to live up to the leader's expectations. The day that Richthofen and Krefft left, Jasta 11 logged three victories: Kurt Wolff's 28th and 29th, and Lothar von Richthofen's 17th.[2]

But the glory time of the Jagdstaffeln was coming to an end. While Richthofen was enjoying his leave, a 6. Armee report published in the Luftstreitkräfte commanding general's weekly summary noted the early signs of change: 'The increase in British fighter squadrons impedes the activity of our reconnaissance and artillery-spotting crews significantly ... Moreover, when our anti-aircraft open fire, the enemy formations twist and turn and fire their machine-guns as if they were in aerial combat; often in this way they succeed in bringing our anti-aircraft fire to an immediate halt.'[3]

The Rise of Kurt Wolff

On 4 May Leutnant Kurt Wolff became the eighteenth fighter pilot to be awarded the *Pour le Mérite*.[4] Under the prevailing rules, Wolff had qualified for Prussia's highest bravery award on 22 April, when his victories – all achieved in less than seven weeks[5] – totalled twenty. Events happened so quickly and April was such a successful month for many fighter pilots, however, that the Orders Chancery in Berlin had not kept pace. Indeed Wolff had not attained the prerequisite awarding of the Knight's Cross of the Royal Order of the House of Hohenzollern until the end of April.[6]

Although small and so slightly built that his comrades nicknamed him *das zarte Blümchen* ('the delicate little flower'), 22-year-old Kurt Wolff was tenacious and resilient. During his first orientation flight at the Döberitz Flying School in 1916, the training aircraft crashed and his instructor was killed. Wolff emerged from the wreckage with only a dislocated shoulder.[7]

His personal bravery was matched by a keen mind capable of clear, concise evaluation. He was quick to recognise the RFC's change in tactics and the emergence of important aircraft that were about to shift the balance of aerial superiority back to the Allies. An early warning by a fighter pilot of Wolff's reputation and accomplishments was taken seriously by Germany's air staff and disseminated to all air units:

'Since the great losses caused by German single-seat fighters in the months of March and April, British airmen have embraced a new tactic in April and May. Ground-support and artillery-spotting crews, who fly low over the British lines, have withdrawn ever farther to the west and have been warned by [their] anti-aircraft and especially ground observation posts. At the appearance of German single-seat fighters, big red flames flare up at the same altitude as [British] tethered observation balloons. Moreover, the British anti-aircraft batteries fire a layer of warning shots at the altitude of their own reconnaissance crews, whereupon [the RFC crews] withdraw behind their balloons.

'During photographic reconnaissance missions they do not send up only small formations of the same type aircraft, as was done earlier; rather, [the two-seaters] are covered constantly by a number of single-seat fighters, some of which fly at about 100 metres higher. The observation and photographic aircraft scarcely allow themselves to fight. One such aircraft used by the British is a new type of B.E. two-seater (probably the Bristol Fighter), which when pressed by our [Albatros] D.III, cannot be forced down.

'For long-range reconnaissance, mostly they use a fast machine which, through its speed alone, is almost impossible to shoot down.

'Single-seat fighters, which had been greatly neglected by the British at the beginning of the year, have in recent times appeared in great numbers over the 6. Armee Front. Nieuports, SPADs, [Sopwith] Triplanes, new F.E. single-seaters and another type, probably a Bristol single-seater, are over and behind the Front in greater numbers. It creates the impression that the British have imitated us and, by using a great number of fighter units, want to snatch back moral superiority from us. Up to 5,000 metres [altitude] one finds small fighter formations, which at times are apparently directed by signals from the ground. Then during an attack on a fighter formation, within a short time there appears a second and a third [fighter formation] from one direction or another.

'Despite their numerical superiority, the British no longer display the daring that they had earlier. Even the [Sopwith] Triplanes, which are superior to the Albatros in speed and climbing and turning ability, with few exceptions, attack only timidly ...'[8]

Seemingly unaffected by British advances, Jasta 11's pilots continued to raise their scores. A 6. Armee report notes that in the week of 27 April to 3 May 1917, 40 enemy aircraft were brought down, of which 23 were credited to Jasta 11.[9] On 6 May, Lothar von Richthofen logged his 18th victory, a two-seater which he sent down in flames south of Givenchy,[10] and the following day he was involved in the most controversial air combat of his career.

Encounter in the Mist

The weather was clear over the Flanders Front during most of Tuesday, 7 May 1917,[11] and aircraft of the RFC's 9th Wing concentrated on hitting German bases in the Douai area.[12] Jasta 11 went up to confront the enemy formations and Lothar von Richthofen opened the day's scoring. At about 0830 hours, he attacked a Nieuport single-seater over Gavrelle, some 15 kilometres south-east of Douai, and sent it down as his 19th victim.[13] Carl Allmenröder claimed to have destroyed two British aircraft that day, but was credited only with his tenth victory.[14]

A good example of the progress desired of newcomers was provided by 22-year-old Leutnant der Reserve Otto Maashoff, who had been in the Staffel for nine days. Another alumni of Feldflieger-Abteilung 5b, an outstanding unit since Max Immelmann's days as its leader, Maashoff quickly proved himself worthy of his assignment to Jasta 11. Following this patrol on 7 May, he was credited with his first confirmed victory, listed as a 'Bristol' shot down over Fresnes. The only RFC casualty that day that approximated to Maashoff's claim, however, was an R.E.8 reconnaissance aircraft brought down while on patrol near Ficheux, south-west of Arras.[15] Maashoff achieved two more victories and showed enough promise to be posted to a single-seat fighter unit dedicated to protecting the German homeland from British and French bombers.[16]

Clouds and mist later in the day offered a protective cloak to British bombers intent on hitting German rear area facilities. With that thought in mind, Lothar von Richthofen led Jasta 11's evening patrol. The air battle that followed has assumed near-epic proportions by virtue of the leading personalities involved.

The official Luftstreitkräfte account claimed: 'The [British] combat pilot Captain Albert Ball, who is said to have shot down 42 enemy aircraft, has been missing since 7 May, according to a newspaper report. (Captain Ball fell on 7 May in an aerial battle with Leutnant Freiherr von Richthofen.)'[17]

It was a propagandist's dream to claim that a brother of Germany's leading fighter ace had shot down the highest-scoring British ace. At the time, 20-year-old Ball had 44 confirmed victories to his credit and was a flight commander with No. 56 Squadron, one of the RFC's most successful fighter units. His illustrious career and more details about his last combat are discussed at length in other current works.[18] Here, suffice it to say that Ball and nine other S.E.5s of No. 56 Squadron were joined by six SPADs of No. 19 Squadron when the leading red Albatros came into view north of Lens at about 2000 hours. In his typically bold and aggressive style, Captain Ball led his wingman, Captain Cyril M. Crowe, and a SPAD in pursuit of the lone red fighter aircraft. The RFC fighters became separated in rain and clouds, each S.E.5 and the SPAD pursuing its own target. It is likely that Albert Ball's intended victim was the red Albatros flown by Lothar von Richthofen.

In the mêlée that followed Leutnant Kurt Wolff shot at an S.E.5, probably Lieutenant Arthur P. F. Rhys-Davids, who was wounded and forced to land in a field at la Hèrlier.[19] Leutnant Wolfgang Plüschow[20] was wounded east of Gouy-sous-Bellonne, probably by Captain Henry Meintjes,[21] who was then most likely hit by Leutnant Carl Allmenröder. During this fight, Allmenröder may have shot down and killed 19-year-old Second Lieutenant Roger M. Chaworth-Musters, but he did not receive credit for either S.E.5 claim.

From various reports, apparently Albert Ball's machine-gun fire disabled Lothar von Richthofen's aircraft and forced the German pilot to land. Lothar was uninjured and flew next day. Ball was not so fortunate. His S.E.5 was seen to be inverted when it emerged from clouds and crashed near Annoeullin, north of Lens. He was found dead in his crashed aircraft. No significant combat damage was discerned among the wreckage and a medical examination of Ball's body showed no combat wounds.[22]

Although the evidence was contradictory – with Lothar claiming a 'triplane', rather than an S.E.5 biplane – the German authorities quickly sought to add lustre to the Richthofen reputation by crediting Manfred's brother with shooting down the RFC's top-scoring ace. To 'legitimise' the claim for this propaganda purpose, photographs of Ball's grave and a note of tribute were dropped over British lines: 'R.F.C. Captain Ball was brought down in a fight in the air on the 7th of May, 1917, by a pilot who was of the same order as himself. He was buried at Annoeullin.'[23]

Lothar as a Leader

The official German account of Albert Ball's defeat by Lothar von Richthofen and an irrational story about a British special squadron dedicated to destroying Manfred von Richthofen were accepted without question by German airmen. Both served to bolster the idea that, like the legendary Teutonic warriors, the Richthofen brothers would remain triumphant in the face of great odds.

This sentiment was evident following Lothar's visit to Erwin Böhme at the Fighter Pilot School at Famars, near Valenciennes, on 9 May. Böhme, who confided much in letters to his prospective fiancée Annemarie Brüning, wrote that evening that Lothar 'wanted to tell me about the new crop [of pilots at Jasta 11] and look over new members [at the school]. The day before yesterday he shot down Captain Ball, the British "Boelcke", after an extremely hard fight. [Ball] had become, we believe, the leader of the plucky Royal Flying Corps' newly formed Anti-Richthofen Squadron. Our pilots have often had to deal with this unit and have already shot down many of [its pilots] ...'[24]

Manfred's absence provided opportunities for Lothar to show his prowess as a fighter pilot. After his visit to Böhme, early that evening the younger Richthofen led a patrol toward the Front. At about 1830 hours, he attacked a Bristol F.2B two-seat fighter which was patrolling the road from Roeux to Gavrelle and sent it down within British lines for his 21st victory.[25]

Thursday, 10 May, exemplified what Lothar wanted to achieve as a fighter pilot. He led a morning attack against Sopwith Pups of No. 66 Squadron patrolling between Douai and Brebières while British forces continued to advance east of Arras. Richthofen and Carl Allmenröder each shot down a Pup, scoring their 22nd and 11th victories, respectively.[26] To crown the achievement, later that day, Richthofen was notified that he had been awarded the Knight's Cross of the Royal House Order of Hohenzollern with Swords.[27]

Lothar knew that by now he had earned the *Pour le Mérite*, but he did not relent in his efforts to catch up with Manfred. On 11 May, while the British Third

Above: In January 1918 Captain Alan P. Maclean and Lieutenant Frederick H. Cantlon, MC, of No. 11 Squadron, RFC, posed in Bristol F.2B C.4844, which they had named 'Rickamadoo'. They were flying this aircraft when they were shot down by Jagdgeschwader I aircraft on 18 March 1918.

Right: A *Pour le Mérite* recipient by the time this photograph was taken, Oswald Boelcke (left) had a brief reunion with his former observer, Heinz-Hellmuth von Wühlisch.

Top: Fokker E.III 210/16 became the first Eindecker captured by British forces when the inexperienced pilot lost his way and landed at the wrong airfield on 8 April 1916.

Above: Early German fighter units operated from good facilities, as seen in this view of Max Immelmann's Fokker E.III on his airfield at Douai in June 1916.

Left: Many German fighter pilots learned their trade in the versatile Albatros C.III two-seat reconnaissance aircraft. The machine seen here is making a tight left turn low over the Front.

Above: A blood-less face-off between two deadly rivals: a Fokker E.III beside a captured F.E.2b. German pilots from Max Immelmann to Manfred von Richthofen found the 'Fee' a formidable opponent.

Below: The wreckage of Oberleutnant Max Immelmann's Fokker E.III after his fatal plunge on 18 June 1916.

Above: Members of No. 11 Squadron, RFC in front of an Airco D.H.2 in June 1916. The rear-engine single-seat fighter had a forward-mounted machine-gun that could successfully engage Fokker monoplanes.

Below: The successors to Boelcke and Immelmann. Five of the next six *Pour le Mérite* fighter aces gather for a commemorative photograph. Front row from left: Oberleutnant Ernst Freiherr von Althaus, Oberleutnant Hans-Joachim Buddecke and Oberleutnant Rudolf Berthold. In the second row between Althaus and Buddecke is Leutnant Wilhelm Frankl, the only Jewish aviation recipient of Prussia's highest award for bravery. Over Berthold's left shoulder is Leutnant Walter Höhndorf. To Frankl's right is a future recipient, Leutnant Otto Bernert.

Right: Wilhelm and Carl Allmenröder (right) flew together in Fliegerabteilung (A) 227 prior to joining Jagdstaffel 11 in November 1916.

Below: The Fokker D.III rotary-engined biplane succeeded the famed Eindecker series, but was outclassed by newer British fighters.

Above: The sesquiplane design of the Albatros D.III led to continual lower wing flutter and breakage even in the later D.V models. Manfred von Richthofen experienced the problem on 24 January 1917.

Left: Leutnant Lothar von Richthofen climbs out of Albatros D.III 789/17, which he was assigned after joining Jasta 11 on 10 March 1917. The largely unpainted aircraft had been flown previously by his brother Manfred.

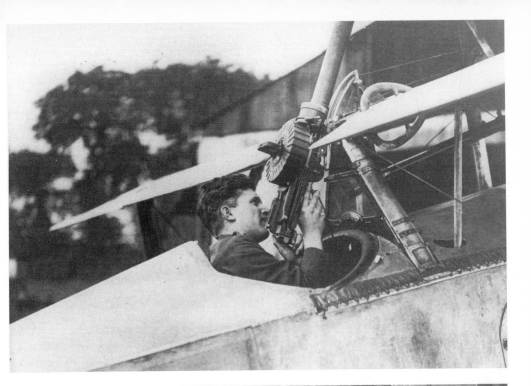

Above: William A. Bishop, then a Lieutenant with No. 60 Squadron, was flying a Nieuport 17 with a top wing-mounted Lewis machine-gun when he encountered Jasta 11 on 30 March 1917.

Right: Jagdstaffel 11's Vizefeldwebel Sebastian Festner is credited with shooting down Captain William Leefe Robinson, VC, of No. 48 Squadron on 5 April 1917. Twenty days later, 23-year-old Festner was killed in a fight with two-seaters of No. 43 Squadron, RFC.

Left: Leutnant Karl Emil Schäfer scored his first victory as an aggressive two-seater pilot with Kampfgeschwader 3 and achieved his next 22 successes with Jasta 11. All but five of his total of 30 victories were British two-seaters defended by a rear-seat gunner.

Below: On Easter Sunday 1917, Leutnant Schäfer achieved his thirteenth victory when he forced Airco D.H.4 A.2140 of No. 55 Squadron, RFC, to land near Epinoy. Lieutenants R. A. Logan and F. R. Henry (seen here wearing leggings) were taken prisoner.

Right: As acting leader of Jasta 11, Leutnant Carl Allmenröder, flew an Albatros D.III, which was all red except for its white nose.

Centre right: Oberleutnant Erich Loewenhardt and a SPAD S.VII which, though forced to land, was counted as a victory. Loewenhardt's 22nd triumph was a SPAD fighter brought down on 16 May 1917. His total of 54 included sixteen SPADs from British and French units.

Below: Leutnant von Hartmann (far left), with his Jasta 11 comrades Wolfgang Plüschow, Konstantin Krefft, Georg Simon, Kurt Wolff, Manfred von Richthofen, Lothar von Richthofen, Hans Hintsch, Otto Brauneck, Matthoff and Carl Allmenröder. Karl Esser is up high behind the group.

Left: Colourful markings of JG I aircraft, such as these Albatros D.V of Jasta 4 in June 1917, gave rise to the Geschwader being called 'the flying circus' by its opponents.

Centre left: Leutnant Carl Allmenröder's awards were displayed on the black velvet *Ordenskissen* placed in front of his coffin. The *Pour le Mérite* takes pride of place, followed by the Iron Cross 1st and 2nd Class, The Knight's Cross of the Order of the House of Hohenzollern with Swords, the Duchy of Oldenburg's Friedrich August Cross 2nd Class and his pilot's badge. He had also received the 1st Class award of the Friedrich August Cross.

Bottom left: Vizefeldwebel Ernst Clausnitzer of Jasta 4 was flying Albatros D.V 1162/17 when he was forced to land and was captured on 15 July 1917. Later, British markings were applied to the aircraft before it was test flown and evaluated.

Right: After Manfred von Richthofen was wounded on 6 July 1917, JG I came under more direct orders from Hauptmann Otto Bufe, the Officer in Charge of Aviation for the 4. Armee. Bufe had been trained as an observer, but as a career officer had command experience of aviation units.

Below: On 28 July 1917 Leutnant Eberhardt Mohnike of Jasta 11 forced down Sopwith F.1 Camel B.3823 of No. 70 Squadron. The aircraft was recovered virtually intact, and the pilot, Second Lieutenant R. C. Hume, was taken prisoner.

Above: During a visit to JG I, Major Albrecht von Richthofen (right) listened with pride and interest as young fighter pilots discussed their work. From left: Leutnant Konstantin Krefft, Leutnant Otto Brauneck, Oberleutnant Ernst Freiherr von Althaus, Manfred von Richthofen and Oberleutnant Erwin Böhme.

Below: SPAD S.VII of Escadrille Spa 31 was the second and last victory of Unteroffizier Hermann Brettel of Jagdstaffel 10. The aircraft was forced down on 10 August 1917; the French pilot, *Maréchal des Logis* Camus is listed only as 'missing in action'. Brettel was killed in action five days later.

Left: Oberleutnant Eduard Dostler led Jagdstaffel 6 from 10 June 1917 until his death in action on 21 August 1917. During that period the 25-year-old Bavarian achieved eighteen of his 26 victories.

Right: Leutnant der Landwehr Hans Adam was an 'old-timer' of 31 when he joined Jagdstaffel 6 in July 1917. He succeeded Oberleutnant Dostler as leader of the Staffel and shot down 21 opponents before being killed in action on 15 November 1917.

Above: Manfred von Richthofen (fourth from left) examines one of three Sopwith Pups of No. 46 Squadron, RFC, brought down on the morning of 3 September 1917.

Below: Enlisted men of Jasta 4 standing before Sopwith Triplane N.5429 of No. 1 Squadron, RNAS. The aircraft was forced down south of Wervicq on 13 September 1917 by Leutnant der Reserve Kurt Wüsthoff of Jagdstaffel 4 and was credited as his 14th victory. The pilot, Flight Sub-Lieutenant J. R. Wilford, was wounded and taken prisoner.

Above: Sopwith Triplane N.5429 of No. 1 Squadron, RNAS, was decorated with German markings and test flown after being captured by JG I.

Below: Jagdstaffel 10 pilots lining up for inspection in front of Voss' Fokker Dr.I and a Pfalz D.IIIa are (from left): Fritz Friedrichs, Erich Lowenhardt, unidentified, Adam Barth, Max Kühn, Paul Aue, unidentified, Werner Voss (with his back to the group), unidentified, and Franz Bohlein.

left: Leutnant Werner Voss signed this photograph for JG I Adjutant Karl Bodenschatz. Voss was killed on 23 September 1917.

Below: F.E.2d aircraft, such as those that bombed JG I airfields at night, carried an assortment of ordnance. Here, an armourer sets the fuse on a 112lb H.E.R.L. bomb. Fitted beneath the wings are 20lb Cooper bombs.

Army moved to secure positions on both banks of the River Scarpe,[28] he led Jasta 11 against a flight of Bristol F.2Bs. Bristol two-seater crews were tough opponents and in this fight No. 48 Squadron claimed several victories,[29] but lost three aircraft. One of the latter was brought down by Lothar at 1710 hours, recorded as his 23rd victory; another went down five minutes later and was credited as Wilhelm Allmenröder's second.[30]

Lothar von Richthofen was superstitious and the events of Sunday, 13 May 1917, only reinforced his belief in the supernatural. It was the first of three occasions, all on the 13th of their respective months, when he was shot down. Just after Lothar and Carl Allmenröder sent down a pair of two-seaters at low altitude over Arleux Forest within British lines – recorded as Lothar's 24th victory and Allmenröder's 12th[31] – they became separated.

Prudence dictated that each find his own way home; while approaching German lines, Lothar's aircraft was hit by groundfire, a bullet struck his hip and he began to lose blood. Crossing the lines, he spotted a place to land and set his Albatros down in a flat meadow and lost consciousness. He woke up in a field hospital, the first of several medical facilities in which he would spend the next four months.

Next day, 14 May 1917, he became the 20th aviation recipient of the *Pour le Mérite*. By now the criterion for a fighter pilot was 20 confirmed victories, which Lothar had attained on 6 May.[32]

Carl Allmenröder succeeded to the position of acting Staffel leader. The number 13 was not at all unlucky to him. While leading the evening patrol on 13 May, he claimed destruction of a Sopwith single-seater near Ostricourt, north of Douai; it was credited as his 13th victory.[33] Soon, he too would receive the *Pour le Mérite*.

Britain's Resurgence in the Air

After a hard struggle Allied troops captured Vimy Ridge in the Battle of Arras,[34] and the RFC's significant achievement in the air was aided by the perseverance of its airmen until new aircraft and better equipment were delivered to the Front.

According to the official Air War Historian H. A. Jones: 'The pilots of the fighting squadrons equipped with the new type aeroplanes, the S.E.5, the Bristol Fighter, the D.H.4, and the Sopwith Pup, had gained confidence and experience in handling their craft, and the squadron mechanics had come to understand the new engines and equipment. There was, from May [1917] onwards, a marked diminution of engine and gun trouble which, throughout April, had been a source of irritation to many pilots and had too often led to a breaking-off of combat. ... From the beginning of May, therefore, the casualties to the corps' aeroplanes dropped appreciably, and the air fighting was pushed away from the lines towards the German back areas.'[35]

The French failure during the Aisne offensive led to the re-organisation of their High Command. For a time Field Marshal Sir Douglas Haig, Commander-in-Chief of the British armies in France, operated more independently and pursued his earlier plans for a major offensive in Flanders. When he moved ground and air units northward, his German counterparts shifted their forces in similar fashion in order to prepare for the Battle of Messines.[36]

The Terrible Triplanes

The growing reputation of the Sopwith Triplanes posed a challenge to many German fighter pilots, who became extraordinarily zealous in targeting them. A newcomer to Jasta 11, Leutnant Gisbert-Wilhelm Groos, pursued a Triplane in the early evening of 19 May and set fire to it near Izel; as the aircraft fell, the pilot jumped or fell out. Groos was credited with his first victory.[37] Four days later, Jasta 11 pilot Leutnant der Reserve Hans Hintsch and Vizefeldwebel Paul Aue of Jasta 10 attacked a Triplane near Carvin at 2115 hours; both men claimed the victory, but it was awarded to Hintsch as his third.[38] On 24 May, there was a big fight between Triplanes of No. 8 Squadron, RNAS, and the red Albatros aircraft. It began shortly before 0900 hours when Jastas 7 and 11 attacked Sopwith Scout biplanes of No. 43 Squadron over Boiry-Notre-Dame, and Carl Allmenröder shot down his 17th enemy aircraft during a spirited encounter. He chased another Sopwith towards Douai and brought it down near Flers for his 18th victory.[39]

From the airfield of No. 8 Naval Squadron at Mont-St-Eloi, some 18 kilometres from where the fight started, Flight-Commander Charles D. Booker, DSC 'observed the combat ... and immediately left and joined the fighting, and drove down a scout, which fell in flames and crashed. Shortly after this Flt-Cdr Booker and Fl-Sub-Lt [Roderick] MacDonald engaged two [enemy aircraft], and drove them both down out of control.'[40]

Leutnant Wilhelm Allmenröder was shot in both knees and forced to land. As the fight continued southward, Hans Hintsch was shot down over Villers-lès-Cagnicourt and killed.[41] No 8 Squadron paid for its success with the loss of Flight-Sub-Lieutenant Harold L. Smith in a Sopwith Triplane over Izel. The victory was credited to Leutnant Otto Maashoff of Jasta 11 as his third.[42]

Irrespective of the credit accorded for the destruction of a Sopwith Triplane, it was clear that German pilots were acquiring too much respect for them to suit the German High Command. The Sopwith's 'phenomenal rate of climb and manoeuvrability apparently suggested to the Germans that there must be some extraordinary quality inherent in the triplane configuration'.[43] Anxious to regain the aerial superiority their pilots had enjoyed in April, the German Inspectorate of Military Aviation set their sights on the triplane to achieve that objective.

No doubt the Inspectorate was spurred on by the report of Manfred von Richthofen, who had shot down a Sopwith Triplane as his 52nd and most recent victory. Moreover one had landed with engine trouble within German lines on 6 April[44] and offered a perfect specimen to study. In short order the Inspectorate ordered triplane prototypes from the Pfalz, Siemens-Schuckert and Fokker aircraft companies. Ultimately, the Fokker Dr.I was selected as the full-production triplane fighter and went on to great fame as an 'acrobatic champion, quite unlike any contemporary fighter'.[45]

Meanwhile the Albatros D.III was still a very effective fighter aircraft, especially in the hands of skilled pilots such as Richthofen's protégé Carl Allmenröder. He achieved Jasta 11's only successes on 25 May by shooting down a Sopwith Scout over Rémy in the morning and a Bristol Fighter over Monchy in the evening, credited as his 19th and 20th victories. The following evening he claimed a Nieuport Scout over Lens.[46]

The day after Carl Allmenröder became a contender for the *Pour le Mérite*, Manfred von Richthofen was welcomed in grand style by a member of the old-line landed nobility of Silesia. He was the guest of honour at the estate of Hans Heinrich XI, Prince of Pless, which had hosted the Supreme Headquarters from 1915 until it was moved westwards to Bad Kreuznach in 1917.[47]

Following his recreational visit in Silesia, Richthofen was sent on a tour of Central Powers' aviation facilities in Austria and in Turkey. Like Oswald Boelcke before him, the latest ace of aces was being kept out of harm's way.

Meanwhile one of his protégés, Leutnant der Reserve Otto Brauneck, was proving himself. With seven Eastern Front victories to his credit, Brauneck was a natural choice to be named a deputy flight leader. He opened Jasta 11's scoring on 1 June by shooting down his eighth enemy aircraft, an R.E.8 over Méricourt.[48]

During an evening patrol On Monday, 4 June, Jasta 11 lost Leutnant Georg Simon, who had only shot down one enemy aircraft although he had been with the Staffel since 7 November 1916. He was forced to land at Fontaine-lès-Croisilles and was taken prisoner; he was recorded as the fifth victory for Captain Charles M. B. Chapman, MC, of No. 29 Squadron.[49] Simon's aircraft was recovered intact and assigned the captured aircraft reference number G 42.[50]

Richthofen Protégés Rise and Fall

The failure of the Second Battle of the Aisne – so demoralising to the French troops that widespread mutinies occurred[51] – shifted the burden of the Western Front offensive on to the British forces in Flanders. In response to this new challenge the British Second Army set out to drive German troops from the high ground of the group of hills forming the Messines–Wytschaete ridge. Increased use of the RFC Corps squadrons drew the attention of German fighter units from neighbouring Armee areas.

Jasta 11 flew some 50 kilometres to reach a late morning fight over the Wytschaete area on 5 June. Once there, the Staffel scored three victories within ten minutes. Carl Allmenröder brought down his 26th opponent, Otto Brauneck his eighth and Leutnant der Reserve Alfred Niederhoff his third; all were listed as Sopwith Pups,[52] but most likely were the larger Sopwith 1½ Strutter two-seaters of No. 45 Squadron, which reported being attacked by '18 H.A. [hostile aircraft] Scouts, led by a red machine with black wheels'.[53]

That afternoon, however, Jasta 11 lost one of its brightest alumni, Leutnant Emil Schäfer, leader of Jasta 28w. The 25-year-old ace with 30 victories was shot down and killed over Zandvoorde by a British two-seater crew. Schäfer must have retained his red Albatros D.III from Jasta 11, for the RFC account noted:

'In a fight between 15 H.A. led by a red machine and seven F.E.s of No. 20 Squadron, one of our aeroplanes was driven down and followed by the red H.A. Lieut H. L. Satchell and 2nd-Lieut T. Lewis at once dived to the assistance of our machine, and a fight lasting about 15 minutes took place in which the German pilot showed great skill and persistence. Eventually, however, after a burst of fire at very close range the enemy scout burst into flames and the wings were seen to fall off before it crashed.'[54]

Emil Schäfer was the fourth of eight victims credited to Lieutenant (later Captain) Harold L. Satchell.[55] Schäfer's body was recovered and sent back to his home town of Krefeld in Westphalia, for a funeral worthy of a national hero. The sad news was relayed and, the following day, Manfred von Richthofen cancelled his appointments in Vienna. He returned to Berlin to use his position and prestige, and very likely the sad news about Schäfer, to persuade the Inspectorate for Military Aviation to provide a successor to the Albatros fighters. He noted that even the improved D.V series continued to suffer wing failures and were less competitive against newer British and French fighters.[56]

Richthofen Returns to Jasta 11

On his way back to the Front, Richthofen stopped at Krefeld for his friend's funeral, at which he led the honour guard. He was all the more convinced of the ineffectiveness of the Albatros series when he learned that his cousin Leutnant Oskar von Schickfuss und Neudorff, an Albatros pilot with Jasta 3, had been shot down in flames[57] near Monchy-le-Preux, behind British lines, only hours after Schäfer perished. Oscar, who was five days past his 23rd birthday when he died, had followed Manfred's example in transferring from a mounted unit[58] into the air service. Freifrau von Richthofen informed Manfred that Oskar's last letter described a recent aerial combat and 'mentioned that often he had to break off the fight due to a jam in his guns; also in some cases the British aircraft seemed to be better than ours ...'[59]

On Thursday, 4 June 1917, Leutnant Carl Allmenröder became the fourth member of Jasta 11 to receive the *Pour le Mérite*. Manfred arrived back at his Staffel just as the good news was circulating. Exercising his usual self-discipline, he put the recent losses out of his mind and concentrated on the tasks ahead of him. He was excited about working with other new pilots and encouraging them to attain Allmenröder's level of achievement.

Among the pilots who benefited from Richthofen's tutelage was Leutnant Gisbert-Wilhelm Groos. The two men had much in common; both were veterans of the Prussian cadet system and Uhlan regiments.[60] Groos later recalled: 'Richthofen was a born leader. Sharp as a razor in service matters; at all times fair, especially in the air over the Front. He saw everything. He gave new men in the Jasta every chance to score a victory. He gave away many victories, if by doing so the young pilot was able to score his first kill. He protected every member of the flight [as much as] possible, but there was no pardon if a pilot sneaked away from a fight. That pilot would be transferred immediately.'[61]

Move to the 4. Armee Front

Hazy weather at the end of the first full week of June 1917 provided a welcome cover on the 9th and 10th of the month, when Jasta 11 was relocated from Roucourt to Bavichove, about 5 kilometres north-north-east of Courtrai. Jasta 11 moved to 4. Armee's Front to follow their British adversaries.[62] On the new Front the chain of command was shortened, as Jasta 11 no longer reported to a group aviation commander (Gruppenführer der Flieger) responsible to an Armee-Korps headquarters.[63] To amass fighter support, the leaders of Jastas 6, 7, 11 and 26 were placed directly under the Officer in Charge of Aviation for 4. Armee,[64] Hauptmann Otto Bufe.

A 33-year-old career officer, Bufe had been one of the top graduates of the Prussian cadet corps system[65] and after being commissioned was on a promising career track. He had joined the Fliegertruppe before the war and by November 1914 had been promoted to Hauptmann, was an aviation observer and was given ever increasing command responsibility.[66] Now, with four fighter units to direct, including the famous Jagdstaffel 11, Otto Bufe had a significant opportunity to bolster his career by displaying his talents as a tactician. A key part of that challenge would be his ability to manage the ever more successful luminary of German military aviation, Manfred von Richthofen.

Jasta 11 settled into new quarters over the weekend and resumed flight operations on Monday, 18 June 1917. Richthofen led a morning flight toward the lines, expecting to meet the RFC's new fighters. Instead the Germans encountered three old Nieuport Scouts which, while less powerful, could out-manoeuvre the Albatroses. In this case, however, there was a brief fight over Zonnebeke, during which Carl Allmenröder drove down one of the biplane fighters. At about 0950 hours it was seen to crash at Valorenhoek and was recorded as his 27th victory.[67]

Three hours later, south of Ypres, Jasta 11 aircraft again clashed with a trio of Nieuports, but with different results. This flight of Nieuports stayed together and, according to the RFC combat report, they fought off 'eight Albatros scouts, new type, painted red fuselage, black wings and black crosses in white circles'.[68] They shot down one of the new Albatros fighters, killing 20-year-old Leutnant der Reserve Walter Bordfeld, a promising pilot who had transferred from Jasta 10 to Jasta 11. But the patrol ended in the Staffel's favour, as Manfred von Richthofen achieved his 53rd victory. North of Ypres, he attacked an R.E.8, which, he reported: 'driven by the wind, it fell into Struywes's [sic] farm, where it began to burn'.[69]

In the last half of June Jasta 11 benefited from the success of the first German daytime bombing raid on London on the 13th. The public outcry for stronger air defences around London was so great that the High Command felt compelled to withdraw two combat-proven squadrons from France to deal with future raids by the big two-engined German bombers. The S.E.5s of No. 56 Squadron returned to England on 21 June and No. 66 Squadron's Sopwith Pups were deployed to Calais. Consequently the RFC's Ninth Wing had only one fighter unit – No. 19 Squadron and its SPAD S.7s – which were experiencing engine problems,[70] and the thinning down of the air defence line in one area meant that neighbouring units had to extend their coverage.

During an evening patrol on 23 June, Richthofen led an attack against a flight of British SPAD single-seaters north of Ypres. He closed in on one SPAD, from above and behind, and fired a stream of bullets into it. After which, he reported: 'My adversary ... did nothing to evade my fire. At first the aircraft began to smoke and then it fell, turning and turning, three kilometres north of Ypres, where it [hit] the ground ...'.[71] Richthofen was credited with his 54th victory.

The British defence line suffered further damage next morning, when Manfred von Richthofen and six of his comrades dived on two reconnaissance aircraft and ten fighter escorts. The fierce battle with what were described as 'Albatros scouts coloured bright red' was related by Flight-Lieutenant (later Air Vice Marshal) Raymond Collishaw, then a flight leader with No. 10 Squadron, RNAS:

'Escorting two D.H.4s of No. 27 Squadron [sic][72] at 11,000 feet in the vicinity of Moorslede [when] four E.A. [enemy aircraft] scouts attacked the D.H.s and I closed immediately on one which got into a spin. I then fired at an E.A. on one D.H.'s tail. While engaged with it, I observed Fl-Sub-Lt [William M.] Alexander attack one on the other D.H.'s tail.

'Fl-Sub-Lt Alexander got away toward the lines with a gun jam. I closed to about 25 yards on E.A.'s tail before I got in position to fire. After about 40 rounds, the enemy machine went out of control and I saw the wings come off one side, and [it] crashed near the road from Moorslede to Passchendaele. About this time we were attacked by about 15 additional scouts and I was chased by four of them down to the ground and was only able to get across the lines at about 50 feet [altitude].'[73]

Another member of the same unit, Flight-Lieutenant John E. Sharman, DSC, reported chasing another Albatros away from a D.H.4, noting: 'I could see the tracers entering his fuselage, and I think I hit the pilot. I was then attacked from behind, and managed to drive down my assailant, though I did not get him. Then I saw, 2,000 feet below me, a light-green coloured E.A. diving out of control. No other machines being near, this one must have been the one I was firing at. His tail-plane flew off, and then his right wing, and the pieces floated down.'[74]

While the two naval Triplane pilots were credited with destroying two Albatros in this fight,[75] 4. Armee reports do not list corresponding casualties. On the other hand, Manfred von Richthofen was credited with shooting down one of the D.H.4s near Beceleare for his 55th victory,[76] while Carl Allmenröder and Gisbert-Wilhelm Groos attended to the escorting Sopwith Triplanes. Allmenröder shot down one, for his 28th victory, and Groos downed another Triplane, his second victory.[77]

Jasta 11 was destined to meet again with the Triplanes of Naval 10 and their leading scorer, Raymond Collishaw. For the moment, however, victory was theirs.

Notes

1 Krefft, *Personal-Bogen*, pp. 1–3; the others were: Ltn.d.R Albert Oesterreicher, Vzfw Alfred Prehn, Uffz Godt, Gefr Sebastian Festner and Flgr Adam Barth (Ref: *Stofl 6. Armee Bericht* Nr. 19257, 10 October 1916).

2 *Kofl 6. Armee Wochenbericht* Nr. 50790, Teil 11, 4 May 1917; Sopwith Triplane N.5474 of No. 8

Squadron, RNAS, Fl-Sub-Lt Edmund D. Roach, aged 25 (KiA); F.E.2b A.815 of No. 25 Squadron, RFC, Lts G. S. French and G. P. Harding, MC (both PoW); and another F.E.2b, most probably from No. 25 Squadron, but not counted as a casualty, because the aircraft returned intact.

3   Kogenluft, *Nachrichtenblatt der Luftstreitkräfte*, Nr. 13, 24 May 1917, p. 5-(2).

4   O'Connor, N., *Aviation Awards*, vol. II, p. 219.

5   Ref: Jasta 11 section of Appendix I of this book.

6   *Kofl 6. Armee*, Nr. 50570, Teil 13, 28 April 1917.

7   Zuerl, W., *Pour-le-Mérite-Flieger*, p. 480.

8   Kogenluft, *Nachrichtenblatt*, op. cit., p. 5-(3); explanations in parentheses are Wolff's; those in square brackets are the author's.

9   *Kofl 6. Armee*, op. cit., Nr. 50790.

10 Kogenluft, *Nachrichtenblatt*, op. cit., Nr. 15, 7 June 1917, p. 12; Armstrong-Whitworth F.K.8 A.9999 of No. 2 Squadron, 2/Lt Geoffrey Wood and Lt John C. G. Coupland, aged 32 (both KiA).

11 RFC *War Diary* entry for this date.

12 Jones, H. A, *War in the Air*, vol. III, p. 376.

13 *Nachrichtenblatt*, ibid., p. 13; Nieuport 17 B.1631 of No. 40 Squadron, Capt William E. Nixon, aged 19 (KiA).

14 Ibid.; B.E.2c 4595 of No. 13 Squadron, 2/Lt Iorweth ap Roland Owen, aged 20 (KiA), and 2/AM Reginald Hickling (DoW).

15 Ibid.; R.E.8 A.3426 of No. 59 Squadron, Capt W. W. Leete and Lt B. A. Wilson (both WiA).

16 Otto Maashoff remained in the Luftstreitkräfte until the end of 1918, went on to university studies in engineering and returned to national service in 1933. He advanced through the Air Transport Ministry and was promoted General-Ingenieur in the Luftwaffe in 1940. He died in a Berlin hospital on 26 October 1941 (Ref: Hildebrand, K., *Die Generale*, vol, II, pp. 331–2).

17 Kogenluft, *Nachrichtenblatt*, Nr. 13, op. cit., p. 8-(c); the parentheses appear in the original German text.

18 See Bowyer, C., *Albert Ball, V.C.* , and Revell, A., *High in the Empty Blue*.

19 Revell, ibid., p. 47.

20 Commissioned into 1. Oberrheinisches Infanterie-Regiment Nr. 97, Plüschow was posted out of Jasta 11 for a long convalescence. Subsequently, he flew with Jasta 39 on the Isonzo Front in Italy, where he scored one victory on 30 January 1918. He died aged 30 in Germany on 5 July 1918.

21 Revell, op. cit., p. 280.

22 Bowyer, op. cit., p. 150.

23 RFC *Western Front Casualty List*, 1917.

24 Böhme, *Briefe eines deutschen Kampffliegers*, p. 111.

25 Kogenluft, *Nachrichtenblatt*, Nr. 15, p. 13; F.2B A.7110 of No. 48 Squadron, 2/Lt William T. Price, MC and Lt Charles G. Claye (both WiA); Shores, et al., *Above the Trenches*, p. 308.

26 Ibid.; Sopwith Pup A.7303, 2/Lt Desmond J. Sheehan (KiA), and Sopwith Pup A.6178, Lt T. H. Wickett (WiA/PoW).

27 O'Connor, op. cit., p. 141.

28 Jones, op. cit., p. 378.

29 RFC *Communiqué* No. 87, p. 7; German documents show no matching losses for these claims.

30 *Kofl 6. Armee*, Nr. 180/I, Teil 11, 18 May 1917; F.2B A.7111, Lt W. O. B. Winkler and 2/Lt E. S. Moore (both PoW); and F.2B A.7101, Capt Arthur T. Cull and 1/AM Arthur Trusson (both KiA).

31 Ibid.; B.E.2e 7150 of No. 13 Squadron, 2/Lt F. Thompson and Lt A. C. C. Rawlins (both of whom made it back to their lines (Ref: Rogers, L., 'RFC and RAF Casualties', in *Cross & Cockade*, 1975, p. 185); and R.E.8 A.4245 of No. 16 Squadron, 2/Lts Vernon F. Stewart, aged 24, and John G. Troup, aged 20 (both KiA).

32 O'Connor, op. cit., pp. 64, 219.

33 Kogenluft, *Nachrichtenblatt*, op. cit., p. 14; *Kofl 6. Armee*, op. cit.; British casualty lists show no Sopwith losses for this date; Allmenröder may have shot down a Nieuport, which has some similarity to a Sopwith Pup, in which case, he may have fought with 2/Lt A. M. Sutherland, Nieuport 23 B.1567 of No. 29 Squadron, who was listed as missing in that area during an evening patrol (Ref: Rogers, ibid.).

34 Falls, C., 'Western Front, Stalemate' in Esposito, *Concise History*, p. 95.
35 Jones, op. cit., pp. 370–1; the reference to the two-seat bomber and reconnaissance D.H.4 as a fighter is apparently a typographical error; perhaps Jones intended to mention the D.H.5 single-seat fighter which became operational in May 1917 (Ref: Bruce, J., *British Aeroplanes*, p. 184).
36 Jones, op. cit., vol. IV, p. 113.
37 *Kofl 6. Armee*, Nr. 270/I, Teil 10, 25 May 1917; Sopwith Triplane N.5488, Fl-Sub-Lt Oliver B. Ellis, aged 18 (KiA) (Ref: Henshaw, T., *Sky their Battlefield*, p. 175).
38 Kogenluft, *Nachrichtenblatt*, Nr. 16, 14 June 1917; Sopwith Triplane N.5481, Fl-Lt Harold A. Pailthorpe, aged 26 (KiA) (Ref: Henshaw, ibid., p. 176).
39 *Kofl 6. Armee*, op. cit., Nr. 270/I, lists both victories only as 'Sopwith' aircraft, while Kogenluft, *Nachrichtenblatt*, ibid., identifies Allmenröder's eighteenth victory as a triplane; it is probable that Allmenröder and/or Ltn.d.R Maashoff shot down an aircraft from No. 8 Squadron, RNAS.
40 RFC *Communiqué* No. 89, 27 May 1917, p. 5.
41 *Kofl 6. Armee*, ibid., Nr. 270/I, Teil 11.
42 Kogenluft, ibid., *Nachrichtenblatt*, ibid.; see Chapter note No. 37 above; Sopwith Triplane N.5450, Fl-Sub-Lt H. L. Smith, aged 19 (KiA).
43 Bruce, J., *Fokker Dr.I*, p. 3.
44 N.5457 of No 1 Squadron, RNAS, Fl-Sub-Lt N. D. M. Hewitt (PoW); Grosz , P. and Ferko, A. E., 'Fokker Dr.I, Reappraisal', in *Air Enthusiast*, 1978, p. 10.
45 Ibid., p. 14.
46 *Kofl 6. Armee*, Nr. 380/I, Teil 12, 1 June 1917 lists the Nieuport as Allmenröder's 21st victory, but it was not confirmed.
47 Showalter, E., *Bad Kreuznach*, p. 8.
48 Schmeelke, M., 'Otto Brauneck, Part II', in *Over the Front*, 1986, p. 196; both Kogenluft, *Nachrichtenblatt*, Nr. 20, 12 July 1917, p. 80, and *Kofl 6. Armee*, Nr. 469 I, Teil 12, 8 June 1917 list Brauneck's first Western Front claim as his seventh confirmed victory; very probably R.E.8 A.3265 of No. 16 Squadron, Lt Wilfred E. McKissock, aged 26, and 2/Lt Arthur W. L. Nixon (both KiA).
49 Shores, et al., *Above the Trenches*, 199., p. 102.
50 Albatros D.III 2015/16; Puglisi, W., 'German Aircraft Down, Part 1' in *Cross & Cockade*, 1969, p. 156.
51 Falls, op. cit., p. 94.
52 *Kofl 6. Armee*, Nr. 469 I, op. cit.; the day's casualties and known status were: Sopwith A.8280, 2/Lt B. Smith and 2/AM S. Thompson (both WiA/PoW); Sopwith A.1925, 2/Lt R. S. Binnie and Lt Thomas A. Metheral, aged 22 (KiA); Sopwith A.8268, Sgt Ernest A. Cook, aged 24, and 2/AM Harry V. Shaw, aged 19 (both KiA); and Sopwith A.8293 in which 2/Lt W. G. Corner was reported to have 'sustained gun shot wound in leg', but returned to his own lines (Ref: RFC *Western Front Casualty List*).
53 RFC *Communiqué* No. 91, 9 June 1917, p. 6; a detailed account of No. 45 Squadron's actions in this fight can be found in Macmillan, N., *Into the Blue*, pp. 71–6.
54 RFC *Communiqué*, ibid.; Jones, op. cit., p. 121; Schäfer's 30th and last victim was F.E.2d A.6384 of No. 20 Squadron, pilot Lt William A. Sawden, aged 26 (DoW), observer Lt R. M. Madill was unhurt (Ref: Hobson, C., *Airmen Died*, p. 248).
55 Shores, et al., op. cit., p. 330.
56 Grosz, P., 'Agile and Aggressive Albatros', in *Air Enthusiast*, 1976, pp. 46–7.
57 Later confirmed in *Kofl 6. Armee*, Nr. 469 I, op. cit., Teil 13; it is most probable that Ltn von Schickfuss und Neudorff was shot down by Major Alan J. L. Scott in Nieuport 17 B.1575 of No. 60 Squadron, whose fourth victory was confirmed as an Albatros brought down near Monchy-le-Preux at 2010 hours (Ref: Shores, et al., op. cit., p. 333).
58 Leib-Kürassier-Regiment Grosser Kurfürst (Schlesisches) Nr. 1.
59 Richthofen, K. von, *Kriegstsagebuch*, pp. 118–19.
60 Groos began his service with Ulanen-Regiment Grossherzog Friedrich von Baden (Rheinisches) Nr. 7.
61 Quoted from Nowarra, H., 'Reminiscences', in *Cross & Cockade*, 1960, pp. 60–1.
62 *Kofl 6. Armee*, Nr. 469 I, op. cit., Teil 1.
63 Air Ministry, *Handbook of German Military and Naval Aviation*, p. 43.

64 *Kofl 4. Armee Wochenbericht*, Nr. 20652/19, Teil 3, 9 June 1917.

65 *Stammliste der Offiziere des 6. Badischen Infanterie-Regiments (Kaiser Friedrich III)* Nr. 114, 1904, list 293, p. 122.

66 Bufe, O., *Personal-Bogen*, 1920, pp. 2–3.

67 Kogenluft, *Nachrichtenblatt*, Nr. 21, 19 July 1917, p. 95; Nieuport 17 B.1638 of No. 1 Squadron, 2/Lt Richard S. Lloyd, aged 29 (KiA).

68 No. 1 Squadron Combat Report, 18 June 1917, filed jointly by Lt L. F. Jenkin in Nieuport B.1681, Lt C. S. T. Reeves in B.3495 and 2/Lt H. G. Reeves in B.1630.

69 Quoted in Gibbons, F., *Red Knight*, p. 278; R.E.8 A.4290 of No. 9 Squadron, Lts Ralph W. E. Ellis and Harold C. Barlow, aged 27 (both KiA). Franks, N., et al., *Guns of the Red Baron*, p. 137 gives the location as 'Stray Farm', east of Pilckem and north of Ypres.

70 Jones, op. cit., pp. 134–5.

71 Quoted in Gibbons, op. cit., p. 281; this claim, unsupported by any other witness, has been questioned by aviation historians. Franks, et al., op. cit., pp. 139–41 makes a strong case for the aircraft's having been SPAD B.1530 of No. 23 Squadron, 2/Lt Robert W. Farquhar, who was unwounded and whose aircraft was not struck off squadron strength because of combat damage and so was not counted as a loss.

72 Collishaw's combat report lists the two-seaters as belonging to No. 27 Squadron, while his book, *Air Command*, notes them as being from No. 25 Squadron; RFC *Western Front Casualty List* identifies the D.H.4 shot down in the encounter as an aircraft of No. 57 Squadron.

73 No. 10 Squadron, RNAS Combat Report of Fl-Lt R. Collishaw in Sopwith Triplane N.5492.

74 No. 10 Squadron, RNAS Combat Report of Fl-Lt J. E. Sharman in Sopwith Triplane N.6307.

75 Shores, et al., op. cit., pp. 115, 335.

76 Kogenluft, *Nachrichtenblatt*, Nr. 21, op. cit.; and *Kofl 4. Armee*, Nr. 20652/19, op. cit.; D.H.4 A.7473 of No. 57 Squadron, Capt Norman G. Naughton, aged 27, and Capt Angus H. Mearns, aged 22 (both KiA).

77 Kogenluft, *Nachrichtenblatt*, ibid.; both from No. 10 Squadron, RNAS: Sopwith Triplane N.5348, Fl-Sub-Lt Robert G. Saunders (KiA) and Sopwith Triplane N.6306, Fl-Sub-Lt Alan B. Holcroft (WiA/PoW) (Ref: Collishaw, op. cit., p. 100).

CHAPTER 7

Germany's First Fighter Wing

BEFORE HAUPTMANN OTTO BUFE COULD TAKE COMMAND OF JAGDSTAFFELN 6, 7, 11 and 26, on 23 June 1917 the four Staffeln were assigned to a new unit designated Jagdgeschwader I (Fighter Wing 1)[1] and commanded by Rittmeister Manfred von Richthofen. Luftstreitkräfte Commanding General Ernst von Hoeppner pointed out that the 'ever-increasing number of aircraft which the opposition were deploying to reach a target made it seem desirable for us to combine several Jagdstaffeln into a Jagdgeschwader ... [and] in the personage of Rittmeister von Richthofen ... [it] received a commander whose steel-hard will in relentlessly pursuing the enemy was infused in every member of the Geschwader.'[2]

To enhance Richthofen's chances of success, two units initially assigned to JG I were replaced: Jasta 7 commanded by the little- known former infantry officer[3] Oberleutnant Fritz Bronsart von Schellendorf, who at the age of 26 had one victory to his credit, and Jasta 26 commanded by the five-victory ace Ober-leutnant Bruno Loerzer, also 26, whose prominence was yet to come.[4] These units were succeeded by Jasta 4, which had had three *Pour le Mérite* recipients among its leaders,[5] and Jasta 10, with two *Pour le Mérite* holders during its short operational life.[6]

Late on the afternoon of 25 June, the day on which he was formally appointed Jagdgeschwader commander,[7] Richthofen accompanied a patrol led by Leutnant Carl Allmenröder, who succeeded him as leader of Jasta 11. Once again, Richthofen demonstrated his skill; over the trenches near Le Bizet he shot down an R.E.8 two-seat reconnaissance aircraft, which was credited as his 56th victory.[8]

Allmenröder's turn came an hour later, when, flying through rain and wet snow, he and his flight pounced on six Sopwith Triplanes. After a brief fight near Quesnoy, the formations were separated by the weather. Two Triplanes did not return; one made an emergency landing at Droglandt,[9] the other crashed within German lines and was recorded as Carl Allmenröder's 29th victory.[10] But Allmenröder's time in a leadership role was brief. On the morning of Wednesday, 27 June 1917, less than two weeks after he had received the *Pour le Mérite*, he was shot down and killed in a fight with Sopwith Triplanes near Klein-Zillebeke.

The pilot often thought to have been Allmenröder's adversary in that fight, 23-year-old Canadian Flight-Lieutenant Raymond Collishaw of No. 10 Squadron, RNAS, stated only that 'it seems likely that it was my fire that sent him down to his death'.[11] In recent times, publication of a German eye-witness account indicates that Allmenröder was most probably hit by British anti-aircraft fire.[12]

Carl Allmenröder's body was retrieved and sent back to his home town in Germany for a traditionally elaborate national hero's funeral.[13] At Richthofen's direction, Leutnant der Reserve Otto Brauneck represented the Staffel and carried his comrade's black velvet *Ordenskissen*, which was crowned by the *Pour le Mérite* which the 21-year-old Rhinelander was wearing when he was killed.[14]

Manfred von Richthofen was in Hamburg to visit his brother Lothar, who was recuperating in hospital,[15] when he was informed of Allmenröder's death. He was unable to attend the funeral, but wrote to his friend's father: 'A British aircraft, that was at least 800 metres away, fired just a few shots from this enormous distance (the usual fighting distances are 100 or 50 metres or only an aircraft's-length away). Carl's machine immediately made a left turn in the direction of our lines. That was a sign that he was still in control of the machine. His comrades observed that he had turned off his fuel [to minimise the danger of fire] and was heading down in a glide. From this glide he went into a dive that could no longer be averted ... I myself could not wish for a more beautiful death than falling in aerial combat; it is a comfort to know that Carl felt nothing at the end ...'[16]

New Leaders Evolve

Given its prominence as an operating unit and as a symbol of German military aviation, Jasta 11 had to have a worthy leader. An obvious choice was Leutnant Kurt Wolff, who, like Carl Allmenröder, was a 30-victory ace. Also Wolff had been one of Richthofen's top students before leaving Jasta 11 to command Jasta 29. With this adjustment, Richthofen's Jasta commanders were now:

Jasta 4: Oberleutnant Kurt-Bertram von Döring, 28 years old and a former cavalry officer,[17] who transferred to aviation in June 1913 and a year later completed pilot training. Promoted to Oberleutnant on 25 February 1915, Döring served with Feldflieger-Abteilung 38 and Sonderstaffel S2 before being assigned command of Jasta 4 on 8 April 1917.[18] He had been a Staffel leader for three months and had three victories to his credit. A Jasta 4 subordinate, Leutnant der Reserve Hans Klein, had 12 confirmed victories at this point.

Jasta 6: Oberleutnant Eduard Dostler, aged 25 and trained as a sapper-engineer,[19] had been a pilot with two-seater 'protection' units Schutzstaffeln 27 and 36, and then with Bavarian Jasta 34. Dostler was credited with 12 victories when he succeeded *Pour le Mérite* ace Leutnant Otto Bernert in command of Jasta 6.

Jasta 10: Oberleutnant Ernst Freiherr von Althaus, 27, was hastily transferred from temporary command of Jasta 14 to succeed fifteen-victory ace and *Pour le Mérite* recipient Leutnant der Reserve Albert Dossenbach, who had been killed in combat while leading Jasta 10 on 3 July 1917. After completing secondary school, in 1909 Althaus began his service as an officer candidate [*Avantageur*][20] with a light cavalry unit.[21] His early bravery in land warfare was recognised by his home state of Saxony in the form of its highest bravery award, the Knight's Cross of the Military St. Henry Order.[22] Althaus entered the aviation service in April 1915 and flew Fokker Eindeckers with Feldflieger-Abteilung 23. After a quick string of eight victories, he became the eighth *Pour le Mérite* recipient,[23] but had not scored since 22 July 1916. Althaus faced a shaky future under the results-oriented Manfred von Richthofen.

Jasta 11: Leutnant Kurt Wolff, 22, came to aviation from a military railway unit.[24] He had been a two-seater pilot at Verdun and on the Somme, and as a Jasta 11 member he became the eighteenth aviation recipient of the *Pour le Mérite*. During his brief command of Jasta 29, Wolff logged his 30th and 31st victories. Of the four Staffel leaders, Kurt Wolff was easily the brightest star.

Manfred von Richthofen was given great latitude in staffing JG I. He had only to ask for someone and the transfer was made. So Leutnant der Reserve Konstantin Krefft, Jasta 11's Technical Officer, was assigned the same post in the Jagdgeschwader.[25] Richthofen's choice for adjutant was 26-year-old Oberleutnant Karl Bodenschatz, a former Bavarian infantry officer who had served well in that capacity with Jasta Boelcke.[26]

On Richthofen's return, quarters and facilities for the Geschwader had been set up in the town of Marcke, just south-west of Courtrai. The estate of Baron Jean de Béthune had been expropriated and its broad green lawns, comfortable castle and nearby buildings were converted to military use for JG I.

Jasta 11 personnel and *matériel* arrived at the new site first, followed by Jasta 4. Jasta 6 was set up at neighbouring Bisseghem, just across the River Lys from Marckebeke, while Jasta 10 was at Heule airfield, a short distance away.

The first days of the new Jagdgeschwader were hectic. Leutnant Erwin Böhme, about to succeed Kurt Wolff as leader of Jasta 29, described the chaos, which was exacerbated by Richthofen's now even greater celebrity status:

'Shortly, I will have the pleasure of seeing my brother's brother-in-law [Professor Hans] Kohlschein, who wants to paint [a portrait of] Richthofen, here on the Western Front. When I was with Richthofen for that reason a few days ago, I found him to be very busy with Jagdgeschwader organisational matters and, moreover, annoyed by the many newspaper reporters and newsreel film maker types who now throng around him. So at first he made rather a sour face – but when I told him that Moritz [his dog] would, of course, be in the portrait, then he became all fired up about it.'[27]

By Monday, 2 July 1917, JG I was firmly settled into the new facilities and, that morning, Richthofen led the first sortie. A pair of R.E.8 reconnaissance biplanes came into view some 20 kilometres south-west of Marcke and the red Albatros fighters headed for them. Over Deûlémont, Richthofen fired at the lead aircraft and hit the observer and then the pilot. As the aircraft went out of control, the ace later reported that he 'fired at the bucking aircraft from 50 metres' distance with a few more shots until flames burst out of the machine and the opponent crashed in flames'.[28] Richthofen was credited with his 57th victory. The second R.E.8 was brought down in a spinning nose-dive by Leutnant Gisbert-Wilhelm Groos and recorded as his third 'kill'.[29]

Although it would have been premature at this juncture to credit the success of these massed operations to Manfred von Richthofen, his reputation was such that his opponents quickly inferred that German air tactics were changing under his direction. In early July, the Luftstreitkräfte Commanding General's weekly intelligence digest reported: 'Many prisoners believe firmly in the existence of the Richthofen Wandering Circus. It is said to fly along the Front from Lille to St-Quentin and to number from 18 to 30 aircraft and more.'[30]

Jagdgeschwader I did not 'wander' that far – some 25 kilometres from their airfield to Lille and another 85 km south to St-Quentin and back. Richthofen was more interested in operational effectiveness than in distance. His approach and sense of organisation became evident during his first meeting with the Jagdstaffel leaders, when he directed that no further individual missions be carried out by pilots on their own initiative. Staffel- or Geschwader-strength sorties would be authorised on the basis of information about enemy air activity that he received from front-line sources, the four Staffel commanders being informed simultaneously by telephone.[31]

Richthofen told his Staffel leaders that increased enemy air activity and seemingly relentless artillery barrages were doing both material and morale damage to German ground forces. During pauses in the shelling, he noted, infantry-strafing aircraft roared over just above the trenches. High above them were formations of bombing squadrons that swung far over German rear areas. Consequently, Jagdgeschwader I's objective would be nothing short of annihilation of enemy ground-strafers, single-seat fighters, and bombing squadrons.[32]

Richthofen deployed the Staffeln carefully. He developed a new plan in steps, as laid out in Wing Order No. 1: 'As of 6 July, the sequence of daily take-off readiness (from daybreak on) in rotation is Jastas 11, 10, 6, 4; the daily midday take-off sequence (from 1330 to 1500 hours) is Jastas 10, 6, 4, 11.'[33]

Richthofen Knocked Out of Action

In keeping with his plan, on the morning of 6 July he sent Jasta 4 due west toward Ypres, where British artillery-spotting aircraft were reported to be very active, despite patchy cloud cover. The intruders were gone when Jasta 4 arrived and the flight returned.

At about 1030 hours, Richthofen was informed that enemy close air support units had crossed the front-line off to the south-west. He led a flight from Jasta 11 towards Armentières in the 6. Armee area to intercept them, but on the way spotted a flight of F.E.2d bombers over Deûlémont and they became the new target. Joining other German fighters in the area, Richthofen led his red Albatros fighters in a wide arc, circling to get behind the bombers and cut off their retreat. The F.E.s turned to meet their attackers.

Reports of the time give the impression that the ensuing combat was a routine exchange of shots, with casualties on both sides. According to a British account:

'An offensive patrol of No. 20 Squadron engaged about 30 Albatros Scouts in several formations. The German machines came much closer than usual and attacked keenly. Capt. [Douglas C.] Cunnell and 2nd-Lieut. [Albert E.] Woodbridge drove down four of their opponents out of control. 2nd-Lieuts. [Cecil R.] Richards and [Albert E.] Wear also drove down one of the [Albatros] Scouts out of control. All of our machines returned ...

'Four [Sopwith Triplane] machines of Naval Squadron No. 10 saw a patrol of No. 20 Squadron engaging 30 Albatros Scouts and at once joined in the fighting. Flight-Lieut. [Raymond] Collishaw drove down one of his opponents out of control, and then attacked five more, each of which he forced down, probably out of control. During the fighting he saw one of the German machines, which was attacked by another Triplane, crash.

'Flight Lieut. ['Mel'] Alexander fired 25 rounds from close range into one of the hostile scouts, which fell out of control, and then he attacked another, which he also drove down out of control.

'Flight Sub-Lieut. [Ellis V.] Reid opened fire at one enemy machine, which turned on its back and fell, and was last seen near the ground out of control.'[34]

Collishaw was credited with six OoCs (out of control) that were counted as victories, Alexander with two and Reid with one.[35] German casualties were very light and no German pilot received credit for the one aircraft from No. 20 Squadron which was damaged and forced to land[36] – albeit within British lines.

German fighter unit casualties reported were: Rittmeister Manfred von Richthofen 'slightly wounded in aerial combat', Vizefeldwebel Fritz Loerzer (Jasta 26)[37] 'wounded in aerial combat' (two shots in the leg) and Vizefeldwebel Hermann Denkhaus (Jasta 7) 'fatally crashed after aerial combat'.[38] Despite the casual reference to Richthofen's wound, he was almost killed while attacking one of the F.E.s.

As the two-seater turned towards the German, the observer stood up to man the forward gun and opened fire. Richthofen scoffed at his naïvety in shooting from such a great distance, but, he recalled: ' ... Suddenly there was a blow to my head! I was hit! For a moment I was completely paralysed throughout my whole body. My hands dropped to the side, my legs dangled inside the fuselage. The worst part was that the blow on the head had affected my optic nerve and I was completely blinded ...'[39]

As his Albatros dived out of control, Richthofen thought he was finished. He could not believe that the F.E.2 could have hit him and, indeed, a recent examination of this fight contends that Richthofen may have been shot unintentionally by a comrade flying behind him.[40] In any event, a primal instinct directed his hand to switch off the engine to lessen the danger of fire. He recovered from the initial shock and regained his vision in time to see the altimeter registering 800 metres. He restarted his engine. The thought that enemy fighters might have followed him down to finish him off was dispelled when he saw that Otto Brauneck and Alfred Niederhoff[41] had stayed with him until he landed in a field of tall grass near Wervicq.[42]

Richthofen's luck held; he had set down near German troops, who summoned help immediately. He was rushed to the field hospital *Feldlazarett* 76 in Courtrai, a short distance from Marckebeke. There, his wound, measuring some ten centimetres across, was cleaned and sutured, although one spot of clear white bone remained exposed and was a long time healing over.[43] The top of his head was shaved and covered with a thick white bandage. When the anaesthetic had worn off, he experienced pounding head pains[44] that would bother him for the ten months he had left to live.

The Chain of Command

That afternoon, as soon as Manfred von Richthofen was declared out of danger, Oberleutnant Bodenschatz and the leaders of Jastas 4, 6 and 11 were at his bedside.[45] He was pale and weak, but he promised them that he would soon be back in service.[46]

During his convalescence, 28-year-old Silesian-born career officer Oberleutnant Kurt-Bertram von Döring became acting Jagdgeschwader commander.[47] A graduate of the Prussian Cadet Corps, Döring had only three confirmed victories to his credit at this point, but his length of service and command experience made him well qualified to lead the Jagdgeschwader on a temporary basis. He reported directly to 4. Armee's aviation staff officer Hauptmann Otto Bufe, but kept Richthofen informed of all Geschwader activities. As will be seen, this arrangement put Döring in a difficult position.

Clear skies and favourable weather the following morning, 7 July, offered good hunting opportunities for Döring and a dozen aircraft representing Jastas 4, 6 and 11. Over Dadizele, 10 kilometres north-west of Marcke, the JG I formation came to the aid of three Albatros from Jasta 24 that were trying to attack two Sopwith two-seaters protected by a flight of Sopwith Triplane fighters. According to the British account of the air combat:

'Six Triplanes of Naval Squadron No. 1 and two [Sopwith] machines of No. 45 Squadron, when on a photographic reconnaissance, engaged 18 Albatros Scouts near Menin and, in the combat which ensued, Capt. [R. M.] Findlay and Lieut. [L. W. M.] Moore in one machine and 2nd-Lieut. Crossland and Lieut. [G. W.] Blaiklock in another machine, drove down two of the opponents out of control.'[48]

German reports state that Ltn Kurt Wolff of Jasta 11, chased a Triplane southward and, at 1100 hours, shot it down over Comines for his 33rd and last victory.[49] West of Wervicq at 1105, Jasta 4's Leutnant der Reserve Richard Krüger shot down another Triplane, which was logged as his first and only victory.[50] Five minutes later, Leutnant der Reserve Alfred Niederhoff of Jasta 11 scored his fourth victory, a Triplane which he sent down near Bousbecque.[51]

A second fight – or perhaps an extension of the first – from 1140 to 1205 hours resulted in confirmations of two R.E.8s and two Sopwith two-seaters brought down east and north-west of Ypres, near the lines at Waasten and over British-occupied Deûlémont. One Sopwith two-seater was credited at 1200 hours north of Warneton to Jasta 6 leader Eduard Dostler, as his 14th 'kill'.[52] Vizefeldwebel Fritz Krebs was credited with his sixth victory, an R.E.8 which came down in flames near Zillebeke at 1135, but there is no matching RFC loss; this claim of a two-seater may have been another Sopwith 1½ Strutter.[53]

The Geschwader's afternoon and evening patrols on 7 July resulted in four more victories: three for Jasta 4 and one for Jasta 11. With a total of nine enemy aircraft shot down and no losses of their own, except for a slight injury Oberleutnant von Döring received when he made a forced landing, this was a day filled with pride for JG I. So much pride, in fact, that many members wanted a share of it. There were a number of disputed claims for victories and, before Geschwader adjutant Bodenschatz could forward them to 4. Armee Headquarters, the claims had to be resolved at the local level. A high victory score was good, but it required a certain measure of decorum in its presentation. There-fore, an Arbitration Committee (*Schiedsgericht*) was convened. Acting commander von Döring was one of the claimants and prudently absented himself from the panel.

Leutnant Konstantin Krefft represented the Geschwader and Oberleutnants von Althaus and Dostler represented the Staffeln. After screening reports from the morning patrol, they disallowed Jasta 11 pilot Vizefeldwebel Josef Lauten-schlager's claim for victory over one of the four Sopwith Triplanes and awarded credit to Leutnant Richard Krüger of Jasta 4. To show that rank did not enter into their decision, the committee accepted Leutnant Alfred Niederhoff's claim over that of Oberleutnant von Döring. From the afternoon and evening patrol reports, they decided that Vizefeldwebel Ernst Clausnitzer (Jasta 4) and not Leutnant der Reserve Alois Heldmann (Jasta 10) had shot down a Nieuport over Gheluvelt at 1430 hours, and that Vizefeldwebel Lautenschlager and not Vize-feldwebel Clausnitzer had brought down an aircraft identified only as a 'Sopwith' between Houthem and Wytschaete at 1810 hours.[54] At the end of the session everyone came away with a credit of one form or another.

Bad Times for JG I

Flight operations were cancelled for the next three days. Low clouds and contin-uous rain offered JG I little prospect for success. In preparation for the coming offensive (known as the Third Battle of Ypres), the Royal Flying Corps intensi-fied its night bombing operations. At the first break in the weather, early on the morning of 11 July, F.E.2s of No. 100 Squadron set out to cripple JG I by bombing its airfields. Unaware of the consolidation of the units and acting on the basis of out-dated information, the 'Fees' bombed Jasta 10's old airfield at Heule, Jasta 4's former facilities at Cuerne and Jasta 6's current airfield at Bisseghem;[55] the latter reported that, at about 0300 hours, three hangar tents and two aircraft were lightly damaged.[56]

Jasta 11 was totally unaffected by the early raid and Leutnant Kurt Wolff led a mid-morning patrol toward Ypres. Just east of the devastated city, the red Albatros fighters were surprised by a flight of British fighters which came down on them with all guns firing. Later Wolff said that his flight had been attacked by 'a squadron of fifteen Englishmen',[57] but it is more likely that a quick strike by four Airco D.H.5 biplane fighters of No. 32 Squadron had caught him off guard. An RFC report states: 'At 9:15 a.m. [British time, then an hour behind German time] 7 E.A. Albatros ... [were] engaged between Hooge and Beselare [*sic*] at 6,000 feet. Lts. [S. C.] Tayler and [C.] Turner drove down the E.A. into the clouds. Both these E.A.s appeared to be out of control, but owing to the clouds, it was impossible to see what happened to them. Lt. Tayler's machine was very badly shot about.'[58]

Five minutes later Kurt Wolff returned to Marcke, his left hand bleeding from a bullet wound sustained during the brief encounter. He was sent to *Feldlazarett* 76 for treatment and ended up sharing a room with his mentor, Manfred von Richthofen.[59]

Wolff was succeeded as leader of Jasta 11 by 26-year-old Oberleutnant Wilhelm Reinhard. A Regular Army officer who had come through the more usual Prussian officer training system after secondary school training,[60] Reinhard was accepted as an officer candidate (*Fahnenjunker*) in an artillery regiment[61] in 1909. He showed great promise in the army, being commissioned Leutnant in 1910 and promoted Oberleutnant in 1915, at which time he also entered the Fliegertruppe. Reinhard began in 1915 as an observer with Flieger-Abteilung (A) 205, and later became a two-seater pilot and flew with Feldflieger-Abteilung 28. After completing fighter pilot training, he was assigned to Jasta 11.[62] Reinhard had no victories to his credit when he was appointed leader of Jasta 11, but he had professional officer's training and command experience.

At this time JG I felt the full force of increasing British air superiority. As described by the Officer in Charge of Aviation for 4. Armee, Hauptmann Otto Bufe:

'Enemy aviation activity shows a further expansion compared with the previous week, although the opponent seems to be holding back his main force. A strong air barrier [*Luftsperre*] has been reported along [our] Armee's entire Front, reaching up to 5,500 metres; according to consistent reports [the barrier] is strongest at Boesinghe, where the objective of the opponent's reconnaissance is especially prominent ...'[63]

Operation 'Beach Party'

To relieve pressure on the 4. Armee Front, a combined German army and naval forces operation was launched to breach Allied lines along the Flanders coast, in the morning fog on Thursday, 12 July 1917. Code-named *Unternehmen Strandfest* (Operation 'Beach Party'), the assault followed intensive artillery bombardment and, according to a German report, 'the [German] naval infantry stormed ... heavily fortified positions ... which were strongly reinforced by the French shortly before being taken over by British defence installations between the coast and Lombardzyte. The enemy was thrown back across the Yser. Over 1,200 prisoners, of whom 27 are officers, were taken; the British casualties in the heavily bombarded terrain between the sea and the river are very high. ...

Again, our airmen contributed to the full success of the day despite intense [rain] storms ...'[64]

Back at the Geschwader, the morning began with the loss of Jasta 4's Vize-feldwebel Linus Patermann, who at the age of 32 had scored his first victory the day before.[65] He was shot down in flames during a fight with five D.H.5s over Gheluvelt; Captain Arthur Coningham of No. 32 Squadron got behind Pater-mann's Albatros and 'followed it down from 15,000 to 1,000 feet and then watched it crash'.[66] JG I more than evened the score that day, logging eight victories, six for Jasta 6 and two for Jasta 4.[67]

Friday, 13 July 1917 was a day of mixed luck for JG I, with six victories claimed by Jasta 6. In a fight with six Sopwith 1½ Strutters of No. 70 Squadron and six Nieuport 17s of No. 29 Squadron, Leutnant Hans Klein of Jasta 4 was wounded. He managed to make a smooth landing at Ghistelles as his comrades tore into the British formation and were credited with bringing down two Sopwiths and two Nieuports.[68] Klein, one of the rising stars of JG I, was out of action for more than two months.

Three days later, Vizefeldwebel Ernst Clausnitzer of Jasta 4 failed to return from a late afternoon sortie against British tethered observation balloons.[69] He had been attacked by three SPADs of No. 23 Squadron and, when he attempted to return fire, both his machine-guns jammed. One of his opponents, Second Lieutenant David Langlands 'followed ... closely and continued firing until the German pilot gave in and landed on our side of the lines S.E. of Poperinghe and was taken prisoner.'[70] Langlands was credited with his fifth victory[71] and Claus-nitzer's Albatros D.V 1162/17, was assigned the captured aircraft reference number G 56.[72]

Early the same evening, Captain Geoffrey H. Bowman of No. 56 Squadron got behind 20-year-old Vizefeldwebel Fritz Krebs of Jasta 4 and shot him down north-east of Zonnebeke.[73] According to Bowman's combat report, the Albatros 'made no attempt to flatten out near the ground and flew into it at the east end of the race course in Polygon Wood and crashed absolutely'.[74]

JG I's two successes helped offset its losses: Jasta 4 pilot Vizefeldwebel Kurt Wüsthoff's fourth victory, a balloon shot down near Kemmel, and Jasta 6's Leut-nant der Landwehr Hans Adam's sixth victory, a Sopwith Camel brought down near Zonnebeke.[75]

On 17 July two more JG I pilots were shot down. In a midday fight over Comines, 25-year-old former infantry officer[76] Leutnant der Reserve Richard Krüger of Jasta 4 was wounded in action and died that evening.[77] During an evening patrol that turned into an extended fight with Sopwith Camels of No. 70 Squadron, Jasta 11's Leutnant der Reserve Karl Meyer was wounded over

Ypres; he was probably Captain Noel W. W. Webb's seventh victim.[78] No. 70 Squadron, in turn, lost two Camels, which, after a review of conflicting claims, were credited as the first success for Leutnant Robert Tüxen of Jasta 6 and the fifth for Vizefeldwebel Kurt Wüsthoff of Jasta 4.[79]

Richthofen versus Bufe

At this time, Manfred von Richthofen developed an intense dislike of his immediate superior, Hauptmann Otto Bufe. From the Jagdgeschwader war diary it is clear that convalescence was the worst possible state for the 'Rittmeister, with his heavily bandaged head and the impatient wish that his loathsome headaches might finally go away. And, next to him, the "delicate little flower" [Wolff], his left hand bandaged and with him likewise the impatient wish to soon have healed fingers holding a control column.' Bodenschatz noted that both men worried incessantly about their Geschwader, a condition not helped when 'every day the Adjutant comes rushing in and brings the [daily action] reports'.[80]

Richthofen began to suspect that his tactical dicta were being subverted by Hauptmann Bufe. As he read Acting Jagdgeschwader Commander von Döring's reports, he seemed to link the Geschwader's rising combat losses with Bufe's orders to send up one Staffel at a time. While Richthofen himself had begun operations that way, his plan was to increase massed operations and bring the Geschwader's full force to bear against its opponents. Now that process seemed to be in limbo and Richthofen knew that Döring could not question the orders of his superior. The Prussian Cadet Corps had instilled in him the virtues of 'a Spartan behaviour, an acceptance of hardship, and devotion to an external superior authority'.[81] Richthofen, however, was able to go beyond the authority of the 4. Armee's Officer in Charge of Aviation, and Döring's report of 17 July surely caused the frustrated fighter commander to perceive emerging danger in the use of current tactics. Döring had written:

'After the experiences of the last few days it has been proven that single flying Staffeln are in no position to do battle successfully with British formations, which appear chiefly in the evening. For this reason, a simultaneous deployment of Staffeln is required ... The Staffeln must appear together over the Front at great height (4,000 to 5,000 metres) and, as much as possible, carry out their attacks together against strong British formations. The Staffeln must make every effort to fly in such a way that they support each other ...'[82]

Confined to his hospital room in Courtrai, Manfred von Richthofen could only seethe with anger over the report. While he adhered to the same code of conduct as Döring, he let his own sense of mission guide his actions when the performance of Jagdgeschwader I was affected. Without going out of the chain of command, he could complain – privately, of course – to friends and contemporaries who could find ways to help him return to the Front, where he knew he was needed.

True, Richthofen was Germany's most successful living air fighter and recipient of many of the highest awards that Prussia and other states could bestow. But his perceived adversary was also a man of considerable achievement within the German military system, as a review of their respective careers shows:

At the Main Cadet Institute, Otto Bufe had earned the highest rank for cadets, *Portepée-Unteroffizier*. He had a good background; born in Alsace–Lorraine, the son of a successful physician, he had had a secondary school education. He was a good example of the meritocracy possible within the cadet system, in which quality of education was as important as bloodlines.[83] Like Richthofen, Bufe had attended the Cadet Institute at Wahlstatt and the Main Cadet Institute at Gross-Lichterfelde, near Berlin. At the latter, he was enrolled among the academic stream, which placed him in an intellectual minority of students qualified for university admission (*Abiturienten*). Other officers in that élite group became generals and field marshals, and Otto Bufe could expect to do the same.[84]

On 2 March 1903, he joined an infantry regiment[85] at Strasbourg as a *Portepée-Fähnrich*. While it took most Prussian officers eighteen months to gain a commission,[86] his better education and standing qualified him for a commission as Leutnant less than a year later, on 27 January 1904, as well as an earlier date of rank, 22 June 1902.[87] He was promoted to Oberleutnant on 16 June 1911 and to Hauptmann on 8 November 1915. On mobilisation in 1914, Bufe was posted to Feldflieger-Abteilung 20 and qualified for his observer's badge on 19 August 1914. He was appointed commanding officer of Feldflieger-Abteilung 40 on 4 May 1915 and to command of Feldflieger-Abteilung 6 on 1 February 1916. His career was advanced further when he was appointed the 4. Armee's Staff Officer for Aviation on 26 September 1916.

Bufe had led troops in battle, and had earned the 2nd and 1st Class awards of the Iron Cross when they were still considered high decorations. The Grand Duchy of Baden, in whose service he was nominally enrolled, awarded Bufe the Order of the Zähringer Lion Knight's Cross 2nd Class with Swords. The Kingdom of Württemberg bestowed upon him its Order of Friedrich Knight's Cross 1st Class with Swords.[88] Both awards were for meritorious service in combat.

Conversely, Manfred von Richthofen admitted that he had been 'no great luminary'[89] as a student at Wahlstatt or at Gross Lichterfelde. Indeed, when he took the examination to qualify for posting to a unit in 1911, he was *not* accepted as an officer into his cavalry regiment.[90] Rather, 'he never appeared in the promotion list of the [weekly chronicle] *Militär Wochenblatt* with his class (1911), [and] the announcement of his transfer to the 1st Uhlans as a sergeant was tucked away in a corner of the publication. Eight months later came the announcement of his promotion to *Fähnrich* in the same regiment.'[91] While Richthofen began his army career with a date of rank behind that of his classmates,[92] he more than compensated his slow beginning by gaining rapid promotion as a consequence of his skill in air fighting and his inspired leadership.

Now, with the rank of Rittmeister and a national hero, he was confronted by a staff officer of equivalent rank who was senior to him, but did not have the influence or recognition that Richthofen had earned in the crucible of battle. Richthofen, the courageous, accomplished warrior, sought to win a test of wills against a solid organisation man.

Among Manfred von Richthofen's friends was Oberleutnant Fritz von Falkenhayn, son of General der Infanterie Erich von Falkenhayn, the former Chief of the General Staff. Young Falkenhayn was also the technical officer on the staff of the Commanding General of the Air Force.[93]

On 19 July 1917 Richthofen wrote to Falkenhayn, telling him that JG I was carrying the burden of air defence in the sector: 'We have sixteen Jagdstaffeln in the [4.] Armee ... [and] when an enemy aircraft has been shot down recently, it was [done] only by the Jagdgeschwader. What are the other twelve Staffeln doing?'[94]

Records reinforce his point and show that three of the four JG I units were, in fact, far more productive than other 4. Armee Jagdstaffeln during the two-week period from the Geschwader's first victories on 2 July to the date of Richthofen's letter. According to the Commanding General's weekly summaries,[95] the numbers of confirmed victories attributed to fifteen army Staffeln and one navy single-seat fighter unit in that sector were:

Jasta 3 3	Jasta 8 2	Jasta 18 2	Jasta 28 0
Jasta 4 13	Jasta 10 0	Jasta 20 4	Jasta 31 2
Jasta 6 13	Jasta 11 7	Jasta 26 3	Jasta 36 6
Jasta 7 1	Jasta 17 4	Jasta 27 3	Marine Jasta...2

In the same letter, Richthofen complained that, while he favoured aggressive attacks on both sides of the lines, Bufe ordered the Jastas only to hinder British aircraft from crossing German lines. According to Richthofen:

'When I came to this Armee, the following was told to me by Bufe: "It does not matter to me that [enemy aircraft] are shot down in my Armee [sector]; rather, that you with your Jagdstaffel [and] by your presence at the Front at a certain time will barricade the air!" This is such an insanely great mistake that one could not make a bigger one in fighter aviation. I explained to Bufe that this was not at all my view of fighter aviation and also gave him a copy [of a report] about what I think about the use of Jagdstaffeln (Geschwader) and have accomplished so far. At the same time I sent it to [Hauptmann Hermann] Kastner.[96] When you peruse it you will realise that it is really a reply to Bufe's remarks.

'Bufe has arranged all the Jagdstaffeln on a time-table whereby each Staffel has a set time, a set area, [and] a prescribed altitude to barricade for an hour and a quarter. It is indeed quite clear, of course, that this will never be a fighter sortie [*Jagdflug*], but rather maintains the character of a barrier flight [*Sperreflug*]. But in Bufe's view there should indeed be no fighter sorties; rather, he wants to have barrier flights.

'The other Jagdstaffeln are ... unhappy about it. The Jagdgeschwader is a thorn in [Bufe's] side, as from the beginning I have not engaged in routine barrier flights. So now he uses the opportunity of my being sick and issues idiotic orders [regarding] how the Geschwader should fly, how the take-off preparations should go, etc., as if he were the commander of the Geschwader.

'I can assure you it is no fun these days to be leader of a Jagdstaffel or in this Armee ... This Bufe is prejudiced in such a way that it is absolutely impossible to deal with him. The [lack of] success is also strikingly clear. For [the past] three days the British have done what they want. They come over, fly wherever they want and absolutely dominate the air [and], not just over their lines, oh no, they dominate the air far over the countryside. Almost none at all are shot down, in any case [few] in proportion to the masses [of aircraft deployed] ...'[97]

While he was impatient to return to the Front, Richthofen did not want his well-placed friend to think that he was complaining just to draw attention to himself; he concluded: 'This letter is not something from overwrought nerves or the boredom that torments me amply [as I lie] here in bed. Also it is no momentary irritation or personal antipathy against certain people; rather, I want only to bring to your attention the conditions in this Armee.'[98]

Apparently independent of Richthofen's criticism of Bufe, a shift of tactics was taking place. The day that Richthofen sent his letter to Falkenhayn, the Commanding General of the 4. Armee, General der Infanterie Friedrich Sixt von

Armin, directed an increase in attacks against British tethered observation balloons and essentially 'turned loose' the fighter units: 'Likewise, Jagdgeschwader I is available to sweep the attack area of enemy aeroplanes.'[99]

Richthofen Returns

A week later, on Wednesday, 25 July 1917, Manfred von Richthofen was back at Marckebeke and in full command of Jagdgeschwader I.[100] He must have felt a sense of personal triumph and validation on reading the 19 July issue of 4. Armee air chief's daily report, which quoted a recently received statement from General von Hoeppner, praising the sector's aviation matters: 'Appreciation on the part of the Commanding General [is extended] to the airmen of the 4. Armee, and above all the Jagdgeschwader, in view of the superiority [gained] over enemy combat airmen in recent days.'[101]

After almost a year on 4. Armee's staff, on 5 August Hauptmann Otto Bufe was re-assigned as Officer in Charge of Aviation for the 8. Armee, on the Eastern Front.[102] It is generally thought that Richthofen was responsible for Bufe's transfer,[103] but more conclusive evidence of his influence has not yet come to light.

Meanwhile Richthofen brought good news upon his return to JG I. Anthony Fokker's new triplanes were in production and JG I would receive the first examples which, Richthofen had been assured, would be able to out-climb and out-fight anything the British could put up.[104]

In return Richthofen received the good news of the Geschwader's recent victories.[105] He was particularly interested in events of the preceding evening, when Jasta 10 leader Oberleutnant Ernst Freiherr von Althaus shot down one of the new Sopwith F.1 Camels south-east of Moorslede, recorded as his ninth victory.[106] Richthofen wanted top pilots, commanded by the most capable people, who would continue to prove their ability, just as he did. As noted in the statistics above, Jasta 10 had the poorest victory record in JG I, a situation that would have to be changed.

On the evening of 26 July, JG I lost a promising pilot and Richthofen protégé. A large formation of S.E.5s, Sopwith Pups, Sopwith Camels and SPADs clashed with a big German fighter group over Polygon Wood.[107] During the fight, at about 2045 hours, an Albatros went down south of Zonnebeke inside the German forward lines, and its pilot, 21-year-old Leutnant der Reserve Otto Brauneck, was killed. That night his mechanic, Gefreiter Schaeffler, and another man crawled out to retrieve his body so that it could be sent home for burial.[108]

The loss of Brauneck on Thursday was assuaged on Friday by the successes of new men. That evening, Vizefeldwebel Kurt Wüsthoff, aged 20, scored his sixth victory and 19-year-old Silesian-born Leutnant Carl August von Schoenebeck[109] his first. The old Teutonic legends tell of the ageless Norns twisting the rope of fate that foreshadows all events.[110] The rope twisted again on Saturday, the 28th, when seven Nieuports of No. 29 Squadron 'encountered and attacked five Albatros Scouts painted red' and the aircraft of Leutnant Alfred Niederhoff of Jasta 11 'was seen to break up in the air and then to crash'[111] south-west of Becelaere at noon; he was 22.[112]

While Niederhoff's body was being prepared for return to his family in Dortmund,[113] Jasta 6 claimed a stunning victory over a half-dozen RFC bombers that had attacked JG I bases. The fight was a classic example of Richthofen's use of massed air power. According to a British report: 'When returning from bombing Heule and Bisseghem Aerodromes, five [Airco D.H.4] machines of No. 57 Squadron encountered 30 enemy scouts. Lieuts. [W. B.] Hutcheson and [T. E.] Godwin fired at one, which fell out of control. Lieut. [D. S.] Hall and 2nd-Lieut. [N. M.] Pizey drove down another out of control, then opened fire and shot the observer in another machine. Lieut. [T. S.] Roadley and 2nd-Lieut. [C. R.] Thomas drove down one of their opponents out of control, and 2nd-Lieuts. [A. C. S.] Irwin and [S. J.] Leete opened fire at about 30 yards at a German scout and the wings of the German machine [were] seen to fold up. They then engaged a second scout which they drove down out of control. 2nd-Lieut. Irwin was wounded in the foot in two places, but returned and made a perfect landing. Capt. [L.] Minot and 2nd-Lieut. [A. F.] Britton shot down one of the German scouts which banked across their front, out of control, and then attacked a second from behind and above. The German pilot looped his machine over the D.H.4, but on flattening out our observer opened fire and the enemy scout fell out of control. After this, a German machine with streamers, apparently the leader, was attacked, and was shot down completely out of control, and was last seen falling upside down.'[114]

A different view of the fight was reported from the ground by Hauptmann Friedrich Ritter von Mann,[115] the 29-year-old leader of Flieger-Abteilung 48b, who was returning to his unit after a conference with 4. Armee's air chief:

'As I drove through Ingelmunster, a few bombs whistled right down on to the town and a huge cloud of smoke rose up from a big garden ... I ordered my driver to speed up and hurry out of the place. In the course of that, I had to cross the railway lines at the station and then understood why the enemy aircraft were dropping bombs. The whole place was crowded with men, horses and baggage waiting to be loaded...

'Away from the station, I ordered the car stopped so that I could view the spectacle calmly. At ... about 5,000 metres' altitude, six Bristol [sic] biplanes were circling in the bright blue firmament as thin whitish threads trailed down from them. From time to time one aircraft after another flew towards the station and dropped bombs, which hit none of the buildings.

'Suddenly ... two of them turned toward the Front, the others seemed hopelessly lost. Just then, machine-gun fire came in rapid succession from all the aircraft. Two German Albatros single-seat fighters surprised them from a higher altitude and pounced like hawks.

'A splendid, frighteningly beautiful picture was presented... An aerial battle as one seldom saw. Here were two masters of German air fighting methods at work.

'One Albatros near one Englishman seemed to pull him backwards. The German machine-gun produced only a short burst and the Englishman dropped out of the fight and went down in wide spirals, with a white ribbon of smoke marking his course. The fuel tank seemed to have been hit. Then flames burst out of the engine, the machine was out of control and dropped on its nose. Then the fire flared out along the fuselage, which was ablaze in a moment. The wings broke away and fell to the ground. A black human form – the unlucky pilot – lurched from the fuselage and, although the wings had scarcely begun to break away, the crew and the rest of the machine fell at great speed to the ground ...'[116]

One after another, the six D.H.4s fell under the guns of Jasta 6 within German lines and were credited as: Oberleutnant Eduard Dostler's 19th victory, Leutnant der Reserve Johann Czermak's first, Leutnant Hans Adam's tenth, Leutnant Robert Tüxen's second, Oberleutnant Dostler's 20th, and Leutnant der Reserve Walter Stock's second.[117]

As a consequence of an earlier victory that day and his role in shooting down the flight of D.H.4s, Hans Adam was nominated for the Kingdom of Bavaria's highest bravery honour, the Knight's Cross of the Military Order of Max Joseph (*Ritterkreuz des Militär Max Joseph Ordens*).[118] The award conferred personal (but not hereditary) nobility and the title of Ritter [Knight] on the Bavarian recipient, who became known as Hans Ritter von Adam.[119]

There was a great celebration at JG I that evening, but the men were reminded of the tenuous nature of their triumph when, shortly after midnight, F.E.2bs of No. 100 Squadron bombed Marcke airfield and other targets in the area. The reported damage to 'von Richthofen's hangars',[120] while not entirely accurate,[121] made it clear that the RFC knew where the Richthofen Geschwader was based and were capable of striking it at will.

Indeed a strange occurrence in the early darkness on 30 July led to speculation that a British ruse might have been employed to lure JG I personnel out on to the airfield as part of an aerial ambush. At 0100 hours, a soldier on night guard duty at Marckebeke sounded the alarm when an aircraft overhead fired a German-type flare, signalling the need to make an emergency landing. All the ground crew responded; some fired acknowledgement flares and, at Jasta 4's airfield, men ignited a landing cross made of fuel-soaked logs to guide the aircraft in. But minutes passed and, as officers gathered to scan the skies, a collective suspicion took hold of the group and many headed for the safety of the bomb shelters. Eventually, some of the men heard distinct German engine sounds drifting southwards. They concluded that it was a German night bomber crew that had become disoriented,[122] but the respite was to be brief. The British night bombers would be back.

Notes

1   Kriegsministerium (organisation manual), Teil 10, Abschnitt B, *Flieger-Formationen*, pp. 208–9.
2   Hoeppner, E. von., *Deutschlands Krieg*, p. 115.
3   With 1. Garde-Regiment zu Fuss.
4   Bruno Loerzer is often linked with Hermann Göring, as both men began their military careers in the 4. Badisches Infanterie-Regiment Prinz Wilhelm Nr. 112, and flew together in Feldfl.-Abt. 25 and Jasta 26. Loerzer received the *Pour le Mérite* on 2 June 1918 and finished the war with 22 confirmed victories. He remained active in aviation and served in the Luftwaffe in the Second World War, attaining the rank of Generaloberst. He died on 23 August 1960 aged 69 (Ref: Hilde-brand, K., *Die Generale*, vol. II, pp. 309–10).
5   Oblt Hans Joachim Buddecke, Ltn Wilhelm Frankl and Oblt Ernst Frhr von Althaus (Ref: Zuerl, *Pour-le-Mérite Flieger*, pp. 32, 124; Theilhaber, F., *Jüdische Flieger*, p. 87).
6   Ltn Albert Dossenbach and Oblt Ernst Frhr von Althaus (Ref: Zuerl, op. cit., pp. 32, 179).
7   Kogenluft directive 62880 Fl.II, quoted in Bodenschatz, K., *Jagd in Flandern*, p. 147.
8   Kogenluft, *Nachrichtenblatt der Luftstreitkräfte*, Nr. 21, 19 July 1917, p. 95; R.E.8 A.3847 of No. 53 Squadron, Lt Leslie S. Bowman, aged 20, and 2/Lt James E. Power-Clutterbuck, aged 23 (both KiA).
9   Collishaw, R., *Air Command*, p. 101; Fl-Sub-Lt Raymond Kent of No. 10 Squadron, RNAS.
10 Kogenluft, op. cit.; Sopwith Triplane N.5376 of No. 10 Squadron, RNAS, Fl-Sub-Lt Gerald E. Nash, aged 25 (PoW).
11 Collishaw, op. cit., pp. 102–3.
12 O'Connor, N., *Aviation Awards*, vol. II, Appendix XIX.
13 Schnitzler, E., *Carl Allmenröder*, p. 7.
14 Schmeelke, M., 'Otto Brauneck', Part II, in *Over the Front*, 1986, p. 197.
15 Richthofen, K. von, *Kriegstagebuch*, p. 124.
16 Ibid., pp. 124–5; the parentheses are Richthofen's.
17 With 1. Grossherzoglich Mecklenburgisches Dragoner-Regiment Nr. 17.
18 Hildebrand, op. cit., vol. I, pp. 203–4; by the end of the war, von Döring was in command of Jagdgruppe 4. He left active duty with the rank of Rittmeister on 4 February 1920, but remained involved in aviation and entered the Luftwaffe as a Major in 1934 and ultimately rose to the rank of Generalleutnant. He was interned from May 1945 until July 1947 when he was released. He died on 9 July 1960 aged 71.
19 With the Bavarian 4. Pionier-Bataillon.
20 Moncure, J., *Forging the King's Sword*, p. 15.
21 1. Sächsisches Husaren-Regiment König Albert Nr. 18.
22 Zuerl, op. cit., p. 30.
23 O'Connor, op. cit., p. 219.
24 Eisenbahn-Bataillon Nr. 4.
25 Bodenschatz, op. cit., p. 147.

26 Ibid., pp. 11–13; as an example of the interconnections within German military aviation, it should be noted that both Oblt Bodenschatz and Oblt Stefan Kirmaier, Boelcke's successor, had come from Bavarian 8. Infanterie-Regiment Grossherzog Friedrich II. von Baden. Kirmaier's successor, Franz Josef Walz, had also been commissioned into this unit. (Ref: *Ehrenrangliste*, vol. II, p. 794).

27 Böhme, E., *Briefe eines deutschen Kampffliegers*, pp. 126–7.

28 Quoted in Bodenschatz, op. cit., p. 15.

29 Kogenluft, *Nachrichtenblatt*, Nr. 24, 9 August 1917, p. 140; These victories were No. 53 Squadron R.E.8 aircraft: A.3538, Sgt Hubert A. Whatley, aged 19, and 2/Lt Frank G. B. Pascoe, aged 20 (KiA); and A.3249, Capt Wilfred P. Horsley, MC, aged 30 (KiA), and 2/Lt A. G. Knight (WiA).

30 Kogenluft, op. cit., Nr. 19, 5 July 1917, p. 61.

31 Bodenschatz, op. cit., p. 17.

32 Ibid., pp. 17–18.

33 Ibid., p. 147.

34 RFC *Communiqué* No. 95, 8 July 1917, p. 5.

35 Shores, C., et al., *Above the Trenches*, pp. 50, 115, 317.

36 F.E.2d 6419, 2/Lt W. Durrand and Lt Stuart F. Trotter, aged 31(KiA).

37 Younger brother of Oblt Bruno Loerzer and ultimately an eleven-victory ace.

38 Kofl 4. Armee, *Meldung*, Nr. 24406/19, Teil 7, 13 July 1917.

39 Richthofen, M. von, *Heldenleben*, p. 148.

40 Ferko, A. E., *Richthofen*, p. 38.

41 Bodenschatz, op. cit., p. 22.

42 It is generally considered that Richthofen was shot down by Capt Douglas C. Cunnell and 2/Lt Albert E. Woodbridge in F.E.2d A.6512 of No. 20 Squadron, although the RFC crew were not officially credited with a victory.

43 Richthofen, M. von, op. cit., p. 150.

44 Bodenschatz, op. cit., p. 30.

45 Ibid., p. 22; it is likely that Oblt Ernst Freiherr von Althaus, leader of Jasta 10, remained at the airfield to provide command-level leadership in the event of JG I being called into action again.

46 Ibid., p. 23.

47 Ibid., pp. 23, 148.

48 RFC *Communiqué* No. 96, 15 July 1917, p. 1.

49 Kofl 4. Armee, op. cit., lists four Triplanes brought down between 1100 and 1110 hours; Kogenluft, op. cit., Nr. 24, 9 August 1917, p. 141 lists aircraft and locations, but not times.

50 Ibid.

51 Ibid.; No. 1 Squadron, RNAS lost three Sopwith Triplanes in this fight: N.6291, Fl-Cdr Cyril A. Eyre, aged 21 (KiA); N.6309, Fl-Sub-Lt Kenneth H. Millward (KiA); and N.5480, Fl-Sub-Lt Donald W. Ramsey, aged 20 (KiA).

52 Kogenluft, op. cit., Nr. 24.

53 RFC *War Diary* for this date lists two Sopwith 1½ Strutters of No. 45 Squadron as missing; further research shows them to have been: A.8281, 2/Lt John V. A. Gleed, aged 20 and Lt John B. Fotheringham, aged 25 (both KiA); and A.1029, Lt Frederick C. H. Snyder, RFC, and 2/Lt Thomas Hewson, AFC, aged 22 (both KiA).

54 Bodenschatz, op. cit., p. 148; no British matching losses support either claim.

55 Jones, H. A., *War in the Air*, vol. IV, p. 156, incorrectly lists the targets as active airfields of the Jastas noted.

56 Bodenschatz, op. cit., p. 149.

57 Ibid., p. 25.

58 RFC, *No. 32 Squadron Record Book*, 11 July 1917, p. 233; despite the indefinite nature of the encounter, Lt St. Cyprian Churchill Tayler was credited with sending down 'out of control' a Jasta 11 aircraft (Ref: Shores, et al., op. cit., p. 358).

59 Bodenschatz, op. cit., pp. 25, 149; one widely used source – Zuerl, op. cit., p. 482 – states that Wolff was injured in a fight with Sopwith Triplanes, but there is no British documentation to support this contention.

60 Moncure, op. cit., p. 15.

61 Badisches Fussartillerie-Regiment Nr. 14.

62 Reinhard, W. *Personal-Bogen*.

63 Kofl 4. Armee, op. cit., Teil 2.

64 *Kriegs-Echo*, Nr. 153, 13 July 1917, p. 664.

65 Kofl 4. Armee, op. cit., Teil 7.

66 RFC *Communiqué* No. 96, p. 5.

67 Ibid.; also see Jasta 4 and Jasta 6 sections of Appendix I of this book.

68 Kofl 4. Armee, op. cit., Nr. 25300/19 Teil 7, 20 July 1917.

69 Ibid.

70 RFC *Communiqué* No. 97, 22 July 1917, p. 3.

71 Shores, et al., op. cit., p. 232.

72 Puglisi, 'German Aircraft Down', Part 1, in, *Cross & Cockade*, 1969, p, 157.

73 Kofl 4. Armee, op. cit.

74 RFC, No. 56 Squadron *Combat Report*, 16 July 1917, Capt G. H. Bowman in S.E.5a A.8900.

75 Kofl 4. Armee, op. cit.; Kogenluft, op. cit., Nr. 25, 16 August 1917, p. 157.

76 With the 9. Westpreussisches Infanterie-Regiment Nr. 176.

77 Kofl 4. Armee, op. cit.

78 Shores, et al., op. cit., p. 378.

79 Kofl 4. Armee, op. cit.; Kogenluft, op. cit.; Bodenschatz, op. cit., pp. 149–50.

80 Bodenschatz, op. cit., pp. 30–1.

81 Moncure, op. cit., p. 188.

82 Bodenschatz, op. cit., p. 28.

83 Moncure, op. cit., pp. 176, 254.

84 Ibid., augmented by comments in correspondence from Col Moncure.

85 6. Badische Infanterie-Regiment Kaiser Friedrich III. Nr. 114.

86 Ibid., p. 15.

87 *Stammliste der Offiziere des 6. Badischen Infanterie-Regiments*, Nr. 114, item 293, p. 122.

88 Bufe, O., *Kriegsranglisten*, p. 4; respective award dates are 15 September 1914, 17 August 1915, 24 March 1915, 20 April 1917.

89 Richthofen, M. von., op. cit., p. 15.

90 Ulanen-Regiment Kaiser Alexander III. von Russland (Westpreussisches) Nr. 1.

91 Moncure, op. cit., p. 241.

92 Ibid.

93 Supf, P., *Deutschen Fluggeschichte*, vol. I, p. 290; commissioned in Kaiser Alexander Garde-Grenadier-Regiment Nr. 1 in Berlin, Falkenhayn became an observer before the war and then a pilot. On 27 November 1914 he was appointed Adjutant to the Fliegerkorps of the German Supreme High Command. He had considerable influence on aviation matters throughout the war, and left military service with the rank of Hauptmann in 1920.

94 Richthofen to Falkenhayn.

95 Kogenluft, op. cit., Nr. 24, pp. 140–2 and Nr. 25, 16 August 1917, pp. 157–8.

96 A well-known pre-war pilot, Hptm Hermann Kastner was in command of Feldfl.-Abt. 62 when Boelcke and Immelmann began their careers, and was associated with later aircraft development. Clearly, he would have supported Richthofen in opposing Bufe's use of the four Jagdstaffeln.

97 Richthofen to Falkenhayn.

98 Ibid.

99 Quoted in Bodenschatz, op. cit., p. 30.

100 Ibid., p. 150.

101 Kofl 4, *Tagesbericht* Nr. 26, quoted in Bodenschatz, op. cit., p. 150.

102 Bufe, op. cit., p. 3.

103 Ferko, op. cit., pp. 39–43.

104 Bodenschatz, op. cit., p. 33.

105 See Appendix I for details.

106 Kogenluft, op. cit.; Sopwith F.1 Camel B.3825, 2/Lt Harold D. Tapp, aged 21 (DoW).

107 RFC *Communiqué* No. 98, 29 July 1917, p. 7.

108 Schmeelke, op. cit., p. 198.

109 Commissioned into 1. Badisches Leib-Grenadier-Regiment Nr. 109, he remained in uniform until 1924. As a civilian, he retained his military contacts and returned to service in 1932. He rose to the rank of Generalmajor in the Luftwaffe and spent nearly two years in captivity after the Second World War. He died in 1989 age 91 (Ref: Hildebrand, op. cit., vol. III, pp. 213–14).

110 For example, in Richard Wagner's The Twilight of the Gods, Act I, Scene I.

111 RFC Communiqué No. 99, 5 August 1917, p. 2.

112 Bodenschatz, op. cit., pp. 35, 151; Franks, et al., op. cit., p. 174; Shores, et al., op. cit., p. 127.

113 Haehnelt, W., Ehrentafel, p. 58.

114 RFC Communiqué, No. 99; this report is inconsistent with information in RFC War Diary and Western Front Casualty List, which note that 2/Lt Noel M. Pizey, aged 18, was KiA the day before this raid, and 2/Lt A. F. Britton was WiA during the earlier mission. Also, there are no German casualties to match the victory claims made by No. 57 Squadron.

115 Bavarian records note the full name of this officer as Friedrich Wilhelm Josef Nepomuk Ritter von Mann Edler von Tiechler; the titles of Ritter (knight) and Edler (nobleman) were hereditary. Prior to joining the Bavarian air service, he served with 11. Infanterie Regiment von der Tann.

116 Mann, F. von, 'Vernichtung eines Bombengeschwaders', in Zeidelhack (ed.), Bayerische Flieger, pp. 134–8.

117 RFC records show these D.H.4 losses on 28 July 1917 from No. 57 Squadron: A.7538, Lt Hew W. B. Rickards, aged 21, and 2/Lt Ronald H. Corbishley, aged 27 (both KiA); A.7540, Capt Lawrence Minot, aged 21, and 2/Lt Sydney J. Leete (both KiA); A.7448, 2/Lt Herbert N. S. Skeffington, aged 33, (KiA) and Lt A. C. Malloch (PoW).

118 O'Connor, op. cit., vol. I, pp. 18, 36.

119 Ibid., p. 9.

120 RFC Communiqué, No. 99, p. 4.

121 Bodenschatz, op. cit.

122 Ibid., pp. 35–6, 151.

CHAPTER 8

The New Fokkers

DESPITE LOW CLOUDS AND RAIN, MONDAY, 30 JULY 1917 MARKED THE BEGIN-ning of further success for Jagdgeschwader I. The interim leader of Jagdstaffel 10, Oberleutnant Ernst Freiherr von Althaus, was transferred to the fighter pilot school in Valenciennes. The young aristocrat was an early *Pour le Mérite* recipient, but he had disappointed his new commander. Richthofen wanted Jasta 10 to be as successful as his other Staffeln, which were led by officers who inspired their men by continuing to shoot down enemy aircraft. He did not know that Althaus was losing his eyesight and eventually would become blind.

Manfred von Richthofen was pleased with the new leader of Jasta 10: Leutnant Werner Voss, only 20 years old and already a 34-victory ace and recipient of the *Pour le Mérite*. He was a brave man who took risks, and he would be dedicated and capable of leading JG I's lowest-scoring Staffel to a high level of success.

Richthofen knew Voss, who had also begun as a cavalryman,[1] from their time together in Jasta Boelcke.[2] There the younger man had scored 25 of his first 28 victories within a four-month period.[3] Richthofen called Voss his 'closest competitor'[4] and welcomed him despite the younger man's erratic command experience: on 20 May 1917 he was appointed acting leader of Jasta 5 after the death in action of Hauptmann Hans von Hünerbein at the age of 38; on 28 June Voss was given command of Jasta 29; five days later he was transferred to Jasta 14 as its leader, and then was requested by Richthofen to command Jasta 10.[5]

His rapid assignments may have been a rehabilitation process, following his involvement in a troublesome event at Jasta Boelcke. Voss and a fellow West-phalian Hussar, Leutnant Rolf Freiherr von Lersner, schemed to have Haupt-mann Franz Josef Walz[6] removed from command of the unit. Trading on the prestige of his victory score (much as Richthofen had done in urging the removal of Hauptmann Otto Bufe from the 4. Armee staff) the younger and less sophisticated Voss wanted the Staffel to have a more daring leader. The scheme worked; Walz felt obliged to request re-assignment, but it had other effects. Voss was transferred to Jasta 5, where he began to redeem himself by scoring another six victories. Lersner was posted out for retraining as a bomber pilot with Kampfgeschwader 3 and perished soon afterwards.[7]

Voss continued to be so successful in the air that his bad behaviour was overlooked and, in the summer of 1917, the Inspectorate of Military Aviation recalled him from the Front to test the Fokker V 4 prototype Triplane. His reports on the new fighter convinced Richthofen that the Fokker Triplane would enable JG I to regain aerial superiority.

Third Battle of Ypres

At 0350 hours on Tuesday, 31 July 1917, a massive combined British–French attack opened the Third Battle of Ypres. Undeterred by constant rain and low clouds, waves of Royal Flying Corps fighters and two-seaters, and Royal Naval Air Service fighters flew over the front line and played havoc with German troops, vehicles and facilities, while the ground forces advanced along the Flanders Front.[8]

In one instance, Lieutenant Richard A. Maybery of No. 56 Squadron, RFC, took off at 0445 hours, his S.E.5a fighter loaded with 20lb bombs, and flew virtually unimpeded over German airfields in the Courtrai area, bombing and strafing at will.[9] Later, Sopwith Triplanes of No. 1 Squadron, RNAS, shot up other German airfields and facilities with apparent impunity.[10]

According to a classified German report: 'On the 4. Armee [Front], extremely strong enemy air forces and almost uninterrupted rain placed the heaviest burden on our airmen during the infantry attack. The enemy airmen were dispersed from the battlefield very soon by our fighters and Schutzstaffeln [low-level protection aircraft] which were sent into action immediately.'[11]

That report is notable for its lack of candour and the attempt to minimise British success. In fact, the RFC and RNAS had gained virtual control of the skies. JG I aircraft, for example, were not sent out until 1100 hours, following a report of an attack in progress at Armee Gruppe Wytschaete, where its infantry lines were being penetrated at numerous points.[12] Even then, Richthofen dispatched only 'small flights' of fighters, rather than the full Geschwader to confront an overwhelming number of intruders. The meagre response may have reflected Richthofen's lack of confidence in the Albatros D.V, which had lost its superior edge over the newest British fighter aircraft. Yet even that minimal effort became a favourable test of pilot skill, as JG I units were credited with five of the six victories confirmed for 4. Armee air units that day.[13]

Rain storms during the next three days kept German and Allied aircraft grounded. With the first clear skies on the evening of 4 August, Leutnant der Reserve Alfred Hübner of Jasta 4 crossed the lines and shot down a French Caudron bomber.

By now news of Hauptmann Bufe's transfer was being circulated to 4. Armee's air units. Whether or not his departure had been hastened by

Richthofen's complaints, Bufe remained a good soldier and sent a dignified, grandly Teutonic farewell message: 'I leave the 4. Armee with the feeling of pride and gratitude for having been commander of a flying force, which through the radiant bravery and discharge of duties by the aircrews, and through the proficiency of pilots in each and every battle made such a splendid name for themselves. I know that this good name will remain secure. Thoughts of our fallen comrades shall live on in our hearts, linked to us by their great deeds. I wish for the activities of the airmen in the 4. Armee to lead to new successes, to new victories and to new glory.'[14]

A day later, JG I's total 'bag' was two enemy aircraft, both shot down by Jasta 4 pilots who were destined to become high-scoring aces and recipients of the *Pour le Mérite*: Leutnant der Reserve Kurt Wüsthoff, who had enlisted in the Fliegertruppe at the age of 16 and worked his way up to commissioned rank at 19, was credited with the eighth of his 33 victories. And Silesian aristocrat Leutnant Oskar Freiherr von Boenigk, three weeks short of his 24th birthday when he scored his third kill, had been a year behind Manfred von Richthofen at Wahlstatt and Gross-Lichterfelde. Badly wounded in combat as a grenadier officer,[15] Boenigk became an aviation observer in 1916 and, after extensive front-line service, became a fighter pilot.[16] He had the experience and the will to fight that the Kommandeur wanted.

Just as Richthofen was quick to post out non-performers, he was fiercely loyal to successful men under his command and continually encouraged them. When Jasta 6 leader Oberleutnant Eduard Dostler was notified that he had been awarded the *Pour le Mérite* but that the decoration itself would be some time in coming, Richthofen took off his own decoration for Dostler to wear for the Geschwader's celebration of the occasion.[17]

Leutnant Kurt Wolff returned to Marckebeke on Tuesday, 7 August. Like Richthofen, he had been discharged from the hospital in Courtrai,[18] but was not yet allowed to fly. His former command, Jasta 11, remained under the leadership of Oberleutnant Wilhelm Reinhard, who had only one victory to his credit.[19] There was no pleading a special case for Wolff, because Richthofen's administrative adversary, Hauptmann Bufe, had departed for the Eastern Front only two days earlier.[20] It would have been unseemly for the celebrated ace to seek a special favour from the new Officer in Charge of Aviation for the 4. Armee, Hauptmann Helmuth Wilberg. A pre-war aviator,[21] he was an admirer of Manfred von Richthofen's, who wished to preserve and cultivate that relationship.

Moreover, that morning an eight-day period began for all 4. Armee units to send Albatros aircraft back to the Armee air depot for repairs and adjustments by a crew of mechanics and riggers from the Albatros factory in Germany.[22] Unit commanders, concerned with rising performance problems with the once vaunted Albatros fighters, had to work out their own schedules of coverage while aircraft were being overhauled. Mindful of Wolff's frustration, Richthofen had to be more concerned that JG I had aircraft on hand to provide coverage at this time.

The High Command hinted at ever greater rewards for Germany's premier air hero, as noted in the JG I war diary entry for 8 August 1917: 'Jasta Boelcke will be set up at Bisseghem airfield and by a verbal agreement will be placed tactically under the command of the Geschwader.'[23] Jagdstaffel 2, established by and named in honour of Richthofen's mentor Oswald Boelcke, would have been the jewel in JG I's crown. Richthofen wanted more aircraft; it was a dream come true for the unit in which he began his air fighting career to come under his command and share an airfield with Jasta 6, just across the Lys from his own residence in the château at Marckebeke.

The night bombers of No. 100 Squadron ended that dream in the early hours of 10 August. Twelve F.E.2bs set out at just after 0200 hours (British Time) to bomb enemy airfields in the Lys valley. The RFC unit reported: 'Two direct hits were made on one of von Richthofen's hangars at Marcke aerodrome.'[24] According to a German account, Jasta Boelcke bore the brunt of the attack, seven of its aircraft being damaged and two hangar tents flattened.[25] The damage dissuaded 4. Armee air chief Wilberg from grouping five fighter units so close together in the Marcke area; subsequently, Jasta Boelcke was trans-ferred to Jagdgruppe Nord commanded by Hauptmann Otto Hartmann at Jabbeke, some 40 kilometres away.[26]

The day was off to a bad start and became worse. At 1015 hours a second F.E.2 formation crossed the lines before Richthofen could order his units into the air. Unfazed, Richthofen turned his explanation of JG I's lack of response into a complaint about the combined inadequacies of the front-line monitoring system and his Albatros fighters. He took the occasion to exert more pressure on 'higher ups' to expedite delivery of the Fokker Triplanes he had been promised, writing: 'To take off against a group that has already broken through is pointless ... [as] British bombing and reconnaissance aircraft groups now fly over our lines at very high altitudes (4,500 to 5,000 metres). Our machines do not have sufficient climbing ability to reach the enemy in time. The possibility of approaching such a formation would occur only when the ground observers report their gathering on the other side of the Front.'[27]

His only consolation on 10 August 1917 was the day's tally of three enemy aircraft brought down – including a 35th victory for Werner Voss – for only one

131

JG I casualty, Jasta 4's Leutnant der Reserve Oskar Rousselle, who was severely wounded in a dogfight. Rousselle managed to land within German lines and was taken to hospital.

JG I's victories were minor, however, in comparison with successes reported by the RFC: 'In the period under review (11th to 16th August inclusive) we have claimed officially 54 [enemy aircraft] brought down and 36 driven down out of control by [British] aeroplanes, and we have dropped 25½ tons of bombs.'[28]

JG I recorded no victories on 11 August, three on 12 August and, although Richthofen ordered all his Staffeln into the air on 13 August, they succeeded in shooting down only two enemy aircraft.[29] On Tuesday the 14th, the Geschwader claimed eight victories – including Wilhelm Reinhard's third and fourth, Hans Adam's twelfth and Eduard Dostler's 24th – but suffered two casualties. In a morning encounter, Leutnant Hans Joachim Wolff of Jasta 11 (although the same age, 21, no relation to the Pour le Mérite ace Kurt Wolff) was wounded in the thigh and came down near Zillebeke Lake; that evening, 22-year-old Leutnant Alfred Hübner of Jasta 4 was killed in a fight with Nieuports over Moorslede.

Hübner was probably the victim of Captain Tom Falcon Hazell, MC, of No. 1 Squadron, who attacked 'Albatros scouts [with] white wings, yellow fuselage [and] black empennage' at 1910 hours (British Time) and reported: 'We saw seven [German] scouts coming from the lines and engaged them at 14,000 feet just south of Moorslede. I got on the tail of one and gave him about 60 rounds [while] closing to about 20 yards. A puff of smoke came out of E.A., which sideslipped, went straight down and burst into flames when close to the ground.'[30]

In less than two months with Jasta 4 and with four confirmed victories to his credit, Alfred Hübner had shown great promise as an air fighter. His body was retrieved at Slypskappelle and sent back to his home town of Dresden for a formal funeral.[31] He had begun his military service there as a Reserve artillery officer[32] and it was only fitting that his body be returned to his native soil.

On the evening of the 15th, Jastas 4 and 6 provided escorts for the big two-engined Friedrichshafen G.III bombers of Kagohl 1 that bombed artillery batteries west and north-west of Loos, but only Jasta 10 was in combat that evening. Leutnant Werner Voss led an attack against three F.E.2s of No. 20 Squadron and scored JG I's single victory that day when, near Zillebeke Lake, he shot down his 36th victim.[33] In the same fight Unteroffizier Hermann Brettel was wounded in the arm and had to land near Moorslede.

This battle was described in an RFC combat report: 'While on [offensive operations patrol], our ... three machines encountered about 20 E.A. Three Nieuports of No. 1 Squadron were above us and were busy keeping the enemy from diving on our machines.

'One of the E.A. managed to get down to our level and attacked F.E.2d A.5152 (Pilot 2/Lt Cameron, Observer Pte. Pilbrow) and shot and killed Pte. Pilbrow[34] and shot away the aileron controls of the machine. F.E.2d A.6359 (Lt Joslyn Pilot, 2/Lt Adams Observer) observed this E.A. on A.5152's tail and dived on same with both front guns firing. This E.A. then went down in a vertical nose-dive and [was] seen to crash by Capt [P. F.] Fullard of No. 1 Squadron at Sheet 28.D.5.

' ... [Joslyn and Adams] observed one E.A. falling past their machine, out of control and smoke coming from same. This E.A. evidently driven down by No. 1 Squadron.[35]

'F.E.2d A.6500 (Pilot 2/Lt McLean, Observer Gunner Owen)[36] was seen to go into a cloud and when next seen was diving for our lines with smoke coming from [the] engine.'[37]

Early the following morning, bomb-laden RFC fighters caught JG I on the ground. It was still dark when Second Lieutenant G. J. Crang in a Sopwith F.1 Camel of No. 70 Squadron dropped several bombs near Jasta 6's hangars at Bisseghem, with little apparent damage. Fifteen minutes later, Lieutenant Walbanke A. Pritt of No. 66 Squadron flew over Marcke in a Sopwith Pup and dropped a 20lb bomb in the middle of a group of aircraft,[38] badly damaging two Jasta 4 Albatros and a nearby hangar.[39]

The Kommandeur Returns to the Air

Following this rude awakening, the entire Jagdgeschwader prepared to engage their attackers. On the morning of 16 August, after a 40-day absence, Manfred von Richthofen was back in his all-red Albatros D.V and leading four Albatros fighters on a patrol. He still showed some residual weakness and was wracked by endless headaches that were made worse by engine noise, but Richthofen craved to be back in the air and in battle.

His wish was fulfilled just before 0800 when he spotted a flight of Nieuport fighters strafing German trenches east of Zonnebeke. Second Lieutenant D'Arcy F. Hilton, a 27-year-old American member of No. 29 Squadron, RFC, reported that the Nieuports had been surprised by five Germans. Hilton dived at one Albatros and 'opened fire at 50 yards' range. [The German] turned to the right, which left me right on his tail, and I fired a drum into him at close range. I clearly saw a number of my tracers hit the enemy pilot and enter the fuselage. The machine turned over on its side and dived, obviously out of control ...'[40]

There were no JG I casualties that day.[41] Richthofen's account of the fight mentions only his own success: ' ... I attacked an opponent and ... shot up his engine and fuel tank. The aircraft went into a spin, [and] I followed right after it until [it was] just above the ground, [and] gave it one more shot, so that the aircraft crashed south-west of Houthulst Forest and went right into the ground.'[42]

The downed Nieuport was credited as Richthofen's 58th victory.[43] But the rigours of the fight had left him exhausted and on his return to Marckebeke he went to bed immediately. He was too tired to object when 4. Armee Headquarters again diverted JG I fighters to escort Kagohl 1's two-seater trench-strafers on an early afternoon raid against machine-gun nests near Zillebeke Lake and later the same Kampfgeschwader's bombers over Poperinghe.

Likewise Richthofen was not on hand to celebrate his own success or the Jagdgeschwader's other three victories, including Werner Voss' 37th, a Sopwith F.1 Camel shot down at 2100 hours over St-Julien. Most probably the RFC pilot was the 14-victory ace Captain Noel W. W. Webb, MC, who is thought to have wounded Leutnant Karl Meyer of Jasta 11 on 17 July and killed Leutnant Otto Brauneck of the same unit on 26 July.[44]

Manfred von Richthofen's rest was interrupted by a single bomb explosion at 2005 hours that evening and a more intensive attack the following morning. The frequency of attacks in the Courtrai area, and Marcke in particular, accelerated long-contemplated plans to move JG I to Jabbeke; indeed, an advance party was sent there on 17 August in anticipation of the relocation.[45]

In the event JG I remained at Marcke. On 17 August four victories were recorded, including a Bristol F.2B brought down near Staden at 2055 hours by Leutnant Hans-Georg von der Osten, a pilot new to Jasta 11. His first triumph[46] also marked Jasta 11's 200th victory during its seven months of operation, and this called for a party at the château at Marckebeke that evening. Like Richthofen, the Silesian-born Leutnant von der Osten was a former Uhlan. Two months earlier a chance meeting with Richthofen in Breslau had made a favourable impression that led to his posting to Jasta 11.[47]

The milestone of the 200th victory offered Richthofen an opportunity to show that, despite modest recent performance, his Staffeln were still the best in the air. He spread the good news and the first response came from Air Force Commanding General von Hoeppner, who equated Jasta 11's triumph to the amount of war booty that a highly successful ground unit might achieve: ' ...[Jasta 11 has] captured 121 aircraft and 196 machine-guns'.[48]

Feeling on top again, Richthofen used the situation to complain that the Jagdgeschwader's effectiveness as an assemblage of fighter units was being diluted. He wrote to Hauptmann Wilberg, 4. Armee's officer in charge of aviation: 'The Geschwader is being split up by deployment as individual Staffeln. Particularly on major combat days the deployment of several Staffeln at the same time in the same place is required. The Staffeln, which [now] must provide escorts for the attack units [Kampfstaffeln], withdraw from the Geschwader formations for the greatest part of the day. A pilot who has already been called upon for protective flights, long-range missions and bombing flights can no longer completely and undividedly fulfil his duty as a fighter pilot on the same day, as, for successful execution of aerial combat, he must be unfatigued and completely fresh.'[49]

Helmuth Wilberg was aware of Otto Bufe's disagreements with Manfred von Richthofen – and their outcome – and had no wish for a repeat performance. He did not order JG I to escort bombers or trench-strafers the following day. Richthofen's success was a double-edged sword, however, and it swung back at him with the next message received from General von Hoeppner. Following words of praise for JG I and Richthofen's 58th victory, the Air Force Commanding General concluded with a thinly veiled warning that the Geschwader Commander needed to be more prudent about his own role in future combats: ' ... I expect that [Richthofen] ... is conscious of the responsibility of the deployment of his person and, until the last traces of his wound are gone, he will fly only when absolute necessity justifies it.'[50]

Richthofen's only comfort that day was the success of his comrade Oberleutnant Eduard Dostler, leader of Jasta 6. During an evening patrol on 18 August Dostler shot down an Airco D.H.4 bomber over Roeselare, near Roulers. It was Dostler's 26th and last victory.[51] Three days later he was killed in combat.

Where are the Fokker Triplanes?

JG I's adjutant wrote that on 19 August: 'General Ludendorff [and his Staff] comes to visit to inspect the most audacious pilots in the German Army and to shake their hands. On this occasion he can also inspect the newly arrived [Fokker] Triplanes, which every fighter pilot awaited longingly and which make an excellent impression.'[52]

This rosy description ignores one essential point: the new fighters had yet to arrive at Marcke. If anything, Richthofen might well have used his increasing influence to ask politely of the *de facto* deputy chief of staff:[53] Where are the Fokker Triplanes? They had been promised for more than a month and their development was already known to the Allies. Six weeks earlier a British intelligence report contained a very accurate description of the aircraft that Richthofen had hoped would turn the tide.[54]

In fact, only three days earlier, the first two prototype V4 Triplanes had made their acceptance flights at the Fokker factory in Schwerin. They were then sent to JG I via Armee-Flugpark 4 at Ghent.[55]

On 21 August, when Jasta 6 leader Oberleutnant Eduard Dostler failed to return from the morning's operations over Ypres[56] Richthofen sent out several flights to look for him. Hopes of finding him hiding in a shell crater were dashed when Hauptmann Wilberg's office reported that 'the British Royal Flying Corps has informed [us] about Oberleutnant Dostler that particulars about his fate cannot be provided. It is known only that on 21.8.1917 at 11 a.m. British Time (12 noon German Time) a British pilot in the vicinity of Frezenberg [north-east of Ypres] brought down a German aircraft and in all likelihood it lies in the forwardmost German lines.'[57]

The report concluded that the circumstances matched the time and place of Dostler's disappearance. The likely scenario, involving an R.E.8 crew, was described in a British report: 'While taking photographs, Lieut. N. Sharples and 2nd-Lieut. M. O'Callaghan, No. 7 Squadron, were attacked by four Albatros Scouts. The observer opened fire at the nearest one, and it burst into flames and crashed. The other three E.A. were driven off by SPADs of No. 19 Squadron, which had arrived on the scene.'[58]

Although the wreckage of Dostler's Albatros D.Va was not retrieved,[59] it was identified as G 64 in the British series designating captured German aircraft. Dostler's body had to be buried where it fell, because the area had come under heavy British artillery fire.[60] The Kingdom of Bavaria honoured Dostler posthumously with its highest award for bravery, the Knight's Cross of the Military Max-Joseph Order; the day of Dostler's last fight was listed as the date of the award.[61]

Fighting Against 'Sub-paragraph II'

Richthofen's sadness at the loss of his friend was compounded by another message from 4. Armee's air chief. Drawing on the power of higher authority, it reminded Richthofen that he was to take no unnecessary risks to attain his personal goals: 'I refer to the Army Order of 12 August, sub-paragraph II and, if necessary, request notification in case this aspect is not being sufficiently taken into account.'[62]

Richthofen knew that 'sub-paragraph II' virtually grounded him. He could command the Geschwader, but could not fly with it in combat unless it were deemed absolutely necessary. Events of the early morning of 26 August put the restriction to a hard test. The airfields at Heule, Bisseghem and Marcke were attacked by SPAD S.7s of No. 19 Squadron, RFC. One of the participants, Lieutenant Alexander A. N. D. Pentland, reported that, at 0545 hours (British Time): ' ... when I got to Marcke aerodrome I went down to within 20 feet of the ground. There were eight Albatros [scouts] on the ground and I fired into these from 500 feet downward. There were a few mechanics about, one of which lay flat on the ground beside his machine. My shots seemed to go right into the machines, and must have done some damage.'[63]

To Manfred von Richthofen, this raid on his airfields was enough for him to disregard 'subparagraph II' and go after the bold attackers. Within 45 minutes of Pentland's strafing run, Richthofen and four comrades caught a SPAD over the German advance lines north of Ypres, between Poelkapelle and Langemarck.

As reported later, Richthofen attacked 'from out of the sun. [The pilot] tried to escape by diving away, whereby I got a good shot at him and he disappeared into a thin cloud cover. Following behind, I saw him below the cloud cover, diving straight down, then at about 500 metres' altitude he exploded in the air ...'[64]

Richthofen was credited with his 59th victory, but at some cost to his red aircraft.[65] Bad rounds of incendiary ammunition had exploded and damaged the pressure line, intake-manifold and exhaust manifold. He could only shut off the engine and hope to glide back to his airfield. He made it, but was still feeling the lingering effects of his wounds. Two days later he wrote: 'I have made only two combat flights [since returning to the Front] and both were successful, but after each flight I was completely exhausted. During the first one I almost got sick to my stomach. My wound is healing frightfully slow ...'[66]

Foul weather at the end of the month had more power than 'subparagraph II' to keep Richthofen on the ground. On 28 August, when the first two Fokker Triplanes arrived, he was tempted to try the new machines during a brief period of sunshine, but gave the honour to Leutnant Werner Voss.

The bad weather did not deter No. 100 Squadron's F.E.2d night bombers from attacking German airfields west of Courtrai in the evening of 31 August.[67] Next morning Richthofen used the occasion to circumvent 'subparagraph II' and make his first combat flight in a Fokker Triplane. At about 0750 hours he and four Jasta 11 comrades attacked what he described as 'a very courageously flown [R.E.8] British artillery-spotting aircraft' which 'apparently ... had taken me for a British triplane, as the observer stood up in his machine without making a move to attack me with his machine-gun.'[68]

The two-seater went down out of control near Zonnebeke, within the German lines and was recorded as Richthofen's 60th victory.[69] Twenty minutes later his protégé Oberleutnant Wilhelm Reinhard claimed a 'Sopwith single-seater' over Frezenberg; it was credited as his fifth victory.[70]

This was more like old times, with combat action and success. Almost symbolic of the beginning of a new era, back on the ground a new man sent from the Fighter Pilot School to Jasta 11 turned out to be an old friend of

Richthofen's – Leutnant Alfred Gerstenberg.[71] He and Richthofen had begun their military careers in the same regiment[72] and then served together in Kagohl 2 in Russia.[73] Gerstenberg was a willing pupil and tried very hard to shoot down enemy aircraft. He was unsuccessful, but was one of the few non-scoring fighter pilots retained in Jasta 11.

During the morning patrol on 3 September, Richthofen and the Geschwader were only some 5 kilometres from their own airfield when they went after a flight of Sopwith Pups over Menin. At 0730 hours, Leutnant Eberhardt Mohnike, also a Kagohl 2 veteran,[74] shot down a Pup south of Tenbrielen, thereby scoring the first of the Geschwader's eleven victories that day and his own sixth triumph.[75]

Moments later Richthofen concluded a prolonged battle with a Pup and forced it to land south of Bousbecque. He acknowledged that his opponent had put up a good fight, but he also commented on his new aircraft in his report: 'The Fokker Triplane F.I 102/17 is absolutely superior to the British Sopwith.'[76]

At the site of the wrecked Pup, credited as the Rittmeister's 61st victory,[77] the victor met his uninjured adversary, 20-year-old Lieutenant Algernon F. Bird of No. 46 Squadron. Aircraft constructor Anthony Fokker was visiting Marcke at the time, and arrived at the crash scene a short time later with his ciné-camera to film Richthofen and his latest victim.

While Manfred von Richthofen was enjoying the company of his former opponent, JG I pilots eluded their enemies and hit a fair number of RFC aircraft. At 0830 Leutnant Kurt Wüsthoff of Jasta 4 sent down an R.E.8 observation aircraft east of Zillebeke for his ninth victory. About an hour and a half later Voss shot down his 39th victim, a Sopwith F.1 Camel north of Houthem. Jasta 11 completed the morning's triumph when two promising air fighters – Leutnants Carl August von Schoenebeck and Eberhard Stapenhorst – claimed a pair of Sopwith Triplane fighters in the vicinity of Hollebeke.[78]

On the morning of 4 September, a Jasta 11 flight engaged Sopwith Pups of No. 66 Squadron and shot down two of them. The tide turned half an hour later, however, when Lt F. A. Smith of the same squadron sent down an Albatros 'out of control'.[79] Apparently Smith's victim was Jasta 11 leader Oberleutnant Wilhelm Reinhard, who was wounded in the thigh in a fight at 0915 hours. He was removed to Bavarian Field Hospital 133 near Courtrai[80] and was out of action for more than two months before returning to his Jasta. Six-victory ace Leutnant Gisbert-Wilhelm Groos became acting Staffel leader until Kurt Wolff returned to active duty.

Flying the other Fokker Triplane prototype,[81] Werner Voss scored his 40th and 41st victories on 5 September. At 1550 hours, he and Jasta 10 newcomer

Leutnant Erich Loewenhardt shot down two Sopwith Pups near St-Julien and, 40 minutes later, Voss was credited with knocking down a French Caudron two-seater between Bixschoote and Langemarck.[82] Loewenhardt, a 20-year-old native of Breslau and former cadet, had served in the infantry[83] before transferring to the aviation service.[84] This flight with Voss resulted in the third of his 54 victories.

As seen by events on 6 September, the High Command had an administrative remedy for Richthofen's disregard of explicit orders to refrain from flying until his injuries had healed completely. He received orders from 'on high' to take a four-weeks' recuperative leave.[85] Once again Oberleutnant Kurt von Döring became Acting Geschwader Leader; Oberleutnant Oskar von Boenigk led Jasta 4 while Döring held the higher post.

In Richthofen's absence, Werner Voss and his new silver-grey Fokker Triplane reigned supreme. Voss recorded his 42nd victory in the late afternoon of 6 September and, four days later, the 20-year-old Rhinelander was credited with shooting down his 43rd, 44th and 45th enemy aircraft, all over Langemarck, north-east of Ypres: at 1750 and 1755 hours, two Sopwith F.1 Camels of No. 70 Squadron, which reported encounters with 'Albatros Nieuports [scouts] and two triplanes',[86] and an F.E.2 at 1815 hours.[87]

The next day Voss added two more 'kills' to his score. The first, according to the JG I war diary, was a 'new type' shot down over Langemarck at 1030 hours and recorded as Voss' 46th victory. This claim remains a mystery. The Luftstreitkräfte's official victory roll listed his 43rd to 47th victories in the accounting for 10 September,[88] which was clearly in error, as the JG I war diary and 4. Armee reports show three Voss victories for that date and two for the next day. But the official list did record Victory No. 46 as a 'SPAD', for which there was no corresponding Royal Flying Corps loss that day.

The most prominent SPAD loss on 11 September 1917 was the aircraft flown by Capitaine Georges Guynemer of Escadrille Spa 3, at that time the highest scoring French fighter ace. Guynemer's aircraft also went down at 1030 hours, just south-east of Poelkappelle, about 2 kilometres east of Langemarck, the site of Voss' fight. Lacking a stronger claim, the German authorities credited Guynemer as the fifth victory of Leutnant der Reserve Kurt Wissemann of Jasta 3,[89] but one wonders whether, in the swirl of events, Werner Voss caught a fleeting glimpse of Georges Guynemer, who typically flew alone? If, as some historians have contended, the War Ministry falsely enhanced the achievements of some prominent German air heroes, it missed an opportunity to add further lustre to Voss' reputation by not crediting him with shooting down the leading French fighter ace.

Voss' second success that day was a Sopwith F.1 Camel of No. 45 Squadron, brought down over St-Julien at 1625 hours[90] and listed as his 47th victory.

The German High Command knew how to motivate its soldiers, whether they fought on land or in the air. On 12 September, Voss received a personally signed photograph of Kaiser Wilhelm II.[91] At the same time, a telegram from the monarch informed Kurt Wolff of his meritorious promotion to Oberleutnant in recognition of his recent achievements. These small gifts were treasured by the recipients and had the effect of binding the two pilots closer to the monarch and the establishment he symbolised.

Flying an Albatros D.V that evening, Kurt Wüsthoff of Jasta 4 claimed a Sopwith single-seater for his 14th victory.[92] At the same time that Jasta 4 was conducting operations south of Ypres, a flight of Airco D.H.4 two-seaters of No. 55 Squadron bombed Jasta 6's airfield at Bisseghem and Jasta 10's facilities at Marcke.[93] No damage was reported,[94] but Wolff and the other Jasta leaders were painfully reminded of their vulnerability.

On Friday, 14 September, JG I was not only scoreless, but suffered losses during several encounters with one of the premier RFC units, No. 56 Squadron. This was the first British unit to deploy the very successful S.E.5 fighter with which it built an enviable record in a short time. With a roster that included such top pilots as Captain James T. B. McCudden, the unit may well have been what German authorities considered to be the 'anti-Richthofen squadron',[95] devoted to the destruction of Germany's most successful air fighter.

Falling Stars

No. 56 Squadron displayed its talents that Friday. In a fight over Ypres at about 0930 hours, Leutnant Wilhelm-Gisbert Groos of Jasta 11 was lightly wounded and forced to return to Marckebeke; he was counted as the 16th victim of Captain Geoffrey H. Bowman.[96] Later that day, at 1725 hours, Oberleutnant Ernst Weigand of Jasta 10 was also lightly wounded and forced to head for home; most likely, his opponent was Captain McCudden who was credited with damaging an Albatros over Roulers at the time.[97]

Late on the afternoon of 15 September, Oberleutnant Kurt Wolff, who was flying Richthofen's Fokker Triplane F.I 102/17, encountered a flight of Sopwith F.1 Camels over Moorslede. One of the British pilots, Flight-Sub-Lieutenant Norman M. MacGregor, reported: 'We were attacked from above by about five Albatros scouts and four triplanes. I got into good position very close on one triplane – within 25 yards – and fired a good burst. I saw my tracers entering his machine. I then had to turn and zoom to avoid hitting him with my machine. I next saw him going down in a vertical dive, apparently out of control.'[98]

The first Fokker Triplane to fall in combat was recorded as the fifth of MacGregor's seven victories.[99] MacGregor miscalculated when he reported seeing 'four triplanes', because the only other Fokker Triplane at the Front was assigned to Werner Voss, who at the time was on a brief visit to the Fokker factory in Schwerin.[100] It is unlikely that any other pilot would have 'borrowed' a Staffel leader's aircraft for a mission.

Wolff's mortal remains were recovered and sent to his one-time home in Memel (now Klaipėda in Lithuania) with all the honours accorded to a knight of the order *Pour le Mérite*.

In Schweidnitz the Richthofen family learned of Wolff's death from the local newspapers. Kunigunde Freifrau von Richthofen recalled the stoic, tightly controlled reaction of her son Lothar, who was at home on convalescent leave and waiting for his brother to arrive from his hunting trip in Thuringia:

'His features became hardened; he sat like that the whole day, glanced into a book and stared out the window at the dark trees in the garden. None of us said anything. None of us dared, [and] each of us stayed busy, as it was absolutely necessary to begin a conversation about something else ... Lothar said nothing, but his face showed the turmoil [within him]. When twilight came, he wanted no light.

'When I went to the door I believe I heard some words. They were spoken very softly, definitely intended for someone far, far away. "So young ... engaged while on leave ... he should not have been allowed to do that ... a combat pilot is not allowed that."'[101]

The day after Wolff's funeral, 19 September, JG I recorded three victories and a casualty; Offizierstellvertreter Paul Aue of Jasta 10 was wounded in a fight over Roulers. He was probably hit by a Sopwith F.1 Camel of No. 10 Squadron, RNAS,[102] at the same time that Jasta 6 leader Leutnant Hans Ritter von Adam was scoring his 15th and 16th victories in the area.[103]

That evening it rained along the Flanders Front, but units of the Royal Flying Corps attacked ground targets at the beginning of the struggle for the Menin Road, an important location in the Battle of Ypres. The German counter-attack which started on the morning of 20 September did not deter the RFC from hitting their opponents hard. At the first break in the weather, according to one German account, a 'numerically superior flying force'[104] was sent into action. A flight of Martinsyde G.102 Elephants of No. 27 Squadron came in low over JG I's airfields at Bisseghem and Marcke,[105] bombing and strafing, and caused considerable damage: ' ... five men were cut down dead, several were badly wounded and nine machines were damaged'.[106] JG I went after the Martinsydes and, while they slipped away, the Geschwader accounted for seven other enemy aircraft and one captive balloon.[107]

Werner Voss' Last Fight

On the morning of 23 September, Werner Voss led Jasta 10 against a formation of Airco D.H.4s that were bombing German positions in Hooglede. He got behind one of the bombers and sent it down in flames. It was his 48th and last victory.[108]

Just over six hours later, Voss and his men were back in action. At about 1930 hours, the Jasta 10 flight encountered a larger force of British aircraft and Voss became separated from his comrades. Leutnant der Reserve Rudolf Wendelmuth of Jasta 8 reported seeing a Fokker triplane attacked from behind by a 'Sopwith', after which the German aircraft smashed into the ground behind British lines, near Frezenberg.[109] According to an RFC account, Voss' last air fight was a mix of bravery and recklessness against a superior force:

'Capt. J. [T. B.] McCudden, No. 56 Squadron ... saw a[n] S.E.5 fighting a triplane, so with others dived at it, and for the next ten minutes the enemy triplane fought the five S.E.5s with great skill and determination. Eventually, however, it was destroyed by 2nd-Lieut. [Arthur P. F.] Rhys-Davids of the same squadron, who had previously driven down a two-seater.

' ... The triplane was seen to crash in our lines by other pilots and the other [sic] occupant proved to be Lieut. Werner Voss, who was killed.'[110]

Voss, five months short of his 21st birthday, was then Germany's second-highest scoring ace. The wreckage of his Fokker F.I 103/17 was assigned the captured German aircraft number G 72 and his body was buried at the site of the crash.[111] According to one report: 'This machine was brought down [at Plum Farm, north of Frezenberg] near St-Julien, and only a few instruments were [salvaged] ... The machine, a single-seater biplane [sic] has a 110-hp Le Rhône [engine], No. 6247, which was missing in a Nieuport scout, in April 1917.'[112]

It was not uncommon for the Germans to set aside captured rotary engines for installation in Fokker triplanes.[113] Of interest in this case, is that the engine for Voss' Triplane came from an aircraft very likely brought down by Jasta 11. Le Rhône rotary engine T6247J was originally fitted in Nieuport 17 A.6693, which had been assigned to No. 60 Squadron.[114] On 5 April 1917, Lt E. J .D. Townesend flew that aircraft and was forced down south-west of Bailleul, most likely by Vizefeldwebel Sebastian Festner, who received credit for his fifth victory.[115]

Almost immediately, Voss was presumed dead[116] and the following day Oberleutnant Ernst Weigand was named acting leader of Jasta 10. A former infantry officer[117] with three victories to his credit, Weigand had been the Staffel's administrative officer, handling the paperwork the younger Voss disdained.

Lothar von Richthofen resumed command of Jasta 11 on 25 September,[118] but bad luck continued to dog the Geschwader. Weigand was leading a patrol of four aircraft over Houthulst Forest that evening and was attacked by a lone S.E.5a. The audacious RFC fighter sent down Weigand's 'yellow-fuselaged V-strutter'[119] in flames at 1740 hours and caused newcomer Unteroffizier August Werkmeister's aircraft to break up in the air two minutes later. Both pilots were killed,[120] most likely as the 15th and 16th victims of Second Lieutenant Leonard M. Barlow of No. 56 Squadron.[121]

Weigand and Werkmeister, both 24 years old, were given a hero's funeral from St. Joseph's Church in Courtrai on 29 September. Heavy, low-hanging clouds and mist added to the sombre atmosphere and seemed to hint at the difficult weather and times to come.

Notes

1   With the 2. Westfälische Husaren-Regiment Nr. 11.
2   Zuerl, W., *Pour le Mérite-Flieger*, p. 461.
3   Franks, N., et al., *Above the Lines*, p. 224.
4   Zuerl, op. cit.
5   Ibid., p. 462.
6   For background on Walz, see Chapter 4, Note 94; Ferko, A. E., *Richthofen*, p. 42.
7   Ltn Rolf Freiherr von Lersner began his service with the 1. Westfälische Husaren-Regiment Nr. 8 and was killed in a training accident at Johannisthal on 25 August 1917 aged 23. Zickerick, W., 'Verlustliste' in von Eberhardt, W. (ed.), *Unsere Luftstreitkräfte*, p. 49 lists his date of birth as 25 May 1897; in fact, it was 26 December 1893.
8   Jones, H. A., *War in the Air*, vol. IV, pp. 160–9.
9   RFC *Communiqué* No. 99, 5 August 1917, pp. 6–7.
10 Ibid., p. 5.
11 Kogenluft, *Nachrichtenblatt der Luftstreitkräfte*, Nr. 23, 2 August 1917, p. 111.
12 Bodenschatz, K., *Jagd in Flandern*, p. 152.
13 Kogenluft, op. cit., Nr. 26, 23 August 1917, p. 174; the other confirmed victory was attributed to Jasta 8, and two other claims were noted as 'not yet decided'.
14 Kofl 4. Armee, *Besonderer Tagesbefehl* Nr. 29171, 4 August 1917.
15 With Grenadier-Regiment König Friedrich III. (2. Schlesisches) Nr. 11.
16 Zuerl, op. cit., pp. 91–6.
17 O'Connor, N., *Aviation Awards* , vol. I, p. 39.
18 Zuerl, op. cit., p. 482.
19 Kogenluft, op. cit., Nr. 25, 16 August 1917, p. 157; Sopwith 1½ Strutter B.2576 of No. 45 Squadron, Capt Geoffrey Hornblower Cock, MC, aged 21, and 2/Lt W. C. Moore (both PoW); Cock was a successful Strutter pilot, credited with at least 13 victories (Ref: Shores, C., et al., *Above the Trenches*, p. 111).
20 Bufe, O., *Kriegsranglisten*, p. 2.
21 Supf, P., *Deutschen Fluggeschichte*, vol. I, p. 562; on 15 September 1910, Wilberg qualified for

Deutsche Luftfahrer Verband licence No. 26. He remained on active duty between the wars and eventually attained the rank of General der Flieger. He was killed in a crash on 20 November 1941, en route to Berlin for the official state funeral of Generaloberst Ernst Udet, who had committed suicide three days earlier (Ref: Hildebrand, K., *Die Generale*, vol. III, pp. 513–14).

22 Kofl 4. Armee, *Tagesbefehl* Nr. 38, 7 August 1917.

23 Quoted in Bodenschatz, op. cit., pp. 36, 152.

24 RFC *Communiqué* No. 100, 12 August 1917, p. 5.

25 Bodenschatz, op. cit., p. 152.

26 Kofl 4. Armee, *Wochenbericht* Nr. 116 op, 30 August 1917, p. 3.

27 Ibid., p. 37.

28 RFC *Communiqué* No. 101, 19 August 1917, p. 1.

29 Bodenschatz, op. cit., pp. 37, 153.

30 No. 1 Squadron Combat Report of Capt T. F. Hazell in Nieuport 17 B.3455; Shores, et al., op. cit., p. 190 lists Ltn Hübner as the eighteenth of Capt Hazell's 43 confirmed victories.

31 Haehnelt, W. (ed.), *Ehrentafel*, p. 35.

32 With 1. Feldartillerie-Regiment Nr. 12 (Ref: Zickerick, op. cit., p. 36).

33 Kogenluft, op. cit., Nr. 29, 13 September 1917, p. 228.

34 Private Stanley E. Pilbrow, MM, was 26 years old; his pilot, Lt C. H. Cameron, was unhurt (Ref: Hobson, C., *Airmen Died*, pp. 82, 253).

35 Apparently Uffz Brettel's aircraft was one of two Albatroses credited as the 20th and 21st victories of Capt Philip P. Fullard, MC.

36 Gunner A. Owen (KiA) and 2/Lt I. M. McLean (WiA) (Ref: Hobson, op. cit., p. 253).

37 No. 20 Squadron Combat Report of Lt Harold W. Joslyn and 2/Lt J. P. Adams in F.E.2d A.6359.

38 RFC *Communiqué*, op. cit., p. 9.

39 Bodenschatz, op. cit., p. 154.

40 No. 29 Squadron Combat Report of 2/Lt D. F. Hilton in Nieuport B.3494.

41 Other 4. Armee reports, however, show these losses: Ltn.d.R Ehlers, Jasta 17 (WiA); Vzfw Anton Schrader, Jasta 31 (KiA); and Vzfw Walter Hoffmann, Jasta 36 (KiA).

42 Quoted in Bodenschatz, op. cit., p. 38.

43 Kogenluft, op. cit., Nr. 30, 20 September 1917, p. 247; Bodenschatz, op. cit., p. 153; Nieuport 23 A.6611, 2/Lt William H. T. Williams (DoW).

44 Shores, et al., op. cit., p. 378; other sources credit Voss with shooting down a D.H.5 of No. 32 Squadron, but his claim of a Sopwith is reinforced by the RFC *Casualty List* entry for this date, which records Capt Webb in Sopwith F.1 Camel B.3756 as 'last seen diving on E.A. over Polygon Wood at 4,000 feet about 7.45 pm [British Time]'. Capt Webb, aged 20, was KiA.

45 Bodenschatz, op. cit., p. 154.

46 Kogenluft, op. cit., possibly F.2B A.7201 of No. 22 Squadron, 2/Lt R. S. Phelan (PoW) and Lt Eric E. White (who had enlisted under the name of James L. Macfarlane), aged 29 (DoW) (Ref: Hobson, op. cit., pp. 68, 106; RFC *Casualty List* notes that this aircraft 'left aerodrome 6 pm and was last seen side-slipping through clouds at 8 pm (British Time; 2100 German Time).'

47 Ltn von der Osten was commissioned into the 3. Garde Ulanen-Regiment in Potsdam; Osten, H-G. von der, 'Memoirs', in *Cross & Cockade*, 1974, p. 221.

48 Quoted in Bodenschatz, op. cit., p. 39.

49 Ibid., pp. 39–40.

50 Ibid., p. 40.

51 Kogenluft, op. cit.; D.H.4 7510 of No. 57 Squadron, Lt John Hood, aged 22, and 2/Lt James R. McDaniel, aged 25 (both KiA).

52 Bodenschatz, op. cit., pp. 41, 154.

53 Haythornthwaite, P., *World War One Source Book*, p. 338.

54 RFC, *Periodical Summary*, No. 7, 2 July 1917, p. 7.

55 Fokker F.I 102/17 and 103/17; Grosz, P., and Ferko, A. E., 'Fokker Dr.I – Reappraisal', in *Air Enthusiast*, No 8, p. 18.

56 Bodenschatz, op. cit.

57 Ibid.

58 RFC *Communiqué* No. 102, 26 August 1917, p. 7.

59 Robertson, B., *British Military Aircraft Serials*, p. 86 notes that G 64 was 'found to be [with]in enemy lines'

60 Zuerl, op. cit., p. 186.

61 O'Connor, op. cit., p. 43; often this pilot is erroneously identified as Eduard Ritter von Dostler, a title he was not able to use in life.

62 Bodenschatz, op. cit., pp. 41–2.

63 No. 19 Squadron Combat Report of Lt A. A. N. D. Pentland in SPAD S.7 B.3620.

64 Bodenschatz, op. cit., p. 42; SPAD S.7 B.3492 of No. 19 Squadron, 2/Lt Collingsby P. Williams (KiA).

65 Albatros D.V 2059/17.

66 Richthofen, M. von, *Heldenleben*, p. 198.

67 RFC *Communiqué* No. 104, 9 September 1917, p. 1.

68 Bodenschatz, op. cit., p. 43.

69 Kogenluft, op. cit., Nr. 33, 11 October 1917, p. 306; R.E.8 B.782 of No. 6 Squadron, 2/Lt John B. C. Madge, aged 25 (WiA/PoW), and 2/Lt Walter Kember, aged 26 (KiA).

70 Ibid.; the only RFC loss in this area was SPAD B.3569 of No. 19 Squadron, 2/Lt Edward M. Sant (KiA), who was credited as the second victory of Ltn Karl Hammes of Jasta 35.

71 Kofl 4. Armee, *Tagesbefehl* Nr. 63, 4 September 1917.

72 Ulanen-Regiment Kaiser Alexander III. von Russland (Westpreussisches) Nr. 1 (Ref: *Ehrenrangliste*, vol. I, pp. 442–3).

73 Richthofen, op. cit., p. 65.

74 Commissioned into Infanterie-Regiment von Boyen (5. Ostpreussisches) Nr. 41.

75 Kogenluft, op. cit.; Sopwith Pup B.1754 of No. 46 Squadron, Lt Kenneth W. McDonald, aged 21 (DoW).

76 Bodenschatz, op. cit.

77 Kogenluft, op. cit.; Sopwith Pup B.1795.

78 Ibid.; British records show one Sopwith triplane loss, N.5381 of No. 1 Squadron, RNAS, Fl-Sub-Lt Gordon G. B. Scott, aged 22 (KiA) (Ref: Hobson, op. cit., p. 13).

79 Bailey, F., and Franks, N., '66 Squadron', in *Cross & Cockade*, p. 4.

80 Bodenschatz, op. cit., p. 156.

81 Fokker D.I 103/17.

82 Kogenluft, op. cit.; of all these claims, the only matching casualty is Sopwith Scout B.1842 of No. 46 Squadron, 2/Lt C. W. Odell, whose aircraft was damaged but brought back intact (Ref: Henshaw, T., *Sky their Battlefield*, p. 221).

83 With Kulmer-Infanterie Regiment Nr. 141.

84 Zuerl, op. cit., p. 315.

85 Bodenschatz, op. cit., pp. 44, 156.

86 No. 70 Squadron Combat Reports Nos. 130, 131 of 2/Lts L. F. Wheeler and F. N. Bickerton in Sopwith F.1 Camels B.3836 and B.2342.

87 Bodenschatz, op. cit., pp. 44, 156–7.

88 Kogenluft, op. cit., Nr. 33, p. 307.

89 Ferko, A. E., 'Guynemer's Last Patrol', in *Cross & Cockade*, 1974, pp. 67–85.

90 Bodenschatz, op. cit.; Kogenluft, op. cit.; Sopwith Camel B.6236, Lt Oscar L. McMaking (KiA), about whom RFC *Casualty List* notes: 'Last seen going down over Langemarck followed by enemy triplane. AA reports Sopwith Camel shot down in flames by enemy triplane over Langemarck.'

91 Bodenschatz, op. cit.

92 Ibid., p. 157; no corresponding RFC loss has been found.

93 RFC *Communiqué* No. 105, 18 September 1917, p. 6.

94 Bodenschatz, op. cit.

95 Jones, op. cit., p. 199.

96 Shores, et al., op. cit., pp. 83–4.

97 Ibid., pp. 268–9.

98 No. 10 Squadron, RNAS, Combat Report No. 139 of Fl-Sub-Lt N. M. MacGregor in Sopwith F.1 Camel B.3833.

99 Shores, et al., op. cit., p. 248.

100 Fokker F.I 103/17; Grosz and Ferko, op. cit., p. 19.

101 Richthofen, K. von, *Kriegstagebuch*, pp. 132–3.

102 No. 10 Squadron, RNAS, Combat Report No. 142 filed by Fl-Lt Desmond F. FitzGibbon and Fl-Sub-Lts Hugh B. Maund, John G. Carroll, Norman M. MacGregor and Johnston, in Sopwith F.1 Camels B.6202, B.6211, B.6357, B.3833 and B.3912.

103 Kogenluft, op. cit., Nr. 34, 18 October 1917, pp. 327–8; Adam's sixteenth victory was probably Sopwith Camel N.6374 of No. 10 Squadron, RNAS, Flt-Sub-Lt Edgar J. V. Grace (KiA).

104 Kogenluft, op. cit., Nr. 31, 27 September 1917, p. 252.

105 RFC *Communiqué* No. 106, 26 September 1917, p. 5.

106 Bodenschatz, op. cit., pp. 46, 158.

107 Ibid., p. 158; Kogenluft, op. cit., Nr. 34, 18 October 1917, pp. 328, 331 lists only four aircraft brought down and credit for one balloon 'not yet decided'.

108 Ibid., pp. 46, 159; D.H.4 A.7643 of No. 57 Squadron (presentation aircraft 'South Africa') (Ref: Vann, R., and Waugh, C., 'Presentation Aircraft 1914–18', in *Cross & Cockade*, 1983, p. 88), 2/Lts Samuel L. J. Bramley, aged 22, and John M. DeLacey, aged 21 (both KiA).

109 Ibid., pp. 47–9.

110 RFC *Communiqué*, op. cit., p. 9.

111 Revell, *Aftermath*, 1975, p. 105.

112 RFC *Periodical Summary*, No. 18, 25 September 1917, p. 13.

113 Grosz and Ferko, op. cit., p. 17.

114 Rogers, L., *RFC/RAF Casualties*, p. 77.

115 Hitchins, F., 'Enemy Aircraft in German Hands', in *Cross & Cockade*, 1969, p. 256.

116 Kogenluft, op. cit., Nr. 31, p. 253.

117 With Füsilier-Regiment Kaiser Franz Joseph von Österreich König von Ungarn (4. Württembergisches) Nr. 122.

118 Kofl 4. Armee, *Tagesbefehl* Nr. 83, 24 September 1917, p. 1.

119 RFC *Communiqué* No. 107, 3 October 1917, p. 3.

120 Bodenschatz, op. cit., p. 159.

121 Shores, et al., op. cit., p. 65.

CHAPTER 9

Grim Winter

DESPITE THE FURIOUS PACE OF GROUND WARFARE IN FLANDERS IN LATE September 1917, Jagdgeschwader I was relatively inactive. Royal Flying Corps aircraft made numerous daily incursions, but from 27 September to 1 October the Geschwader recorded no successes. During intermittent flying weather, JG I flew 76 sorties on 27 September, 79 on the 28th, 51 on the 29th, and 66 on the 30th – all without tangible success.[1]

Finally, as a heavy morning mist cleared on Tuesday, 2 October, Jasta 10 attacked a flight of Airco D.H.4 two-seaters that had bombed Jasta 11's airfield at Marcke. When the yellow Albatros fighters caught up with them, however, success was hard earned: former infantry officer Leutnant Friedrich Römer,[2] aged 21, who had been in the Staffel for only eleven days, was shot down in flames over Westroosebeke by a D.H.4.[3] Minutes later, the newly appointed leader of Jasta 10, Leutnant der Reserve Hans Klein, shot down a D.H.4 over Meulebeke; it was confirmed as his 17th victory.[4]

In Manfred von Richthofen's absence, JG I's performance slipped. Lothar was unable to inspire the pilots in the same way as his brother; indeed, after his recuperation and return to the Geschwader, he did not have any success in the air for another month.

Bad weather in early October curtailed aerial success over the Flanders Front for both sides,[5] a notable exception being provided by three new men in JG I, who demonstrated their potential ability as fighter pilots worthy of the connection to the Richthofen name and reputation. On 5 October a Jasta 4 newcomer identified only as Leutnant der Reserve Wilde achieved the first and only confirmed victory of his career when he shot down a Sopwith Triplane[6] over Dadizele. On the 7th, Leutnant Carl Galetschky of Jasta 6 was credited with the first of his three victories, an R.E.8 reconnaissance aircraft which he brought down within British lines along the Ypres–Menin road.[7]

Tuesday, 9 October 1917, was a blustery day, but with British formations out in force to support renewed ground assaults, Jasta 11 rose to the challenge. During a midday fight over Gheluwe, Leutnant der Reserve Franz Müller shot down his second enemy aircraft, a Nieuport.[8] While closing in on his victim, Müller was attacked by No. 1 Squadron's Second Lieutenant Guy B. Moore, who reported: ' ... seeing two E.A. Scouts on 2/Lt Peacock's tail, I attacked and drove both off. Following one, I fired 50 rounds into it. E.A. stalled, then went over on his back, fell into a spin and went down and crashed about Kaelberg [Koelenberg].' Moore's victim, confirmed as his fifth, was an Albatros described as being decorated with a 'red nose, black rudder, white fuselage, [and] dark wings'.[9] While the red-coloured nose might have applied to Jasta 11, Moore could not have shot down Müller,[10] who, after shooting down Second Lieutenant Martin A. Peacock, returned safely to his own airfield.

Little in Name, Big in Achievement

The JG I war diary records 'scant enemy air activity' on 10, 11 and 12 October.[11] In fact, a strong British attack was launched at 0525 hours on 12 October, during driving rain and supported by RFC units making low-level strafing and bombing attacks. At least 41 pilots from ten squadrons[12] were involved, and eleven RFC aircraft fell on 4. Armee Front's that day.[13] One of them, a Sopwith single-seater brought down at midday, was credited to Leutnant Hans Klein as his 18th victory.[14] Klein, whose family name is also the German word for 'little', proved to be a man of no 'small' accomplishments.

Despite heavy winds next morning, Klein's Jasta 10 flight accompanied Albatros fighters of Jastas 2 and 8 north-west, beyond Roulers. Near Dixmude, the Germans split up; four aircraft headed low to 'invite' enemy fighters and eight climbed higher to spring the trap. Over the town of Zarren, six Sopwith Pups of No. 54 Squadron[15] flying at about 12,000 feet took the bait. They were soon outnumbered and outmanoeuvred. A member of the RFC flight, Captain F. J. Morse, later reported: 'Owing to very high west wind high up, [our] patrol were unable to make much ground toward the lines. By this time the first four E.A. [enemy aircraft] had climbed up again and joined the eight. E.A. then pressed [the] attack and came to close range, but always keeping above [us].'[16]

Captain Morse and Second Lieutenant T. L. Tebbit made it back to their airfield, but their four comrades fell within German lines,[17] one of them being Hans Klein's 19th victim.[18] This successful aggression, despite adverse weather, explains why the 26-year-old native of Stettin in Pomerania (now Szczecin in Poland) was one of Richthofen's favourites. He described Klein as being 'one of my most successful and best qualified Staffel leaders. His courageous gallantry, vigorous aggressive spirit and relentless daring know no bounds. As a leader in the air [he is] an ideal example of courage and bravery [who] requires of his subordinates the exertion of all strengths and relentless determination of the individual. Despite numerous severe wounds, his iron will-power would not let him be inactive at home. Barely recovered, he returned to the Geschwader early.

'Military through and through in bearing and conduct, energetic, prudent and indefatigably effective, he had the best resources of the Staffel under control. He was concerned about the well-being of every one of his men.'[19]

Hans Klein had interrupted his studies at the Charlottenburg Technical College (*Technische Hochschule*) in Berlin when the war began in 1914. He served in the trenches[20] during early battles in France and received a Reserve commission on 25 March 1915. Transferred to the aviation service eleven months later, his daring and skill while flying with the single-seat fighter element of Feldflieger-Abteilung 43[21] led to his transfer to Jasta 4, then commanded by the early ace Hans-Joachim Buddecke. Klein scored 15 victories within four months and his consistent performance was interrupted only when he was wounded on 13 July 1917. His return to active duty and appointment as leader of Jasta 10[22] was a portent of greater deeds to come.

Manfred von Richthofen had objected strenuously when the units of JG I were not deployed together during his convalescence in July. During his enforced autumn leave, however, there is no record of complaint about Jasta 10's mission with Jastas 2 and 8 on 13 October or with Jastas 3 and 7 on 18 October.

On the latter flight, Hans Klein and a future leader of Jasta 10, Leutnant Erich Loewenhardt, achieved the Geschwader's only triumphs of the week. During an early morning break in the weather the three Jastas each sent up four fighters to intercept two RFC bombing formations heading toward Ingelmunster.[23]

While other fighters attacked a flight of Airco D.H.4 bombers and their Sopwith Scout escorts, Klein and Loewenhardt went after a pair of Bristol F.2B two-seat fighters. Loewenhardt chased one over Roeselare and sent it crashing down into the grounds of the château at Ardooie. Klein followed his adversary westward and brought him down near Staden.

Other RFC aircraft fell in the course of the furious mêlée.[24] One F.2B pilot reported that north-east of Roulers he 'dived on the tail of one E.A. and in turn was dived on by two more [Albatros]. I got a burst into the E.A. and my observer also put a burst into him and he went down in a spin and was last seen by my observer spinning at 3,000 ft.'[25] German records show no losses that day, but do credit Loewenhardt with his seventh victory and Klein with his 20th.[26]

JG I Pounded by the RFC

To counter night bombing raids by long-range twin-engined aircraft from the 4. Armee, RFC units targeted the bombers' operating facilities. Late on the morning of 20 October, bomb-laden Sopwith F.1 Camels escorted by other Camels and SPAD S.7s – 45 aircraft in all – from 22nd (Army) Wing used the cover of thick fog to attack Kagohl 4's airfield at Rumbeke, as well as Abele and neighbouring airfields.[27] Other German fighter aircraft brought down two of the raiders, while JG I had two casualties to show for its efforts: Leutnant Alfred Gerstenberg of Jasta 11 took a bullet through the lung but managed to make a 'controlled crash' at Vossemolen; friendly troops rushed him to a field dressing station at Rollegemcappelle.

JG I's luck was little better next day. Good visibility on 21 October led to considerable RFC photo-reconnaissance activity in preparation for an infantry assault.[28] A Jasta 6 sortie against the RFC formations resulted in the loss of an aggressive and successful newcomer, Vizefeldwebel Fritz Bachmann. This 24-year-old pilot already had a Sopwith single-seater and a balloon to his credit. On this bright Sunday morning, however, he was so intent on increasing his score that he became the third victim of Captain Frederic H. Laurence of No. 70 Squadron.[29]

Laurence was leading six Sopwith F.1 Camels eastwards towards the Roulers–Menin Road when he saw five Albatros going down in front of him. He later reported: 'I dived on the rear machine and fired about 50 rounds at him from 100 yards' range; he nose-dived with smoke coming out of his machine ...'[30]

The score was evened that afternoon when Acting Geschwader Commander von Döring, led a flight from Jasta 4 into battle alongside Albatros fighters led by his future chief in this war and the next, Leutnant Hermann Göring, commander of Jasta 27. Near Roulers they went to the aid of a German two-seat reconnaissance aircraft under attack by a patrol of six S.E.5a single-seaters headed by Captain Kenneth M. St.C G. Leask of No. 84 Squadron.

This 21-year-old flight commander was credited with shooting down the two-seater, after which, as he reported: ' ... patrols of E.A. Scouts approached from various directions and a big fight ensued ... I attacked four separate E.A. and drove them down with bursts from both guns ... The fight lasted from 2.40 to 3.20 p.m. [British time] and we dispersed all the E.A., those under control going due East, noses down ...'[31]

Of the three RFC fighters that went down during this action, one was credited to Oberleutnant von Döring, his ninth victory, and one to Göring, his 15th.[32] But JG I had not seen the last of the RFC that day. After the Germans had settled in for the evening of the 21st, F.E.2bs of No. 102 Squadron bombed targets from Roulers to Courtrai, including Marcke and Bisseghem airfields.

The following evening, a rainy Monday, F.E.2bs from the same squadron bombed Marcke and Bisseghem airfields again, clearly demonstrating that bad weather offered no respite from their attacks.[33] Five Jasta 11 aircraft in one hangar were damaged and the roof was knocked off the Geschwader's orderly room.[34]

The Rittmeister Returns

By the time Manfred von Richthofen returned from leave on 22 October, the airfield had been put in order again, and a new Fokker Triplane[35] was waiting for him. The loss of Werner Voss and Kurt Wolff left Richthofen as the only JG I pilot with a depth of experience on the Triplane. The new aircraft could indeed 'climb like apes and [were] as manoeuvrable as the devil', as Richthofen said,[36] but only a skilled pilot could handle it properly. The controls were very sensitive and required constant attention; the Fokker Dr.I was not an aircraft for novices.[37]

As part of JG I's transition to the Triplane – equipped with rotary engines, which had a different 'feel' from the in-line, stationary engines in the Albatros – Richthofen ordered orientation flights in the older rotary-engined Fokker D.V biplane. Rain and violent gales kept JG I on the ground for the next few days, but when the weather improved, RFC night bombers resumed their disruption of German airfields north of Courtrai. On the night of 25/26 October, No. 102 Squadron returned to bomb Jasta 6's airfield at Bisseghem and Jasta 11's field at Marcke.[38] No damage was reported, but, as the Jastas had no night-fighting capability, the 'Fees' flew off with only the wind to trouble them on their long south-westerly journey home to Treizennes, west of Merville.

Richthofen made good use of the clear skies on Saturday, 27 October, sending Jasta 4 out on a morning patrol and Jasta 6 in the afternoon, while Jasta 11 pilots trained on Fokker D.Vs. The day's first success was recorded by Leutnant Kurt Wüsthoff, whose flight was working with Jasta 2 north-east of Ypres. The German formation dived on RFC artillery-ranging two-seater biplanes protected by RNAS Sopwith Triplanes.

The British fighter patrol leader, Flight-Commander Richard P. Minifie, struck first, thinking that he was attacking a new type of German fighter. Minifie reported that he let it 'come in and then attacked from in front and above firing 50 rounds at him from a close range. The E.A. dived vertically and crashed on a house in Westroosebeke, disappearing right through the roof. This was a new type rotary [engined biplane] scout with an overhang on the top plane, bright unpainted cowl, and much like the Nieuport Scout, only the bottom plane had a much wider chord.'[39] In fact, Minifie's victim was Leutnant Czaslea, a Jasta 2 pilot who imprudently had chosen to fly an old Fokker D.V on a combat patrol. German records list him only as 'missing'[40] and he is not named in Luftstreitkräfte necrologies, but he was the last pilot to cross the front line in a Fokker D.V.

Jasta 4's Wüsthoff then attacked a Sopwith Triplane and reported sending it down over British lines between Poelkapelle and Hooge. The RNAS aircraft was logged as his 22nd victory,[41] although the pilot escaped with a minor wound and got back to his own airfield at Bailleul.

Jasta 11 lost a promising air fighter that morning when Leutnant Franz Müller fatally crashed just short of the airfield during an orientation flight in a Fokker D.V.[42] Müller, a 21-year-old former cavalry officer,[43] had come to the Staffel from Feldflieger-Abteilung 18, one of Richthofen's favourite recruiting sources. His body was sent to Cologne for burial.

In the afternoon a new member of Jasta 6, Vizefeldwebel Franz Hemer, claimed an R.E.8 reconnaissance aircraft shot down north of Gheluvelt. It was credited as his first victory.[44] There was little to celebrate that evening, however, as once again F.E.2s from No. 102 Squadron flew the well-known route to JG I facilities. At 2130 hours the raiders dropped five 112lb bombs on Marcke airfield,[45] including one right outside the Geschwader's telephone exchange which killed one of the telephonists on duty.[46] Early the following morning, the F.E.2s again hit Bisseghem.

More Bad Luck

Two days later, Jasta 11's Vizfeldwebel Josef Lautenschlager, flying a new Fokker Dr.I north of Houthulst Forest, was shot down and killed. An official German report confirmed that the 25-year-old Bavarian had been attacked by another German fighter pilot who apparently mistook the Fokker for a Sopwith Triplane.[47]

On the morning of Tuesday, 30 October, Manfred and Lothar von Richthofen made their first flight together for more than five months. Both were fit and eager to prove to their comrades and themselves that they were still formidable in the air. Despite heavy clouds and rain, they led the Jasta 11 flight in new Fokker Triplanes. Suddenly, for no apparent reason, Lothar's Dr.I went into a glide with engine off. Manfred circled as Lothar made a successful landing near Zilverberg, just south of Roeselare. Minutes later, when Manfred set down nearby, his new machine[48] began to crack and burst and literally fall apart. He emerged from the wreckage unharmed, but the Triplane was a total loss.

Richthofen was shocked at the destruction caused by a seemingly minor incident. But he was luckier than Leutnant Heinrich Gontermann – a 39-victory ace, former infantry officer[49] and *Pour le Mérite* recipient – who also crashed that day in a Fokker Triplane.[50] Gontermann was making a test flight over Jasta 15's airfield at La Neuville when all the ribs broke away from the top wing spar and the aircraft crashed within 50 metres of the crowd that had gathered to watch his display of flying skill. Staffel leader Gontermann, aged 21, died of his injuries that evening.[51]

The following afternoon, Jasta 4's Leutnant Kurt Wüsthoff shot down an S.E.5a north of Bellewaarde Lake and was credited with his 23rd victory.[52] Three hours later, however, Jasta 11 lost another Fokker Triplane[53] and pilot. Leutnant Günther Pastor, a 19-year-old former gunnery officer[54] who had joined the Staffel five weeks earlier,[55] went down under circumstances similar to Gontermann's. One kilometre north of Moorseele, his Triplane's top wing structure collapsed and the aircraft crashed fatally .[56] The official daily summary noted Wüsthoff's success, but made no mention of Pastor's demise; only the loss of a German two-seater hit by anti-aircraft fire.[57]

This series of accidents was too costly in manpower and *matériel* to allow operations with the Fokker Triplane to continue and on 2 November 1917 all of them were grounded until the Inspectorate of Aviation determined the cause of the recent crashes and instituted corrective measures. During the course of the investigation by the Inspectorate's Central Acceptance Commission, JG I's pilots flew only Albatros D.III and D.V and new Pfalz D.III biplanes.[58]

Then, while Richthofen was planning the Geschwader's move to 2. Armee's Front in anticipation of a major Allied assault in that area, another aircraft problem emerged. On the morning of 6 November, the day that Canadian troops took Passchendaele, Jasta 10 ace Leutnant Erich Loewenhardt made an emergency landing at St-Eloi-Winkel with a broken wing on his Albatros D.V. If, in addition to the removal of the Triplanes, the Albatros had to be withdrawn or if pilots lost confidence in them, JG I would be left with only its Pfalz D.III fighters, which had sleek good looks that belied their air-fighting inferiority to the Albatros.[59]

To the Geschwader's good fortune, two Albatros fighters of Jasta 6 shot down British fighter aircraft[60] during the driving wind and rain that hindered progress on the battlefield and in the air that morning. It is difficult to match victory claims and losses for the early morning fight because analysis of RFC combat reports shows that three different types of rotary-engined biplane fighters were deployed: Nieuport 27s of No. 1 Squadron,

Airco D.H.5s of No. 32 Squadron, and Sopwith F.1 Camels of No. 65 Squadron. It is fairly certain, though, that a Nieuport or similar fighter fell near Zonnebeke at 0845 hours and was credited to Vizefeldwebel Gottfried Stumpf as his first and only triumph. Five minutes later Leutnant Hans Ritter von Adam claimed a Sopwith Camel west of Passchendaele for his 21st and last success in battle.

While British and Canadian troops expanded their positions at Passchendaele on the morning of 9 November, two JG I stalwarts – Lothar von Richthofen and Kurt Wüsthoff – encountered increasingly worsening weather and greater numbers of enemy aircraft. At 1030 hours, flights from Jastas 4 and 11 were at the perimeter east of Passchendaele when they attacked RFC two-seaters between Zonnebeke and Bellewaarde Lake. Lothar von Richthofen claimed a Bristol F.2B as his 25th victory, and Wüsthoff was credited with an R.E.8 reconnaissance aircraft for his 26th.[61]

JG I's bad luck resumed two days later, when Leutnant Robert Tüxen of Jasta 6 crashed while making an orientation flight in a rotary-engined biplane.[62] He lost control of it during a tight turn and ended up in a tree near the airfield. Tüxen was uninjured, but his Fokker was a total loss.

Heavy fog over the Flanders Front on 14 November caused RFC flight operations to be cancelled. In marginally better weather next day many aircraft were over the lines to make up for the previous day. German 'aircraft were active in the morning and endeavoured to stop our artillery machines working, while fifteen of theirs attempted to work on the [British] Second Army Front', according to one source.[63]

A Knight Falls

Jasta 6 leader Leutnant Hans Ritter von Adam saw five British fighters attacking a lone German two-seater over Houthulst Forest and led six comrades to the rescue. Upon their arrival, however, the Rumpler artillery-spotter was on fire[64] and the Germans attacked the Sopwith F.1 Camels that had sent it down. Then, as the fight moved northwards toward Langemarck, Albatros scouts of Jasta 18 and a flight of Nieuport 17s of No. 29 Squadron joined in. Camel pilot Second Lieutenant Kenneth B. Montgomery of No. 45 Squadron, the victor in nine previous dogfights, claimed to have shot down one Albatros in flames.[65] Second Lieutenant J. M. Leach in a Nieuport was credited with saving one of the Camels by shooting down the Albatros that was chasing it.[66]

The first German fighter pilot confirmed as lost in that fight was 31-year-old Ritter von Adam. Victorious in 21 fights, he was the only fighter pilot to become a Knight of Bavaria's Military Max-Joseph Order who did not also receive Prussia's highest bravery award, the Orden *Pour le Mérite*.[67]

Where is Richthofen?

Adam's body was retrieved and prepared for return to his home town, where a state funeral was being organised. As a commoner elevated to the nobility, he was *the* local hero in Eisenstein, Bavaria. With the loss of another top pilot from JG I, the unasked questions of the time had to be: Where is Richthofen? Why isn't *he* leading the Geschwader into battle?

Certainly Richthofen had the personal courage, but he also had propaganda value and, with the Fokker Triplane sidelined and the Albatros again in question, he could not be risked in a fight such as the one in which von Adam had met his end. Manfred von Richthofen was trapped by his own fame, as observed by his old friend Erwin Böhme, by now leader of Jasta 2. Böhme's letter of 19 November to his fiancée contrasted his own joy of flying with a cynical commentary by Richthofen, who had become 'public property' with the various press reports bolstered by publication of his autobiography *Der rote Kampfflieger*.

Böhme wrote that Richthofen's Geschwader 'also belongs to our Armee and is right in the neighbourhood, but is at the disposal of the [4.] Armee High Command for special missions, while we have a prescribed sector at the Front. Of course, we do not have to stay within it meticulously; when the situation requires, very often we hunt even in the neighbouring sectors – that is what is so great indeed about fighter aviation, that one finds new tasks on every flight and then pursues them based on one's own decision.

'Yesterday afternoon on the flight back from the Front, I stopped for a coffee at Richthofen's airfield – they always have the best cakes there. Richthofen is now constantly spied on by artists, who want to paint his likeness. Yesterday, he said he wanted to give up flying altogether and busy himself with self-portraiture, which is less dangerous and at least makes one famous just as quickly.'[68]

Move to the 2. Armee Front

Heavy fog in Flanders on the day after Böhme's visit gave JG I good cover to prepare to move south to 2. Armee's Front. Leutnant Konstantin Krefft, the Technical Officer, and advance elements took advantage of the weather to begin setting up facilities at Avesnes-le-Sec, 14 kilometres north-east of Cambrai.

They had barely unpacked when, at 0620 hours on 20 November, British forces initiated the Battle of Cambrai in an attempt to crack the stabilised front in that sector. Departing from the usual opening artillery barrage, this offensive began with 381 British tanks attacking German lines from Gonnelieu to Havrincourt, less than 15 kilometres south-west of the city. The tanks were followed out of the mist and low clouds by infantry and aircraft of British First and Third Armies, south and south-west of Cambrai.[69] The British aerial onslaught was so complete that an Airco D.H.4 of No. 57 Squadron penetrated the ground fog that morning, descended to within 300 feet of the ground and dropped two bombs on the railway station at Cour-trai[70] just after the funeral cortège for Leutnant Hans Ritter von Adam had placed his coffin on a train bound for Bavaria.

While the ground fighting raged during the next two days, JG I's men and equipment headed south under cover of bad weather to their new airfields, all within 5 kilometres of one another: Jastas 4 and 6 at Lieu- St-Amand, Jasta 10 at Iwuy, and Jasta 11 and the Geschwader staff at Avesnes-le-Sec.

Finally, on Friday, 23 November 1917, Rittmeister von Richthofen was back in combat in the repaired Albatros fighter in which he'd been shot down in July.[71] He led combined flights from JG I and Jastas 5 and 15 on a mission to clear the skies over Bourlon Wood, which had been taken by the British 51st Division, supported by low-flying fighters from Nos. 3, 46 and 64 Squadrons, RFC, and No. 68 (Australian) Squadron.[72]

Richthofen attacked two Airco D.H.5 fighters over Fontaine-Notre-Dame and chased them back to British lines. Later, he reported forcing one fighter to land and then closing in on the second: 'After the first shots, the Englishman started to glide downward, but then fell into the south-east corner of Bourlon Wood ...' Although the second D.H.5 was not seen to crash, it was recorded as Richthofen's 62nd victory[73] and he later received the patch of fabric with the serial number on it.

At about the same time Lothar von Richthofen achieved his 26th victory by bringing down a Bristol F.2B near Séranvillers.[74] West of Cambrai, 19-year-old rising star Leutnant der Reserve Kurt Küppers of Jasta 6 claimed a 'Sopwith biplane' which, more likely, was one of the D.H.5s involved in the fight with Manfred von Richthofen; like Richthofen's victim, Küppers' adversary crashed within British lines, but was still recorded as a victory, his fifth.[75]

On the whole, it had been a good day for JG I, although Jasta 11 recorded two bad incidents: Leutnant Hans Joachim Wolff ground-looped while landing at Avesnes-le-Sec and was slightly injured. Leutnant Carl August von Schoenebeck, who had fought with an S.E.5 east of Cambrai and whose Alba-tros was hit, withdrew to Epinoy. Although he returned with no personal injuries or aircraft damage, Schoenebeck has been counted as the 21st victory of No. 56 Squadron's Captain Geoffrey H. Bowman.[76]

JG I completed the move to its new airfields during the next few days of wind and rain. While the Geschwader coped with the weather, fierce ground fighting resulted in the Allies' capture of Bourlon village on 24 November – and the loss of it the following day. The heavy winds were a blessing for JG I because they minimised the danger of personnel and equipment being strafed by enemy fighters or low-flying two-seaters looking for targets of opportunity. A casualty of the move was an Albatros, badly damaged when it nosed over in the mud upon the first landing at Iwuy on 25 November; the pilot, Hans Klein, was uninjured.[77]

On the same day Lothar von Richthofen wrote to his mother: 'We have moved, but at the moment I cannot tell you where – it is secret. When you read the reports: there, where the British attacks are taking place – that is where we are!'

'On the second day of our move, Manfred and I each shot down an Englishman on the new Front.

'Here there is so much to do – Manfred doesn't know whether he is coming or going. (At the moment a violent storm is beginning, and my aircraft are standing out in the open.)'[78]

The move was not a well-kept secret. Allied intelligence officers learned about it from prisoner interrogations, which, although imperfect, provided valuable clues about important German air combat units and their leaders. Even before the move was completed, British air units were informed: 'The 2nd and 11th Pursuit Flights [Jastas 2 and 11] (looked upon as "Star" units) were recently withdrawn from the Flanders Front, where they had suffered many casualties, as they were unable to make much headway on such an active Front.'[79]

The Richthofen Factor

The presence of JG I and its famous commander had a marked effect on RFC air operations during the last week of November, the commanders feeling that additional fighter escorts were necessary for their bomber units. On the 26th, for example, the first Western Front bombing raid by a dozen D.H.4s of No. 49 Squadron was scheduled to be escorted by fourteen S.E.5a fighters,[80] which was twice the number usually assigned. Bad weather probably kept the fighters from linking up with the bombers; in any case, despite JG I's 37 sorties that day, no air contacts were made between the opposing elements.[81]

In the next few days, however, increasing German low-level air activity – marked by the appearance of 'the coloured aircraft of the Richthofen "Circus"'[82] – strongly indicated that a German counter-attack was being prepared along the Cambrai Sector.

Improved weather on 29 November brought aircraft out in force on both sides and JG I's morning patrol claimed three British aircraft within fifteen minutes: an S.E.5a forced to land at 0945 hours near Wambaix by Feldwebelleutnant (Sergeant-Lieutenant) Friedrich Schubert of Jasta 6, and two fighters identified as Sopwiths brought down fifteen minutes later near Crevecoeur by Leutnants der Reserve Hans Klein and Alois Heldmann of Jasta 10.[83]

But bad news came for Manfred von Richthofen from the 4. Armee Front, where his old friend Erwin Böhme had been killed in combat. Following Böhme's 24th success that day, he was shot down by a two-seater. Awaiting him on his desk at Jasta 2 was his newly awarded Orden *Pour le Mérite*.[84]

At 0700 hours on 30 November, heavy artillery fire heralded the German counter-offensive at Cambrai. Two-seater Schutzstaffel [Protection Flight] aircraft came in low, bombing and strafing British positions. As Jasta flights followed, the danger of many aircraft operating within a confined space was seen at 1135 hours, when the Pfalz D.III of Leutnant Wilhelm Schulze[85] of Jasta 4 collided with the Albatros D.V of Leutnant der Reserve Rudolf Wendelmuth, leader of Jasta 20 and a 14-victory ace,[86] over Fontaine-Notre-Dame; both pilots perished.[87]

During the morning's fierce ground and air fighting the British 3rd Balloon Wing launched one of its tethered observation craft just behind the front line, some 10 kilometres south-west of Cambrai. The French-made 'gas bag' provided its crewman a good view of the battle area, but was a tempting target, swaying on a heavy steel cable just under the low cloud cover. Alerted to its presence, Hans Klein clambered into his Albatros and went after it.[88] At 1230 hours the balloon fell in a ribbon of flame and smoke west of Ribécourt; it was recorded as Klein's 22nd victory.[89]

In the early afternoon Manfred von Richthofen led an attack against a formation of Airco D.H.5 fighters. He stayed above the fray to observe his pilots at work and, at 1345 hours, south of Bourlon Wood, he watched a D.H.5 fall to the guns of one of his protégés, Leutnant Georg von der Osten of Jasta 11, who was credited with his fourth victory.[90]

Forty-five minutes later and a few kilometres away, the JG I flight attacked a formation of ten S.E.5a fighters over Moeuvres. Just over the front line, the Richthofen brothers and Leutnant Siegfried Gussmann charged into the RFC intruders. Manfred got behind one British fighter, fired a stream of bullets into it and sent it down on fire into a small quarry in the woods. He was credited with his 63rd victory,[91] which would be his last during 1917.

Gussmann was credited with his second victory, listed as an Airco D.H.5 sent down over Moeuvres fifteen minutes after Richthofen's victim had crashed.[92] There is no corresponding loss for that type of rotary-engined biplane, but in the heat of battle a Sopwith F.1 Camel could have been mistaken for a D.H.5, and two Camels of No. 3 Squadron went down nearby while on a low-level bombing mission between Inchy and Bourlon that after-noon.[93]

An hour later, Jasta 10's Erich Loewenhardt brought down a Sopwith Camel between Moeuvres and Bourlon Wood. It is difficult to determine who shot down which aircraft; activity over that area was intense and some aircraft seemed to disappear. Fifteen minutes later, Leutnant der Reserve Friedrich Demandt, a one-month veteran with Jasta 10, was last seen in a fight over Flesquières, south-east of Moeuvres. The 25-year-old native of Rastatt in the Grand Duchy of Baden simply never returned.[94]

Bad news was not allowed to linger. Successful combat pilots learned to 'steel' themselves to the sight of vacant chairs in the mess and to look forward to the morrow's successes or a comrade's personal achievement. In addition to Richthofen's great victory, a telegram brought good news for Hans Klein. He was to be the seventh Richthofen protégé to receive Prussia's highest bravery award, the Orden *Pour le Mérite*.[95]

As part of the Geschwader commander's system for developing promising air fighters, on 1 December, another Richthofen student, Leutnant Karl Meyer, was rotated from Jasta 11 to Jasta 4. The 22-year-old former cavalry officer[96] had been wounded in two dogfights and had two victories to his credit and it was time for him to move on. Meyer was succeeded in Jasta 11 by another ex-cavalryman and brother of a former Richthofen flying comrade, Leutnant Friedrich-Wilhelm Lübbert. Like his elder brother Eduard, a Jasta 11 member when he fell in combat on 30 March 1917, Friedrich-Wilhelm had served in the cavalry[97] and in the much admired Feldflieger-Abteilung 18. Indeed, Lübbert's Observer from that unit, Oberleutnant Hans-Helmut von Boddien, had been recruited to Jasta 11 four months earlier. Both men displayed the fighting spirit Richthofen wanted, as evident in a citation from 6. Armee's commander, General Ludwig Freiherr von Falkenhausen, after they had blown up an impor-tant bridge.[98]

A devoted student of the Rittmeister, Lübbert recalled that his mentor 'possessed all of the qualities that a successful fighter pilot must have: flies well, shoots well, sees everything, [and] always stays calm and alert when approaching the enemy.

'[But] he was absolutely opposed to unnecessary escapades in the air – he never in his life made a loop just for fun – and never followed the unhealthy impulse that cost many another good fighter pilot his life. "Slow but sure" seemed to be his motto. "I prefer to shoot down fewer [enemies] than to be shot down myself; for then I can perform no duties for the Fatherland."

'When his Staffel or Geschwader was embroiled in an aerial combat, he saw everything and everyone. He concerned himself not only with his own opponent, but at the same time watched over his pilots, whether to come to one's aid just in time or, during the critique afterwards, to tell him what he should not have done.'[99]

Strong winds, ground fog and snow showers made the training of new pilots in winter weather especially difficult. In addition to the 55 combat sorties flown on 4 December, Leutnant Siegfried Gussmann led an orientation flight on the sector for two former cavalry officers who had arrived at Jasta 11 a week earlier: Leutnant Hans Karl von Linsingen, a son of Generaloberst Alexander von Linsingen and a friend of Manfred von Richthofen's from their Kampfgeschwader 2 days, and Leutnant Traugott von Schweinitz.[100] The flight was uneventful, but all three men damaged their aircraft on landing.[101]

There was hope for success, however; on 5 December two new pilots achieved their first victories: at 1120 hours Vizefeldwebel Adam Barth of Jasta 10 brought down a Bristol F.2B north of Cambrai,[102] and at 1235 Leutnant der Reserve Egon Koepsch of Jasta 4 claimed a Sopwith F.1 Camel over Graincourt on the Bapaume–Cambrai road.[103]

British withdrawal from hard-won positions in Bourlon on 7 December ended the Battle of Cambrai. Despite worsening weather, Richthofen continued to send JG I out to patrol the Front. He ordered 39 sorties on the final day of the battle and eighteen the following day. There were no flight operations on Sunday, 9 December, because of heavy rain, but 64 sorties were launched when the weather cleared on the 10th. For all that activity JG I inflicted only one casualty – an S.E.5a south-east of Gonnelieu claimed by former Hussar Leutnant Johann Janzen[104] of Jasta 6 on 10 December – and lost two Jasta 11 aircraft. During one of the day's seven fights, Leutnant Eberhardt Mohnike[105] flew into the tail of Oberleutnant von Boddien's Albatros and knocked off the elevator. Mohnike plunged to the ground, but although his aircraft was completely demolished he emerged uninjured. Demonstrating great piloting skill, Boddien managed to get his aircraft home to Avesnes-le-Sec by throttling back the engine in order to descend gradually.[106]

Although construction and design problems with the Fokker Triplanes had been identified and were being corrected,[107] Manfred von Richthofen was casting about for a suitable replacement. The Pfalz Flugzeugwerke in Speyer am Rhein had also developed a triplane and its management invited Richthofen to consider it for use by JG I. His endorsement would have led to a sizeable contract for the company, hence the direct appeal to Germany's leading air fighter. The Pfalz Dr.I had a more powerful engine and was supposed to be able to climb faster than the Fokker Triplane.

On 12 December, during the winter lull, Richthofen went to the factory with high hopes, but returned ten days later to report that the Pfalz aircraft did not handle as well as the Fokker Dr.I, and its Siemens-Halske Sh III rotary engine did not fulfil the manufacturer's claims.[108] Until the Fokker Dr.Is with modified wings arrived, the Geschwader had to face increasing British superiority with its old Albatros and Pfalz D.III biplane fighters.

Whither the Weather?

Bitter weather provided a needed respite for airmen on both sides of the Front. But the slightest hint of mildness prompted the pilots of JG I to bundle up in heavy flight clothing and take to the air. On Wednesday, 12 December, for example, JG I flew 45 sorties and provided cover when Leutnant der Reserve Erich Just of Jasta 11 went after an observation balloon near Hermies. The 19-year-old newcomer succeeded and was credited with his first victory.[109] Three days later, Jasta 11's Hans-Georg von der Osten claimed his fifth and last victory: an S.E.5a brought down near Havrincourt.[110]

Raw, windy conditions on Tuesday, 18 December 1917 kept the Jagdgeschwader on the ground. Indeed, Manfred von Richthofen was the only JG I pilot who flew that day; he was still in Speyer, testing the Pfalz Dr.I. But his bogey-man image is discernible in the day's diary entry of Lieutenant A. G. Richardson, an officer of the 116th Siege Battery assigned as liaison to No. 21 Squadron, RFC. He recorded the destruction of an R.E.8 two-seat artillery-spotter near Zonnebeke, in JG I's former operating area on the 4. Armee Front:

'A truly ghastly thing happened this morning. An R.E.8 observing with the 286th S.B. caught fire at 3,000 feet directly over our battery position shortly after 10.00 a.m. Immediately the whole machine was enveloped in flames and was soon looping, stalling, and diving completely out of control. The observer fell or jumped out of the plane from a terrible height – landing about 100 yards away to our left; it was a terrible sight. The aircraft fell half a mile away and was completely wrecked; the pilot being burned to death ... I did not know [the crew] personally, but had the gruesome task of recovering the charred and mutilated bodies. I think their R.E.8 was pounced on by [an aircraft] of ... Richthofen's Circus, then opposite our lines, but I cannot confirm this.'[111]

In fact it was a fairly inactive time for JG I. Flight operations the following day centred on providing cover for the train bringing Kaiser Wilhelm II and his entourage for a Christmas visit to 2. Armee's Front. And, on 22 December, Geschwader aircraft patrolled the skies above Solesmes, east of Cambrai, during the Kaiser's review of his troops.

All was quiet when Manfred von Richthofen returned to the Front and that uncharacteristic peace on earth afforded an opportunity for him to spend Christmas with Lothar and their father, Major Albrecht von Richthofen.[112] The presence of the family patriarch brought a warmth that was generally missing from the front line. He was fondly referred to as the *Fliegervater* (father of the airmen) by the men of JG I, as Jasta 6 leader Hauptmann Wilhelm Reinhard recalled:

'It was a marvellous sight when Father Richthofen spent time with us in the company of his two sons. Three solid soldier figures! Father Richthofen, tall and broad-shouldered, despite his age [58] still straight as a reed, [and with] a striking profile; our Rittmeister, somewhat compact, but a powerful figure; and Lothar, slender and sinewy, a cavalry figure. And, as their outward appearance showed them to be old-line Prussian officers, their character and conduct was soldierly through and through.'[113]

Bad weather made Christmas Day 1917 a little less disagreeable on both sides of the lines; a British report noted: 'Very little work was possible owing to snow and mist.'[114]

Jagdgeschwader I scored no further victories during the lull, but did suffer two losses on 27 December. At 1435 hours, Leutnant Traugott von Schweinitz was flying over Jasta 11's airfield in the same aircraft in which he had had a minor crash three weeks earlier. Suddenly the wings collapsed and the sleek fighter plunged to the ground, where it caught fire on impact. Schweinitz was killed. Total destruction of the aircraft prevented the Geschwader's Technical Officer from determining whether the crash had been caused by the all-too-frequent Albatros wing weakness or was related to earlier damage to the aircraft.

Also that day, Jasta 10 reported that Vizefeldwebel Hecht had failed to return from his patrol.[115] In looking for targets, Hecht had drifted to the southern part of the Front and crossed the lines inadvertently. Second Lieutenants A. S. Hanna and R. A. Burnard in an Armstrong Whitworth F.K.8 reconnaissance aircraft of No. 35 Squadron[116] attacked Hecht and forced him to land at Vermand, west of St-Quentin. He made a smooth landing in his Pfalz D.III, which was assigned captured aircraft identification number G 110.[117] Apparently Vizefeldwebel Hecht confirmed for British Intelligence that Jasta 10 was now in the vicinity of St-Quentin, the unit last having been reported at Heule on the Flanders Front on 19 July.[118]

Aircraft from the third and final production batch of Fokker Triplanes[119] began to arrive at the Front in late December, but by then Manfred von Richthofen had left the Geschwader again. He and Lothar were on their way to Brest-Litovsk in Russia as guests of Prince Leopold of Bavaria, Commander in Chief of German Forces in the East. There the war was over and the Central Powers were dictating peace terms to the revolutionary government of V. I. Lenin. Manfred von Richthofen, now a victorious field commander, was among the luminaries invited to the peace conference to witness Germany's great triumph. Peace with Russia would free men and *matériel* for deployment on the Western Front and in Italy before American forces arrived to shift the balance against Germany and Austria–Hungary.

Furthermore, the Battle of Cambrai had ended favourably for Germany. As the High Command sought to conserve Western Front resources for the spring offensive, there was no urgency for JG I and its noted commander to be placed at risk during the last week of December and into the early period of 1918. Their RFC adversaries, on the other hand, could not let down their guard.

Inclement weather provided a respite for the Jagdstaffeln, but not for German reconnaissance and low-level support crews. When those two-seaters flew over 2. Armee's Front, the RFC's third-highest scoring fighter pilot at that time,[120] Captain James T. B. McCudden, accomplished the kind of stunning results that Richthofen had recorded in 'Bloody April'. McCudden shot down four German two-seaters on 23 December, three on the 28th and two on the 29th to bring his score up to 37 confirmed victories.

In reporting his latest successful combat, McCudden wryly concluded: 'E.A. not very active west of the lines.'[121]

Notes

1   Bodenschatz, K., *Jagd in Flandern*, p. 161.
2   Commissioned into Infanterie-Regiment von Winterfeldt (2. Oberschlesisches) Nr. 23 (Ref: Zickerick, W., 'Verlustliste', in von Eberhardt, W. (ed.), *Unsere Luftstreitkräfte*, p. 67), Römer reported to Jasta 10 on 22 September 1917 (Ref: Kofl 4. Armee *Tagesbefehl* Nr. 82, 23 September 1917).
3   2/AM S. Leyland and Lt M. Jones of No. 55 Squadron (Ref: RFC *Communiqué* No. 108, 11 October 1917, p. 2).

4 Kogenluft, *Nachrichtenblatt der Luftstreitkräfte*, Nr. 38, 15 November 1917, p. 397; D.H.4 A.7642 of No. 55 Squadron, 2/Lt William R. Bishop, aged 22, and Lt Douglas F. Mackintosh (who enlisted under the name of George Mathews), aged 27 (both KiA) (Ref: Hobson, C., *Airmen Died*, pp. 24, 69, 72, 257).

5 Kogenluft, op. cit., Nr. 38; RFC *Communiqués* Nos. 108, pp. 3–5, and 109, 17 October 1917, pp. 1–3.

6 Kogenluft, ibid.; N.5377 of No. 1 Squadron, RNAS, Fl-Sub-Lt Malcolm J. Watson (PoW).

7 Ibid.; RFC *Western Front Casualty List* identified no lost or damaged R.E.8 aircraft that day.

8 Ibid.; B.3577 of No. 1 Squadron, RFC, 2/Lt Martin A. Peacock (PoW).

9 No. 1 Squadron Combat Report No. 76 of 2/Lts W. W. Rogers and G. B. Moore in Nieuports B.3629 and B.1508.

10 It is possible that Moore's victim was Jasta 26 pilot Ltn.d.R Richard Wagner, aged 27, who was shot down at about that time over Zonnebeke (KiA).

11 Bodenschatz, op. cit., p. 160.

12 Jones, H. A., *War in the Air*, vol. IV, p. 206.

13 Kogenluft, op. cit.; including aircraft that got back to their own lines, the RFC recorded eighteen aircraft casualties that day (Ref: Henshaw, T., *Sky their Battlefield*, pp. 237–8).

14 Ibid.; probably Sopwith Scout A.635 of No. 66 Squadron, 2/Lt M. Newcomb (PoW).

15 RFC *Communiqué*, No. 109, p. 4.

16 No. 54 Squadron Combat Report No. 66 of Capt F. J. Morse in Sopwith Scout A.6156.

17 No. 54 Squadron *Record Book*, 13 October 1917; Sopwith Scout B.5918, 2/Lt W. W. Vick (PoW); A.7344, 2/Lt P. Ch. Norton (PoW); B.1800, 2/Lt Frederick W. Gibbes (KiA); and B.2161, 2/Lt John H. R. Salter, aged 18 (KiA).

18 Kogenluft, op. cit.

19 Letter of 26 February 1918 quoted in Zuerl, W., *Pour le Mérite-Flieger*, p. 267.

20 With Reserve-Infanterie-Regiment Nr. 210.

21 Hans Klein's service record lists his first unit assignment as Festungsflieger-Abteilung 6, which went into action as Feldfliegerabteilung 43 (Ref: Hildebrand, K., *Die Generale*, vol. II, p. 180).

22 Zuerl, op. cit., p. 268.

23 Kogenluft, op. cit., Nr. 35, 25 October 1917, p. 334.

24 Losses in RFC *Casualty List* include three F.2B aircraft from No. 22 Squadron: A.7125, 2/Lts B. B. Perry and C. H. Bartlett (both PoW); A.7247, 2/Lts Charles E. Ferguson, aged 25, and Alexander D. Lennox, aged 22 (both KiA); and A.7264, Capt Henry Patch, aged 23 (DoW) and Pte Richard Spensley (KiA).

25 No. 22 Squadron Combat Report of 2/Lt H. G. Robinson and Lt F. J. B. Hammersley in F.2B A.7230.

26 Kogenluft, op. cit., Nr. 39, 22 November 1917, p. 414.

27 Jones, op. cit., pp. 207–8.

28 Ibid., p. 208.

29 Shores, C., et al., *Above the Trenches*, p. 234.

30 No. 70 Squadron Combat Report No. 157 of Capt F. H. Laurence in Sopwith Camel B.2423.

31 No. 84 Squadron Combat Report of Capt K. M. St.C G. Leask in S.E.5a B.4874; German records show no matching casualties.

32 Kogenluft, op. cit.; No. 84 Squadron S.E.5a aircraft lost were: B.547, 2/Lt A. E. Hempel (PoW); B.560, 2/Lt F. L. Yeomans (PoW); and B.551, 2/Lt Robert B. Steele, aged 31 (PoW/DoW).

33 RFC *Communiqué* No. 111, 31 October 1917, p. 1.

34 Bodenschatz, op. cit., p. 161.

35 Fokker Dr.I 114/17.

36 Quoted in Bodenschatz, op. cit., p. 33.

37 Grosz, P., and Ferko, A. E., 'Fokker Dr.I Reappraisal', in *Air Enthusiast*, 1978, p. 22.

38 RFC *Communiqué*, No. 111, p. 3.

39 No. 1 Squadron, RNAS, Combat Report No. 86 of Fl-Cdr F. P. Minifie, DSC, in Sopwith Triplane N.5454.

40 Ref: 4. Armee notes compiled by the late Dr. Gustav Bock.

41 Kogenluft, op. cit., p. 415; Sopwith Triplane N.5455, Fl-Sub-Lt W. M. Clapperton (WiA) (Ref: Henshaw, op. cit., p. 244).

42 Bodenschatz, op. cit.

43   With Kürassier-Regiment Graf Gessler (Rheinisches) Nr. 8.

44   Kogenluft, op. cit.; there is no corresponding RFC casualty.

45   RFC *Communiqué*, No. 111, p. 5.

46   Bodenschatz, op. cit.

47   Kogenluft, op. cit., Nr. 36, 1 November 1917, p. 351; Lautenschlager died in Fokker Dr.I 113/17.

48   Fokker Dr.I 114/17 (Ref: Bodenschatz, op. cit., pp. 54–5).

49   Commissioned into Füsilier-Regiment von Gersdorff (Kurhessisches) Nr. 80 (Ref: Zickerick, op. cit., p. 26).

50   Fokker Dr.I 115/17.

51   Zuerl, op. cit., pp. 203–4; Kogenluft, op. cit., p. 355 noted the death of Gontermann by name, but made no mention of the aircraft type in which he perished.

52   Kogenluft, op. cit., Nr. 39, p. 416.

53   Fokker Dr.I 121/17.

54   Born on 5 August 1898 and commissioned into Fussartillerie-Regiment von Dieskau (Schlesisches) Nr. 6.

55   Kofl 4. Armee, *Tagesbefehl* Nr. 86, 27 September 1917, p. 1.

56   Vanoverbeke, L., *Moorsele – één dorp*, p. 165.

57   Kogenluft, op. cit., Nr. 37, 8 November 1917, p. 367.

58   Bodenschatz, op. cit., p. 162.

59   Gray, P., *Pfalz D.III*, p. 8. This *Profile* monograph quotes a German comparison of the Pfalz D.III: 'It is slower than the Albatros D.III; it is fast in a dive and is then faster than the Albatros D.V. The climbing performance of Pfalz D.III varies greatly, sometimes almost as good as the average Albatros D.V, but never better ...'

60   Kogenluft, op. cit., Nr. 42, 13 December 1917, p. 455.

61   Ibid., p. 455; no RFC losses match the German claims.

62   Fokker D.V 2642/16.

63   RFC *Communiqué* Nr. 114, 29 November 1917, p. 1.

64   According to No. 45 Squadron Record Book entry of 15 November 1917, credit was awarded to 2/Lt Peter Carpenter in Sopwith F.1 Camel B.5782; there is no matching German casualty.

65   Ibid.; Shores, op. cit., p. 284 credits Montgomery with shooting down Ltn Hans Ritter von Adam.

66   No. 29 Squadron Combat Report No. 106, Nieuport B.6800; Leach's adversary may have been Jasta 18 pilot Ltn Richard Runge, who was shot down and killed near Langemarck.

67   O'Connor, N., *Aviation Awards*, vol. I, p. 34.

68   Böhme, E., *Briefe eines deutschen Kampffliegers* , pp. 186–7.

69   RFC *Communiqué* No 115, 29 November 1917, p. 1.

70   Ibid.

71   Albatros D.V 4693/17.

72   Jones, op. cit., pp. 244–5.

73   Kogenluft, op. cit., Nr. 43, 20 December 1917, p. 469; D.H.5 A.9299 of No. 64 Squadron, Lt James A. V. Boddy, aged 22 (WiA).

74   Ibid.; most probably F.2B B.1116 of No. 11 Squadron, 2/Lts Erland D. Perney, aged 22 and Ewan J. Blackledge, aged 20 (both KiA).

75   Bodenschatz, op. cit., p. 164, and later in Kogenluft, op. cit., Nr. 48, 24 January 1918, p. 532; other D.H.5s of No. 64 Squadron brought down in that area were: A.9235, Capt A. C. St. Clair Morford (WiA); A.9295 , Lt A. A. Duffus; A.9313, Lt R. C. Hardie; A.9490, Capt H. T. Fox Russell; and A.9508, 2/Lt V. W. Thompson.

76   Shores, op. cit., p. 84.

77   Bodenschatz, op. cit., p. 164.

78   Quoted in Richthofen, K. von., *Kriegstagebuch*, pp. 142–3.

79   RFC *Periodical Summary*, No. 23, 16 November 1917, p. 7.

80   Jones, op. cit., p. 248.

81   Bodenschatz, op. cit.

82   Jones, ibid., p. 249.

83   Kogenluft, op. cit., p. 469 lists three 'Sopwiths' brought down south of Cambrai – Klein's 20th

victory and Heldmann's third – but events suggest that both pilots received separate credit for D.H.5 A.9517 of No. 68 (Australian) Squadron, Lt R. W. Howard, whose aircraft was damaged, but brought him back safely to his own airfield.

84 Zuerl, op. cit., p. 81.

85 Commissioned into Infanterie-Regiment von Wittich (3. Kurhessisches) Nr. 83, Schulze served with Jasta 4 for 14 months and was 21 years old when he died.

86 Initially assigned to Reserve Infantrie-Regiment Nr. 233, he was killed at the age of 27.

87 Bodenschatz, op. cit., pp. 57–8, 165; Kofl 6. Armee, *Wochenbericht* Nr. 2070/6472, Teil 5, 7 December 1917.

88 The balloon belonged to 41st Section, 15th Company, 3rd Balloon Wing (Ref: Bailey, et al., *Analysis of German Balloon Claims*, p. 323.

89 Kogenluft, op. cit., Nr. 43, 20 December 1917, p. 470 lists this balloon as Klein's 21st victory.

90 Ibid.; D.H.5 A.9509 of No. 24 Squadron, 2/Lt Ian D. Campbell (KiA).

91 Ibid.; S.E.5a B.644 of No. 41 Squadron, Lt Donald A. D. I. MacGregor, aged 22 (KiA).

92 Ibid.

93 B.2496, 2/Lt L. W. Timmis, and B.6336, Capt D. B. King (both PoW).

94 Kilduff, P., 'Honor Roll', in *Over the Front*, p. 367.

95 Bodenschatz, op. cit., pp. 58, 165; O'Connor, op. cit., vol. II, p. 219 lists the date of award as 4 December 1917.

96 Commissioned into Kürassier-Regiment Graf Gessler (Rheinisches) Nr. 8.

97 Both commissioned into Dragoner-Regiment König Carl I. von Rumänien (1. Hannoversches) Nr. 9.

98 See Chapter 4, Note 124.

99 Lübbert, F. W., 'Richthofen als Vorgesetzer und Kamerad', in Richthofen, M. von, *Heldenleben*, p. 311.

100 Linsingen had been commissioned into Kürassier-Regiment Königin (Pommersches) Nr. 2, and Schweinitz began his service in Husaren Regiment Graf Goetzen (2. Schlesisches) Nr. 6.

101 Bodenschatz, op. cit., p. 165; Linsingen was flying Albatros D.V 2161/17, Schweinitz was in D.V 5313/17 and Gussmann was in D.V 4628/17.

102 Recorded in Bodenschatz, op. cit., but Kogenluft, op. cit., Nr. 46, 10 February 1918, p. 496 lists 'not yet decided' for the victor of a Bristol shot down over Abancourt, north of Cambrai; most probably F.2B A.7143 of No. 11 Squadron, Sgt M. H. Everix and Lt H. Whitworth (both PoW).

103 Kogenluft, op. cit., Nr. 46, 10 February 1918, p. 496; there is no matching RFC loss.

104 Commissioned into 1. Leib-Husaren-Regiment Nr. 1.

105 Commissioned into Infanterie-Regiment von Boyen (5. Ostpreussisches) Nr. 41.

106 Bodenschatz, op. cit.

107 Grosz and Ferko, op. cit., pp. 19–21.

108 Lamberton, W., *Fighter Aircraft*, p. 158.

109 Kogenluft, op. cit., Nr. 47, 17 January 1918, p. 515.

110 Listed only in Bodenschatz, op. cit., p. 166 and not in Kogenluft, ibid.; there is no corresponding RFC casualty.

111 Quoted in Waugh, C., 'History of No. 21 Squadron', in *Cross & Cockade*, 1983, p. 316; R.E.8 B.5899, 2/Lt Frederick G. Flower, aged 23, and 2/Lt Charles W. Cameron, aged 25 (both KiA); probably the fifth victory of 24-year-old Ltn Hans Gottfried von Haebeler of Jasta 36.

112 Richthofen, M. von, op. cit., p. 199.

113 Quoted in ibid., pp. 318–20.

114 RFC *Communiqué* No 120, 2 January 1918, p. 1.

115 Bodenschatz, op. cit., pp. 60, 166.

116 Usually misidentified as '2/Lts Hanna and Burnand' because of spelling errors in both RFC *Communiqué*, ibid., and the RFC *War Diary* entry, A. S. Hanna (pilot) and R. A. Burnard (observer) flew together often as a team in No. 35 Squadron's 'C' Flight; according to the RFC *Casualty List*, on 31 March 1918, they were brought down in Armstrong Whitworth F.K.8 C.8482; Burnard (identified also as 'Burmand' and 'Burmard') was slightly wounded and both men were taken prisoner.

117 Pfalz D.III 1370/17 (Ref: Puglisi, W., 'German Aircraft Down', Part 1, in *Cross & Cockade*, 1969, p. 160).

118 RFC, *Periodical Summary*, No. 26, 31 December 1917, p. 1.

119 Designated as the series Fokker Dr.I 400–599/17 (Ref: Grosz and Ferko, op. cit., pp. 21–3).

120 As of 20 December 1917, Major William A. Bishop, VC, had achieved 47 victories, Sqn-Cdr Raymond Collishaw, DSO, 40 and Capt McCudden 27 [Ref: Shores, et al., op. cit., pp. 77, 116, 269).

121 RFC *Communiqué*, No. 120, p. 3.

CHAPTER 10
Germany's Last Big Push

MANFRED VON RICHTHOFEN HAD TIMED HIS ABSENCE FROM THE FRONT badly. Foul weather did not deter his adversaries, beginning on New Year's Day 1918 when the level of Royal Flying Corps activity required Jagdgeschwader I to respond with 34 sorties.[1] Two days later, 'despite heavy mist, air activity was brisk on both sides', noted the weekly bulletin of the German Air Force Commanding General.[2]

JG I's first verified victory of 1918 came on the afternoon of 5 January, when, in rain and fog, French observation balloons were raised opposite the 2. Armee Front. Geschwader pilots flew thirteen sorties that day, but only Leutnant Erich Loewenhardt of Jasta 10 achieved success; he shot down a balloon near Attilly, west of St-Quentin, and it was confirmed as his ninth success.[3]

JG I pilots flew as the weather allowed, but in the absence of their noted leader they seemed unable to score, although RFC units flew into their area continually and offered opportunities for combat. Oberleutnant Kurt-Bertram von Döring, again acting Geschwader commander,[4] did not provide Richthofen-type leadership; his most recent victory had been on 21 October 1917 (and he would not score again until October 1918). He had been promoted to Rittmeister [Cavalry Captain] on 28 November 1917[5] and, at the age of 28, 'the old man' may have felt that his talents were best used on the ground.

Furthermore, there was a value in conserving Germany's best fighter pilots; wherever German air combat leadership was applied at that time, it suffered grievous losses. On Sunday, 6 January, Jagdstaffel 2 – better known as Jasta Boelcke – lost its fifth commanding officer when Leutnant Walter von Bülow-Bothkamp, a 28-victory ace who had succeeded Leutnant Erwin Böhme as Staffel leader,[6] failed to return from patrol. The 23-year-old former cavalryman[7] and recipient of the Orden *Pour le Mérite*[8] was killed in a dogfight north of Ypres and had lain in an unmarked grave for almost a month before his death was confirmed.[9]

He had been succeeded by Leutnant Max Müller, at 31 the highest-scoring Bavarian fighter pilot of the war,[10] with 36 confirmed victories. Müller, the 24th *Pour le Mérite* fighter pilot,[11] went down in flames three days after taking command of Jasta Boelcke. His body was returned to his home at Rottenburg an der Laaber, for burial with military honours.[12]

The war machine was so well tuned that fighting continued without a break, irrespective of individual losses. For Jasta 11, the focal point was balloon hunting, using newly arrived Fokker Triplanes. Under clear skies on the afternoon of Sunday, 13 January, Triplanes flown by Leutnants Werner Steinhäuser and Eberhard Stapenhorst joined biplanes from Jasta 20 and headed south-west, past Cambrai and over the lines to the British 5th Brigade area, where, from their wicker basket battle stations, balloon observers had an unrestricted view of German positions.

Even at the high altitude necessary to begin their long diving attacks, the German fighters attracted anti-aircraft fire. The two Triplanes and an Albatros piloted by Leutnant Hermann Stutz of Jasta 20 plunged through intense fire, directing their bullets at a balloon raised near Heudicourt. Within minutes the gas bag was set on fire and the crew went overboard, parachuting to safety. As the three fighters turned away towards their own lines, ground fire hit Stapenhorst's Triplane and the 22-year-old ex-cavalryman[13] had to land within British lines. He was taken prisoner and his machine, assigned captured aircraft identification number G 125, provided British intelligence specialists with their first look at a Fokker Triplane intact.[14] Previously, they had examined only salvaged instruments and the engine from Werner Voss' wreck.[15] Leutnant Stutz claimed the balloon, but it was awarded to Steinhäuser, a one-time field artillery officer[16] who already had one balloon to his credit.[17]

On the morning of 18 January Jastas 6 and 10 were on patrol in mist and rainstorms halfway between Cambrai and St-Quentin when they spotted and attacked a formation of British single-seaters and two-seaters within German lines. Leutnant Erich Loewenhardt of Jasta 10 claimed to have sent down a two-seater near Le Catelet and was credited with his tenth victory – but there is no corresponding RFC loss recorded. Minutes later, a pilot new to Jasta 6, Leutnant Otto von Breiten-Landenberg, fought with a Sopwith Camel over British lines to the south-west and reported sending it down near Hargicourt; later and without independent confirmation, he was credited with his fifth victory.[18] RFC casualty information suggests that the aircraft claimed by Breiten-Landenberg was a Sopwith F.1 Camel from No. 54 Squadron flown by Lieutenant William G. Ivamy, who was wounded. Two months later, Ivamy would fall to JG I again: as the 66th victory of Manfred von Richthofen (as noted in Chapter 1 of this book).

On this day, however, Ivamy's commanding officer, Major R. Stuart Maxwell, MC, achieved the tangible victory. Over the town of Beaurevoir, a German fighter attacked Maxwell, who reported that he 'turned underneath path of E.A.'s dive and E.A. [Enemy Aircraft] continued diving, followed by [Maxwell's]

Camel. After a burst at about 70 yards, E.A. turned over and right bottom wing came partly away and folded back. E.A. went down in spiral.'[19] German infantrymen near the crashed fighter[20] recovered the body of 27-year-old Flieger [Private] Helmuth Riensberg of Jasta 10.

While the Richthofen brothers were attending tests of new fighter types at Adlershof airfield outside Berlin, JG I suffered further losses and achieved no success. In mid-afternoon on 24 January, poor visibility forced Jasta 11's Leutnant Hans Karl von Linsingen to fly low along the road to Iwuy when suddenly his aircraft[21] dropped and crashed. He suffered extensive injuries and was rushed to a nearby military hospital. Linsingen had already survived a bad crash during a night bombing mission while he was with Kampfgeschwader 2 in May 1917 and had been in hospital for two months. The Jasta 11 incident aggravated old injuries and he spent the next nine months recuperating. Following convalescence, he was posted to Jasta 59.[22]

Less fortunate was Jasta 10's Vizefeldwebel Adam Barth who was with three comrades during a morning patrol south-west of Cambrai on 30 January when a lone S.E.5a boldly attacked them. Their adversary was Captain James T. B. McCudden of No. 56 Squadron, whose courage, skill and cool methodology was equal to Richthofen's. McCudden reported later: 'I dived and secured a firing position behind and below an Albatros scout and fired a short burst from both guns at 50 yards' range, when pieces of what looked like three-ply fell off the E.A., who turned to the left and went down in a vertical dive emitting smoke, absolutely out of control ...'[23] McCudden's 20-year-old victim fell near Anneux, within German lines; he was the RFC ace's 45th victory.

Preparations for Battle

JG I's recent performance had been imperfect, but it had shown the potential effectiveness of grouping fighter units into a Wing to counter numerically superior squadrons of the RFC. So two additional fighter Wings were formed on 2 February 1918 in preparation for the spring offensive.[24] As with JG I, the new units were built on the leadership of two successful, strong-willed veterans[25]:

Jagdgeschwader II (comprising Jastas 12, 13, 15 and 19) was formed in the 7. Armee sector under the command of Hauptmann Adolf Ritter von Tutschek. A recipient of the highest bravery awards of his native Bavaria and of Prussia – Knight [Ritter] of the Military Max-Joseph Order and the Pour le Mérite – Tutschek had survived severe wounds and had a passion for air fighting.

JG III (Jastas 2, 26, 27 and 36) was established in the 4. Armee under Hauptmann Bruno Loerzer's leadership. He had joined the aviation service in the early months of the war and had progressed from aerial reconnaissance to prototypical fighter units and then to Jagdstaffeln. His 20th victory had gained him the *Pour le Mérite*.

Manfred von Richthofen's return to the Front complemented the new fighter organisation. Added to the other fighter Wing leaders, the presence of the first Jagdgeschwader commander, now deployed in support of the 2. Armee, would show a unity of force at key points on the Western Front.

The mist that covered JG I's airfields on Sunday, 3 February, was pierced by an incident decidedly *déjà vu*. Leutnant Hans Joachim Wolff of Jasta 11 was flying north to Avesnes-le-Sec when the leading edge and ribs of the top wing of his Fokker Triplane collapsed. He made a successful emergency landing at Villers-Outréaux,[26] but the wing failure in a new aircraft[27] raised fresh doubts about the Fokker Triplanes with only about six weeks to go before the long-awaited offensive was to begin.

Richthofen knew that his men had to have supreme confidence in their own ability and the soundness of their aircraft. There could be no room for doubt. They had to believe that they were 20th-century reincarnations of the Teutonic Knights, fully equipped and glorying in the thrill of the fight, even against overwhelming odds. In the weeks ahead, one of his greatest challenges would be to have the Geschwader perform as an organised fighting force. Group effort would have to be paramount for German airmen to triumph over the air combat strength of Britain, France and – soon enough – the United States of America.

Richthofen was keenly devoted to what he felt was his mission in life, and his views about aerial combat were highly regarded in German aviation circles. His adversaries, however, took a different view of his public pronouncements, as noted in a Royal Flying Corps report of the time: 'A good deal of propaganda work is being carried out in the German Army in order to maintain a good feeling between the infantry and the air service. Rittmeister von Richthofen's book *Der rote Kampfflieger* has been extensively circulated. (In this book Richthofen gives vain-glorious accounts of his career as an airman.).'[28]

In February, JG I's glory was meagre, indeed. On the 16th, Jasta 6 leader Wilhelm Reinhard shot down his eighth opponent, a Bristol F.2B.[29] But next day an S.E.5a evened the score by wounding Leutnant Friedrich-Wilhelm Lübbert of Jasta 11 in a midday fight south of Cambrai. It is very probable that Lübbert's sleek-looking Albatros was the 'Pfalz [sic] scout with red nose' brought down by No. 40 Squadron,[30] the unit that had caused the demise of his elder brother Eduard, Jasta 11's first casualty.[31]

On 19 February Richthofen suffered a great blow when his friend and former pupil Hans Klein, leader of Jasta 10, was wounded during a fight. One bullet caused a flesh wound to Klein's right arm, and another smashed the index finger of his right hand,[32] which made further flying difficult.

JG I sank into another non-productive period for the rest of the month as bad weather again hampered flying on 2. Armee's Front. Under low cloud on Friday, 1 March, a flight of Jasta 11 Fokker Triplanes encountered a formation of Sopwith F.1 Camels south of Cambrai, but could not manoeuvre into a suitable attack position; they sustained two casualties and scored no victories. As he later described it, Lieutenant George C. Cuthbertson, MC, of No. 54 Squadron, 'was going over on Special Reconnaissance at 9,000 ft. Four triplanes approached the formation about 1,000 ft below and climbed up towards it. The Camels climbed up [heading] West owing to presence of other E.A. formations. When south of Masnières they dived on the triplanes. [I] shot at one at very close range and he appeared to go down out of control. [I] then engaged another E.A. triplane, which when shot at at close range went down in a spin.'[33]

The Geschwader recorded that two 20-year-old triplane pilots, Leutnants Eberhard Mohnike and Erich Just, were wounded during the fight with the Camels, but their aircraft were undamaged.[34] Mohnike, an East Prussian infantry veteran,[35] had to be sent to a field hospital, but Just's wounds were slight and he remained with the Staffel.

When the United States of America entered the war on 6 April 1917, the British and French were seen by the Germans as overly optimistic in their expectations of American resources. 'The columns of the enemy press were crammed with fantasy-like statements ... [that] thousands of American aircraft would flow over Germany and force it to seek peace,'[36] recalled German Air Force Commanding General von Hoeppner.

German military planners were not swayed by Allied propaganda. They recognised America's vast potential in men and *matériel*, but they felt that they still had time to achieve a decisive victory in Europe. 'In consideration of all this, [I] came to the conclusion that a quite substantial increase in enemy air power must be counted on by spring 1918 at the latest,' von Hoeppner wrote.[37] In June 1917 the *Amerikaprogramm* was approved and focused on expanding aircraft procurement and the Air Force itself in several ways, including doubling the number of Jagdstaffeln from 40 to 80, even at the expense of other military production and deployment programmes.[38]

German forces in France and Belgium were reinforced by fresh and enthusiastic troops from the Eastern Front,[39] where an armistice went into effect on 3 March 1918. Three attack plans were formulated: 'Michael', on both sides of St-Quentin; 'Mars', near Arras; and 'Georg', near Armentières. 'Michael' was selected by General Erich Ludendorff[40] and German units within the broad operational area began preparing for their roles in that plan.

JG I had begun to prepare for the coming offensive as early as 28 February. Because of increasing RFC reconnaissance patrols a forward airfield had been established at Awoingt, south-east of Cambrai. On the morning of 6 March, the first sunny day for more than a week, A Fokker Triplane patrol took off from there but was caught by higher-flying enemy fighters and Leutnant der Reserve Erich Bahr was shot down north of St-Quentin.[41]

As in previous encounters with Jasta 11, No. 54 Squadron pilots used altitude to advantage. Twenty-four-year-old Captain Abdy H. G. Fellowes was 'leading the patrol north-east from St. Quentin and about three miles behind the enemy's lines at 13,500 ft, [and the] patrol dived on three triplanes. [I] attacked the leading machine[42] and fired a long burst while on his tail. The triplane commenced to spin and then fell apparently out of control. [I] followed the machine down to 6,500 ft.'[43]

Bahr, who was the same age as his opponent and had been with Jasta 11 since late November 1917, crashed between Nauroy and Etricourt. He had not been a pilot of great achievement and his remains were not sent to his birth place of Beuthen, Silesia or even back to his airfield for a funeral; he was buried in the Soldiers' Cemetery at Etricourt.[44]

The Pace Quickens

While formations of two-engined bombers from Bombengeschwaders 1, 2, 5 and 7[45] prepared for a night raid on Paris on 8 March, a Jagdstaffel 10 flight joined Jastas 8 and 17[46] in attacking a flight of single-engined Bréguet 14B.2 bombers over German territory. During a midday battle north-east of St-Quentin on the 9th, Leutnant Heldmann of Jasta 10 destroyed two French bombers and Jasta 17 pilots were credited with bringing down two more.[47]

On the afternoon of Monday the 11th, Jasta 11 regained its old form when Lothar von Richthofen led a patrol south towards St-Quentin to begin another string of successes. He scored his 27th victory, a Bristol Fighter, north-west of St-Quentin.[48] A short distance away, 19-year-old Vizefeldwebel Edgar Scholz, who had shot down his first enemy aircraft while flying as a bomber pilot seven months earlier,[49] logged his second victory: an S.E.5a which crashed in Holnon Wood.[50]

During the weeks before the offensive, JG I members coined a word to describe their desire to meet their adversaries. Often they interjected into conversations the word 'kuk', short for 'komme und kämpfe' (come over and fight).[51] Their wish was fulfilled late on the morning of 12 March, when ten

Bristol F.2B fighters were observed south-east of JG I's airfields, heading for Le Cateau. As fast and manoeuvrable as single-seats and equipped with front and rear machine-guns, the F.2B two-seaters were tough opponents. The Richthofen brothers and Leutnant Werner Steinhäuser attacked the formation. Lothar fired at the first one and, as he turned to attack again, he reported, 'a sea of fire in the form of the British [aircraft] whizzed right by me. The observer stood up and stared into the flames. The British machine, completely on fire, made yet another turn. Both crewmen jumped out on the way down. The rest of the machine fluttered [down] in the air.'[52]

Having achieved victory No. 28, Lothar engaged a second F.2B and fired at it until it went down near Clary. Steinhäuser's opponent fell at about the same time; it was his fourth victory. The triplanes chased the Bristols south-west and then Manfred von Richthofen, flying a new, mostly red, Fokker[53] for the first time, forced down an F.2B for his 64th triumph. The crew were taken prisoner.[54]

It had been a good day for the Geschwader, and not only on 2. Armee's Front. To relieve pressure on the Flanders Front, Jastas 4 and 10 had been assigned to patrol areas of 6. Armee's Front for the previous four days. Their successes on 12 March were added to JG I's overall score: an S.E.5a brought down between La Bassée and Béthune at mid-day by Jasta 4 leader Leutnant Kurt Wüsthoff for his 28th and last victory; and, in the early evening, a balloon each at Lacouture, west of La Bassée by Leutnant Erich Loewenhardt and Leutnant der Reserve Franz Bohlein of Jasta 10.[55]

Unlucky 13

Lothar von Richthofen was superstitious and carried good-luck charms. Although he had scored his fourth and fifth victories on Friday, 13 April 1917, his belief in the supernatural was reinforced when he was shot down a month later, on Sunday, 13 May. He claimed that he was not overly concerned about flying on the morning of Wednesday, 13 March 1918, but he was given much to think about when he and more than 30 JG I comrades[56] encountered a large formation of British bombers and fighter escorts south-east of Cambrai. Just as the fight began, Lothar went down minus the top wing of his Fokker Triplane.

According to one RFC account: 'Capt [Geoffrey] F. Hughes and Capt H. Claye, [in a Bristol F.2B of] No. 62 Squadron, in a general engagement between his patrol and a very large formation of E.A. scouts, shot down one E.A. triplane, which ... went down vertically; the top plane was seen falling away in pieces. Capt Hughes was then attacked by at least six other Albatros scouts and triplanes. The observer's gun was out of action and [Hughes] found it impossible to keep the E.A. off his tail, but he finally out-distanced all the E.A. except one Fokker triplane which was handled remarkably well. Capt Hughes managed eventually to out-manoeuvre this machine by diving with the engine full on and succeeded in recrossing the lines at 3,000 ft.'[57]

One of the RFC Sopwith Camel single-seat fighter escort pilots attracted the attention of Manfred von Richthofen, who came within 20 metres of him and opened fire. Richthofen's bullets punctured the small fighter's fuel tank and wounded the pilot, who crashed within German lines near Gonnelieu. Moments later, Vizefeldwebel Scholz shot down a Camel in flames north of Vaucelles.[58] After hours of anxious waiting for firm news about Lothar – one report said that he was dead and another reported him seriously injured – Manfred flew to the crash site. There he confirmed that Lothar had been injured and taken to a hospital in Cambrai.

A Jagdgeschwader Commander Falls

Intermittent rain and low clouds curtailed most flight operations for the next two days, and on 15 March Manfred von Richthofen took the opportunity to 'recruit' a very successful fighter pilot and leader of another unit to take charge of Jasta 11 during Lothar's convalescence. Although entitled to a chauffer-driven Mercedes touring car, he preferred to remain inconspicuous and set off alone in a small car that any junior officer might have used.

It was only a 20-kilometre drive eastwards along the main road from his own facilities near Cambrai to Jasta 37's airfield outside Le Cateau. He soon found the flat field where the newly arrived Staffel was being set up and sought out Leutnant der Reserve Ernst Udet. At the age of 21, Udet had twenty victories to his credit, had qualified for the *Pour le Mérite* and was known as a brave and tenacious Staffel leader. Udet, who was overseeing the erection of new hangars in drizzling rain, recalled:

'Someone tapped me on the shoulder. I turned around. [It was] Richthofen. The rain dripped off of his peaked cap and streaked down his face.

'"Hello, Udet!" said the Rittmeister and touched the brim of his cap. "Beautiful beastly weather today, eh?"

'"I saluted him silently and looked at him. A calm, completely dominating face, [with] big, cold eyes, half covered by heavy lids. This was the man who had already brought down 67. The best of all of us.

'His car stood down below, by the side of the road; he had scrambled up the slope through the rain. I waited.

'"How many have you actually shot down now, Udet?"

'"Nineteen confirmed, one [more] reported," I replied.

'He poked his oak walking-stick into the wet leaves. "Hmmm. So twenty in all," he repeated. He glanced up and looked at me in a scrutinising way. "Then you would really be ready for us. Would you like to [join us]?"

'Would I like to? Of course I would like to. I would like it enormously. And if I had any say in the matter, I would have packed up immediately and gone back with him ...

'"Yes, indeed, Herr Rittmeister," I said. We shook hands. I watched as he – small and slender – almost elegantly scrambled down the steep slope. He climbed into his car and disappeared in the next wave of the cloak of rain.'[59]

That evening another rising star, Jasta 10's Erich Loewenhardt, used the weather to advantage and shot down a British balloon at aptly named Villers-Faucon [which translates as Falcon Town], opposite the 2. Armee's positions between Cambrai and St-Quentin. It was the 12th kill for Loewenhardt, who was becoming JG I's balloon specialist.

The day's positive developments were offset by bad news from 7. Armee's Front. Hauptmann Adolf Ritter von Tutschek, commander of Jagdgeschwader II, had been killed that morning when his Fokker Triplane[60] was shot down by an S.E.5a south of Laon. Tutschek, who was almost a year older than Richthofen, was credited with shooting down 27 enemy aircraft. His body was recovered and sent to Munich for an elaborate state funeral.[61]

Richthofen could not know that he himself had less than seven weeks to live and perhaps it is just coincidence that later that evening he handed a sealed envelope to Geschwader adjutant Karl Bodenschatz; to be opened if Richthofen did not return from a patrol, it nominated his successor.[62]

Another preparation for the uncertain future occurred the following day when Richthofen transferred Kurt Wüsthoff from command of Jasta 4 to the Geschwader staff. Wüsthoff, a 27-victory ace and *Pour le Mérite* recipient, was reported to be suffering from a nervous disorder,[63] but his successor, Hans-Georg von der Osten, remembered that: 'Leutnant Wüsthoff was a most dashing and successful fighter pilot. For this reason he had been assigned command of Jasta 4 by Richthofen, at the age of 19! ... I heard that they did not like him very much there. He was ... younger than all his pilots, and he had a very cheeky way. Apart from not being a very sympathetic man, he reported victories which he did not always check. So Richthofen relieved him as Staffel leader.'[64]

Richthofen tried to place the best-qualified men in command of his Staffeln. Just as he replaced the high-scoring Wüsthoff with the less successful von der Osten, the Geschwader commander did not appoint Ernst Udet as leader of Jasta 11 immediately. Until the new man proved himself, Leutnant Otto von Breiten-Landenberg would serve as interim leader.

It is a tribute to Richthofen's training and strength of character that, as a 25-year-old captain, he was able to juggle his administrative responsibilities, plodding through the grim routine of daily life at the Front while maintaining a high success rate as a fighter pilot. With the achievements of 16 March came the bad news that a promising new man, 21-year-old former two-seater pilot[65] Leutnant Franz Bohlein of Jasta 10, had been killed in a morning fight near Marcq.[66]

An inspection of JG I by the Commanding General of the Air Force next day was marred by the occurrence of another casualty. Werner Steinhäuser was wounded in the foot and had to land at Jasta 3's airfield.[67] The Geschwader demonstrated its readiness for the offensive late on the morning of 18 March when a large formation of RFC aircraft crossed 2. Armee's front line. JG I pilots brought down nine of them[68] without loss (see Chapter 1 of this book). Rain and low clouds curtailed most flying for the next two days and Richthofen took advantage of the lull to have the Geschwader's equipment moved by night from Avesnes-le-Sec and Lieu-St-Amand to the advance airfield at Awoingt. On the eve of the offensive all aircraft were flown to the new field and quickly put into hangar tents, ready for important events to come.

Operation 'Michael' Begins

During the early morning darkness made murkier by heavy ground fog, the German spring offensive began at 0445 hours on Thursday, 21 March 1918. For the next five hours German heavy artillery along the 70-kilometre line of 17., 2. and 18. Armees' Front pounded enemy positions.[69]

Hauptmann Wilhelm Haehnelt, Officer in Charge of Aviation for the 2. Armee, anticipated massive aerial action and designated two zones that would merit special attention. Richthofen was made responsible for Zone North, an area of about 160 square kilometres bounded by Marcoing and Vendhuille on the German side and Ytres and Longavesnes across the lines. For this operation he would lead Jagdgruppe 2 (Jastas 5 and 46) in addition to his own four Staffeln. Zone South was assigned to another Regular Army officer,[70] Oberleutnant Hermann Kohze, who had only three confirmed victories, but was a veteran fighter pilot; under Kohze's command were Jagdgruppe 9 (Jastas 3, 37, 54 and 56) and Jagdgruppe 10 (Jastas 16b and 34b).[71] In all, 150 German fighter aircraft were readied for a massive assault on their adversaries.[72]

Richthofen and Jasta 11 were scheduled to take off at 0900 hours to escort German reconnaissance aircraft and to knock out RFC aircraft and observation balloons. But the heavy mist that protected the German infantry also hampered early flight operations and kept JG I aircraft from taking off until 1230. JG I Staffeln flew 52 sorties that day, but had only Jasta 10's two balloon victories to show for their efforts: Erich Loewenhardt's 14th victory and Leutnant Fritz Friedrichs' first.[73]

The Geschwader units had no luck on 22 March, but farther south another cycle of events began. Captain Thomas S. Sharpe, DFC, led a formation of Sopwith F.1 Camels of No. 73 Squadron against five LVG two-seater reconnaissance aircraft[74] south-west of St-Quentin and was credited with shooting down two of them. German troops at the crash site of one LVG, north-east of Nesle, discovered that the dead pilot had been a man of some prominence: Leutnant Erich Pernet, the 20-year-old step-son of General Erich Ludendorff and the second of his wife's sons to die as an airman.[75] Pernet and his Observer, Leutnant Karl Westphal, members of Flieger-Abteilung 29, were buried in a nearby field. Five days later, Captain Sharpe was to be defeated by another prominent German, Manfred von Richthofen, but at least he would live to tell of it.

Meanwhile, during the morning patrol on 24 March, a new Jasta 11 pilot, Leutnant Keseling, was brought down in his Fokker Triplane by anti-aircraft fire over British Third Army's Front. He was taken prisoner and his aircraft, recovered nearly intact, was assigned captured identification number G 158.[76]

That afternoon Manfred von Richthofen logged his 67th kill. Flying a new, mostly red, Fokker Triplane,[77] he led a flight of some 25 aircraft south-east of Bapaume and overwhelmed ten S.E.5a single-seaters. Richthofen closed in like a hawk on one British fighter, as if he sensed that the pilot was a newcomer and unable to escape him or his superior force. The Rittmeister's stream of machine-gun fire caused the S.E.5 to break up and fall in pieces near Combles.[78]

In an endeavour to retard the swift advance of German ground forces, a number of RFC fighters carried small bombs. This ordnance had little effect on the German offensive and generally interfered with the effectiveness of the British aircraft carrying it. The weather was turning cloudy and windy on the afternoon of 25 March when Richthofen and five Jasta 11 aircraft attacked a flight of low-flying Sopwith F.1 Camels north-east of Albert, searching for German troops. In Richthofen's claim for his 68th victory, he reported: 'I came up to within 50 metres of one of the Englishmen and fired a few shots [that] set him on fire. The burning aircraft crashed between Contalmaison and Albert and continued to burn on the ground. The bombs that he was apparently carrying exploded some minutes later.'[79]

On Tuesday, 26 March, RFC units continued their low-bombing attacks from Bapaume south to Péronne. Major-General John M. Salmond, RFC commander in

France, ordered 'every available machine ... [to] bomb and shoot up' the area west of Bapaume.[80] A large aerial force was attacking German ground units when Richthofen and his late afternoon flight arrived in the area. Being sure to mention the latest addition to JG I's eyrie of hunters, Richthofen reported: 'Leutnant Udet and I encountered a Sopwith single-seater. At the beginning the opponent attempted to escape by skilful flying. I fired from an aircraft's length away and set him on fire. During the fall it broke into pieces, [and] the fuselage fell into the small woods at Contalmaison.' The British fighter went down at 1645 hours and was confirmed as Richthofen's 69th victory.[81]

Fifteen minutes later Richthofen and Leutnant Siegfried Gussmann attacked an R.E.8 reconnaissance two-seater and a fighter escort over the same area. Richthofen dived on the R.E.8, which because of its flexible rear machine-gun was a more dangerous opponent, and Gussmann fired at the single-seater. Both aircraft went down north-east of Albert. Richthofen's second kill of the day was recorded as his 70th triumph and Gussmann was credited with shooting down a Sopwith F.1 Camel as his fourth victory.[82]

Eager to keep pace with the advancing infantry, Richthofen arranged for JG I to move from Awoingt to Léchelle.[83] As an early combatant in the war, who recalled progress measured in metres, he considered it a real achievement for his Staffeln to move some 15 kilometres westwards.

A Memorable Day

On the morning of Wednesday, 27 March, RFC aircraft came in low to bomb and strafe German infantry at Cambrai, Bapaume, Péronne and Chaulnes[84] – and JG I was waiting for them. Four flights of Fokker Triplanes and Albatros and Pfalz biplanes headed for a large formation of Airco D.H.4 two-seater bombers and Bristol F.2B fighter escorts en route to Albert, where beleaguered Allied troops were trying to hold the line against overwhelming numbers of fresh German troops who were sweeping across the shell-pocked terrain.

At 0745 hours Richthofen led his pilots in attacking the British formation. As the fighters closed on the bombers, each pilot selected a target. The day's first victory went to Vizefeldwebel Franz Hemer, who manoeuvred his Fokker Triplane in low behind a Bristol Fighter. Staying in the safe spot behind the gunner's own rudder and tail-planes, Hemer fired short, effective bursts at the F.2B, which went down as his fifth victory.[85]

Erich Loewenhardt achieved his 15th 'kill' by following Richthofen's admonition of using short bursts of machine-gun fire against a D.H.4. The incendiary rounds hit the fuel tank and the bomber caught fire and crashed west of Miraumont.[86]

Then Richthofen set out in his red Triplane;[87] this day would see his last triple victory. He and five Jasta 11 aircraft attacked Sopwith F.1 Camels covering the bombers at higher altitude and he sent down the first one at about 0900 hours. It crashed at Aveluy and was recorded as his 71st 'kill'.[88]

Twenty minutes later, Jasta 6's Leutnant Johann Janzen brought down an R.E.8 two-seater south of Aveluy Wood for his fourth victory.[89] About an hour after that the JG I swarm caught a flight of the square-nosed S.E.5a fighters near the main road from Arras to Cambrai. Fritz Friedrichs of Jasta 10 scored his third victory by shooting down one of them within German lines.[90]

Other successes that morning were earned by Wilhelm Reinhard, whose tenth victory was an R.E.8[91] shot down at 1140 hours while patrolling between the Somme Canal and the Ancre, and Leutnant Ernst Udet, who dispatched an R.E.8 south of Albert for his 21st victory. Edgar Scholz of Jasta 11 shot down a Bristol Fighter in the same area for his sixth.[92]

Switching to another red Fokker Triplane[93] for the afternoon patrol, Richthofen led the Geschwader back to the Albert area. There, the first kill went to a newer member of Jasta 10, 21-year-old Leutnant Hans Kirschstein, who got into a protracted fight with an Armstrong Whitworth F.K.8 that was bent on bombing German infantry near Bray-sur-Somme.[94] Finally, he set fire to the two-seater and pulled away as the doomed aircraft's Observer climbed out on to the bottom wing in a futile attempt to continue to defend the aircraft. It was recorded as Kirschstein's second victory.[95] Minutes later, he claimed his third triumph, a Sopwith F.1 Camel.[96]

At 1630 hours, Richthofen led six Jasta 11 fighters against a formation of RFC two-seaters south of the winding Somme Canal near Bray and expended 100 rounds to send one down near Foucaucourt, along the main road from Amiens to St-Quentin. He identified his opponent – credited as his 72nd victory – as a Bristol F.2B, but recent research suggests that it was an Armstrong Whitworth F.K.8 of the same squadron[97] as Kirschstein's adversary of an hour earlier. Indeed, at 1645 another F.K.8 crew of that unit reported a fight with 'six Triplanes and one Albatros scout' in that area.[98]

Richthofen's third victory of the day came five minutes later. North-east of Chuignolles, a short distance away from where he had dispatched the two-seater, he claimed a Bristol Fighter. He reported later that he 'saw a Bristol Fighter attack one of my gentlemen, got behind and, from 50 metres, shot him down in flames. In so doing, I noticed that only one crewman was present. The observer's compartment was closed and I presume filled with bombs. I [had] just shot the pilot dead and the aircraft was in a stall. I fired a few more shots, then the aircraft caught fire, broke up in the air [and] the fuselage fell into a wood and continued to burn.'[99]

Richthofen's description of his 73rd combat success has long puzzled aviation historians. There is no matching loss of an F.2B that crashed and burned at that time and place. Nor is there another Armstrong Whitworth casualty in that area. A possibility advanced is that it was a Sopwith 5.F1 Dolphin single-seat fighter that was mistaken in the afternoon haze for a two-seat bomber.[100] Whatever the final historical judgement on these match-ups may be, the indisputable fact is that 27 March 1918 was a memorable day for JG I and its commander.

The German armies in the field seemed to be an unstoppable Juggernaut that would finally crush its opponents. German airmen, despite being outnumbered by superior aircraft, appeared to be on the verge of a victory that would be the stuff of future legends. Capping that triumph, Germany's greatest living air fighter had performed at a level not seen since his previous triple victory, on Friday, 13 April 1917.

One question remained: Could the German success continue?

Notes

1 Bodenschatz, K., Jagd in Flanderns, p. 166.
2 Kogenluft, Nachrichtenblatt der Luftstreitkräfte, Nr. 46, 10 January 1918, p. 490.
3 Ibid., Nr. 52, 21 February 1918, p. 602; French records confirm a balloon lost by 53ème Compagnie d'Aérostières (Ref: Bailey, F., et al., 'German Balloon claims', in Cross & Cockade', 1983, p. 223).
4 Bodenschatz, op. cit., p. 166.
5 Hildebrand, K., Die Generale, vol. I, p. 203.
6 Bolle, C., 'Jagdstaffel Boelcke', in Neumann, G. (ed.), In der Luft unbesiegt, p. 44.
7 Commissioned into Braunschweigisches Husaren-Regiment Nr. 17.
8 O'Connor, N., Aviation Awards, vol. II, p. 222.
9 Zuerl, W., Pour le Mérite-Flieger, p. 143.
10 Commissioned into the Bayerischer Flieger-Bataillon.
11 O'Connor, op. cit.
12 Zuerl, op. cit., p. 13.
13 Commissioned into Ulanen-Regiment Grossherzog Friedrich von Baden (Rheinisches) Nr. 7, as was his Staffel comrade Ltn Gisbert-Wilhelm Groos.
14 Fokker Dr.I 144/17; RFC Periodical Summary, No. 29, 27 January 1918, p. 9.
15 Fokker F.I 103/17; assigned the captured aircraft identification number G 72, it was noted briefly in the Technical Section of Periodical Summary, No. 18, 25 September 1917, p. 13.
16 Commissioned into 2. Grossherzoglich Hessisches Feldartillerie-Regiment Nr. 61.
17 Kogenluft, op. cit., Nr. 47, 24 January 1918, p. 497, credited one balloon each to Steinhäuser and Stutz; op. cit., Nr. 52, p. 602, confirmed only Steinhäuser's victory.
18 Bodenschatz, op. cit., p. 167.
19 No. 54 Squadron Combat Report No. 75 of Major R. S. Maxwell in Sopwith F.1 Camel B.6403; confirmed as his fifth victory.
20 Pfalz D.III 4059/17.
21 Pfalz D.III 4223/17.
22 Albedyll, K. von, Gedenkblätter, p. 84.
23 Quoted in Revell, A., High in the Empty Blue, p. 240.
24 Kriegsministerium (organisational manual), Teil 10, Abschnitt B, Flieger-Formationen, p. 208; Möller, H., Kampf und Sieg, p. 15.
25 Hoeppner, E. von, Deutschlands Krieg, p. 145.

26 Bodenschatz, op. cit., p. 168.

27 Fokker Dr.I 155/17.

28 RFC *Summary of Air Intelligence*, No. 4, 15 February 1918, p. 1; the parenthetical comment appears in the original report.

29 Kogenluft, op. cit., Nr. 2. Jahrgang Nr. 10, 2 May 1918, p. 180; F.2B A.7229 of No. 48 Squadron, Sgt Ernest F. Hardeman and Lt George W. Croft, aged 24 (both KiA).

30 Bodenschatz, op. cit., p. 169; No. 40 Squadron Combat Report No. 138 of 2/Lt H. C. Wade in S.E.5a C.5336.

31 See Chapter 5, Note 50.

32 Ibid., p. 169; Shores, C., et al., *Above the Trenches*, p. 295, credits Lt Robert J. Owen of No. 43 Squadron with shooting down Klein, but Owen's first victory, an Albatros D.V, went down in flames and Klein's Pfalz D.III 4283/17 did not catch fire.

33 No. 54 Squadron Combat Report No. 87 of Lt G. C. Cuthbertson in Sopwith F.1 Camel B.6293. Cuthbertson was WiA on 1 April and DoW a week later, aged 23 (Ref: Hobson, C., *Airmen Died*, pp. 132, 273).

34 Fokker Dr.I 155/17 (the same aircraft in which Hans Joachim Wolff had a mishap on 3 February) and Fokker Dr.I 110/17 (Ref: Bodenschatz, op. cit., pp. 61, 169).

35 Commissioned into Infanterie-Regiment von Boyen (5. Ostpreussisches) Nr. 41.

36 Von Hoeppner, op. cit., p. 140.

37 Ibid.

38 Ibid., p. 141.

39 Esposito, V. (ed.), *Concise History*, p. 104.

40 Jones, H. A., *War in the Air*, vol. IV, pp. 264ff.

41 Bodenschatz, op. cit., p. 170.

42 Fokker Dr.I 106/17.

43 No. 54 Squadron Combat Report No. 88 of Capt A. H. G. Fellowes in Sopwith F.1 Camel C.1568. He died five days later aged 24 (Ref: Hobson, op. cit., pp. 45, 269).

44 Haehnelt, W. (ed.), *Ehrenliste*, p. 4.

45 Kogenluft, op. cit., 2. Jg. Nr. 3, 14 March 1918, p. 26.

46 Kofl 18. Armee, *Wochenbericht*, Teil 4, 14 March 1918.

47 Kogenluft, op. cit., 2. Jg, Nr. 16, 13 June 1918, p. 233; *État Nominatif*, No. 15863, 15 April 1918, p. 4, reports only three crews missing, all from Escadrille Br107: Sergent Larroucau and Brigadier Bouet; Maréchal des Logis Connie and Soldat Cador; Caporal Michel and M.d.L Hertzog.

48 Kogenluft, op. cit.; F.2B A.7114 of No. 48 Squadron 2/Lts Herbert H. Hartley, aged 19, and John H. Robertson (both KiA).

49 Franks, N., et al., *Above the Lines*, p. 204.

50 Ibid.; S.E.5a B.54 of No. 56 Squadron, 2/Lt Douglas Woodman, aged 20 (KiA).

51 Bodenschatz, op. cit., p. 64.

52 Richthofen, L. von, 'Berichte von Manfreds Bruder' in Richthofen, M. von., *Heldenleben*, (1920), pp. 232–3; Bristol F.2B B.1247 of No. 62 Squadron, Capt Douglas S. Kennedy, MC, aged 30 and Lt Hugh G. Gill, aged 28 (both KiA).

53 Fokker Dr.I 152/17.

54 Kogenluft, op. cit.; the other three F.2Bs, all from No. 62 Squadron, were: B.1250, 2/Lt C. B. Fenton and Lt H. B. P. Boyce (both PoW); C.4824, Lt J. A. A. Ferguson and Sgt L. S. D. Long (both WiA/PoW); and B.1251, 2/Lt Leonard C. F. Clutterbuck (PoW) and 2/Lt Henry J. Sparks, MC (WiA/PoW).

55 Kofl 6. Armee, *Wochenbericht*, Nr. 1437, Teil 5, 15 March 1918; no matching casualty for Wüsthoff's claim has been found; two balloon losses were confirmed by 1st Balloon Wing (Ref: Bailey, et al., op. cit., p. 225).

56 Jones, op. cit., vol. IV, p. 289.

57 RFC *Communiqué* No. 131, 20 March 1918, p. 3.

58 Kogenluft, op. cit.; No. 73 Squadron suffered two losses in that fight: Sopwith F.1 Camel B.5590, 2/Lt James N. L. Millet (KiA), was reported 'brought down in flames by Fokker triplane', which was surely Vzfw Scholz; the other Camel, B.2523, Lt Elmer E. Heath (WiA/PoW), was most probably Richthofen's 65th victim.

59 Udet, E., *Fliegerleben*, pp. 65–6; Udet was in error about Richthofen's score; at this juncture he had 65 confirmed victories.

60 Fokker Dr.I 404/17.

61 Zuerl, op. cit., p. 447.

62 Bodenschatz, op. cit., p. 70.

63 Zuerl, op. cit.., p. 486.

64 Osten, H-G von der, *Memoirs*, p. 224

65 With Flieger-Abteilung (A) 213.

66 Bodenschatz, op. cit., p. 171.

67 Ibid., pp. 65, 171.

68 Kogenluft, op. cit., Nr. 16, p. 234.

69 Jones, op. cit., pp. 292–3.

70 Commissioned into 4. Lothringisches Feldartillerie-Regiment Nr. 70.

71 Duiven, R., *Jagdstaffel*, p. 145.

72 Bodenschatz, op. cit., pp. 72–3, 172; Bodenschatz, K., 'Das Jagdgeschwader Frhr. v.Richthofen', in Neumann, G., *In der Luft*, pp. 227–8.

73 Kogenluft, op. cit.

74 No. 73 Squadron Combat Report No. 20 of Capt T. S. Sharpe in Sopwith F.1 Camel C.1619.

75 Goodspeed, D., *Ludendorff*, pp. 250–1; Margarethe Ludendorff's eldest son, Franz Pernet, a pilot with Jagdstaffel 2, was KiA on 5 September 1917, in a fight with 2/Lt [later Air Chief Marshal Sir] Keith R. Park and 2/AM H. Lindfield of No. 48 Squadron (Ref: Shores, et al., op, cit., p. 297).

76 Fokker Dr.I 147/17 (Ref: Puglisi, W., ' German Aircraft Down', Part 1, in *Cross & Cockade*, 1969, p. 158).

77 Fokker Dr.I 477/17, which had a red top wing, cowling and fuselage upper decking.

78 Bodenschatz, op. cit., p. 74; S.E.5a C.5389, 2/Lt Wilson Porter, Jr., aged 25 (KiA); Porter's death has also been attributed to Jasta 34b's encounter with S.E.5s that day, but their records show that the fight took place near Péronne, south-east of Combles.

79 Ibid., pp. 74–5; most probably Sopwith F.1 Camel C.1562 of No. 3 Squadron, 2/Lt Donald Cameron, aged 18 (KiA).

80 Quoted in Jones, op. cit., p. 323.

81 Kogenluft, op. cit., 2. Jg, Nr. 17, 20 June 1918, p. 250; the identity of this victim is unclear, but recent research suggests that it was S.E.5a B.511 of No. 1 Squadron, 2/Lt Allan McN. Denovan, aged 23 (KiA) (Ref: Franks, N., et al., *Under the Guns*, pp. 177–9).

82 Ibid.; Richthofen's victim was R.E.8 B.742 of No. 15 Squadron, 2/Lts Vernon J. Reading, aged 22 and Matthew Leggat, aged 22 (KiA); no RFC fighter losses match Gussmann's claim.

83 Bodenschatz, op. cit., pp. 75–6, 173.

84 RFC *Communiqué* No. 133, 10 April 1918, p. 2.

85 Kogenluft, op. cit.; probably an aircraft of No. 48 Squadron, from which four crewmen were wounded in this fight, including 2/Lt Henry J. Finnemore, aged 21 (DoW) (Ref: Hobson, op. cit., pp. 45, 271).

86 Ibid.; D.H.4 A.7664 of No. 25 Squadron, 2/Lt Charles G. Pentecost (KiA) and Lt Alex Rentoul (WiA/PoW).

87 Fokker Dr.I 127/17.

88 Ibid.; Sopwith F.1 Camel C.6733 of No. 73 Squadron, Capt Thomas S. Sharpe, aged 29 (WiA/PoW).

89 In Fokker Dr.I 403/17; ibid.; R.E.8 B.7722 of No. 59 Squadron, 2/Lt W. L. Christian and Lt J. E. Hanning.

90 Ibid.; S.E.5a D.4507 of No. 40 Squadron, Lt F. C. B. Wedgwood (WiA/PoW).

91 Ibid.; B.6528 of No. 42 Squadron, Lt J. V. R. Brown and 2/Lt C. F. Warren (both WiA).

92 Ibid.; both difficult to confirm because of large numbers of two-seaters operating in the area at that time.

93 Fokker Dr.I 477/17.

94 Bowyer, C., *For Valour*, p. 108.

95 Ibid.; Armstrong Whitworth B.5773 of No. 2 Squadron, 2/Lt Alan A. McLeod [later VC] (DoW), aged 19, and Lt Arthur W. Hammond, MC (WiA).

96   Ibid.; Kirschstein's victim was most probably C.1570 of No. 3 Squadron, 2/Lt Thomas F. Rigby, aged 23 (KiA).

97   Franks, et al., op. cit., pp. 184–6; F.K.8 B.288 of No. 2 Squadron, 2/Lt Edward S. Treloar, aged 20, and Lt Kenneth P. Barford, aged 19 (both KiA); their aircraft took off at 1520 hours, which would have put it in proximity to the Jasta 11 flight at the time claimed (Ref: RFC *Western Front Casualty List*).

98   No. 2 Squadron Combat Report No. 33 of 2/Lt H. I. Pole and Lt L. C. Spence, MC, in F.K.8 C.3575.

99   Quoted in Bodenschatz, op. cit., p. 77.

100 Franks, et al., op. cit., pp. 187–8; C.4016 of No. 79 Squadron, 2/Lt George H. Harding, aged 24 (KiA).

CHAPTER 11

Grinding Down

NEW PILOTS WERE ARRIVING AT JAGDGESCHWADER I WHILE MANFRED VON Richthofen and his comrades were enjoying their great triumph of 27 March 1918. The mood of the time was recorded by Leutnant der Reserve Richard Wenzl, who had transferred from the artillery to the air service[1] and then worked his way up to what he considered the zenith of fighter aviation – JG I. After being dropped off by a re-supply lorry, he got a first glimpse of his new comrades in action that convinced him that his efforts had been worth-while:

'As I walked up an incline to the airfield just outside Léchelle, Staffel 11 took off in their triplanes. I will never forget this sight! I had already seen a lot of flying, but was astonished by the manoeuvrability and performance of these fearsome machines that rose from the earth in the last rays of the setting sun.

'At the 'field I found a few old friends, among whom was my old technical college comrade [Leutnant Hans] Weiss, with whom I had trained in Darmstadt in the summer of 1916. He had done well for himself and by then had twelve victories ...'[2]

After Richthofen returned from his flight, Wenzl went to the staff hut to report in. The Geschwader commander was looking at a map with his adjutant, Oberleutnant Karl Bodenschatz, and complaining that Léchelle was not close enough to the front line. Wenzl sensed that Richthofen 'wanted to see the enemy air activity with his own eyes and make his own judgement. When he saw me, he asserted; "Well, now we have managed for you to get here." After attending to the official formalities, he said: "You have been transferred to Staffel 11 and are joining a nice circle of comrades in which you will surely feel at home. You will fly the triplane. There are enough machines, [and] there is no lack of ammunition. Therefore you will have opportunity [to succeed]. I culti-vate just a few aces." Period. That was all.'[3]

The Officers' Mess at Léchelle was in a cramped corrugated metal Nissen Hut left by No. 15 Squadron, RFC, when it withdrew from the area a few days earlier. Wenzl recalled that 'only right at the table could one stand upright, but when we were seated there was room enough. A gramophone donated by the Albatros Company provided the necessary noise and was played frequently by [Jasta 11's Leutnant Erich] Just and even today my ears ring with the devas-

185

tating tunes of the bagpipes, which were on some of the captured British recordings. Once I settled in, some really nice evenings were spent with my beloved tunes. Then the *"Manzanareslied"* [Song of Manzanares] took hold and became the constantly requested Geschwader song ...'[4]

Udet Leads Jasta 11

After Ernst Udet's first patrol that day, Richthofen approached him and said: 'By the way, you can take over Staffel 11 tomorrow.' Udet was surprised at the informality of the assignment, but a new comrade nearby was not. Vizefeldwebel Edgar Scholtz smacked Udet on the shoulder and said: 'Man, you made a big impression on the Rittmeister!'[5]

Udet did even better next morning. He and Leutnant Siegfried Gussmann were searching for targets between Bapaume and Albert when they were jumped by Sopwith Camels. Gussmann dived with one British fighter on his tail and, as Udet followed in pursuit, a second Camel charged at him head-on. They were only 20 metres' distant, Udet recalled, and 'it looked as though our machines would ram into each other in the next few seconds. Then, in a slight movement, he leapt past me by a hair's breadth. The blast of his propwash shook me, [and] a mist of castor oil lubricant covered me.'[6]

The small, manoeuvrable Camel was the better aircraft, but Udet was the more experienced pilot and stayed close to his opponent: 'Again we pounced at each other.The thin white threads of tracer ammunition hung in the air like curtain cords. He swept by me only a hand's breadth away ... [I saw] the black numbers "8224" on the fuselage of his aircraft.'[7]

The two fighters came at each other again and again. Finally, as the Camel dipped, Udet's machine-gun fire pounded into it and sent it down into a shell-hole between Thiépval and Courcelette. There, German infantrymen ran to the wreckage, pulled out the dead pilot and gathered souvenirs from Udet's 22nd victory.[8]

Farther south, at Suzanne-sur-Somme, a former cavalryman began his string of air combat successes. Leutnant Viktor von Pressentin *genannt* von Rautter of Jasta 4 shot down a Sopwith Camel.[9] Later, Leutnant Hans Weiss of Jasta 10 claimed a Bristol F.2B as his 13th victim.[10] The day was capped when Rittmeister von Richthofen, leading the afternoon flight, attacked an Armstrong Whitworth F.K.8 and sent it down in flames by a small wood at Méricourt in the Somme valley; the big two-seater was listed as his 74th confirmed 'kill'.[11]

During the protracted morning fight, however, Second Lieutenant Cecil F. King of No. 43 Squadron[12] gained the advantage over Jasta 4 leader Hans-Georg von der Osten and sent him crashing down east of the road from Albert to Bray; he was King's eighth victim. The German pilot was severely injured and sent to hospital in Le Cateau. Later, von der Osten noted that he 'was flying a Pfalz D.III, not an Albatros, as stated by Bodenschatz[13] ... and these Pfalzes had a nasty habit of side-slipping in a turn, so it can be assumed that I crashed while slipping in a turn'.[14] He was succeeded as leader of Jasta 4 by Leutnant Johann Janzen.

A clear signal of the rising prominence of Jasta 11's new leader, 21-year-old Ernst Udet, came in the following week's Air Force activity summary, in which General von Hoeppner was quoted: 'I have expressed my and the Luftstreitkräfte's congratulations to the father of Rittmeister Freiherr von Richthofen on [the occasion of] the 100th aerial victory of both brothers. To Leutnants Udet and Loewenhardt, who in rapid succession and [with] exemplary craving for action have increased the numbers of their victories continuously, I convey my sincere appreciation. The 27th of March was again a proud day for Jagdgeschwader I.'[15]

To assure more such days, JG I continued to receive new pilots who had characteristics that the Geschwader commander liked. One arrival was Oberleutnant Walther Karjus, who might seem to have been an odd choice for a fighter pilot, but had been personally selected by Richthofen and was readily accepted by his new comrades. Karjus had transferred from an East Prussian artillery unit[16] to an aviation observation squadron, where he ranged the big guns from a two-seater. He was an outstanding combatant and had been awarded the Knight's Cross of the House Order of Hohenzollern for his valour, but had been so badly wounded in the air that his right arm had to be amputated. Even with a prosthetic device, Karjus could no longer perform aerial photography and other Observer duties, but he remained on active duty and became a pilot and then a flight instructor.

Richthofen had met him at 2. Armee's air depot and when he asked how he could fly with one hand, Karjus explained that the control column and the gun firing lever had been modified to be worked with one hand.[17] He often flew with Richthofen, and was called 'the Götz von Berchlichingen of the air',[18] the current incarnation of the medieval poet and knight who, after losing an arm in battle, continued to fight while wearing an iron claw.

April Showers

Bad weather at the end of March offered JG I a brief respite from the furious pace of combat which had followed the opening of the offensive. Clear skies on Monday, 1 April 1918 – the day the Royal Flying Corps and the Royal Naval

Air Service were amalgamated to create the Royal Air Force[19] – had the Geschwader out in force to resume the struggle for the skies over the battlefield. JG I's 106 sorties resulted in five confirmed victories: a first[20] for Leutnant der Reserve Eugen Siempelkamp of Jasta 4, sixth[21] for Jasta 6's Vizefeldwebel Franz Hemer, second and third[22] for Leutnant Hans Joachim Wolff of Jasta 11, and 11th[23] for Jasta 6 leader Wilhelm Reinhard, recently promoted to Hauptmann.

On 2 April Richthofen led the scoring. Just past midday he shot down an R.E.8 reconnaissance aircraft over the woods at Moreuil and watched as it caught fire. In his usual dispassionate manner he reported later: ' ... When the flames shot out, I was only five metres away from him. I could see the pilot and observer twisting out of their seats to escape the flames. The machine did not burn in the air, but gradually burned [on the way] down. It fell out of control to the ground, where it exploded and burned to ashes.'[24]

That afternoon, a flight of Bristol F.2Bs pounced on a Jasta 11 patrol flying along the old Roman road west of Amiens. In response, Hans Joachim Wolff shot down one of the two-seat fighters near Framerville; it was his fourth victory. Minutes later, Hans Weiss scored his 14th success, an F.2B that broke up in the air near Harbonnières.[25] F.2B Observer Sergeant Sydney Belding of No. 22 Squadron 'fired a drum into an E.A. (Triplane) which went down and ... [crashed] west of Vauvillers'. His pilot, Second Lieutenant George N. Traunweiser, verified the claim, although there is no corresponding German loss.[26] An hour later Jasta 6 recorded two kills: A Bristol F.2B by Leutnant der Reserve Paul Wenzel and an S.E.5a by Leutnant Hans Kirschstein.[27]

At the end of the day, Leutnant Wolff's victory provoked a lively discussion. The 22-year-old pilot, like Richthofen, a former Uhlan,[28] wished to emulate his idol and build a reputation distinct from that of Oberleutnant Kurt Wolff, the 33-victory ace who had been killed six months earlier. On this occasion, 'Wölffchen' [wolf cub], as he was nicknamed, became the object of verbal horseplay. Oberleutnant Peter Martin Lampel, a visiting bomber pilot, recounted the story:

'"Wölffchen", said [Richthofen]. "I saw your victory. I could make it out clearly. A Tommy came down burning and someone right behind him, sideslipping away on one wing." He winked behind [Wolff's] back.

'"No!, no!," Wölffchen denied it, of course. But then asserted: "It was my fourth, Herr Rittmeister, and at the same time the 250th [victory] of Jagdstaffel 11." He secretly hoped for a signed photograph of Richthofen. Usually that came with one's tenth victory, [as] the Rittmeister gave them out very sparingly.

'Then he thumped [Wolff] on the shoulder and his whole face broadened into a smile [and he said]: "Until your victories are out of the laughable single-digit numbers, *Wölffchen*, you will never be a *Kanone* [ace]."

'But Leutnant Wolff (who followed his master in death four weeks later) shoved both fists deep into his trousers pockets and smiled self-consciously ...

'Later on, [Wolff] came to dinner late, along with another gentleman. "You two sit in the corner," said the Rittmeister, "and eat your bowl of soup there, but with your faces toward the wall." Then, after a while [he said]: "All right, come on over here!"

'The gentlemen all got on very well together. [For a military unit] there was an unusually relaxed atmosphere at Staffel 11.'[29]

The usual round of jokes and antics was followed by a serious note. As the airmen were celebrating Richthofen's 75th triumph, adjutant Bodenschatz burst in with a telegram from Air Force Headquarters announcing that Richthofen had been awarded the Order of the Red Eagle Third Class with Crown and Swords.

'It is again a great joy for me to ... express to you my congratulations [upon attaining] this high and seldom-bestowed decoration,' the Commanding General had written. 'Wear it as a mark of the very highest recognition for what you have proved in three years of war, of the glittering successes that have crowned your flying actions and of the gratitude of your King for [all] that you have accomplished in the mighty battles of the last two weeks at the head of your Geschwader as the champion of German air power.'[30]

Usually this high honour was accorded to regimental commanders (colonels or lieutenant-colonels) and, as Richthofen was the only airman to have received the distinction for bravery in the face of the enemy[31] he blushed at the announcement. Later, however, he recognised that the award was a 'consolation' arranged by high-ranking admirers when their request for a higher honour was denied. He confided: 'I know that on my 70th victory, [General der Infanterie Erich] Ludendorff himself forwarded a nomination for me to be awarded the Oak Leaves to the *Pour le Mérite*. But the Cabinet Council members proved quite clearly that I could not receive this award because it was [to be presented] only for winning a battle. General Ludendorff, of course, said: "Richthofen has won more than a battle."'[32]

The fame and the recognition were gratifying, but Manfred von Richthofen was a realist and understood that his current success was short-term and could not last without long-term help. At that time on the battle front south of Arras, German units had 822 aircraft opposing the RAF's 645 machines; the numerical superiority, however, compensated little for the qualitative advantages of the

Allied aircraft. The situation was different on other Fronts[33] and Richthofen knew that the balance would change when Allied squadrons received projected supplies of new aircraft. To maintain German superiority, the Jagdgeschwader commanders needed new, improved fighter aircraft.

That evening Richthofen wrote to his friend at Air Force Headquarters in Berlin, Oberleutnant Fritz Falkenhayn, to inquire about the status of the new fighter aircraft he had seen at the Adlershof competition in January. In particular, Richthofen asked when he could expect delivery of the new Fokker biplane fighter, noting: 'The superiority of British single-seater and reconnaissance aircraft makes it even more perceptibly unpleasant here. The single-seaters fight coming over [at high altitude] and stay up there. One cannot even shoot at them. The two-seaters drop their bombs without our being able to reach them. Speed is the most important point. One could shoot down five to ten times as many [enemy aircraft] if one were faster. During the offensive we liked the low cloud ceiling (100 metres), because at low altitude the triplane has its advantages ... So please give me news soon about when we can count on [receiving] new machines.'[34]

On the Move Again

Meanwhile Richthofen maximised the effectiveness of his Fokker Triplanes by having them stationed close to the front line. Taking advantage of rainy weather on 5 April, he had an advance airfield set up at Harbonnières, south-west of Léchelle. From this field, south of the old Roman road from Amiens to St-Quentin and only 8 kilometres from the front line,[35] JG I units could respond more quickly and so spend more time in the air.

The next day's operations took the Geschwader close to Amiens, as Richard Wenzl recalled of his own first flight with Ernst Udet, 'who was then leader of Jasta 11 and had 22 victories. He wanted to go on leave to see his fiancée and was very keen on shooting down another opponent, which would assure him of "the Blue Max" [Pour le Mérite]. Therefore Udet went all out on this flight and flew until his fuel tank was almost completely dry, when at last he shot down a Sopwith Camel in flames [over Hamel Wood].'[36]

Udet returned to Harbonnières to refuel and Richthofen led five Triplanes against another group of Sopwith Camels over the same wooded area. Low clouds and rain were no obstacle when the Rittmeister had such otherwise favourable conditions: a position above his adversary and at relatively low altitude. The red Fokker Triplane[37] closed in and sent out a burst of bullets which hit the Sopwith's fuel tank. Later, Richthofen reported: 'The British aircraft ... started to burn after only a few shots from my guns. Then it crashed burning near the little wood north-east of Villers-Bretonneux, where it continued burning on the ground.'[38]

Sunday Victories

On Sunday, 7 April 1918, JG I reportedly accounted for four British aircraft within 35 minutes in a small area straddling the Roman road east of Amiens. Manfred von Richthofen began the day's successes by bringing down an aircraft which he identified as an 'S.E.' near Hangard at 1130 hours. Fifteen minutes later Jasta 6's Hans Kirschstein sent down a Sopwith F.1 Camel not far from the Geschwader's advanced airfield at Harbonnières. At 1150, Hans Joachim Wolff claimed an S.E.5a north of Domart-sur-la-Luce and at 1205 Richthofen claimed a SPAD north of Villers-Bretonneux.

Sorting out results of intense combat activity almost eight decades later is an exercise in map-reading and comparing combat reports and other accounts to make a judgement. In this case, information from a participant in the events offers insight.

The late Wing Commander Ronald Adam, OBE, then a Sopwith Camel pilot with 'B' Flight of No. 73 Squadron, recalled that he and his four comrades joined with 'A' and 'C' Flights that morning on an offensive patrol near Amiens, looking for 'the Richthofen Circus'. As the eighteen Camels headed east, Adam's fuel pump malfunctioned and he was busy with a hand pump when his squadron encountered Fokker Triplanes and Albatros fighters east of Villers-Brettoneux.[39]

A Triplane began the fight and three of Adam's comrades reported attacking it. The chaotic circumstances of air fighting can be seen in the Squadron records which show that two Camel pilots received full credit for shooting down the Triplane, while one was acknowledged as sending it down out of control.[40] Under the system used then, two victories and a 'partial' were awarded for destroying the same aircraft.[41]

The confusion was endemic to both sides. Richthofen claimed to have attacked an 'S.E.' (noted in quotes in his combat report), but no S.E.5s were in that area at the time; it is more likely that he tangled with a Sopwith Camel from No. 73 Squadron. Recent research makes a strong case for the aircraft flown by Second Lieutenant Albert V. Gallie,[42] which fell apart, and from which Gallie was fortunate enough to emerge unhurt, as being Richthofen's 77th victory.

Hans Kirschstein's opponent was surely Ronald Adam, who has also been suggested as Richthofen's 78th victim.[43] Adam came down some 12 kilometres north-east of the position of the aircraft claimed by Richthofen, and right where Kirschstein reported his sixth victory. According to Adam's account at the time, his fuel pump problem caused him to withdraw from the fight and: 'No sooner had I tried to turn for our lines when, with a crash behind me, a bullet entered my tank and the pressure disappeared forever. True, I had a gravity tank, which did not need pressure. I had not turned it on before, as it held only a half-hour's petrol, but on to it I turned now.

'Nothing happened and 200 ft below me I saw Richthofen's airfield [at Harbonnières], with machines and mechanics out in front of the sheds. In a last despairing effort I pointed the nose of my machine at them and pressed my useless triggers. I shouted with idiot laughter as the mechanics scattered and fell about in fear of me, and then madness seemed to take hold of me. Better dead than captured – and all the time the triplane was firing into me. Better dead than captured – and I saw a railway line below me. I put my nose straight down and ... I went into the lines. There was one colossal crash, a series of somersaults, and I came to, upside down and dangling in the machine by my feet, while my head and shoulders rested on the sleepers. The triplane had at last stopped firing.'[44]

The result of Wolff's fight, five minutes after Kirschstein's victory and just 2 kilometres from the scene of Richthofen's earlier fight, was recorded as 'forced to land' and not credited as a victory.[45] It, too, may have been a Sopwith Camel mistaken for an S.E.5a. Richthofen's second victim that day was probably another Sopwith Camel from No. 73 Squadron, but not that of Second Lieutenant Ronald Adam. Two other members of Adam's flight – Captain M. LeBlanc Smith in D.1839 and Lieutenant Albert N. Baker in D.1823 – were 'holed' during the fight but made it back to their airfield at Beauvois.[46] Moreover, Richthofen's report noted that the combat ended at a point east of Hill 104, some 2 kilometres north-east of Villers-Brettoneux and 10 kilometres from the site of Adam's crash – but right along the gauntlet of a route taken by the Camels fighting their way home. Richthofen's description of the opposing aircraft as a SPAD adds confusion to the claim, but German authorities accepted it as his 78th triumph.[47]

For a brief time Manfred von Richthofen must have felt that April 1918 would be a repetition of his and Jasta 11's success of a year earlier. Fuelling the sentiment was this citation from the Commanding General of the Air Force: 'In the 2. Armee area, despite bad weather from 3 to 7 April, 943 combat flights were carried out and 29 enemy aircraft [were] shot down, 12 of which by Jasta 11 of Jagdgeschwader I ...'[48]

Then, a combination of bad weather and a shift of emphasis to the Second German Drive of 1918 (the Lys Offensive) on the 4. and 6. Armee Fronts brought

Above: Like Manfred von Richthofen's, 21-year-old Leutnant Max Römer's Albatros had a 'wash applied over the national markings. It was most probably yellow, the Jasta 10 colour. The lightning bolt was Römer's individual insignia. Previously a pilot with Flieger-Abteilung (A) 208, Römer had been with JG I just four weeks when he was killed on 2 October 1917.

Right: Leutnant Johann Janzen joined Jagdstaffel 6 on 16 October 1917, succeeded to command of the unit and had thirteen victories to his credit when he was shot down and captured in June 1918.

Top: A sentry guards the wreckage of Fokker Triplane 113/17 in which Jasta 11 pilot Vizefeldwebel Josef Lautenschlager was killed on 29 October 1917.

Above: Leutnant Heinrich Gontermann, leader of Jasta 15, was flying Fokker Dr.I 115/17 when it crashed as a result of structural failure on 30 October 1917. Manfred and Lothar von Richthofen had problems with their triplanes the same day, but survived. Gontermann, a 39-victory ace and *Pour le Mérite* recipient, was killed.

Left: Leutnant Robert Tüxen's rotary engine familiarisation flight ended abruptly on the morning of 11 November 1917. The Jasta 6 pilot banked too steeply in Fokker D.V 2642/16 and 'slid' into a tree. He was uninjured and descended from the wreckage on a long ladder.

Above: Fokker Dr. I flown by Leutnant Robert Tüxen of Jasta 6.

Below: Pfalz D.III 1370/17 of Jasta 10 was captured undamaged when its pilot, Vizefeldwebel Hecht, was forced to land by the crew of an Armstrong Whitworth F.K.8 of No. 35 Squadron, RFC.

Above: On 13 January 1918 four-victory Leutnant Eberhardt Stapenhorst of Jasta 11 was forced to land by anti-aircraft fire. He was taken prisoner and his aircraft, Fokker Dr.I 144/17, was captured intact.

Below: Jagdstaffeln were highly mobile when Geschwader commanders such as Manfred von Richthofen wanted to move closer to the Front. Equipment and men could be packed into lorries very rapidly.

Right: Aircraft that were not flown to a Staffel's new airfield were disassembled and, like the Fokker Triplane seen here, were towed by small cars typically provided to units in the field.

Bottom right: Jasta 10 pilot Leutnant der Reserve Franz Bohlein survived a crash in Albatros D.V 4571/17. He shot down a balloon on 12 March 1918, but his luck ran out four days later when he was killed in action.

Above: Prior to joining Jasta 11 on 30 March 1918, Oberleutnant Walther Karjus (bottom row, left) was an Observer with Flieger-Abteilung (A) 207. In this Christmas 1916 photograph with his comrades, he made a joke about his prosthetic right arm by posing a toy car on it.

Below: Hauptmann Wilhelm Reinhard (left) was leader of Jasta 6 when he posed for this photograph with Leutnant Otto Mangold (second from left) and two other members of Flieger-Abteilung 33 at the airfield at Moorsele in the spring of 1918.

Top right: Jasta 11 pilots Leutnant Werner Steinhäuser (left) and Leutnant Richard Wenzl with the Fokker Dr.I in which Wenzl scored the second of his twelve victories, an S.E. 5a of No. 56 Squadron, brought down on 16 May 1918.

Bottom right: Fokker Dr.I flown by Leutnant der Reserve Robert Tüxen of Jasta 5.

Above: Rank did not matter when four Jasta 11 pilots were united in death at the Heroes' Cemetery in Cappy. A broken propeller was the centrepiece for the graves of Unteroffizier Robert Eiserbeck and Leutnants Hans Weiss, Edgar Scholz and Hans Joachim Wolff.

Below: Sergeant Otto Schmutzler of Jasta 4 wore a Heinecke parachute when he flew in his Fokker Triplane, but he had no time to deploy it when his aircraft crashed from a low altitude on 16 May 1918.

Opposite page, topleft: Leutnant Viktor von Pressentin gen. von Rautter, who scored fifteen victories while flying with Jasta 4.

Opposite page, top right: Oberleutnant Hermann Göring, the last commander of JG I, poses by a Fokker D.VII which he flew when he led the unit in action.

Opposite page, bottom: Pfalz D.XII 2603/18 was inspected at the factory in Speyer, Germany for possible use by JG I. Seen here are (from left): Oberleutnant Seibert, Jasta 10 leader Hans Klein, Pfalz company owner Alfred Everbusch, Jasta 4 leader Ernst Udet, Geschwader technical officer Konstantin Krefft, Austrian Oberleutnant Lucas and Speyer Bürgermeister Dr Moericke. JG I declined delivery of the aircraft.

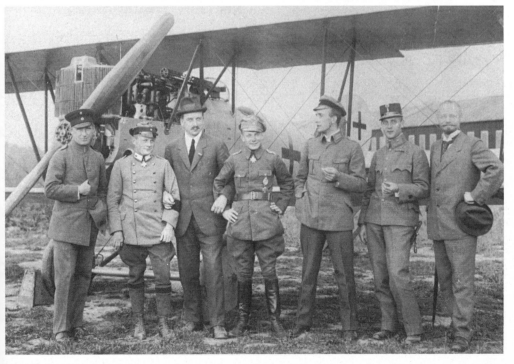

Above: Just as he had been tutored by his brother, Lothar von Richthofen (left) tried to refine Leutnant Otto Förster's air-fighting skill. Förster had scored three victories while with Jasta 15, but had no success with Jasta 11 and was posted out on 4 September 1918.

Below: The coffin of Oberleutnant Erich Lowenhardt of Jasta 10 lies in state at the airfield at Bernes. It was flanked by an Honour Guard and the bottom wings of a Fokker D.VII. The black velvet *Ordenskissen* displays the *Pour le Mérite* above his other awards.

Above: Leutnant Fritz Friedrichs of Jasta 10, seen here in a Pfalz D.IIIa, was awaiting arrival of his *Pour le Mérite* when he was killed in action on 20 July 1918.

Below: Fokker E.V aircraft supplied to Jasta 6 in early August 1918 were Germany's last hope for attaining superiority over increasing numbers of newer British- and French-built fighters.

Top left: High losses by JG I resulted in its being joined with JG III and Jagru 9 on 12 August 1918. Reflecting that combination, JG I adjutant Karl Bodenschatz (left) and Jasta 4 leader Ernst Udet planned operations with Rittmeister Carl Bolle, leader of Jasta 2.

Opposite page, bottom left: American First Lieutenant George V. Seibold of the 148th Aero Squadron claimed only one victory, but his victim was Leutnant Lothar von Richthofen, brought down on 13 August 1918.

Opposite page, bottom right: Anglo-American adversaries of JG I, Captain Tom Falcon Hazell, RAF (left), and First Lieutenant Hilbert Leigh Bair,

USAS, both members of No. 24 Squadron, RAF. The eighteenth of Hazell's 43 confirmed kills was Leutnant der Reserve Alfred Hübner of Jasta 4, killed on 14 August 1917. Hazell was brought down on 21 August 1918 by Leutnant Ernst Udet of Jasta 4, but survived. Bair's six victories included four 'assists' in RAF comrades' triumphs.

Above: Victorious German pilots examine the wreckage of a French Bréguet 14B.2 shot down on 20 August 1918.

Below: Leutnant Friedrich Noltenius (right) with his brother and a mechanic in front of Fokker D.VII 5056/18 in which he scored his first six victories.

Above: Leutnant Friedrich Noltenius's Fokker D.VII 5056/18 after he shot down a balloon on 14 September 1918. His target ignited so quickly that Noltenius had to fly through the explosion, which caused extensive damage to his aircraft.

Left: Leutnant Wolfram Freiherr von Richthofen, a cousin of JG I's first commander and a member of Jasta 11, was involved in the air action on 21 April 1918, but emerged unscathed. With his eighth victory, on 5 November 1918, he concluded his air-fighting career.

Above: JG I ordered twelve Siemens-Schuckert D.IV aircraft on 5 October 1918, much too late to regain the superior edge once held by Germany's first fighter air wing.

Right: Leutnant der Reserve Alois Heldmann of Jasta 10 was the kind of pilot Richthofen liked. A steady producer of results, Heldmann shot down fifteen aircraft from 22 July 1917 to 6 November 1918. The latter victory was one of the last recorded by JG I.

Above: Siemens-Schuckert D.III and D.IV aircraft were armed with twin Spandau machine-guns, standard equipment on German fighter aircraft following their use by the Fokker Eindecker series.

Below: Leutnant Ulrich Neckel flew this black-and-white striped Fokker D.VII during his time as last wartime leader of Jasta 6.

another relatively quiet period to 2. Armee's Front. The new drive, beginning on 9 April, General Erich Ludendorff's 53rd birthday, was Germany's last chance to split the British forces and thereby postpone Allied prospects of victory in the land war.[49]

Meanwhile, Richthofen lost his highest-scoring fighter ace when Ernst Udet developed a severe ear problem which impaired his flying ability and required specialised treatment in Germany. Udet left for home in Bavaria on 8 April and – which must surely have relieved his distress at having to leave the Front – next day he became the 35th fighter pilot to be awarded the *Orden Pour le Mérite*.[50]

Udet was succeeded as leader of Jasta 11 by another Bavarian, 25-year-old Leutnant der Reserve Hans Weiss. Another one of Richthofen's personal choices, Weiss knew the war from a ground soldier's perspective and had been an aggressive two-seater pilot. During his first assignment to a fighter unit – Jasta 41 – he shot down 12 enemy aircraft in six months. He had earned rapid promotion, a Reserve commission and Bavaria's Military Merit Cross.[51] He was ready for the long, hard struggle ahead.

Also new to Jasta 11 was Leutnant Wolfram Freiherr von Richthofen, the Rittmeister's 22-year-old cousin, a Silesian cavalry veteran[52] of the Eastern and Western Fronts. Although he did not achieve his first success in the air until June 1918, Wolfram was retained in Jasta 11 which meant that the unit had a member of the family serving with it until the end of the war. He proved to be a dedicated fighter pilot and scored eight confirmed victories.

Other pilots were transferred in and out of JG I on an almost whimsical basis – some lasted for months, others for only weeks or even days – and these cross-postings continued while JG I was moving, beginning on 8 April, from Léchelle and Harbonnières to an airfield south-east of Cappy, only 6 kilometres from the Front. Two days later, Leutnant Eugen Siempelkamp, who had been with Jasta 4 for less than a month but had one victory during his time there, was posted to Jasta 29; by the end of the war he had five victories to his credit.[53] Vizefeldwebel Kurt Delang, who had shot down two opponents while flying as a bomber pilot,[54] was sent back to the 2. Armee air depot after two barren months with Jasta 10. Similarly, Vizefeldwebel Ernst Bürggaler ended six months of undistinguished service with Jasta 10 by being returned to the air depot. Next day he was joined there by Leutnant Joachim Kortüm, whose three weeks with Jasta 10 had not been as productive as his work as a two-seater pilot; Kortüm, who had been on the staff of the Commanding General of the Air Force when he was posted to JG I, was assigned to Flieger-Abteilung (A) 242w and later became a Luftwaffe general.[55] With the exception of Wolfram von Richthofen, numerous combat successes within a short time became the key to remaining in JG I.

During a brief spell of favourable weather on 12 April, Geschwader patrols exemplified the performance expected. At 1225 hours, Leutnant Loewenhardt of Jasta 10 shot down a Sopwith Camel north-west of Péronne for his 16th victory and, an hour later, Jasta 6 leader Hauptmann Reinhard scored his 12th, a SPAD brought down north of Roye. At 1400 hours two Jasta 4 pilots – Leutnants Hübner and von Pressentin *genannt* von Rautter – shot down two SPADS over Bayonvillers for their first successes.

Jasta 11's afternoon patrol south of Albert was totally unsuccessful and resulted in the loss of Unteroffizier Robert Eiserbeck. The pilot, new to the Staffel, crashed fatally into a hill south of Méaulte; he was a month short of his 22nd birthday.

The German Air Force was losing the battle of attrition. JG I's total of four victories during the period from 8 to 14 April was meagre within the overall German claim of 58 confirmed victories.[56] And that number compared poorly with the period's total RAF claim of 69 enemy aircraft shot down and another six brought down by anti-aircraft or ground machine-gun fire,[57] despite the unfavourable weather which hampered air operations along the Front.

By this time, however, Manfred von Richthofen knew that, except in the hands of a superior pilot, the Fokker Triplane was inferior to most current British fighters. The new Fokker D.VII biplane fighters he had seen in January were still not ready for front-line service. Furthermore, Germany's top-scoring fighter pilot was beginning to feel the effects of what would later be diagnosed as combat fatigue.

A private commentary he wrote at this time indicates that Richthofen was running out of momentum while the spring offensive was grinding down to failure: ' ... The battle now taking place on all Fronts has become dreadfully serious ... Now we must arm ourselves against despair so that the enemy will not violate our country.

' ... I have been told by [people in] high places that I should give up flying, for one day it will catch up with me. [But] I would be miserable with myself if now, burdened with glory and decorations, I were to become a pensioner of my own dignity in order to save my precious life for the nation, while every poor fellow in the trenches endures his duty as I do mine.

'I am in wretched spirits after every combat. But that is surely one of the consequences of my head wound. When I put my foot on the ground again at the airfield, I go to my [room], I do not want to see anyone or hear anything. I believe that [the war] is not as the people at home imagine it, with a hurrah and a roar; it is very serious, very grim ...'[58]

Sunday Defeat

Richthofen's mental attitude was not helped by the unusually severe weather. On 19 April, strong wind, hail and snowstorms kept the skies over the Somme virtually clear of aircraft. A Jasta 6 patrol returned with no victories and a new pilot, Leutnant der Reserve Wolff, was wounded slightly and sent to a hospital in Péronne. A luckless fellow, 'Wolff III', as he was called to distinguish him from Oberleutnant Kurt Wolff and Leutnant Hans Joachim Wolff, had been wounded in a fight a week earlier.[59] This time, the combination of wounds kept him out of the air until August.

Taking advantage of calmer but cloudy skies early on the evening of the 20th, Richthofen's red Fokker[60] was at the head of five other triplanes from Jasta 11 flying south, seeking targets near the old Roman road. He was not disappointed; a flight of Sopwith F.1 Camels from No. 3 Squadron was also out, possibly looking for him.

The RAF flight leader, Captain Douglas J. Bell, MC, claimed that he engaged and shot down one of the triplanes: 'I saw one Camel in flames, and another catch fire, but [the] fire appeared to go out. The 'plane, when last seen, was absolutely out of control.'[61]

Bell witnessed the swift attack of Richthofen and Weiss, each of whom shot down a Camel at about the same time.[62] It is possible that one of the Camels was on Weiss' tail and the Rittmeister saved his comrade, because he reported: 'During the fight I observed that a triplane was [being] attacked and shot at from below by a Camel. I positioned myself behind the adversary and brought him down, burning, with only a few shots. The enemy aircraft crashed near Hamel Wood, where it burned ...'[63]

Having determined that his first victim of the day was finished, Richthofen set his sights on another from the same flight. It was to be his 80th and last victory. He noted that the second Camel 'went into a dive, pulled out and repeated this manoeuvre several times. As he did that, I came up to the closest fighting distance and fired about 50 rounds at him [until his machine] caught fire. The fuselage burned in the air, the rest of the aircraft crashed north-east of Villers-Bretonneux.'[64]

Richthofen strictly forbade all manner of stunt flying by his pilots. On the return flight home after his 80th victory, however, he modified this rule slightly. Hans Joachim Wolff recalled later that Richthofen 'went down very low so that everyone could recognise his red machine and waved to the infantrymen [in the trenches] and the columns of men [on the roads]. Everyone knew who was in the machine and all of them had seen the burning Englishmen shortly before. Enthusiastically, they all waved and flung their caps into the air.'[65]

For all his honours and decorations, meetings with the Kaiser and other national leaders, Manfred von Richthofen never lost touch with the ground troops from whence he had come. Their jubilation lifted his own spirits, if even briefly.

Next morning, Sunday, 21 April 1918, a heavy grey fog covered the airfield at Cappy, but it did not dampen the spirits of anyone in Jagdgeschwader I. There was a high level of joy, enthusiasm and excitement that this day might see the beginning of a new era. Having doubled the victory score of his mentor Oswald Boelcke, Richthofen could go on to unimaginable triumphs in the aerial arena over the battlefield.

When adjutant Bodenschatz suggested that it might be time for Richthofen to assume a new role, such as Inspector of Fighter Aviation, to make his vast experience available to all German fighter pilots, the Rittmeister laughed. He knew that well-meaning people at Air Force HQ had urged Bodenschatz to deliver that message. Richthofen responded curtly: 'A paper-shuffler? No! I am staying at the Front!'[66]

Ever the competitor, Manfred von Richthofen could not retire now. His closest German air-fighting rival had been Werner Voss, now dead after scoring 48 victories. Of the British aces, Captain James T. B. McCudden, VC, DSO and Bar, MC and Bar, MM, had 57 victories, but had been posted back to England to become an instructor.[67] Major William A. Bishop, VC, DSO, had 48 victories to his credit before he had gone home to Canada in September 1917;[68] and naval ace Flight-Commander Raymond Collishaw, DSO, DSC, had scored 40 before he, too, was sent back to Canada.[69] The RAF's other ranking fighter ace, Captain Edward Mannock, MC and Bar, had only eighteen victories and was relatively unknown at that time.[70] The leading French ace, Capitaine Georges Guynemer, had scored 54 victories at the time of his death in combat in 1917.[71] Manfred von Richthofen was the war's supreme air fighter and planned to remain at the Front. He would be faithful to his comrades until the end.

Any discussion about his future ended at about 1030 hours, when word was received from the Front that British aircraft were heading toward their sector[72] from the south. Two flights of Fokker Triplanes were soon under way, heading toward the old Roman road. The first was led by the Rittmeister's all-dark red machine,[73] accompanied by Wolfram von Richthofen, Walther Karjus, Edgar

Scholtz and Hans Joachim Wolff. The second flight was distinguishable by a mostly white-and-black-striped Triplane[74] flown by Hans Weiss.

A High Offensive Patrol (HOP) from No. 209 Squadron, RAF, was on a course that would intersect the Triplanes. Three flights of Sopwith F.1 Camels – a total of fifteen aircraft – had flown from their airfield at Bertangles, south to Hangard and then swung north toward Albert. En route three aircraft from 'B' Flight initiated the day's action,[75] as American-born flight leader Captain Oliver C. LeBoutillier reported: 'I observed two Albatros two-seaters over Le Quesnel. Lieuts. Foster, Taylor and myself fired on one ... [and then] he burst into flames and crashed at Beaucourt [-en-Santerre].'[76]

While most of 'B' Flight attended to the German reconnaissance aircraft, 'A' Flight's leader. Captain A. Roy Brown, DSC, led the rest of the squadron north toward the Somme. Fifteen minutes later, the Jasta 11 Fokker Triplanes and a flight of Albatros fighters from Jasta 5 appeared near Cérisy.

A member of 'A' Flight, Lieutenant [later Sir] Francis J. W. Mellersh, reported: 'I followed Captain Brown down on to a large formation of Fokker Triplanes and Albatros D-5s. A dogfight ensued and I managed to get on the tail of a triplane with a blue tail. I fired about 50 rounds into him when he turned and I got a long burst into him when he was turned up. The triplane then dropped his nose and went down in a vertical dive. I followed, still firing, and saw the machine crash near Cérisy.

'The other triplanes then dived on to me and I was forced to spin down to the ground and return to our lines at about 50 ft. Whilst so returning, a bright red triplane crashed quite close to me and in looking up I saw Captain Brown.'[77]

Flight Leader Brown reported that he 'dived on [a] large formation of 15 – 20 Albatros Scouts D-5 and Fokker Triplanes, two of which got on my tail and I got out. Went back again and dived on a pure red triplane which was firing on Lieut. May. I got a long burst into him and he went down vertical and was observed to crash by Lieut. Mellersh and Lieut. May. I fired on two more but did not get them.'[78]

The object of the red triplane's attention, Sopwith F.1 Camel pilot Second Lieutenant Wilfrid R. May, reported that after he had fired at one of the German fighters, 'I then went down and was attacked by a Red triplane which chased me over the lines low to the ground. While he was on my tail, Captain Brown attacked it and shot it down. I observed it crash into the ground.'[79]

Hans Joachim Wolff was probably the last German to see the red Fokker Triplane in that fight. Later, he wrote to Lothar von Richthofen: 'While Oberleutnant Karjus and I fought against two or three Camels, suddenly I saw the red machine near me, as he fired at a Camel that first went into a spin, [and] then slipped away in a steep dive toward the west. This fight took place on the other side over the heights of Hamelet.

'We had a rather strong east wind and Herr Rittmeister had not taken that into account. As I now had clear air around me, I got closer to a Camel and shot it down.[80] As the Camel went down, I looked over at Herr Rittmeister and saw that he was at extremely low altitude over the Somme near Corbie, right behind an Englishman. I ... wondered why Herr Rittmeister was following an opponent so far on the other side.'[81]

Machine-gun fire from another British fighter drew Wolff's attention away from watching his leader descend into the Somme valley in pursuit of victory No. 81. By the time Wolff had slipped away from his latest adversary, the red triplane was out of sight. Wolff circled the area for a time and then returned to Cappy where, he noted: 'Reports had already come in. A red triplane had landed smoothly north-west of Corbie. That another Englishman could have shot him down from behind was out of the question – that I would vouch for – And, indeed, should Herr Rittmeister have shot down the Englishman, then he would have pulled up, but he suddenly went into a steep dive and landed smoothly. Now there were two possibilities. The machine was overstressed, a valve let go, and the engine quit. The other possibility [is] that shots fired from the ground hit the engine ...'[82]

Hauptmann Wilhelm Reinhard, about to become the new commander of Jagdgeschgwader I, directed Richard Wenzl, Walther Karjus and Wolfram von Richthofen to fly back to the area of the fight. They made a thorough search that afternoon, but found no trace of the red Fokker Triplane or its pilot.

Major Wilhelm Haehnelt, Officer in Charge of Aviation for the 2. Armee, arrived at Cappy airfield next day to inform the Geschwader of the certainty that their commander had disappeared behind the British lines.[83] He and they could only await official notification from their adversaries.

Who Shot Down the Red Baron?

Historical records are clear that Rittmeister Manfred Freiherr von Richthofen was killed at about 1145 hours (German Time) while chasing Second Lieutenant Wilfrid May's Sopwith F.1 Camel along the Somme valley from Sailly-le-Sec to Vaux-sur-Somme. Richthofen had been hit by one bullet which, entering his chest, passed through his heart and killed him.[84]

The question as to who it was that fired the fatal bullet has been debated for nearly as long as Richthofen has been dead. His last pursuer, Captain A. Roy

Brown, DSC, claimed to have 'got a long burst into him ... [after which] he went down vertical ...'[85]

Adding to reports by Lieutenants Mellersh and May, Captain LeBoutillier stated: 'Engaged Fokker Triplane over Cérisy (about 15 – 20 machines) and fired about 100 rounds at a mottled coloured one but did not get him. Also fired on red triplane which was shot down by Captain Brown and crashed [on] our side of the lines.'[86]

The 53rd Australian Field Artillery Battery, 5th Division, and the 24th Machine-gun Company also claimed to have shot down Manfred von Richthofen. Their accounts do not mention Brown's aircraft, only May's Sopwith being pursued by Richthofen's Fokker: 'Then one machine dived for the ground with the other on its tail. They darted about wildly for a few seconds. Suddenly the pursued aeroplane, evidently in desperate straits, made straight for the crest of the ridge near the [field artillery] battery. The gunners saw that it was a British machine and its pursuer a red triplane. The Lewis [machine-] gun on the nearer flank of the battery made ready to fire, but at first could not, for the machines were flying so low and close that the fleeing Camel blocked the gunner's sight of the German. The German was firing rapid short bursts at the Camel just beyond his nose, and the hunted British machine was making no attempt to turn and fire ...

'The machines flew on right overhead, careless of everything else except their own duel and ... at about a hundred yards' range, the artillery, Lewis gunners and other machine-guns from Australian camps on or behind the crest opened fire on the German. Splinters of wood were seen to fly off immediately near his engine. The triplane wobbled, side-banked up, swerved across to the left in a half-circle, obviously crippled, then dived straight into the ground about 400 yards away and was smashed to pieces ...'[87]

Richthofen's triplane came down in a fertiliser beet field at Vaux-sur-Somme, along the road from Corbie to Bray. From scrutiny of photographs of the wreckage, it appears that the undercarriage collapsed; the abrupt stop caused the pilot's face to strike the machine-gun butts, thereby breaking Richthofen's top front teeth. By that time, however, the Rittmeister was life-less. Australian soldiers removed his body from the Triplane wreckage, which was picked over thoroughly by hordes of souvenir hunters.[88]

What was left of the wreckage was retrieved and listed as G/5th Brigade/2, the second enemy aircraft captured within 5th Brigade's area.[89] Richthofen's body was taken to an airfield at Poulainville used by No. 3 Squadron, Australian Flying Corps. This R.E.8 unit had a connection with the day's events because some of its two-seaters had engaged JG I Fokker Triplanes at about the time of Richthofen's death.[90]

At Poulainville, Richthofen's corpse underwent a 'surface examination'[91] by British and Australian medical officers. The doctors did not perform a complete autopsy, but pushed a steel rod through the wound to determine the trajectory of the fatal bullet. They reported that it had entered at about the ninth rib on the right side, just behind the arm, and exited near the left nipple.[92] The finding made a compelling case in favour of the ground gunners, many of whom were firing at a low angle as opposed to the pursuing Sopwith Camel, which would have been firing from a high angle, above the German pilot.

At this late date, no one can prove conclusively just who shot down the red Fokker Triplane at Vaux-sur-Somme. Most probably an Australian gunner, possibly even a rifleman, fired the shot that ended the life and career – but not the legend – of the Red Baron. Even if the .303 calibre bullet had been recovered, it would have been of a type common to rifles and machine-guns used by British troops. And so the controversy continues.

On the afternoon of 22 April 1918, Manfred von Richthofen's remains were buried in accordance with military custom. An honour guard of officers from No. 3 Squadron, AFC, accompanied the Crossley tender which bore the coffin to the cemetery at nearby Bertangles, which was also home to No. 209 Squadron. All the putative 'victors' were represented.

Notes

1   Wenzl enlisted in the 5. Badisches Feldartillerie-Regiment Nr. 76 at the beginning of the war, gained a Reserve commission, transferred to the air service in December 1915 and flew with Flieger-Abteilung (A) 236, Kampfeinsitzer-Kommando Ost and Jagdstaffel 31 before being selected for Jasta 11 (Ref: Wenzl, R., *Richthofen-Flieger*, pp. 5–6).

2   Ibid., p. 16; at that time Ltn Hans Weiss had ten confirmed victories and was on the eve of scoring his first 'kill' with JG I (Ref: Franks, N., et al., *Above the Lines*, pp. 227–8).

3   Ibid., pp. 16–17.

4   Ibid., p. 17; an allusion to the old Spanish town and castle near Madrid.

5   Udet, E., *Fliegerleben*, p. 70.

6   Ibid., p. 76.

7   Ibid.

8   Kogenluft, *Nachrichtenblatt der Luftstreitkräfte*, 2. Jg, Nr. 17, 20 June 1918, p. 251; Sopwith F.1 Camel C.8224 of No. 43 Squadron, 2/Lt Charles R. Maasdorp (KiA).

9   Ibid.; C.8259 of No. 43 Squadron, 2/Lt Robert J. Owen (PoW); Ltn Viktor von Pressentin was descended from the Counts of Rautter-Willkamm in East Prussia, and to continue that lineage his family affixed to its own name '*genannt*' (known as) von Rautter'; Viktor was commissioned into 3. Garde-Ulanen-Regiment at Potsdam (Ref: Perthes, J., *Ehrentafel*, p. 185).

10   Ibid.; F.2B B.1273 of No. 48 Squadron, 2/Lts E. R. Stock and W. D. Davidson.

11   Ibid.; F.K.8 C.8444 of No. 82 Squadron, Lts Joseph B. Taylor, aged 19, and Eric Betley, aged 21 (both KiA).

12   RAF *Communiqué* No. 133, 10 April 1918, p. 3.

13   Bodenschatz, K., *Jagd in Flanderns*, p. 174 lists von der Osten has having been shot down while flying Albatros D.V 4566/17.

14   Osten, H-G. von der, *Memoirs*, p. 225.

15   Kogenluft, op. cit., 2. Jg, Nr. 6, 4 April 1917, pp. 80–1.

16 3. Ostpresussisches Feldartillerie-Regiment Nr. 79.

17 Quoted in Lampel, P., 'Als Gast beim Rittmeister Frhr. v. Richthofen' in Neumann, G. (ed.), *In der Luft*, p. 215.

18 Zuerl, W., *Pour le Mérite-Flieger*, p. 546; Götz von Berchlichingen is also remembered for scatalogical contributions to German literature that Oblt Karjus' comrades would have known.

19 Cole, C. (ed.), *Royal Air Force 1918*, p. 9.

20 Kogenluft, op. cit., 2. Jg, Nr. 19, 6 June 1918, p. 280; Sopwith F.1 Camel D.1811 of No. 65 Squadron, 2/Lt Percy R. Cann, aged 28 (DoW).

21 Ibid.; Airco D.H.4 A.7401 of No. 57 Squadron, 2/Lt Edgar Whitfield, aged 22, and Lt William C. F. N. Hart (both KiA).

22 Ibid., erroneously listed as his first and second victories; Airco D.H.4 A.7872 of No. 57 Squadron, 2/Lt Douglas P. Trollip, aged 23, and Lt James D. Moses, age 28 (both KiA), and S.E.5a B.174 of No. 84 Squadron, 2/Lt Stanley H. Winkley, aged 25 (KiA).

23 Ibid.; S.E.5a C.6351 of No. 56 Squadron, 2/Lt Barclay McPherson (PoW).

24 Public Record Office, Air 1/686/21/13/2250 XC15183; R.E.8 A.3868 of No. 52 Squadron, 2/Lts Ernest D. Jones, aged 19, and Robert F. Newton (both KiA).

25 Kogenluft, op. cit.; No. 22 Squadron's only loss in that fight was F.2B A.7286, 2/Lt Frederick Williams and 2/Lt Roland Critchley, aged 23 (both KiA).

26 No. 22 Squadron Combat Report of 2/Lt G. N. Traunweiser and Sgt S. Belding in F.2B C.4808; Traunweiser and Belding, aged 32, were KiA in the same F.2B on 15 April (Ref: Hobson, C., *Airmen Died*, pp. 116, 197); RFC *Western Front Casualty List* notes that they were 'fired at and brought down by British Infantry near Haverskerkue'.

27 Kogenluft, op. cit.; F.2B C.4862 of No. 11 Squadron, 2/Lt Arthur R. Knowles, aged 24, and Lt Ernest A. Matthews, aged 22 (both KiA), and S.E.5a B.8236 of No. 60 Squadron, 2/Lt Edgar W. Christie (KiA).

28 Commissioned into Schleswig-Holsteinisches Ulanen-Regiment Nr. 15.

29 Lampel, op. cit., pp. 222–3.

30 Quoted in Bodenschatz, op. cit., pp. 79, 176, which states that the telegram was received on 6 April.

31 O'Connor, N., *Aviation Awards*, vol. II, p. 18, which also notes that princes of the Prussian royal house – e. g., the combat pilot Prince Friedrich Karl – received the Red Eagle Order as a matter of course in their youth.

32 Quoted in Lampel, op. cit., p. 216.

33 Jones, H. A., *War in the Air*, vol. IV, pp. 349–50.

34 Letter from the Falkenhayn family via a private source.

35 Bodenschatz, op. cit., p. 176.

36 Wenzl, op. cit., p. 18; Udet's opponent was probably Sopwith F.1 Camel C.8247 of No. 43 Squadron, Lt Henry S. Lewis, aged 24 (KiA).

37 Fokker Dr.I 127/17.

38 PRO, op. cit.; Sopwith F.1 Camel D.6491 of No. 46 Squadron, Capt Sydney P. Smith, aged 21 (KiA).

39 Adam, R., 'Episodes', in *Cross & Cockade*, 1972, pp. 263–7.

40 No. 73 Squadron Combat Reports Nos. 30, 31 and 29 of Sopwith F.1 Camels flown by 2/Lt O. M. Baldwin (D.1832), Capt G. A. H. Pidcock (D.1812) and 2/Lt R. R. Rowe (D.1855).

41 Most probably Uffz Paul Fricke, aged 26, who was killed that day at Framerville-Rainecourt, north-east of Harbonnières.

42 Sopwith F.1 Camel D.6550 (Ref: Franks, N., et al., *Under the Guns*, pp. 196–7).

43 Ibid., pp. 198–9.

44 Quoted from Ronald Adam's PoW Diary (unpubd.); 2/Lt R. G. H. Adam crash-landed in Sopwith F.1 D.6554 and became PoW.

45 Kogenluft, op. cit.

46 Adam's account lists Hesdingneul as No. 73 Squadron's airfield; RAF *War Diary* of 2 April 1918 shows it as being at Beauvois.

47 Kogenluft, op. cit.

48 Ibid., 2. Jg, Nr. 8, 18 April 1918, p. 110.

49 Esposito, V. (ed.), *Concise History*, p. 111.

50 O'Connor, op. cit., p. 220.

51 Zuerl, op. cit., pp. 544–5.

52 Commissioned into Husaren-Regiment von Schill (1. Schlesisches) Nr. 4; after the war Wolfram von Richthofen earned a doctorate in engineering, joined the early Luftwaffe, became commander of the Condor Legion during the Spanish Civil War, and was appointed Field Marshal on 16 February 1943. He commanded Luftflotte 2 and earned the Knight's Cross of the Iron Cross (17 May 1940) and Oakleaves (17 July 1941). He was operated on for a brain tumour on 27 October 1944 and never returned to service. He was taken into custody by American forces at the end of the war, and died of a cerebral haemorrhage on 12 June 1945 aged 49 (Ref: Hildebrand, K., *Die Generale*, vol. III, pp. 107–8).

53 Franks, op. cit., p. 210.

54 Kilduff, P., *Germany's First Air Force*, pp. 71–4.

55 He was promoted Generalmajor on 1 March 1944 and was on the staff of Luftflotte 4 at the end of the war. General Kortüm was interned by the Americans until 3 March 1947; he died on 21 October 1982 (Ref: Hildebrand, op. cit., vol. II, pp. 219–20).

56 Kogenluft, op. cit., Nr. 19, pp. 280–1.

57 RAF *Communiqué* No. 2, 18 April 1918, p. 1.

58 Richthofen, M. von, *Rote Kampfflieger*, pp. 203–4.

59 Bodenschatz, op. cit., pp. 177, 178.

60 Fokker Dr.I 425/17.

61 No. 3 Squadron Combat Report No. 55 of Capt D. J. Bell, MC, in Sopwith F.1 Camel C.6730; there is no corresponding German loss.

62 Most probably Weiss' opponent was 2/Lt George R. Riley, aged 19, in Sopwith F.1 Camel D.6475, who was 'wounded in combat' but returned to his own airfield (Ref: RAF *Western Front Casualty List*).

63 PRO, op. cit., p. 44; Sopwith Camel D.6439 of No. 3 Squadron, Maj Richard Raymond-Barker, MC, aged 24 (KiA).

64 Quoted in Bodenschatz, op. cit., p. 179; Sopwith Camel B.7393 of No 3 Squadron, 2/Lt David G. Lewis, aged 19 (PoW).

65 Wolff, 'H., Briefe des Leutnants Hans Joachim Wolff', in Richthofen, M. von, *Heldenleben*, pp. 260.

66 Bodenschatz, op. cit., p. 81.

67 Shores, C., et al., *Above the Trenches*, pp. 268–70; this source notes that Major McCudden's score at the time of his death was 57 victories.

68 Ibid., pp. 76–7; this source notes that Lt-Col Bishop finished the war with 72 victories.

69 Ibid., pp. 114–16; this source notes that Lt-Col Collishaw finished the war with 60 victories.

70 Ibid, pp. 255–7; this source notes that Major Mannock had 61 victories at the time of his death.

71 Joly, P., *Victory List, Guynemer*, pp. 187–8.

72 Bodenschatz, op. cit., p. 81.

73 Fokker Dr.I 425/17.

74 Fokker Dr.I 545/17.

75 Jones, op. cit., p. 389.

76 No. 209 Squadron Combat Report of Capt O. C. LeBoutillier in Sopwith F.1 Camel B.3338; recorded as his fifth victory, the crew were most likely Uffz Karl Meyer, aged 28, and Ltn d. R. August Wurm, aged 27, of Flieger-Abteilung 33 (both KiA).

77 No. 209 Squadron Combat Report of Lt F. J. W. Mellersh in Sopwith F.1 Camel B.6257; there is no German casualty corresponding to this claim.

78 No. 209 Squadron Combat Report of Capt A. R. Brown, DSC, in Sopwith F.1 Camel B.7270.

79 No. 209 Squadron Combat Report of 2/Lt W. R. May in Sopwith F.1 Camel D.3326.

80 Most probably Sopwith F.1 Camel B.7245 of No 209 Squadron, Lt W. J. Mackenzie (WiA).

81 Wolff, op. cit., p. 261.

82 Ibid., p. 262.

83 Ibid.

84 O'Dwyer, W., 'Post-Mortem', in *Cross & Cockade*, 1969, pp. 302–4.

85 Brown's Combat Report., op. cit.
86 LeBoutillier's Combat Report, op. cit.
87 Cutlack, F., *Official History*, vol. VIII, (1933), p. 251.
88 Carisella, P. and Ryan, J., *Who Killed the Red Baron?*, pp. 133–149 chronicles in detail items pilfered from von Richthofen's clothing and aircraft.
89 Puglisi, W., 'German Aircraft Down', Part 2, in *Cross & Cockade*. 1969, p. 278.
90 Cutlack, op. cit., vol. VIII, pp. 249–50.
91 McGuire, R. (ed.), 'Documents', in *Over the Front*, 1987, p. 172.
92 O'Dwyer, op. cit., p. 301.

CHAPTER 12

Too Few, Too Late

DESPITE A CAREFUL SEARCH OF THE AREA AROUND VAUX-SUR-SOMME, AND numerous radio messages – including one in uncoded text to a British post[1] – inquiring about Manfred von Richthofen, for almost two days there was no definite word as to the fate of JG I's commander. Frustration gave way to a reckless urge for vengeance late on the morning of Monday, 22 April 1918, when Leutnant Hans Weiss led a Jagdstaffel 11 flight southwards, over the Somme.

The Fokker Triplanes had just passed the old Roman road when they were attacked by a flight of Sopwith F.1 Camels.[2] The fight drifted southwards toward Hangard and within two minutes a couple of Camels went down, one credited to Hans Weiss and the other to Hans Joachim Wolff.[3] It was a bittersweet victory for Wolff, whose courage and determination had made him Richthofen's favourite;[4] on the 24th he and the Rittmeister were scheduled to begin a short leave to go hunting in the Black Forest[5] and Wolff would have enjoyed recounting how his ninth victim had gone down in flames and smashed into the ground to die as befitted a warrior.

Instead of preparing for the great honour and joy of a brief sojourn with his idol, on the 23rd, Wolff read and re-read the official notification from the office of the Commanding General of the Air Force. It repeated the Reuters News Service report that the manner of Richthofen's descent 'gave the appearance that he fell victim to fire of an Australian battery gunner whose Lewis machine-gun was directed at him ...'[6]

Honours for the Fallen Hero

Lothar von Richthofen was still convalescing from his wounds of 13 March when he received news of Manfred's death. Although he was to remain in the Aaper Wald Clinic in Düsseldorf until July, he was named commanding officer of Jagdstaffel 11, as of 24 April.[7] This formal assignment ensured that the Rittmeister's old unit would have 'a' Richthofen in charge, if even nominally.

Meanwhile the Air Force Commanding General's office continued to honour the late Rittmeister's requests for certain pilots and, on 23 April, another old friend of his arrived at Jasta 11. Oberleutnant Erich-Rüdiger von Wedel, who had been in the same Uhlan regiment at the outbreak of war,[8] would live up to expectations and attain 13 confirmed victories.[9]

There was a general feeling of melancholy following Richthofen's death, but the sadness did not hinder the Geschwader's mission. At 0655 hours Jasta 4's Leutnant Egon Koepsch shot down an S.E.5a[10] north of Sailly-Laurette and, 95 minutes later, the new leader of Jasta 10, Erich Loewenhardt, forced down a 'Bristol Fighter' near Morisel.[11] A short time after that two Jasta 10 pilots – Offizierstellvertreter Paul Aue and Gefreiter Alfons Nitsche – who were listed as missing the day before, returned to Cappy in fine fettle, having run out of petrol and landed to refuel at other airfields.[12] The overnight hospitality extended to them, as was common practice, was made all the warmer given their link to Richthofen's Geschwader.

As expected, on 27 April Hauptmann Wilhelm Reinhard was appointed commander of Jagdgeschwader I. While the Commanding General and others in the Air Force took some cold comfort that Richthofen had not fallen to the guns of an enemy airman, Reinhard applied his venerated leader's own Nietzschean view to the Geschwader's great loss at Vaux-sur-Somme. He wrote to his mother: 'It seems now to have been proved definitely that he has fallen due to ground machine-gun [fire], a lucky hit in the heart area. For an airman that is no beautiful death. One would prefer to fall in aerial combat.'[13]

Reinhard's new duties required him to remain at the Front, so he was unable to attend the memorial service for Richthofen in Berlin. Jasta 6's chief administrative officer Hauptmann Kurt Lischke, and Leutnant Hans Joachim Wolff of Jasta 11 were dispatched to escort Lothar von Richthofen from Düsseldorf.[14]

The service was held on Thursday, 2 May 1918, the 26th anniversary of Manfred's birth. The ceremonies became a national outpouring of grief, intended to comfort family and comrades. At a reception later, maternal instinct drew Kunigunde Freifrau von Richthofen to a distraught young airman wearing an Uhlan's jacket similar to Manfred's. Hans Joachim Wolff poured out his grief to his hero's mother: 'I, especially, am deeply unhappy. I have lost more in him than the great model, which he was to all of us. I loved him like a father. I was happy when I could be with him ...'[15]

Try as she might, Freifrau von Richthofen could not console Wolff and help him expiate his guilt; he could not shake off the feeling that he should have 'covered' her son during that fateful dive after a Sopwith Camel. For reasons far different from those of Reinhard, Wolff's devotion was such that he could not accept the theory that ground fire had brought down his commander; no doubt he wished that he himself had been hit by the 'lucky shot'.

More Falling Stars

Just before the memorial service began in Berlin, one of Manfred von Richthofen's most promising protégés faced his own entry to Valhalla. Back in the same ominous area over the Somme that had claimed the Rittmeister, Hans Weiss' Fokker Triplane[16] was targeted by a Sopwith F.1 Camel flown by another Canadian member of No. 209 Squadron.

In his combat report, Lieutenant Merril S. Taylor described his battle with 'Fokker Triplanes [of] various colours' and how he achieved his fifth victory: 'Flight dived on eight E.A. at 7,000 ft. just south of Cérisy and I got a burst into several at close range. One white E.A., into which I got a burst at about 20 yards' range, turned over on its back and went out of control. This machine was seen to crash by Lieut. [Oliver N.] Redgate, also confirmed by [No.] 65 Squadron.'[17]

A comrade wrote to Weiss' father: 'About 1:30 p.m. he and his Staffel took off to fight against the enemy. Just as they arrived at the Front, our pilots were attacked by a squadron of British single-seaters. In the course of the combat it was observed in the air and from the ground that your son's aircraft suddenly went down, first in a glide, then plunging and finally at 1.45 p.m., north of Méricourt-sur-Somme, it crashed into the ground. I drove there immediately, but there was nothing more to be done. A shot in the forehead and a shot in the left [side of his body] through his pilot's badge ended his life ... With admirable valour he followed in death his beloved master, Rittmeister Manfred Freiherr von Richthofen, and thereby sealed his love, his devotion and his admiration for [Richthofen] ...'[18]

Late that afternoon, Vizefeldwebel Edgar Scholz crashed while taking off from Cappy. His aircraft[19] stalled and plunged to the ground, killing the 20-year-old, 6-victory pilot immediately. An hour later the Geschwader's adjutant Bodenschatz was notified that Scholz had been promoted to Leutnant der Reserve.

On 3 May JG I pilots settled scores for their recent losses by bringing down seven enemy aircraft in nine hours. Among the successes were first-time victories for former cavalry officers Leutnant der Reserve Moritz-Waldemar Bretschneider-Bodemer of Jasta 6 and Leutnant Joachim von Winterfeld of Jasta 4.[20] During a midday fight over Proyart, Jasta 10's Offizierstellvertreter Paul Aue shot down a Bristol Fighter[21] which was reconnoitring the area near Villers-Bretonneux, but fire from an RAF fighter wounded Leutnant der Reserve Erich Just and put him out of action for two months.

At 1400 hours on 4 May, a double funeral was held for Edgar Scholz and Hans Weiss. Scholz was buried under an officer's grave marker next to Weiss at the

Heroes' Cemetery in Cappy.[22] Weiss had been nominated for the *Pour le Mérite*, an unusual circumstance for a pilot with fewer than 20 victories, but normally Prussia's highest decoration for bravery was not awarded posthumously.[23] Hence, during final honours for the 16-victory ace, the velvet pillow (*Ordenskissen*) placed on his coffin bore the Knight's Cross with Swords of the Royal House Order of Hohenzollern as his highest military award. Next to it was the Bavarian Military Merit Cross he had earned when he was an enlisted pilot.

The sad occasion enabled Leutnant der Reserve Kurt Wüsthoff to depart quietly from the Geschwader. A *Pour le Mérite* recipient, one-time Staffel leader and 27-victory ace aged 20, Wüsthoff had progressed too rapidly and was on the verge of nervous collapse.[24] A brief rest period had done little good and now he was being placed 'at the disposal of the Inspectorate of Aviation'.[25] Five weeks later he became temporary leader of Jasta 15, and shortly afterwards was shot down and taken prisoner.[26]

Later that day Leutnant Bretschneider-Bodemer of Jasta 6 achieved his second victory, Leutnant Alois Heldmann of Jasta 10 his fifth and the new leader of Jasta 6, Leutnant Johann Janzen, also his fifth.[27]

A period of bad weather gave way to clear skies on the 9th, when Janzen's Staffel and Jasta 4 were attacked by Sopwith F.1 Camels from No. 209 Squadron. The Fokker Triplanes had 'blue tails and yellow wings', according to Captain Oliver G. LeBoutillier, who reported: 'When over Bray, [I] observed nine triplanes going south; they turned west and I opened fire at long range. I got on the tail of one and fired about 150 rounds at 50 yards' range. He then went down vertical and I later observed him crashed ...'[28]

LeBoutillier's victim was Janzen, who was lucky enough to walk away from the crash. His JG I comrades brought down four enemy aircraft that day and eleven the next. In the Richthofen style of leadership, Geschwader commander Reinhard was with his men, scoring his 14th victory on Thursday[29] and watching as newcomers demonstrated their skill on the evening of Friday, 10 May. On the latter occasion, JG I attacked a flight of Sopwith F.1 Camels and sent six of them down. Among the victories were the second for Leutnants Joachim von Winterfeld and Paul Wenzel, and the first for Oberleutnant Erich-Rüdiger von Wedel.[30]

The day's performance was singled out for praise by the Commanding General of the Air Force: 'I heartily congratulate the Geschwader for its successes of 10 May, among which was the 300th aerial victory of the Geschwader ...'[31]

The Commanding General's office had carefully noted and publicly recognised Jasta 11's 100th and 200th victories[32] under Manfred von Richthofen's leadership. It is interesting that after his death, official recognition was accorded to JG I's 300th victory, linked to Oberleutnant Erich Loewenhardt's 20th victory, a key factor in qualifying for the *Orden Pour le Mérite*. The recognition was based on faulty mathematics, however; from 5 July 1917 to 10 May 1918, JG I had attained 320 confirmed victories (71 by Jasta 4, 84 by Jasta 6, 59 by Jasta 10, 77 by Jasta 11, in addition to Rittmeister von Richthofen's 28 victories and Hauptmann Reinhard's first success as JG I commander, which were not included in individual Staffel tallies).[33] In any event, publicising the victory total was intended to inspire other German fighter units to emulate JG I.

On 11 May, Hauptmann Reinhard had the difficult task of posting out of the Geschwader a pilot who had been hand-picked by Richthofen. Oberleutnant Walther Karjus was brave and audacious, but during his six weeks with Jasta 11 the one-handed pilot had not been able to shoot down a single enemy aircraft. He went to 2. Armee's air depot,[34] and was assigned to Schlachtstaffel 17, where his courage was put to good use as a low-level ground support pilot.[35]

Even successful Jasta 11 pilots were pressured to achieve more victories or quit. Leutnant der Reserve Richard Wenzl recalled: 'Various things, obviously caused by [my] superiors, nurtured my wish to ... be transferred to Staffel 6. At that time Staffel 6 was led by [Leutnant Johann] Janzen, with whom I had a good understanding and who would gladly have me ... and so on the 15th [of May] I went to Staffel 6. I kept my living quarters at Staffel 11 with [Leutnant Werner] Steinhäuser. That helped me get over the parting, which in effect meant that I flew with another Staffel and ate my meals in another tent.

'It must be clarified ... [that] the other Staffeln were not worse [performers]. In terms of pilot replacements, unlike Staffel 11, they did not always have the advantage of being regarded with the power and high status of the old Richthofen Staffel. But the transitory quality of the Staffeln changed very quickly. At that time, Staffel 6 was indisputably at the top. [Leutnant Hans] Kirschstein blossomed into a big ace there.'[36]

Living up to his reputation, on 15 May Kirschstein shot down three British aircraft in six hours – a Sopwith F.1 Camel and two Bristol F.2Bs – as part of JG I's overall total of 13 confirmed victories that day.[37] Among these successes were first-time victories by two Fokker Triplane pilots who had been with Jasta 4 since December. They demonstrated the 'equalising' effect of the new aviation branch: one was a Silesian nobleman from an estate that has long since been dispersed by war and enforced social change, the other a Thuringian metalsmith who made the iron gate that still stands at the entrance to his home town of Zimmritz. Leutnant Heinz Count von Gluszewski-Kliwicki, a 22-year-old former cavalryman[38] who gravitated to the cavalry of the air, shot down a Bréguet 14B.2 bomber[39] north of Harbonnières at 1115 hours. Less than an hour later, Sergeant Otto Schmutzler, aged 28, shot down a Sopwith F.1 Camel south of the Roman road outside Villers-Bretonneux. The Sopwiths were escorting Airco D.H.4 bombers to Rosières-en-Santerre;[40] three fighters went down in that encounter, all from No. 209 Squadron,[41] the unit that claimed victory in Manfred von Richthofen's last fight.

A Tale of Three Triplanes

In clear skies during the afternoon and evening of Thursday, 16 May, Hans Kirschstein added his 12th and 13th victories to his list. The day was marked by significant loss, however, beginning with the morning patrol. The body of Hans Joachim Wolff was found in the wreckage of his Fokker Triplane near Lamotte Ferme not far from the Roman road and some 10 kilometres from where Richthofen's triplane had come down. Bullet wounds just below his heart were the sole evidence of his demise. Two days later he was buried at Cappy beside Hans Weiss and Edgar Scholz.[42]

That afternoon, Leutnant Fedor Hübner of Jasta 4 went down behind British lines in a fight with old opponents, as described: 'Capt [Stearne] T. Edwards, No. 209 Squadron, attacked one of a large formation of E.A. triplanes. Lieut M. S. Taylor of the same squadron also attacked the same E.A. together with Lieut W. R. May and forced it to land just west of Corbie.'[43] Hübner was taken prisoner and his aircraft was assigned the captured aircraft identification number G/5th Brigade/8.[44]

In the evening Jasta 4 Triplanes attacked a flight of Airco D.H.4 bombers of No. 205 Squadron which were approaching the German line near the Roman road, en route to Chaulnes. The two-seaters were escorted by S.E.5a fighters, which fended off the German fighters. According to a British report: 'Lt [Horace] D. Barton, No. 24 Squadron, engaged one of several E.A. triplanes which were diving on a D.H.4; he fired 50 rounds into one E.A., which went down in a spin and crashed south of Proyart.'[45] Jasta 4's Sergeant Otto Schmutzler plunged to the ground at about that time. He died later that evening at Field Hospital 303 in Rosières.[46]

The brief life and harsh death of Otto Schmutzler followed the trail of many pilots who fell in combat. The details of his death and simple funeral were sent to his family by his brother, Sergeant Friedrich Schmutzler. A year younger than Otto, Fritz was in the field with the reserve element of Thüringisches Fussartillerie-Regiment Nr. 18 when he learned of his brother's death. Two days later he wrote home:

'This morning the Staffel sent a driver to bring me ... information that Otto would be buried this afternoon at 3 o'clock at the Cemetery of Honour near the [former] "British Field Hospital" in Rosières ...

'I got dressed immediately and went there to see my dear brother one last time. Something unspeakably grievous had happened to me, but it is what one has to suffer through in this sad existence. I would shake his hand for the last time when he was already dead ... Then I received a sturdy oak coffin in which he would be laid to rest. Now I had to wait until 3 o'clock, when the Division chaplain came. I introduced myself to the chaplain as Otto's brother, then [he] preached a beautiful sermon, which I did not comprehend at all, as I was too upset.

'From Jagdstaffel 4 there were two cars [bearing] five officers, the First Sergeant [Otto's best friend, a man named Albrecht], another Sergeant and two of Otto's mechanics, a non-commissioned officer and a non-rated man. They brought with them a cross-shaped oak grave marker, as well as the propeller from Otto's triplane and two large wreaths. At the time I could do nothing further, as the grave had not yet been prepared; there were no men free to do it and I had to get under way. I wrote my last greetings and wishes on a piece of parchment paper and put it into a flask that went to the grave ...

'Now I will describe brief circumstances of what happened ... Shortly before, Otto had shot down an opponent and on the 15th of May he was awarded the Iron Cross 1st Class. As [the Staffel] returned from a flight at quite low altitude, suddenly he crashed. Leutnant von Rautter told me he must have had engine failure, as Otto had been so proficient and reliable [as a pilot], he could not think of any other cause. In general, the officers praised Otto highly ...'[47]

The Great German Hope

F.E.2b bombers of No. 101 Squadron struck German aviation and other facilities at Rosières, Méharicourt, Harbonnières, Bray and Cappy on the night of 16/17 May 1918.[48] In the morning French Bréguet bombers followed up with a raid on the airfield at Cappy. Only slight damage was caused by the bombers, and the second flight of marauders met with stiff opposition. Leutnant Hans Kirschstein led the defence and scored his 14th victory. Minutes later, Jasta 6 leader Janzen shot down another Bréguet.[49]

In the afternoon JG I had an unexpected 'guest' after Second Lieutenant Victor W. Hillyard of No. 70 Squadron was shot down in the area.[50] The British pilot recalled: 'I came down near Bray-sur-Somme. I was roughly handled [by German troops] until an officer came, who dispersed the crowd and took me and another officer in a car to the Richthofen Staffel at Cappy, [and] then to another officer who spoke English quite well. He had lived in England quite a time. He gave me some tea, no milk, black bread toasted with jam, but no butter. Then I went to Péronne by light railway at 5.00 p.m. Then on a Red Cross train to Cambrai.'[51]

Less fortunate was Lieutenant Edward Harrison of No. 24 Squadron, who was shot down in flames by Ltn Viktor von Pressentin *gennant* von Rautter of Jasta 4. Harrison's aircraft crashed near Foucacourt, on the north side of the Roman road, where he was found dead; he was buried at Soyécourt, less than 3 kilometres away.[52] Rautter's 11th victim was from the squadron that his Staffel had fought just prior to Otto Schmutzler's death.

JG I's four 'kills' of 18 May included an Airco D.H.4 shot down by Rautter. This encounter also had a link to Jasta 4's loss two days earlier, as the German nobleman's 12th victim was a two-seat bomber from No. 205 Squadron, RAF.[53]

Later that day, Leutnant Richard Wenzl flew his Fokker Triplane to 2. Armee's air depot to exchange it for a new Fokker D.VII, the steel-framed fighter with which the High Command had great hopes of regaining air superiority. The first production models were delivered with a 160hp Mercedes engine; other, more powerful engines were supplied later. In the words of one eminent aviation historian: 'The Fokker D.VII was the best fighter of the war.'[54] The sentiment was reinforced by Wenzl, who wrote later: 'Although the new biplane was not as manoeuvrable as the triplane, it was still a bit faster; it climbed slower at lower altitude, [but] better at higher altitude; above all, as we had to work at higher altitudes, it was fitted with a super-compressed engine ...'[55]

Hauptmann Wilhelm Reinhard also cultivated protégés and one of the first was Vizefeldwebel Willi Gabriel, a two-seater pilot who had shot down an aircraft while flying with Schlachtstaffel 15.[56] Reinhard was impressed by the 24-year-old enlisted pilot and pulled strings to have him transferred. Upon his arrival on 19 May, however, the Kommandeur told the new pilot in blunt terms what he expected. That evening, Gabriel proved his worth by shooting down an Airco D.H.9 two-seat bomber north of Marcelcave.[57] He ended the war with 11 confirmed victories.

In contrast to the pressure that Reinhard reportedly put on other pilots, including transferring out 'non-producers', the treatment of Leutnant Wolfram von Richthofen is interesting. The cousin of Manfred and Lothar, Wolfram had arrived at Jasta 11 on 4 April and would not score his first victory until 4 June. Apart from attending a one-week course at the Armourers' School in August,

Wolfram von Richthofen must have had other qualities in order to be retained in Jasta 11. Eventually, he shot down eight enemy aircraft.

Move to the 7. Armee Front

In mid-month, JG I was ordered to prepare for transfer south to 7. Armee's Front to help support the forthcoming Aisne Offensive. On the Geschwader's last day at Cappy, 20 May, Ernst Udet returned from convalescent leave and was eager to fly the new Fokker D.VII in combat. That afternoon he and Reinhard drove around the area to discuss Udet's future role as leader of Jasta 4. At length they came to the Heroes' Cemetery and stopped to pay final tribute to comrades who would remain behind. They stood thoughtfully in front of the graves of Robert Eiserbeck, Hans Weiss, Edgar Scholz and Hans Joachim Wolff. Then both officers saluted. Reinhard's only comment was: 'They had a good death.'[58]

A tribute to JG I's deployment to Cappy came in a telegram from Air Force Commanding General von Hoeppner, announcing that, at the Kaiser's direction, henceforth the unit would bear the name Jagdgeschwader Freiherr von Richthofen Nr I.[59]

JG I pilots were given a week's rest at Guise, east of St-Quentin and well behind German lines, while their new airfield was being prepared at Puisieux Farm, outside Laon. To avoid alerting their adversaries to the new assignment prior to the offensive, the four Staffeln were spread out: Jasta 4, now commanded by Udet, was based at a field north-west of Guise, along the road to Longchamps; Jasta 6 was on the outskirts of Guise; Jasta 10 along the road to Etreux; and Jasta 11 at Lamotte Farm, south-west of the city. The quiet time was used for orientation flights in the new Fokker D.VIIs, and the pilots were ordered to fly only over German rear areas.

The Allied forces were taken by surprise when the German offensive began at 0200 hours on Monday, 27 May. The German 7. and 1. Armees attacked the French 6éme and 5éme Armées and made swift progress. Three days later German forces were at Château-Thierry on the Marne, some 37 miles from Paris.[60] The initial success was so great that there was little for German air units to do. On the opening day of the offensive, JG I reported only two successful fights, both attributed to Leutnant von Rautter of Jasta 4; only one, a Bréguet 14B.2 over Pont-Arcy, was confirmed.[61]

With the German Army advancing again, Hauptmann Reinhard wanted JG I to be moved closer to the Front. He sent Oberleutnant Bodenschatz on an aerial tour of suitable locations on 30 May and then decided on a former French airfield at Beugneux, north of Château-Thierry, which had three usable hangars. Heavy fighting was in progress when Bodenschatz flew over the area, but it was clear that German forces were prevailing. He also spotted a flock of more than 300 sheep, grazing unattended and made certain arrangements, as he noted: 'In a flash, these prospective soup and meat dishes for Jagdgeschwader Richthofen were secured in a pen.'[62]

The change in airfield locations must have been confusing because next day Leutnant der Reserve Rademacher, who had been with Jasta 10 for only two weeks, inadvertently landed at a British-held airfield and was taken prisoner. His Albatros D.Va was assigned the captured aircraft identification number G/2nd Brigade/13.[63]

Another loss on 31 May was Leutnant Viktor von Pressentin *genannt* von Rautter of Jasta 4. A fast-rising ace, the 22-year-old East Prussian had shot down 15 enemy aircraft in his ten-weeks' service with Jasta 4. Rautter's final victory, a Bréguet 14B.2 bomber, was brought down south-west of Soissons at 1255 hours.[64] While he was pursuing the French two-seater, however, he was attacked by Adjudant (Warrant Officer) Gustave Daladier, piloting a SPAD S.XIII of Escadrille Spa 93, and went down in flames near his latest victim.[65]

Minutes later Leutnant Ernst Udet proved that his absence from the Front had not dulled his air-fighting ability. He shot down a Bréguet – his 24th 'kill'.[66] That evening former artillery officer Leutnant Martin Skowronski[67] of Jasta 6 achieved his first success when he, too, shot down a Bréguet.[68]

The Geschwader's move to Beugneux was completed on 1 June, and the initial observation was that the previous French occupants had left no comfort for their successors. They had torched or rendered useless aircraft, hangars and other supplies that could not be taken with them. Richard Wenzl recalled that one apparently overlooked treasure – fuel – also turned out to be useless: 'The French gasoline was too light and made our engines run exceedingly hot [as a result of the] bad mixture.'[69]

Quality of materials was of utmost concern to the pilots. The next day, during Jasta 6's first flight from the new airfield, they attacked several SPAD two-seaters on patrol south of Fère-en-Tardenois. Wenzl lined up a target, following Richthofen's technique, and closed in when, he wrote, 'at the decisive moment my guns jammed [because of faulty ammunition] and I had to let [Staffel leader] Janzen finish the job. Also ... Leutnant [Fritz] Heidenreich, who was covering me from above, seemed to have lost his sense of direction. Apparently he developed engine trouble and headed south [instead of north] and ended up in French captivity.'[70]

Overall, though, the Geschwader had a good day, with ten triumphs shared by Jastas 4, 6 and 10. Three were credited to Wilhelm Reinhard's personal score, making him an air combat leader in the Richthofen mould. That evening, when word was received that Erich Loewenhardt – who had scored his 25th victory during the day[71] – had been awarded the *Pour le Mérite*, there was a general expectation that Reinhard would receive that honour soon.

As if to prove the point, late in the afternoon of 4 June Reinhard shot down a SPAD two-seater which was confirmed as his 18th victory. He needed two more 'kills' to qualify for the highly prized 'Blue Max'. In the same fight, Wolfram von Richthofen achieved his first success by sending down another SPAD two-seater.[72]

The Third German Drive (or Aisne Offensive) was so successful initially that the territorial gains of Generaloberst (Colonel-General) Max von Boehn's 7. Armee expanded into a salient south towards the Marne. To help hold that line, Jagdgeschwaders I and III combined forces on 5 June to keep Allied aircraft from reconnaissance and attacks that might weaken the rapid advance. Particular emphasis was placed on tethered observation balloons, whose observers could see far behind German lines.[73] Of the eight captive balloons shot or forced down that day, three were credited to Jasta 10.[74]

Machine-gun units dedicated to protecting the balloons were a constant danger to fighter pilots attempting to shoot down the high-flying lighter-than-air craft. That point was driven home to Leutnant Heinrich Otto, who had been with Jasta 10 just over a month. On the morning of 6 June he and Leutnant Fritz Friedrichs, who had already shot down five balloons, were heading due west when they spotted a couple of French balloons. Friedrichs shot down one at Fontaine-Croix and Otto achieved his first victory by firing incendiary bullets into a balloon at Villers-Cotterêts. As he flew away from the flaming wreckage, Otto was hit in the right arm by ground fire.[75] His wounds were so severe that he had to be sent to a military hospital and was then posted out of JG I.

The Fourth German Drive

Still intent on securing his gains during the Aisne Offensive, General Erich Ludendorff launched a two-pronged attack by the 7. and 18. Armees on 9 June. This time, however, French forces were prepared and they mounted a much stronger ground and air defence, as Richard Wenzl noted about the initial move against Noyon:

'We met up with a flight of five SPADs and went "round and round" with them. This time we were dealing with plucky fellows. They took up the fight and in an instant were joined by six to eight others from above us. The wind was not in our favour and we were already far over the other side of the lines, so we had to be careful.

'Suddenly I saw [Jasta 6 leader] Janzen going like crazy and roaring by me right behind a SPAD. I did not see what happened beyond that, as suddenly I found myself alone with four SPADs. In any case, Janzen was missing when we landed. As it was revealed later, during his pursuit he was forced down and ended up in French captivity.'[76]

In an attempt to balance the loss of Leutnant Janzen, the JG I war diary noted that six French fighters fell to the guns of Jastas 10 and 11: a SPAD XIII each was credited to Hauptmann Reinhard, Oberleutnant von Wedel and Leutnant Steinhäuser during the morning patrol; a SPAD each by Steinhäuser and Wolfram von Richthofen at midday; and a Bréguet 14B.2 bomber late in the afternoon by Friedrichs. The official Geschwader chronicle also recorded that JG I's 300th victory had been achieved that day.[77]

Next day, Leutnant der Reserve Hans Kirschstein was appointed acting leader of Jasta 6. With 24 confirmed victories to his credit, the 21-year-old Rhinelander was well qualified for the new position. At the outbreak of war he had enlisted in a sapper unit, 3. Pionier-Bataillon 'von Rauch', at Spandau and transferred to the air service a year and a half later. His service with three two-seater units was marked by such distinguished conduct that in December 1917 he was posted to the Fighter Pilots' School and thence to Jasta 6, where he became the Staffel's highest scoring pilot.[78]

Geschwader commander Wilhelm Reinhard reached a milestone on 12 June when he shot down a SPAD two-seater. It was his 20th victory, which made him eligible for the *Pour le Mérite*. As it turned out, his protégé Vizefeldwebel Willi Gabriel claimed victory over the same French reconnaissance aircraft. Rather than ask the Geschwader commander to submit to an arbitration panel (*Schiedsgericht*) to decide which pilot should get the credit, Oberleutnant Bodenschatz prevailed upon Gabriel to relinquish this claim and thereby enhance Reinhard's eligibility for Prussia's highest bravery award. Bodenschatz promised that if the same thing happened again the credit would go to Gabriel.[79] The enlisted pilot agreed to the bargain and Reinhard's nomination was forwarded up the chain of command with all the necessary qualifications. Next day Gabriel shot down a SPAD single-seater, as if to prove that he was a successful air fighter. It was recorded as his fifth victory without question.

Less successful was the German Noyon–Montdidier Offensive, which stalled on its fifth day. While preparations were being made for the next offensive, JG I commander Reinhard reflected on his new French adversaries in his regular report to Hauptmann Hugo Sperrle,[80] the Officer in Charge of Aviation for the 7. Armee:

'In the first days after the [most recent] breakthrough, almost no enemy airmen showed themselves. During the advance, extensive bomber formations were deployed, apparently to replace artillery. Since the beginning of the planned assault, the Frenchman has been very cautious, completely on the defensive and only seldom crosses the lines. The individual French airman is very skilled technically, but avoids serious fighting. Normally, enemy captive balloons are deployed 10 km on the other side of the lines at relatively low altitude and are protected by enemy single-seat fighters. [Balloon] attacks are very difficult and are successful only [when carried out] by surprise.'[81]

With all these factors taken into account, on the morning of 14 June, Hans Kirschstein led a Jasta 6 flight over Villers-Cotterêts and shot down his first balloon, and one of the SPAD fighters assigned to protect it. But one of his new pilots, Vizefelwebel Josef Degen, was brought down and taken prisoner. More balloons in the French 6éme Army sector were destroyed two days later in a sweep by Paul Aue and Fritz Friedrichs of Jasta 10 and Willy Gabriel of Jasta 11.

Despite these successes Hauptmann Reinhard realised that new and better aircraft were needed to maintain the current position and overcome the newly combined forces of Great Britain, France and the United States. He was invited to attend the latest round of aircraft type tests of new fighters at Adlershof, near Berlin, and brought with him an experienced Staffel leader, Hans Kirschstein, to offer his expertise.

When the two pilots left Beugneux, on 18 June, it was the end of one era and the beginning of another. Karl Bodenschatz wrote in the Geschwader war diary: ' ... Richthofen himself had called for such tests to be carried out only and exclusively by front-line pilots, [as] they alone were in a position to determine which types were useful at the Front and which were not. All of the Jagdstaffeln ... sent representatives ... [who] flew the individual machines thoroughly and then handed in their opinions. As Hauptmann Reinhard took leave of his Geschwader no one could know that the parting would be forever.'[82]

Notes

1   Bodenschatz, K., *Jagd in Flanderns*, p. 84 notes that the commander of the 2. Armee, General Georg von der Marwitz, authorised transmission of the message: 'Rittmeister von Richthofen has landed on the other side [of the lines], request news of his fate.'
2   No. 201 Squadron Record Book entry this date.
3   Both Sopwith F.1 Camels from No. 201 Squadron: B.6428 flown by Capt Gerald A. Magor, aged 21, and B.6377 flown by 2/Lt Walter H. Easty, aged 26 (both KiA).
4   Bodenschatz, op. cit., pp. 93–4.

5   Osborn, M., 'Wie Richthofen fiel', in Richthofen, M. von, *Heldenleben*, p. 267.
6   Later disseminated broadly in Kogenluft, *Nachrichtenblatt der Luftstreitkräfte*, 2. Jg, Nr. 9, 25 April 1918, p. 128-A.
7   Bodenschatz, op. cit., p. 180.
8   Richthofen, M. von, *Rote Kampfflieger*, pp. 29, 31, 36.
9   Franks, N., et al., *Above the Lines*, p. 226.
10   Kogenluft, op.cit., 2. Jg, Nr. 19, 4 July 1918, p. 281; C.1086 of No. 56 Squadron, Capt Kenneth W. Junor, MC, aged 24 (KiA).
11   Ibid.; Airco D.H.4 D.8406 of No. 57 Squadron, 2/Lts William H. Townsend, aged 24 (DoW), and Charles C. Souchotte, aged 20 (KiA).
12   Bodenschatz, op. cit., p. 178.
13   Quoted in Zuerl, W., *Pour-le-Mérite-Flieger*, p. 535.
14   Bodenschatz, op. cit., p. 180.
15   Richthofen, K. von, *Kriegstagebuch*, p. 171.
16   Fokker Dr.I 545/17.
17   No. 209 Squadron Combat Report of Lt M. S. Taylor in Sopwith F.1 Camel B.3329; he was killed in the same aircraft on 7 July 1918 (Ref: No. 209 Squadron Record Book entry that date).
18   'In Memoriam Hans Weiss', *Hofer Anzeiger*, 14 May 1918.
19   Fokker Dr.I 591/17.
20   Bretschneider-Bodemer was commissioned into the 1. Ulanen-Regiment Nr. 17 Kaiser Franz Joseph von Österreich, König von Ungarn; Winterfeld was commissioned into Kürassier-Regiment Kaiser Nikolaus I. von Russland (Brandenburgisches) Nr. 6; air combats on this date are given in Appendix 1 of this book.
21   F.2B C.814 of No. 48 Squadron, 2/Lt Alexander C. G. Brown, aged 27 (PoW/DoW), and A. W. Sainsbury (WiA/PoW).
22   Bodenschatz, op. cit., p. 181.
23   O'Connor, N., *Aviation Awards*, vol. II, pp. 64–5, 95.
24   Zuerl, op. cit., p. 486.
25   Bodenschatz, op. cit., p. 181.
26   Möller, H., *Kampf und Sieg*, p. 47.
27   See Appendix 1 for details.
28   No. 209 Squadron Combat Report of Capt O. C. LeBoutillier in Sopwith F.1 Camel D.3338; confirmed as his eighth victory.
29   Kogenluft, op.cit., 2. Jg, Nr. 22, 25 July 1918, p. 328; possibly Sopwith F.1 Camel D.1821 of No. 43 Squadron, Lt Anthony H. Whitford-Hawkey, aged 18 (KiA); also claimed by Loewenhardt.
30   Ibid., pp. 328–9; Sopwith F.1 Camels from No. 80 Squadron lost or damaged in that fight were: D.6591, 2/Lt H. V. Barker (WiA but returned); D.6457, 2/Lt A. V. Jones (WiA/PoW); B.2463, 2/Lt Alfred W. Rowden, aged 23 (KiA); D.6419, Lt George A. Whateley, aged 24 (KiA); D.6619, 2/Lt Colin G. S. Shields (KiA); and B.9243, Lt T. S. Nash (aircraft damaged, but returned).
31   Kogenluft, op.cit., 2. Jg, Nr. 12, 16 May 1918, p. 169.
32   Ibid., Nr. 9, 26 April 1917, p. 2, and Nr. 26, 23 August 1917, p. 164.
33   Individual Jasta scores are noted in Appendix I; including all Jasta 11 victories since 1916, as done previously, the JG I total would be 467 victories.
34   Bodenschatz, op. cit., pp. 97, 182, 185.
35   Oblt Walther Karjus was appointed leader of Jasta 75 on 21 August 1918 and achieved a victory on 21 October when he shot down one of seven Airco D.H.9As of No. 110 Squadron of the Independent Force during a raid on Cologne and Frankfurt; he died on 14 June 1925 (Ref: *Ehrenrangliste*, p. 527).
36   Wenzl, R., *Richthofen-Flieger*, p. 35.
37   Kogenluft, op.cit., Nr. 22, p. 329; further details of the day's combat activities are given in Appendix I.
38   Commissioned into the 3. Garde-Ulanen-Regiment, as were his JG I comrades Ltn Viktor von Pressentin *gennant* von Rautter and Ltn Hanns-Georg von der Osten.
39   Maréchal des Logis de Guerre, pilot, of Escadrille Br 111; no word on the observer/bombardier

(Ref: *Etat Nominatif*, No. 25466, 21 June 1918, p. 1).

40 No. 209 Squadron Combat Report of Lts M. S. Taylor and W. R. May in D.3329 and B.6398.

41 B.5666, 2/Lt Oswald G. Brittorous, aged 19 (KiA); B.6257, Lt Geoffrey Wilson, aged 23 (KiA); and D.3373, Capt Oliver W. Redgate, aged 19 (WiA).

42 Bodenschatz, op. cit.

43 RAF *Communiqué* No. 7, 23 May 1918, p. 6.

44 Fokker Dr. I 546/17; Puglisi, W., 'German Aircraft Down', in *Cross & Cockade*, p. 278.

45 RAF *Communiqué*, op.cit., p. 5.

46 Bodenschatz, op. cit., p. 183.

47 Letter from the Schmutzler family.

48 RAF *Communiqué*, op.cit., 23 May 1918, p. 7.

49 Two French aircraft lost that day were: Bréguet 14B.2 of Escadrille Br 117, pilot unknown and Maréchal des Logis Bombardier (Corporal bombardier) Mont; and Bréguet 14A.2 of Escadrille Br 45, Sergent-Pilot Viex and M.d.L Mitrailleur (Corporal gunner) LaMere (Ref: *État Nominatif*, p. 2).

50 While flying in Sopwith F.1 Camel C.8242.

51 Quoted in Waugh, C., 'Short History', in *Cross & Cockade*, 1979, p. 313.

52 S.E.5a C.1105; grave site is noted in RAF *Western Front Casualty List* entry for that date; but the annotation 'no known grave' appears in Hobson, C., *Airmen Died*, p. 148.

53 D.H.4 D.8401, Lt Hatton C. R. Conron and 2/Lt Joseph Finnnigan, aged 19 (both KiA).

54 Grosz, P., 'Fokker D.VII', in *Windsock Datafile 9*, 1989, p. 2.

55 Wenzl, op. cit., p. 38; the over-compressed engine mentioned was the 185hp BMW.IIIa issued later (Ref: Grosz, ibid., p. 5).

56 Kogenluft, op.cit., 2. Jg, Nr. 17, 20 June 1918, p. 250 credits (then) Unteroffizier Gabriel and his gunner, Gefreiter Hilsebein, with shooting down a SPAD.

57 D.H.9 C.6181 of No. 49 Squadron, Lt C. G. Capel and 1/AM J. Knight (both WiA).

58 Udet, E., *Fliegerleben*, pp. 98–9.

59 Bodenschatz, op. cit., p. 184.

60 Esposito, V. (ed.), *Concise History*, p. 113.

61 Kogenluft, op.cit., Nr. 22, p. 330.

62 Bodenschatz, op. cit., p. 103.

63 Ibid., pp. 103, 185 and Wenzl, op. cit., p. 41 contend that Rademacher landed in a two-seater at an unnamed French airfield, which is unlikely because his single-seat Albatros D.Va fighter was seized by British forces (Ref: Puglisi, op. cit., p. 273).

64 Aircraft from Escadrille Br 29, Sous-Lt Berenger and his gunner, Sergent Wolff, were KiA (Ref: *État Nominatif*, p. 6 and Kilduff, P., 'Groupes 4 and 9', in *Cross & Cockade*, 1974, p. 19).

65 Chamberlain, P. and Bailey, F., 'Escadrille Spa 93' in *Cross & Cockade*, 1978, p. 70.

66 Kogenluft, op.cit.; aircraft from Escadrille Br 29, Sergent Martin and his gunner, Soldat Galbrun, were KiA (Ref: *État Nominatif* and Kilduff, op. cit.).

67 Commissioned into Fussartillerie-Regiment von Linger (Ostpreussisches) Nr. 1.

68 Kogenluft, op.cit.; twelve Bréguet 14s (including both reconnaissance and bomber versions) were reported missing that day and lack of further details precludes matching those losses with German victory claims.

69 Wenzl, op. cit., pp. 42–3.

70 Ibid., p. 43 notes 1 June 1918 as the date Ltn Heidenreich inadvertently landed within French lines; Bodenschatz, op. cit., p. 186 gives the date as 2 June and Kofl 7. Armee *Fliegertagesmeldung* Nr. 111, Teil VI, 9 June 1918, p. 8 gives the date as 30 May 1918.

71 Kogenluft, op.cit., 2. Jg, Nr. 23, 1 August 1918, p. 363 listed this victory as Loewenhardt's 26th.

72 Further information appears in Appendix I.

73 Bodenschatz, op. cit., p. 186.

74 Kogenluft, op.cit., p. 366.

75 Bodenschatz, op. cit., p. 187.

76 Wenzl, op. cit., pp. 45–6.

77 Bodenschatz, op. cit.; again, the figure is understated, because the previous JG I total of 320 was augmented by 89 additional victories at this point, bringing the Geschwader total to 409 victo-

ries; see Appendix I for the various Jasta totals.

78 Zuerl, op. cit., pp. 259–61.

79 O'Connor, op. cit., vol. II, p. 67.

80 Hugo Sperrle began his aviation career as an observer at the beginning of the war. He commanded several front-line units and training facilities prior to his appointment as Kommandeur der Flieger der 7. Armee on 21 January 1918. He remained on active duty between the world wars and was promoted Generalmajor in 1935 and Generalfeldmarschall in 1940. He was interned after the Second World War, released in 1946 and died on 2 April 1953 (Ref: Hildebrand, K., *Die Generale*, vol. III, pp. 325–6).

81 Quoted in Bodenschatz, op. cit., p. 108.

82 Ibid., p. 109; Wenzl, op. cit., p. 46 states that Feldwebelleutnant Fritz Schubert, JG I's technical officer and the victor of four combats, accompanied Reinhard and Kirschstein to Adlershof for the fighter competition.

CHAPTER 13

Elusive Victory

THE LEADERSHIP OF THE GERMAN AIR FORCE ENCOURAGED COMPETITION between its fighter pilots and offered incentives – from medals to important assignments – to motivate pilots to continue to perform at high levels of success. When Hauptmann Wilhelm Reinhard departed for Adlershof, the prospect of higher command was raised between two pilots well qualified to lead Jagdgeschwader I on an interim basis: Leutnant Erich Loewenhardt, credited with 27 air triumphs, and 30-victory ace Leutnant der Reserve Ernst Udet. Both men were *Pour le Mérite* recipients and Staffel leaders. With his air combat record, Udet seemed to be a natural choice to lead JG I, but he held the post for only a day. With no explanation, however, on 19 June Loewenhardt became the acting Geschwader commander.[1] He was a year younger than Udet, but he was a product of the Prussian Cadet Corps and no doubt more familiar with military procedures.

Losing the prestigious post of Geschwader commander did not seem to affect Udet. He was more comfortable in a cockpit than sitting at a desk for long hours and wrangling with superiors, as was proved 23 years later when, as a Luftwaffe General, he was driven to suicide by political in-fighting coupled with his basic unsuitability for high-level command.[2]

Already in possession of all the medals he wanted and now free to make the best use of his talent in 7. Armee's sector, Udet went 'hunting' in his all-red Fokker D.VII and shot down two Bréguet 14B.2 bombers on 23 June, one Bréguet on the 24th and two fast, rugged SPAD fighters the following day. During the same period, Loewenhardt shot down a Bréguet and a SPAD, raising his score to 28 as against Udet's 35 confirmed victories.[3]

The arrival of new Fokker D.VIIs equipped with the more powerful 185hp BMW engines contributed to their success, as Leutnant der Reserve Richard Wenzl pointed out: 'On 22 June, the first BMW-Fokkers arrived and were assigned to Staffel 11. Each of the aces of other Staffeln also received one. While Kirschstein was in Berlin, I led Staffel 6 and was able to fly his BMW-engined aircraft, which gave me great pleasure. This machine could reach 6,000 metres' altitude in 24 minutes, which at that time was excellent performance. The effect of these new machines was seen immediately. Staffel 11 shot down many [enemy aircraft], for now it was easy to reach the extraordinarily high-flying French reconnaissance aircraft and shoot them down. Loewenhardt and Udet made especially good use of their new machines and, as was seen at this time, increased the number of their victories ... Udet flew far behind the lines at high altitude and in this way surprised the unsuspecting homeward bound "lone wanderers". In this way he once shot down a Bréguet in flames over Compiègne.'[4]

The arrival of Fokker D.VIIs augured well for Germany's hard-pressed fighter units. But there were still many Fokker Triplanes in front-line service and their deficiencies became all the more glaring when their performance was compared with the new biplane fighters. On the morning of 26 June, Wenzl's friend Leutnant Werner Steinhäuser of Jasta 11 was flying a triplane when he attacked a SPAD S.XVI two-seater, bent on achieving his 11th victory. The French gunner was quicker, however, and killed Steinhäuser. The former artillery officer was buried in Beugneux on 28 June, the day before his 22nd birthday.[5]

Since early in the war, balloon observers had used parachutes of a size and bulk that required them to be attached to the wicker baskets that held crewmen and equipment. By 1918, the more portable Heinecke parachutes had been issued to aircrew[6] and, while Steinhäuser did not live long enough to use his, three days later Jasta 4 leader Udet saved himself by bailing out.

It was a clear morning on Saturday, 29 June, when Udet's flight headed for the front line. They could see German infantry units being pounded by a French barrage. Then far below, Udet spotted a Bréguet on a low-level close air support mission. To avoid meeting Steinhäuser's fate, Udet dived on the two-seater and targeted the observer, who disappeared quickly. He thought he had knocked out the back-seat crewman and came at the French aircraft from the side to finish it off. Then, as stated in his combat report: 'I noticed that the French observer appeared again from within the fuselage and, at the same moment, I took several hits, including one in the machine-gun and one in the fuel tank. Simultaneously, my elevator and aileron control cables must have been severed, for my Fokker D.VII plummeted down out of control. I tried everything possible to bring the aircraft back under my control, partly using the throttle and partly the rudder, but to no avail. At about 500 metres' altitude the machine was in a vertical nose dive and could not be brought out [of it].'[7]

The new and untried parachute was Udet's only hope for survival. He unbuckled himself from the seat and stood up to jump and activate the static line that would deploy the parachute. A rush of air blew him out of the Fokker so swiftly that he did not have time to get completely clear of it. His parachute harness became caught on the rudder but he kicked himself free. He thought the parachute had failed to open until a sudden deceleration brought the comforting feeling that he would live. Udet landed near a Westphalian ground unit[8] and was eventually taken back to his airfield.

He returned in time to celebrate a happier event that day. Leutnant der Reserve Hans Kirschstein, who had returned to the Geschwader briefly on 24 June and used his new Fokker D.VII to achieve his 27th victory, was back again. This time he wore the distinctive blue and gold Maltese Cross badge that identified him as the 41st aviation recipient of the *Pour le Mérite*.[9]

The Red Aircraft Legacy

Udet's crashed Fokker was unsalvageable and he received a new BMW-powered one,[10] with which he shot down five Frenchmen during the next four days. With this aircraft, Udet went a step beyond the all-red paint scheme established by Manfred von Richthofen. Udet's new machine had an all-red fuselage with red and white diagonal stripes on the top wing. In the event of an opponent getting close enough to read it, the solid red tail elevators were decorated with a bold challenge in equally prominent white letters: *'Du doch nicht!!'* ('Certainly not you!!')[11] The audacious colour scheme seems to have achieved the recognition that Udet desired.

A tribute to Udet's tenacity and skill was found in a letter taken from a French PoW and circulated within the German Air Force to reinforce morale: 'A comrade was attacked twice while at 5,000 metres' altitude and within our lines. The second time by a single Fokker which was painted red all over [and was] quite far behind our lines. (Over the Reims mountain forest, according to reports.) Despite all manner of aerobatics by our pilot, who was the best in our squadron, the Fokker did not relent [during the descent from] 5,000 to 3,000 metres and fired his machine-gun three times at our man from the somewhat great distance of 150–200 metres and put 30 holes into [our] crate. They had to land with the engine switched off because of a hit that emptied the fuel tank. The machine had to be dismantled [as usable only for spare parts]. The observer believed that they were as good as shot down when he saw how this German sprang about him and shot up his crate. Furthermore, this red-painted machine has been talked about several times recently. In any event, in it sits a pilot equal to our Fonck.'[12]

Major Harold E. Hartney, commanding officer of the US 27th Aero Squadron, was also aware of his illustrious adversary. He wrote: 'Richthofen had been killed ... but his "Flying Circus" ... as they nicknamed those waspish camouflaged little ships, had been taken over by Udet [sic], Germany's greatest flyer at that moment, and I had a tip from "Intelligence" that they were about to swarm the skies and put on a grand show for us.'[13]

On the morning of Tuesday, 2 July 1918, nine American Nieuport 28 biplane fighters set out for German-held territory. First Lieutenant Donald Hudson led the low flight while First Lieutenant Fred W. Norton and his three men covered them from a higher altitude. Just north of Château-Thierry, nine Fokkers representing Jastas 4, 10 and 11 took the bait and pounced on Hudson's five-aircraft formation. Immediately Norton's flight came down and evened the odds.

Norton's valour during this patrol led to his being awarded the Distinguished Service Cross. The citation noted that 'as flight commander, [he] led a patrol of eight machines, the first large American formation to encounter a large German patrol. His command gave battle to nine enemy battle planes, driven [sic] by some of the leading aces of the German army. Although both of his guns jammed at the beginning of the fight and were, therefore, useless, Lieut. Norton stayed with the formation, skilfully maneuvering his machine to the best advantage. He was attacked by enemy planes at four different times, but skilfully avoided them or dived at them. His continued presence was a great moral help to his comrades, who destroyed two of the enemy planes.'[14]

Major Hartney later wrote: 'This dizzy battle lasted for 35 minutes, then both sides, getting low on gasoline, broke away. Our boys had engaged in 32 combats. We had definitely brought down four Boche machines. We got official credit for only two, but by this time the boys were getting accustomed to this ...'[15]

Ernst Udet reached an important milestone on 3 July, when he shot down a French SPAD fighter that was credited as his 40th victory. He had become the air-fighting equal of Oswald Boelcke and was halfway to matching Manfred von Richthofen's final tally. As a citizen of Bavaria, Udet should have been proposed for that kingdom's highest bravery award, the Knight's Cross of the Military Max-Joseph Order, which carried with it a title of nobility, but he had upset the Bavarians. Having been refused entry into their aviation arm, he had paid for his own flying lessons and then joined the German Air Service. After Udet had gained prominence, he was invited to join a Bavarian squadron, but, recalling the earlier slight, he refused the assignment, saying: 'I stay with the Prussians who accepted me in 1915. The Bavarians rejected me then.'[16] After that, Udet had no chance of the Bavarian award and everything that went with it.

A Death in Berlin

Udet's great achievement that day was eclipsed by a radio message from Air Force Headquarters: 'The Commander of Jagdgeschwader Richthofen, Hauptmann Reinhard, crashed fatally on 3 July 1918 during a test flight at Berlin-Adlershof.'[17]

Later, his comrades learned that the 27-year-old Reinhard had perished while testing the new duralumin-skinned Dornier D.I, a proposed successor to the Fokker D.VII. Jasta 27 leader Hermann Göring had flown the aircraft first and then handed it over to Reinhard. During his test flight, the JG I commander put it into a steep dive, the top wing came off and the D.I smashed into the ground.[18] Wilhelm Reinhard's body was returned to his home town of Düsseldorf for a hero's funeral.

Condolences poured into the Geschwader. Reinhard's death came less than two and a half months after Richthofen's and, with the German advance bogged down once more, it was a severe blow to the morale of the hard-pressed German fighter pilots. Reinhard was succeeded by Göring, who wrote the obituary notice and phrased the sad event in classic Teutonic terms:

'His exemplary life as a German soldier and his fidelity to King and Fatherland were sealed with [his] heroic death ... He followed his great master in death rapturously. He led the Geschwader, which he took over as Richthofen's heir, with the old spirit from victory to victory.'[19]

More Losses at the Front

From the time of Reinhard's death until Göring assumed command on 14 July, JG I was mostly dormant. Routine flights were carried out, but were not rich with the spirit of success that Reinhard had worked so hard to create. The greatest achievement of that period took place at midday on 8 July, when Leutnant der Reserve Fritz Friedrichs of Jasta 10 shot down an American Nieuport 28.[20] Having achieved his 21st victory, the former infantry officer was qualified to receive the *Pour le Mérite* and had only to wait for it to be authorised by the Orders Chancellery in Berlin.[21]

Meanwhile, current *Pour le Mérite* recipient Hermann Göring arrived at Beugneux and made a strong impression from the outset. 'He was the best model of a young career officer,' Karl Bodenschatz recalled. 'In the quiet, well-proportioned features of his face there dwelled cool-headedness and energy. His eyes were clear, compelling and calm ... The man was tough, as one saw in the way he moved, heard in what he said and felt it breathing from his entire being. In short order he had the Geschwader in hand.'[22]

Göring was a product of the Prussian Cadet Corps and might have remained in the infantry,[23] had he not been urged to join the Air Service by Bruno Loerzer, a regimental friend who had become a pilot. When Göring was in hospital early in the war, Loerzer visited him and extolled the benefits of aviation. By the end of 1914 Göring was in training to become an Observer. Later he became a pilot and, on 16 November 1916, began a string of victories that led to his receiving the *Pour le Mérite* on 2 June 1918. Always a very ambitious man, he reached the zenith of his First World War career when he was appointed to lead JG I.

On Monday, 15 July, the fifth German drive of 1918 (the Champagne–Marne Offensive) began and among the day's casualties was Fritz Friedrichs. He had taken off in a Fokker biplane at 2100 hours and, as later determined, experienced premature ignition of the phosphorous ammunition loaded as 'tracer' rounds; sparks flew back to his fuel tank and set it alight.[24] Friedrichs jumped out to activate the static line parachute, but the 'chute became entangled in the Fokker's empennage' and the 23-year-old pilot was dragged down with his flaming aircraft.[25]

Next evening, Julius Bender of Jasta 4 experienced a similar in-air fire while flying his Fokker, but parachuted successfully from his burning aircraft.[26] The saddest news of the day was the death of Leutnant der Reserve Hans Kirschstein, who at the age of 21 was a 27-victory ace, recipient of the *Pour le Mérite* and leader of Jasta 6. A new pilot of about the same age, Leutnant Johannes Markgraf,[27] had been sent to fly Kirschstein back from Fismes in a Hannover two-seater. The aircraft stalled at 50 metres' altitude and crashed, killing both men. Later it was learned that this flight was Markgraf's first in a Hannover and he was unfamiliar with the controls.[28]

Leutnant Paul Wenzel became acting Staffel leader 'until a new *Pour-le-Mériter* [could be] found', sardonically observed Leutnant Richard Wenzl,[29] who had held the post when Kirschstein went to Berlin with Reinhard. No doubt he felt slighted at not being re-appointed to lead the unit. As usual, the victory score was a critical factor in promotion: at that time 31-year-old Paul Wenzel had six 'kills' to his credit and Richard Wenzl, a year younger, had only three.

The German offensive ended on 17 July, a day on which Jastas 4 and 6 brought down five Bréguet bombers. Among them was Paul Wenzel's seventh victory, which further confirmed for Geschwader commander Göring that he had picked the right man to lead Jasta 6.

When the Allied counter-offensive began the following day, Göring led the morning patrol in a Fokker D.VII made distinctive by being painted bright red from nose to cockpit, the remainder of the fuselage being yellow.[30] His 22nd and last victory was among the thirteen 'kills' confirmed for that operation.

The day's successes were offset by the loss of Jasta 6's Leutnant Moritz-Waldemar Bretschneider-Bodemer, aged 26, and Gefreiter Ludwig Möller of Jasta 10. The 27-year-old Möller had scored his first victory, a SPAD S.XIII, two days earlier.

The Allied armies made such gains on the ground that by early afternoon of 18 July, Allied observation balloons could be seen by JG I members standing out on the airfield at Beugneux. By evening, the balloons were directing artillery fire at the German airfield and, rather than have his pilots attempt to shoot down the tethered observation posts, Göring ordered the Geschwader to be evacuated to a safer location. Under cover of darkness the men and equipment of the four Staffeln were moved by lorries to Monthussart Farm, north-east of Braine and along the River Vesle .[31]

Before the field hospital at Beugneux was evacuated, the bodies of Leutnants Kirschstein, Markgraf and Bretschneider-Bodemer underwent the limited mortuarial preparation available and were transported to the new area. Two days later, they were buried in the Cemetery of Honour at Courcelles.

Lothar Returns

Poor weather greeted Jagdgeschwader I upon arrival at its new base. As the groundcrew secured tent hangars for the aircraft, a two-seater landed in their midst and into the pouring rain stepped the familiar figure of Lothar von Richthofen. After complaining to everyone he knew in the Air Force, he had been allowed to return to the Front. Lothar was at Maubeuge in Belgium when his clearance came through and he convinced a pilot that he needed a 'ride' to his airfield, irrespective of the weather.

The younger Richthofen's first request of the new Geschwader commander was to be placed on active flying status. He was reminded that first he needed to become familiar with the Fokker D.VII and 7. Armee's Front. Lothar's limitations became apparent on his first flight, when he nearly got lost and his vision was so blurred that he 'could scarcely tell friend from foe'.[32] But he persisted and flew on every possible occasion.

His tenacity paid off during the early evening of 25 July. While leading aircraft from Jastas 4, 10 and 11, he came upon a formation of Airco D.H.9 bombers and Sopwith F.1 Camels. Lothar chased one of the British fighters and shot it down near Fismes, thereby scoring his 30th victory.[33] According to German Air Force calculations, this 'kill' was the 500th victory for Jagdgeschwader Freiherr von Richthofen Nr. I.[34]

The triumph came at the cost of one of Jasta 11's newer pilots, 22-year-old Leutnant Friedrich-Franz Count von Hohenau. It is most likely that he was shot down by a Canadian, Lieutenant (later Sir) William S. Stephenson, MC, who reported: 'While leading "A" Flight on Offensive Patrol escorting D.H.9s, we were attacked by Fokker Biplanes and Triplanes, but could not get a decisive engagement. When D.H.9s were over the lines, we circled back, got height, and dived on a formation of three Fokker Biplanes with seven Fokkers below. Two Fokkers went under the main formation; the remaining one turned and fired, then turned back and started to dive. I got on his tail and fired a burst at short range. He dived vertically, then pulled up slightly and turned West, and dived again [this time] into the ground.'[35]

The young German nobleman, one of so many airmen who came from the cavalry,[36] was removed from his aircraft and taken to Field Hospital 103 in Grugny, where he died the following evening. Apparently the rear area hospital had better mortuary facilities, and Count von Hohenau's body was prepared for the long journey across Germany to his family's estate in Oschelhermsdorf bei Grünberg in Silesia for burial.[37]

The Allied counter-offensive continued to advance and JG I moved again as part of the orderly German withdrawal from the Marne salient, this time back to Puisieux Farm, north-east of Laon. Although it was an inauspicious time, on 26 July Oberleutnant Hermann Göring transferred acting command of the Geschwader to Lothar von Richthofen and went on leave. Appropriately enough, Manfred's old regimental comrade Erich-Rüdiger von Wedel was placed in charge of Jasta 11. The fortunes of war had changed, but 'the old guard', the Prussian élite, was there to carry on. Indeed, three days later, Wedel proved himself a fitting Jasta 11 leader in the Richthofen tradition by shooting down a Bréguet bomber, his ninth victory.

On 30 July, the Geschwader's top scorer, Jasta 10 leader Erich Loewenhardt, enhanced his stature by shooting down two Sopwith F.1 Camels, one in the after-noon and one in the evening, for his 47th and 48th victories. Leutnant der Reserve Heinrich Drekmann of Jasta 4 also scored that day, shooting down a French SPAD fighter for his 11th victory. During the same fight, however, 22-year-old Drekmann was shot down and killed by two SPADs of Escadrille Spa 75.[38]

The 7. Armee withdrew to more secure positions behind the Vesle, where it had eighteen fighter units well positioned to defend its air space: Jagdgeschwader I (Jastas 4, 6, 10 and 11) at Puisieux Farm, JG III (Jastas 2, 26, 27 and 36) south of Chambry, Jagdgruppe 4 (Jastas 21, 39, 60 and 81) at Boncourt, and JaGru 5 (Jastas 1, 8, 41, 45, 50 and 66) at Sissone.[39]

Demonstrating the ability to respond to increased enemy air activity, on 1 August 1918 Jastas 4, 6 and 11 brought down eleven aircraft. Among them were some of the six SPAD S.XIII fighters that the American First Pursuit Group's 27th Aero Squadron lost that day.[40] Lothar's 31st and 32nd victims were most likely French SPADs, because there were no other American losses in that sector on that day.[41] Lothar believed that he had encountered elements of the US Air Service and wrote of one of his victims:

'The American was just a beginner. There were four of them and three of us. I was somewhat higher than the American. In a moment I was near him, fired about 50 shots and the enemy aircraft fell out of control. A gentleman who flew with me also thought that he would like to shoot down the American. He recognised the enemy just as he saw me behind him [and pulled away] and then the Yankee fell. A quick grasp of the situation means life for a *Jagdflieger*. Thus, the American did not notice me at all and really had a beautiful death.'[42]

Richthofen noted that his second victim that day 'lived a little longer' but finally succumbed to the classic relentless attack from behind. More worrying to the veteran air fighter were the two new pilots with him; the spirit of competition made them eager for victories and so intent on shooting down their leader's quarry that one almost rammed into Lothar and the other put a few holes in his aircraft.[43]

Yet again, these victories came at a cost. Leutnant der Reserve Walter Lehmann of Jasta 10 was shot down over Fère-en-Tardenois and taken prisoner. Acting Jasta 6 leader Leutnant Paul Wenzel was lightly injured, but remained with his unit.[44]

The New Fokker Monoplane Arrives

German fighter pilots had hoped that in this dark hour of their history they would receive an entirely new type of aircraft to provide the advantage needed to defeat their numerically superior foe. But the dream was short-lived. Richard Wenzl recalled: 'On 5 August we in Staffel 6 received a new type, the Fokker "Parasol", a [high-wing] monoplane with a 110hp Oberursel-Le Rhône rotary engine. We picked up the machine at the air depot in Clermont and flew it back immediately. In terms of aviation technology, the machine was outstanding, despite the fact that it had been designed for the more powerful 140hp rotary engine. In about a minute and a half it climbed to 1,000 metres and in eight minutes to 3,000 metres, but then, [as a consequence of] a characteristic of engine torque, the performance fell off. Nevertheless, in terms of climbing ability and technical performance, this machine was superior to all previous [fighters], even the much slower [Fokker] Triplane.'[45]

Before the new aircraft – the Fokker E.V (later redesignated D.VIII) – could be tested in combat, JG I was ordered to return to the 2. Armee Front, the area fraught with the Geschwader's worst memories. Lothar von Richthofen took some small comfort in his new relationship with Erich Loewenhardt who had recently been promoted to Oberleutnant. Although two years younger than Lothar, Loewenhardt had become a 'big brother' figure. Both men came from Breslau and had much in common. Loewenhardt had come from the infantry,[46] but he displayed Manfred's air of confidence, which surely touched in Lothar memories of a happy time that he yearned to re-live.

The German Army's 'Black Day'

The next Allied counter-offensive began at 0420 hours on Thursday, 8 August 1918. Under cover of thick fog, British Fourth Army, supported by French 1ère Armée slashed into the Amiens Salient[47] so effectively that Quartermaster-General Erich Ludendorff called this 'the black day of the German Army in the history of the war'.[48]

The evening before, Lothar von Richthofen had been summoned to the area to arrange for the relocation to 2. Armee's Front. He brought Loewenhardt with him and they proved to be a formidable team, each scoring triple victories – Lothar's 33rd, 34th and 35th, and Loewenhardt's 49th, 50th and 51st – as they literally fought their way across 2. Armee territory and back to Puisieux Farm.

Lothar recalled: 'It was nice to fly with Loewenhardt, almost the way it had been with Manfred ... We had got to know each other well in a short time and we had a splendid understanding of each other in the air. Since Manfred [was gone], I was happy to have again found someone on whom I could rely. Loewenhardt expressed a similar view about me.'[49]

Next day, Lothar von Richthofen in his 'red bird'[50] scored Victories Nos, 36 and 37, two Airco D.H.9 bombers in flames. Erich Loewenhardt in his yellow Fokker D.VII shot down two Sopwith F.1 Camels for his 52nd and 53rd triumphs.[51]

JG I's move on 10 August from Puisieux Farm on the 7. Armee Front to Ennemain, west of St-Quentin, on the 2. Armee Front, put the Geschwader close to its new operating sector. The new airfield was still being prepared when, at about 1100 hours, Richthofen and Loewenhardt took beginners from Jastas 10 and 11 over the Front for air combat lessons. A dozen Fokkers crossed the lines at 3,000 to 4,000 metres. They avoided a formation of S.E.5s and found a more favourable target: a single Sopwith F.1 Camel. Loewenhardt signalled his flight to follow him and watch the master at work.

From a distance Lothar von Richthofen saw Loewenhardt line up behind the Camel for the kill. He also saw that one of the other Fokkers was too close to Loewenhardt, but in those days before aircraft had radios, he could only watch and hope that all the pilots were aware of their proximity to one another. Eagerness prevailed, however, and other new men came in behind their leader, each looking to share in the victory. The Camel began to trail smoke behind him and go into a steep dive.

Then, Lothar recalled: 'At about the same moment, what's this! Loewenhardt is no longer flying behind the falling Englishman; instead there is a wild confusion of thousands of splinters. Immediately, I make a steep dive to see what is really wrong. It is immediately clear – Loewenhardt has been rammed!'[52]

The German pilots so focused their attention on the two falling Fokkers that the intended victim got away. One man fell like a stone, his parachute unopened. The parachute that did open was that of Leutnant Alfred Wenz, whom Lothar officially cleared of any responsibility in the incident.[53]

The Sopwith F.1 Camel pilot saved by the collision of the Fokkers was probably a member of JG I's old adversary, No. 209 Squadron, RAF. Lieutenant M. A. Toomey of that unit returned 'shot up [and] damaged' from a patrol in that area at about that time.[54]

Loewenhardt's aircraft came down in a hotly contested area near Chaulnes and his corpse could not be recovered for a week.[55] Then his body was sent home to Breslau for burial with all the honours due to JG I's leading air fighter of the time.[56]

JG I Driven Back

On 11 August the Geschwader had to move to Bernes, about 12 kilometres north-east of Ennemain. Heavy Allied air activity helped to drive German forces ever eastward and, as in the case of JG I, to give up advantageous forward airfields.

Under these conditions the command structure was more vital than ever, and 9-victory ace Leutnant der Reserve Alois Heldmann was named acting leader of the yellow-nosed Fokkers of Jasta 10. Lothar von Richthofen led a full Geschwader formation that day and was credited with shooting down an Airco D.H.12 (sic) bomber for his 38th victory.[57] This gain was marred by three casualties however: Jasta 6's acting leader Leutnant Paul Wenzel, wounded in a fight with S.E.5s; and two new men, Leutnant der Reserve Max Festler of Jasta 11 and Leutnant Bodo von der Wense of Jasta 6, were killed in a sprawling aerial brawl with old, by now almost traditional foes: Sopwith F.1 Camels of No. 209 Squadron, RAF.[58]

Richard Wenzl, who became acting leader of Jasta 6, wrote: 'West of Péronne, all of a sudden the sky was black with Englishmen. A concentration of bombers under the strongest protection of single-seat fighters approached, easily 50 aircraft in all. We were still far too low, and all the [opposing] single-seaters were much higher, so I pulled up to gain altitude.

'To my horror, Wense ... simply flew right at the Englishmen and away from us. By the time he realised his mistake, they were all over him. The "pennant man", i. e., the leader of the British flight, was right on his tail and shot him down as I tried to intervene. Then there was a hot battle, as all the single-seaters, easily 25 of them, came down at us ... [and] the British "pennant man" came down and fired at me. I can still see his big red cowling

... his red insignia and his two red pennants [streaming from the interplane struts].'[59]

Wenzl was lucky; he managed to slip away from the British flight leader and fought off the numerically superior Sopwith fighters. When he realised that the 'warm' feeling in his hip was blood soaking into his flight suit, he withdrew and flew back to his own airfield. He was only lightly wounded, but counted 58 holes in his Fokker.[60] Leutnant Bodo von der Wense, a 23-year-old nobleman and veteran of an élite Hessian life-guards regiment,[61] was buried where he fell, alongside the road from Herbécourt to Péronne.[62]

It had become clear that the German Air Force – like other German military branches – was being forced to withdraw on various Fronts. By 12 August, JG I's losses had been so high that it was condensed into a Staffel and joined with Hauptmann Bruno Loerzer's JG III and Jagdgruppe 9 (Jastas 34b, 37 and 77b)[63] commanded by Oberleutnant Robert Greim and based at Hervilly, just a few kilometres from Bernes. At the same time 1. Armee sent Leutnant Emil Thuy's Jagru 7 (Jastas 28w, 33, 57 and 58) to an airfield at Mons-en-Chaussée, south-west of Bernes.[64] JG I recorded five victories that day – including Lothar von Richthofen's 39th and 40th – and recorded no losses. Lothar led the morning flight accompanied by his cousin Wolfram, Erich Just and Eberhardt Mohnike[65]. One of Lothar's victims that day was Captain John K. Summers, MC, the 23-year-old leader of 'B' Flight of No. 209 Squadron. He was captured and taken to JG I's airfield, where he was treated cordially as a guest at dinner. Lothar's other victim was Lieutenant Kenneth M. Walker, aged 24, a member of Summers' flight who a day earlier had shot down and killed Leutnant Max Festler,[66] a man of his own age; Walker perished in his fight with Richthofen.

Unlucky '13' Again

The next morning – Tuesday, 13 August – Lothar von Richthofen had an uneasy feeling. He had been shot down twice before on the 13th, but he was determined not to give way to his superstitions. Later he wrote that he wanted 'to dispel the last misgivings. If it were another day, perhaps I would not have taken off at all, for I had three different pressing car trips that had to be made. But ... the spell of the 13th had to be broken. There were a lot of Englishmen at the Front ...'[67]

Lothar led five comrades over the lines at about midday. He attacked an unidentified two-seater, disabled the Observer and was about to shoot the pilot when he had a rude surprise. 'I looked back to see where my Staffel was and saw instead that I was being pursued by six "Lords" [British fighters]. Quickly I broke away from my victim to get back over to my own side,' he recalled. He dived at full speed, but one Sopwith F.1 Camel stayed with him, leaving no room for him to turn and manoeuvre to return fire. 'Suddenly there was a terrible pain in my right leg,' he wrote. 'I almost got away. It was the only shot [to hit] the whole machine. Then I had such pain that I was unable to work the rudder. My right leg was stuck on the rudder bar and I couldn't move it. I had to pull it free with both hands ...'[68] Trapped and diving fast, Lothar was unable to climb out to use the parachute. He headed for a flat area in the lunar landscape of the Somme Front.

Behind him was First Lieutenant George V. Seibold of the 148th Aero Squadron, whose account of his first and only victory stated simply: 'Flight attacked six E.A. I fired 150 rounds into one [German] scout at 50 yards' range, which was diving down trying to get away, apparently out of control, and followed him down to under 2,000 ft, when I saw him crash.'[69]

The young American witnessed the abrupt conclusion of Richthofen's last combat flight. Lothar returned to Germany for medical treatment and enforced retirement with 40 confirmed victories – half as many as Manfred. The mantle of achieving greater glory was passed to Ernst Udet, the charming, mercurial Bavarian who decorated his aircraft with 'LO', the nickname of his fiancée, Eleanore Zenk. He shot down an enemy aircraft on each of the next three days, which raised his score to 56, surpassing Loewenhardt and attaining the final position among German fighter pilots: second only to Manfred von Richthofen.

A Different 'Fokker Scourge'

In the glory days of 1915 and 1916, Fokker E.I, E.II and E.III Eindeckers became known to the RFC as 'the Fokker scourge'. When the remnant of JG I settled in at their airfield at Bernes, Jasta 6 retrieved its allotment of the latest Fokker monoplanes – E.V Parasols – from storage at Chambry with a view to opening a new era of Fokker successes. On 16 August, Leutnant der Reserve Emil Rolff flew a Parasol on a combat patrol and shot down a Sopwith F.1 Camel,[70] for his third victory. A sign of future problems with the new Fokker fighter came later that day when, inexplicably, Vizefeldwebel Lechner crashed during a test flight; he was uninjured.[71]

Two days later RAF Intelligence staff alerted Western Front units 'that Fokker monoplanes have been issued to at least two pursuit flights now working in the Somme area'.[72] Next day, Emil Rolff was putting the new fighter through its paces over Bernes airfield when, at 300 metres' altitude, the aircraft broke apart and the 22-year-old pilot fell to his death. The Fokker E.V was grounded immediately and a 'crash commission', similar to the one that had investigated the Fokker Triplane, was convened. Like the previous panel, this *Sturz-Kommission* found shoddy workmanship to be the cause of a series of Fokker E.V crashes.[73]

While the technical experts were investigating Fokker's flawed master-piece, on 21 August, Jasta 4 leader Ernst Udet achieved his 57th and 58th victories in his all-red Fokker biplane.[74] Next day he shot down two more RAF aircraft to raise his score to 60 – the last twenty having been brought down since 1 August 1918.[75]

But victory No. 60 was a hard-won fight. Udet's Staffel had been sent to head off five S.E.5s that were approaching a row of German balloons west of the airfield at Bernes. He led six aircraft towards Brie, along the old Roman road, to catch the intruders, but was too late. Below and off to his right, still some kilometres away, a German balloon was on fire and an S.E.5 was framed by the burning hydrogen. He went after the fast, square-nosed RAF fighter, which dived for the ground to shake him off.

The two fighters roared over telegraph poles and roads lined by small trees. The church tower at Maricourt loomed ahead and the two aircraft – flown by highly skilled pilots – zoomed around it with aerobatic precision. Udet concentrated his machine-gun fire on the flight leader's red pennants flapping madly from the S.E.5's struts. Finally, Udet wrote: 'The machine shook, wavered, swirled into a turn, hit the ground, rose up like a stone skipping across water and disappeared with a mighty bound behind a small stand of birch trees. A cloud of smoke and steam rose up.'[76]

Udet's comrades had been dispersed and now he had three S.E.5s chasing him. None was as good as the pilot he had shot down, and by deft manoeuvring he slipped across the lines. Just when he thought he was safe, phosphorous ammunition ignited in the belts and threatened to set fire to his aircraft. A hard whack on the trigger guard freed the breech and sent the burning rounds tumbling behind him, still igniting and sending grey smoke trails arcing across the sky. He was amused by the thought that an opponent might view the action as some new rear-firing weapon.[77]

Once back on the ground at Bernes, Udet was helped out of his Fokker by mechanic Walter Behrend. On hearing that Geschwader commander Göring was due to return, Udet replied 'Yes, yes' and headed for his quarters. He had survived a harrowing fight and was scheduled to go on leave. In his typically single-minded way, he felt no need to chat with his new superior.

Udet knew that his latest opponent had been no novice, but he did not know that he and a major RAF ace had engaged in one of the war's last duels between high-scoring fighter pilots. RAF records reveal that Udet's opponent had been Captain Tom Falcon Hazell, DSO, DFC, leader of No. 24 Squadron's 'A' Flight, who ended the war with 43 victories. A report from Hazell's squadron confirms Udet's account:

'Capt Hazell dived on the balloon thinking the E.A. [enemy aircraft] would not come down, and put in 150–200 rounds of [incendiary ammunition] in two bursts down to ten yards, first at the nose and then from rear to front. [It] went down in flames after the second dive and one observer was seen to get clear.

'Capt Hazell was then seen home by the E.A., who shot his [fuel] tank, longerons and propeller to pieces.

'Lt [John H.] Southey tried to get on to a red E.A. which was attacking Capt Hazell, but could not do any good. He then attacked a grey one and fired 30 rounds at 50 yards' range and [it] retired.

' ... Lt [Ernest P.] Crossen and Lt [William C.] Sterling each had some indecisive fighting and the latter then separated [out after] a red E.A. at 1,500 ft and fired 130 rounds at close range and the E.A. went down vertically out of a turn. The result could not be observed as other E.A. then attacked Lt Sterling.'[78]

Jagdfliegerdämmerung

Oberleutnant Hermann Göring returned from leave and resumed his appointment as Kommandeur on 22 August. There was no hope of victory or a ceasefire to enable the German Army to prepare for a spring 1919 offensive. Ever the realist at the end, both in 1918 and in 1945, Göring must have sensed that his mission was to preside over a final, valiant but futile effort at least to preserve the honour of his pilots. Like Wagner's 'Götterdämmerung' (Twilight of the Gods), the final months of air fighting would be a heroic immolation, as the Jagdflieger sought to eliminate their foes, despite the impossibility of achieving an overall victory. But a realist also puts aside something for another day and, even then, Göring began to plan for the future.

Göring assured his own niche in the history of Jagdgeschwader I by breaking with the tradition of flying a Kommandeur's red-coloured aircraft. He left that hallmark for Udet and established his own identity by flying an all-white Fokker.[79] After achieving his 22nd victory – the only one scored while flying with JG I – Göring took a less active personal role in the air war. Certainly he did not lack in bravery, but he knew that he had qualifications to revel in and, it was to be hoped, capitalise on by being the 'successor' to Manfred von Richthofen in the years to come.

At the moment, JG I's withdrawal further behind the 18. Armee Front at the end of August was of greater concern to Göring; he left matters of individual achievement and glory to underlings such as Leutnant Richard Wenzl. After forcing down a Sopwith F.1 Camel, his seventh opponent, on the morning of 4

September, Wenzl was quick to seize a 'souveniring' opportunity worthy of Richthofen, as he described after the war:

'When I approached his machine ... he had already been taken away by a military police crew. So I did not learn his name, only that he was a British Lieutenant who had shot down 24 German aircraft. His [air fighting] technique could attest to that. His machine bore the serial number "5434". I took with me as souvenirs his telescope gunsight and a [fuselage] cockade, as well as his cockpit clock. The latter has been nicely mounted, now reposes on my writing-desk and keeps very good time.'[80]

Wenzl was a good, hard-fighting pilot who would score a total of 12 victories by the end of the war. But he was not the 'steady performer' that Udet had been and, as Göring did not attract and cultivate emerging talent in the manner of Manfred von Richthofen, JG I's performance dropped.

The Geschwader's situation was made worse by the steady loss of pilots. On 5 September, Jasta 6's Wenzl and a Silesian-born former Uhlan from Jasta 4, Leutnant Egon Koepsch,[81] scored their eighth victories, but Koepsch's wingman was lost that day. Leutnant Joachim von Winterfeld, the scion of a centuries-old German family, who entered the war as a cavalry officer,[82] was in an evening fight over Avesnes-le-Sec and Lieu-St-Amand, both old JG I airfield locations, when his aircraft was set alight. Winterfeld jumped out, but his badly damaged parachute did not fully deploy and he was in a critical condition when he was found and taken to an aid station, where he died a few hours later.[83] The victor of three combats, Winterfeld was eleven days short of his 22nd birthday when he died.

When no high-scoring fighter pilot emerged from the ranks of JG I, on 1 September Leutnant Ulrich Neckel was brought in as leader of Jasta 6. In less than a year Neckel had shot down a mix of 24 British and French aircraft. The 20-year-old ex-artilleryman[84] had flown on the Eastern and Western Fronts and had risen to command Jasta 12 before being given a prestigious position in the Richthofen Geschwader.

As Allied offensives in September continued to push back the German line, the need of better aircraft grew proportionately. Fortunately for many German pilots, Fokker D.VIIs were available at the Front. Newer types such as the stubby-looking but promising Siemens-Schuckert D.III could not be supplied in the numbers needed as the war drew to a close. Indeed, many German air units were hampered by a lack of spare parts, fuel and engine lubricants.

Still in good supply, however, were high awards to recognise achievement. JG I moved to Metz in Armee-Abteilung C's sector on 20 September and on the 29th three Geschwader pilots were awarded the Hohenzollern House Order with Swords:[85] Eberhardt Mohnike, who had nine victories to his credit when he was sent on convalescent leave on 8 September, but who had served as acting leader of Jasta 11 on three occasions; Erich-Rüdiger von Wedel of Jasta 11, who had 12 victories; and Arthur Laumann, who had scored the last five of his 28 victories as leader of Jasta 10 and would receive the *Pour le Mérite* within a month.

The Geschwader's reputation was well known to the High Command of the American Expeditionary Force, which alerted its air units to JG I's shift to an area directly opposite them: 'From latest information, [JG I] was reported to be equipped with Fokker biplanes. Losses in machines seem to be made good immediately with the best machines obtainable. This [air wing] seems to have taken part in the fighting wherever the Germans or Allies have started an offensive, and its transfer to the Conflans area would ... indicate that this sector is now regarded as an active one by the enemy.'[86]

JG I Meets the Yanks

Soon after moving to Marville, north of Verdun, in the 5. Armee sector on 7 October, the Geschwader clashed with American aircraft. On the afternoon of the 10th, five Fokkers dived on a flight of SPADs from the 147th Aero Squadron before they could attack a German balloon at Dun-sur-Meuse. After the fight began, the Germans discovered that their adversaries were part of a larger formation led by Captain Edward V. Rickenbacker, commanding officer of the 94th Aero Squadron, who reported that the Fokkers had 'the red noses of the von Richthofen Circus'.[87]

Rickenbacker and his comrades tried to distract the Fokkers from the balloon attackers, but to no avail. Leutnants Justus Grassmann and Wilhelm Kohlbach of Jasta 10 each claimed a SPAD.[88] Moments later, however, Rickenbacker set fire to Kohlbach's aircraft and recalled: 'I was ... gratified the next second to see the German pilot level off his blazing machine and with a sudden leap overboard into space let the Fokker slide safely away without him. Attached to his back and sides was a rope which immediately pulled a dainty parachute from the bottom of his seat. The [canopy] opened within a 50-ft drop and lowered him gradually to earth within his own lines.'[89]

After this fray, air combat activity wound down as the approach of winter made flying more difficult. But in any case the Germans had accepted American President Woodrow Wilson's 'Fourteen Points' on 20 October, which included the evacuation of all occupied territories.[90] The German Army's major challenge now was the conducting of an as orderly withdrawal as possible, and the salvaging of as much honour as conditions would allow. Two days later, Hermann Göring went on leave, as did Ernst Udet, who had been promoted to Oberleutnant der Reserve on 14 September and then scored his 61st and 62nd victories almost three weeks later. With the impending dissolution of Imperial Germany's military might, firm hands were needed at all levels of command. Thus, Göring was succeeded by another professional officer, Oberleutnant Erich-Rüdiger von Wedel and Udet by the 6-victory ace Leutnant Heinrich Maushake.[91]

The next day, two balloons and a SPAD were credited to Leutnant der Reserve Friedrich Noltenius, a strong JG I performer whose accomplishments were eclipsed by more flamboyant personalities. The SPAD, Noltenius' 18th victory, was piloted by an American, Sergent Edwin B. Fairchild, of Escadrille Spa 59, who had enlisted in French service prior to the US entry into the war, had one German balloon to his credit and remained with his Gallic comrades to the end.[92] The war had devolved to the point where idealistic young men such as Noltenius and Fairchild struggled to get in the last shots, irrespective of the results.

Noltenius' 21st and final victory, an American D.H.4 of the 11th Aero Squadron, shot down on 4 November, qualified him for the *Orden Pour le Mérite*,[93] but it was too late in the war for the Prussian Orders Chancellery in Berlin to process such honours properly. The German capital was in turmoil, as Bolshevik-inspired revolutionary fever swept the all but defeated Second Reich of Kaiser Wilhelm II.

For Jagdgeschwader Freiherr von Richthofen Nr I, the last day of battle was Wednesday, 6 November 1918. Still operating from Marville, Leutnants Ulrich Neckel, Justus Grassmann and Alois Heldmann shot down three American SPAD S.XIIIs near Woevre Wood.[94] The feeling of triumph did not last, because next day the Geschwader withdrew even further to Tellancourt.

On Friday, 8 November, Ulrich Neckel became the final JG I recipient of the *Pour le Mérite*. Next day, Kaiser Wilhelm II abdicated and left Germany in a shambles for a comfortable exile in Holland. There, he would write his memoirs and mention Oswald Freiherr von Richthofen, the geographer whose work led to establishment of a German enclave in Qiangdao, China in 1897[95] – and not a word about the 'Red Baron', his most worthy aerial knight and highest decorated airman, or the valiant members of JG I who risked everything for the last Kaiser's misplaced ambitions.

On the day his emperor quit, the recently returned Oberleutnant Hermann Göring began organising JG I's withdrawal to Germany. Men and *matériel* were readied for loading into lorries bound for the next, as yet undecided, destination. Next day, wearying and confusing orders and counter-orders came in, directing and redirecting the units. Finally, on 11 November the Armistice took effect and Göring decided that the aircraft would go to Darmstadt, followed by the lorries.

En route to Darmstadt, a flight landed in Mannheim, where the pilots and aircraft were seized by a local soldiers' and workers' council, a communist-style collection of would-be revolutionaries and military deserters. The pilots were disarmed and held until other Geschwader officers landed and gave the council leaders an ultimatum from Göring: 'If the officers are not allowed to take off immediately, with their weapons, the airfield [at Mannheim] will be razed to the ground.'[96] Fokkers circling overhead reinforced the message and the aircraft were released quickly.

Geschwader pilots performed one final defiant act against their victors. Having left the Front and avoided turning over their aircraft to the Americans, they were directed to fly to Strasbourg and surrender them to French authorities. Hermann Göring said that he could not carry out such an order and his pilots made things easier for him: they had 'accidents' while landing at Darmstadt and wrecked all their aircraft.

From Darmstadt it was a short distance to the Geschwader's ultimate destination, Aschaffenburg, where the men were welcomed as heroes. A paper factory was converted to a barracks for the enlisted men, and the officers were honoured guests of the factory's owner, Commercial Privy Councillor Schmitt-Prym.

At its final meeting in a monastery wine cellar (*Stiftskeller*) in the historic city along the River Main, Jagdgeschwader I had – like the contents of the casks on the walls – been distilled to its essence, the men who fought in the air and the groundcrews who supported them. Fifty-three officers and 473 non-commissioned officers and non-rated men[97] sat in a form of perversely satisfied silence as the last Kommandeur made an impassioned speech, which stirred the survivors, many of whom had a personal link to Manfred von Richthofen.

Göring also planted a poisoned seed in their minds: that they had been totally victorious and undefeated in the air. His final report noted that JG I had accounted for 644 British, French and American aircraft at a cost of 56 officers and enlisted pilots and six groundcrew killed and a further 52 officers and pilots and seven enlisted men wounded.[98] It was a record to be envied and the stuff of legend that future propagandists would exploit when they prepared for the 20th century's second world war.

Göring assured the JG I survivors that they had acquitted themselves well on their aerial battlefield. His comments presaged Erich Ludendorff's later sentiment that the German military had been 'stabbed in the back' by the politicians – ignoring the reality of having been overwhelmed by a force superior in numbers and resources. It was the concluding allusion to the Siegfried legend; the great hero, unvanquished in battle, but struck down from behind by his trusted armourer.

The post-war period gave rise to a new pantheon of German air heroes, of whom Manfred von Richthofen would be extolled as the greatest. Even greater than his mentor Oswald Boelcke. Richthofen was remembered in the Second World War when the Luftwaffe had Geschwaders named for him, Boelcke, Immelmann and Udet. But of all these heroic figures, Manfred von Richthofen remains at the top of the list. Today, the much smaller Luftwaffe of the Federal Republic of Germany has only one Geschwader of fighter/attack aircraft for its role within NATO and it bears the time-honoured name of Rittmeister Manfred Freiherr von Richthofen. Its members are proud that their unit is the direct descendant of the Richthofen Combat Wing established on 24 June 1917.

Notes

1 Bodenschatz, K., *Jagd in Flanderns*, p. 188.
2 Ishoven, A. van, *Fall of an Eagle*, p. 208.
3 See Appendix 1 for details.
4 Wenzl, R., *Richthofen-Flieger*,p. 47.
5 Commissioned into 2. Grossherzlich Hessisches Feldartillerie-Regiment Nr. 61; Haehnelt, W., *Ehren-liste*, p. 84.
6 Kromer, 'Fallschirme', in Neumann, G. (ed.), *Deutschen Luftstreitkräfte*, pp. 219–27.
7 Kogenluft, *Nachrichtenblatt der Luftstreitkräfte*, 2. Jg, Nr. 20, 11 July 1918, p. 292; this source lists the date as 28 June 1918; Bodenschatz and other sources identify 29 June as the date.
8 Ibid.; a squad from Infanterie-Regiment Freiherr von Sparr (3. Westfälisches) Nr. 16.
9 Bodenschatz, op. cit., p. 110; O'Connor, N., *Aviation Awards*, vol. II, p. 220.
10 Fokker D.VII 4253/18.
11 VanWyngarden, G., *Flying Circus*, p. 14.
12 Kogenluft, op. cit., 2. Jg, Nr. 30, 19 September 1918, p. 467; Capt René Fonck, who by now had scored 49 of his 75 victories, was the leading French fighter ace (Ref: Franks, N., and Bailey, F., *Over the Front*, p. 160).
13 Hartney, H., *Up And At 'Em*, , p. 169; Udet was thought to be the Geschwader commander because his reputation was so far greater than Göring's at that time.
14 *Air Service Bulletin*, 31 October 1918, p. 5.
15 Hartney, op. cit., p. 172; JG I recorded no losses from this fight, but two Americans were brought down: 1/Lt Edward Elliott (KiA) and 1/Lt Walter B. Wanamaker (WiA/PoW).
16 Quoted in O'Connor, op. cit., vol. I, p. 18.
17 Bodenschatz, op. cit., pp. 112, 190.
18 Dornier D.I 1751/18; Terry, G., 'Dornier Landplanes', in *Cross & Cockade*, 1981, p. 112.
19 Quoted in Zuerl, W., *Pour le Mérite-Flieger*, p. 537.
20 From 147th Aero Squadron, USAS, 2/Lt Maxwell O. Parry (KiA).
21 Commissioned into the 2. Thüringisches Infanterie-Regiment Nr. 32; Zuerl, op. cit., p. 508; O'Connor, op. cit., p. 93.
22 Bodenschatz, op. cit., p. 114; this is not an unbiased account,because Bodenschatz was Göring's adjutant when JG I's war diary was published, and served on his staff until the end of the Second

World War, by which time he held the rank of General der Flieger. He was interned for two years after the war and died on 25 August 1979 aged 88 (Ref: Hildebrand, K., *Die Generale*, pp. 89–90).

23 Commissioned into the 4. Badisches Infanterie-Regiment Prinz Wilhelm Nr. 112.

24 Fokker D.VII 309/18; Wenzl, op. cit., p. 57.

25 Bodenschatz, op. cit., pp. 115–17.

26 Commissioned into the 1. Badisches Leib-Dragoner-Regiment Nr. 20; Fokker D.VII 2063/18; Bodenschatz, op. cit., pp. 116–17, 191.

27 Commissioned into Eisenbahn-Regiment Nr. 1.

28 Zuerl, op. cit., p. 261.

29 Wenzl, op. cit., p. 53.

30 Fokker D.VII 294/18 (Ref: Bodenschatz, op. cit., p. 192).

31 Ibid., pp. 118–20, 188.

32 Richthofen, L. von, 'Das letzte Mal an der Front', in Dickhuth-Harrach, G. von (ed.), *Im Felde unbesiegt*, vol. I, p. 279.

33 Lothar's victim was one of three Camels lost by No. 73 Squadron in that fight: B.7874, 2/Lt K. S. Laurie (PoW); D.1794, 2/Lt William A. Armstrong (KiA); and D.9398, Lt Richard F. Lewis, aged 20 (KiA).

34 Kofl 7. Armee *Fliegertagesmeldung* Nr. 211, 26 July 1918 credits Lothar with scoring JG I's 500th victory, as do other sources.

35 No. 73 Squadron Combat Report No. 77 of Lt W. S. Stephenson in Sopwith F.1 Camel C.8296; During the Second World War he played a prominent role in Allied counter-intelligence, using the cover name 'Intrepid', for which he was knighted by King George VI.

36 Commissioned into Leib-Kürassier-Regiment Grosser Kurfürst (Schlesisches) Nr. 1, the same unit as a Richthofen cousin, Ltn Oskar von Schickfuss und Neudorff, who was killed aged 23 while flying with Jasta 3.

37 Haehnelt, op. cit., p. 34.

38 Franks, N., et al., *Above the Lines*, p. 102.

39 7. Armee-Oberkommando, *Befehl über die Rückverlegung und Aufklärung der Fliegerverbände bei der Einnahme der Vesle-Stellung*, 29 July 1918, p. 7.

40 Puglisi, W., '27th Aero Black Day', in *Cross & Cockade*, 1962, pp. 229–38; see Appendix I for details.

41 Hartney, op. cit., pp. 322–33; conversely, Escadrille Spa 215 recorded the loss of four 'SPAD S.XI [fighters] *au cours combat*' that day and, as there was no SPAD S.XI, they were S.XII or S.XIII aircraft (Ref: *État Nominatif*, No. 29488, 21 September 1918, p. 1).

42 Richthofen, op. cit., p. 281.

43 Ibid.

44 Bodenschatz, op. cit., p. 195.

45 Wenzl, op. cit., p. 58.

46 Commissioned into Kulmer Infanterie-Regiment Nr. 141.

47 Esposito, E. (ed.), *Concise History*, pp. 118–19.

48 Quoted in Bodenschatz, op. cit., p. 123.

49 Richthofen, op. cit., p. 288.

50 Ibid., p. 287.

51 Bodenschatz, op. cit., pp. 125, 196.

52 Richthofen, op. cit., p. 289.

53 Zuerl, op. cit., p. 322.

54 Henshaw, T., *Sky Their Battlefield*, p. 378.

55 Richthofen, op. cit., p. 290.

56 Haehnelt, op. cit., p. 50; Bodenschatz, op. cit., p. 132.

57 Bodenschatz, op. cit., p. 198; there was no D.H.12 aircraft (Ref: Bruce, J., *British Aeroplanes*, pp. 157–215); Ltn Ernst Udet of Jasta 4 also claimed a 'D.H.12' as his 55th victory that day (Ref: Udet, *Fliegerleben*, p. 183); these two-seaters might have been D.H.9s, of which RAF *Casualty List* notes four were lost that day – but all in the 4. Armee area; they remain 'mystery victories'.

58 RAF *Communiqué* No. 19, 14 August 1918, p. 5.

59 Wenzl, op. cit., p. 65.

60 Ibid., p. 66; Wenzl claims that his opponent was 'the famous British ace Collinhow' (Major Raymond Collishaw, then commanding officer of No. 203 Squadron, who claimed no victories that day), but it is more likely to have been Captain John K. Summers of No. 209 Squadron.

61 Commissioned into Leibgarde-Infanterie-Regiment (1. Grossherzoglich Hessisches) Nr. 115.

62 Haehnelt, op. cit., p. 92.

63 Zuerl, op. cit., p. 210; O'Connor, op. cit., p. 82.

64 Bodenschatz, op. cit., p. 130.

65 Commissioned into Infanterie-Regiment von Boyen (5. Ostpreusssisches) Nr. 41, Mohnike died on 14 October 1930.

66 Shores, C., et al., *Above the Trenches*, p. 373; Festler had been commissioned into Feldartillerie-Regiment König Karl (1. Württembergisches) Nr. 13.

67 Richthofen, op. cit., p. 292.

68 Ibid.

69 148th Aero Squadron Combat Report of 1/Lt G. V. Seibold in Sopwith F.1 Camel D.8803; several sources report Lothar von Richthofen as the fourth victory of 1/Lt Field E. Kindley, who flew Sopwith F.1 Camel D.8245 in this fight, but Kindley claimed credit for a German two-seater, not a single-seat Fokker D.VII, as did Seibold.

70 D.9595 of No. 203 Squadron, Sgt P. M. Fletcher (PoW); Wenzl, op. cit., p. 67.

71 Kofl 2. Armee, *Wochenbericht* Nr. 1668, Teil 5, 22 August 1918.

72 RAF *Summary of Air Intelligence* No. 179, 18 August 1918, p. 1.

73 Bruce, J. M. *Fokker D.VIII*, pp. 6–7.

74 Fokker D.VII 4253/18.

75 Udet, op. cit., pp. 182–4; Franks, et al., op. cit., pp. 220–21.

76 Udet, ibid., pp. 111–13.

77 Ibid., p. 114.

78 No. 24 Squadron Combat Report of Capt Hazell, Lts Southey, Crossen and Sterling in S.E.5as B.8422, C.1813, C.6913 and C.6967. RAF records make no mention of injuries to Capt Hazell or destruction of his S.E.5a, as claimed by Udet; but Hazell's next victory, on 4 September 1918, was achieved in S.E.5a E.1269 (Ref: RAF Combat Report).

79 Fokker D.VII 5125/18; Nowarra, H., *Eisernes Kreuz*, p. 114.

80 Wenzl, op. cit., p. 71; his opponent was Sopwith F.1 Camel B.5434 of No. 46 Squadron, 2/Lt C. H. P. Killick (PoW), who, despite Wenzl's information, appears on no list of RAF fighter aces.

81 Commissioned into Ulanen-Regiment von Katzler (Schlesisches) Nr. 2, Koepsch was an observer in Flieger-Abteilung (A) 256 before transferring to Jasta 4 where he accounted for nine enemy aircraft. Later trained as an attorney, he entered the German military legal system in 1935 and rose to the rank of Judge Advocate General in the Luftwaffe. He was interned for two years after the Second World War, and died on 26 November 1976 (Ref: Hildebrand, K., *Die Generale*, vol. II, pp. 204–5].

82 Perthes, J., *Ehrentafel*, p. 274; commissioned into Kürassier-Regiment Kaiser Nikolaus I. von Russland (Brandenburgisches) Nr. 6.

83 Winterfeld family chronicle, which also notes that the pilot's body was sent to the family estate in Saxony for burial. The estate was expropriated by the post-Second World War Communist state and the family cemetery was paved over and used as a tractor repair station.

84 He enlisted in Holsteinisches Feldartillerie-Regiment Nr. 24.

85 Bodenschatz, op. cit., p. 204.

86 GHQ AEF, *Summary of Air Information*, No. 58, 28 September 1918, p. 175.

87 Rickenbacker, E., *Flying Circus*, p. 282.

88 The 147th Aero Squadron lost two SPADs that day, one flown by 2/Lt William E. Brotherton (KiA) and the other by 2/Lt Wilbur W. White, Jr. (KiA). But White collided with a Fokker D.VII of Jasta 60 and is not numbered on any German victory list (Ref: Parks, J., 'No Greater Love', in *Over the Front*, 1986, p. 46).

89 Rickenbacker, op. cit., p. 285. He shot down two Fokker D.VIIs that day, recorded as the 19th and 20th of his 26 victories; Ltn Wilhelm Kohlbach, commissioned into Grenadier-Regiment König Wilhelm I. (2. Westpreussisches) Nr. 7, was an Observer with Fl.-Abt. (A) 255 before being posted

to JG I. He returned to the Luftwaffe in 1935, rose to the rank of Generalmajor and died aged 50 as a PoW in Britain on 11 February 1947 (Ref: Hildebrand, op. cit., pp. 207–8).

90 Esposito, op. cit., p. 131.

91 Bodenschatz, op. cit., p. 207.

92 Hall, J. and Nordhoff, C., (eds.), *Lafayette*, vol. I, pp. 230–1.

93 Ferko, A. E., 'Noltenius', in *Cross & Cockade*, 1966, p. 309; Zuerl, op. cit., p. 528.

94 Bodenschatz, op. cit., pp. 139, 209; the fight was with aircraft of 28th Aero Squadron, USAS, which lost 1/Lt Ben E. Brown and 1/Lt Hugh C. McClung (both PoW) (Ref: 'History of the 28th' in *Cross & Cockade*, pp. 344–5).

95 Kaiser Wilhelm II, *Memoirs*, p. 62.

96 Bodenschatz, op. cit., p. 141.

97 'Göring musterte 1918 in Aschaffenburg ab' in *Aschaffenburger Volksblatt*, 26 November 1988.

98 Bodenschatz, op. cit.

Daily Victory and Casualty Lists of JG I Units

Many German aviation records of the First World War in the Reichsarchiv at Potsdam were destroyed by Allied bombing during the Second World War. Rumours persist that some – or even most – of this material was seized by the Red Army in 1945 and taken to unknown locations in the former Soviet Union. Until this issue is resolved, German squadron war diaries, record books, combat reports and other documentation are not as complete as those of other belligerents of the 1914–18 war.

To present an overview of Jagdgeschwader I's operations, the following chronologies have been assembled from existing German Army and Air Force records. A noteworthy and relatively complete source is the weekly *Nachrichtenblatt der Luftstreitkräfte*. Often, air combat victories were calculated differently by individual Armees and the staff of the Commanding General of the Air Force. The differences are reflected in the tables below, where the first figure given is that reported in the *Nachrichtenblatt* and the second is from an Armee, Gruppe or other local source. The following information is based on the latest available archival material. For consistency, abbreviations are used: Ac (accident); C/Ui (crash, uninjured); EA (enemy aircraft); DoW (died of wounds); FtL (forced to land); I/A (injured in an accident); IiC (injured in a crash); KiA (killed in action); KiC (killed in a crash); n/c (not confirmed); PoW (prisoner of war); SD/P (shot down, parachuted to safety); and WiA (wounded in action).

JASTA 4

Date	Time	Pilot & Victory Number	Aircraft Type	Location	Status
1916					
6. 9.		Lt Bernert – 4	Caudron	Dompierre	1
7. 9.		Lt d R Frankl – 9	Nieuport	Allennes	2
17. 9.		Oblt Berthold – 7	Martinsyde	Cambrai	3
22. 9.		Lt. d R Frankl – 10	B.E.12		4
22. 9.		Lt Bernert	B.E.2		FtL
* 23. 9.		Lt d R Fügner	WiA		
26. 9.		Lt d R Frankl – 11	Caudron	Rancourt	6
.10.		Lt d R Frankl – 12			7
10.10.		Lt d R Frankl – 13	Nieuport	Villers-Carbonnel	8
20.10.		Vzfw Clausnitzer – 1	F.E.2b	Barleux	9
22.10.		Lt d R Frankl – 14	Sopw 2-seater	Metz/Ortschofer	10
9.11.		Lt Bernert – 5	D.H.2	Adinfer/Le Sars	11
9.11.		Lt Bernert – 6	D.H.2	Adinfer/Havrincourt	12
9.11.		Lt Bernert – 7	B.E.2	Arras	13
1917					
* 4. 3.	1600	Oblt d R von Althaus	WiA		
6. 3.	1645	Lt d R. Kralewski –1	Sopw 2-seater	Ransart	14
24. 3.	1040	Vzfw Patermann – */1	F.E.[2b]	Heudicourt	15
		(contested by Lt Schulte, Jasta 12)			
(25 March 1917: German time synchronised with Allied time)					
4. 4.	0900	Lt d R Klein – 1	B.E.[2e]	Arras	16
4. 4.	0950	Lt Malchow – 1	F.E.[2b]	SW of Arras	17
5. 4.	0230	Lt d R Frankl – 19/15	F.E.2b 7714	Douai airfield	18
6. 4.	0850	Lt d R Frankl – 15/16	F.E.[2b]	Arras	19
6. 4.	0850	Lt d R Frankl – 16/17	F.E.[2b]	between Feuchy & Arras	20
6. 4.	1000	Lt d R Frankl – 17/18	B.E.[2d]	between Boiry & Sailly	21
7. 4.	1700	Lt d R Klein – 2	Balloon	W of Arras	22
7. 4.	1710	Vzfw Patermann – 1/2	Nieuport 17 A.6692	Neuvireuil–Fresnes– Biaches	23
7. 4.	1925	Lt d R Frankl – 18/19	Nieuport 17 4635	Fampoux	24
8. 4.	0420	Lt d R Klein – 3	F.E.[2b]	Douai	25

Date	Time	Pilot & Victory Number	Aircraft Type	Location	Status
8. 4.	1330	Lt d R Frankl – */20	EA [R.E.8]	Arras	26
†8. 4.		Lt d R Frankl	KiA	between Vitry & Sailly	
11. 4.	1020	Lt d R Klein – 4	B.E.[2e]	between Biaches & Vitry	27
11. 4.	1050	Lt d R Klein – 5	B.E.[2e]	Roeux	28
13. 4.	0856	Lt d R Klein –6	F.E.[2b]	NW of Vitry (between Biaches & Hamblain)	29
13. 4.	1910	Lt d R Klein – 7	F.E.[2b]	Vimy	30
14. 4.	0934	Oblt von Döring – 1	Nieuport	between Willerval & Fresnoy	31

(17 April 1917: German time one hour ahead of Allied time)

Date	Time	Pilot & Victory Number	Aircraft Type	Location	Status
30. 4.	1200	Lt d R Klein – 8	F.E.[2b]	Ribécourt	32
1. 5.	1020	Oblt von Döring – 2	Sopw Triplane	Arleux-en-Gohelle	33
6. 5.	1615	Lt d R Klein – 9	B.E.[2]	between Lens & Liéven	34
19. 5.	2055	Lt Groos – 1	Sopw Triplane	between Droucourt & Izel	35
†19. 5.		Lt d R Fügner	KiA	Izel, near Douai	
25. 5.	1850	Vzfw Schmelcher – */1	B.E.[2]	Arras	
26. 5.	1035	Vzfw Schmelcher – */2	B.E.[2]	Oppy	
9. 6.	1525	Oblt von Döring – 3	Nieuport	Zandvoorde	36
15. 6.	2130	Vzfw Wüsthoff – 1	Sopw/SPAD	Vormezelle	37
18. 6.	1530	Lt d R Klein – 10	R.E.8	Messines	38
23. 6.	1443	Lt d R Klein – 11	Balloon	Wytschaete	39
23. 6.	1443	Vzfw Clausnitzer – 2	Balloon	Wytschaete	40
23. 6.	1443	Vzfw Wüsthoff – 2	Balloon	Wytschaete	41
24. 6.	1240	Lt d R Klein – 12	Balloon	W of Wytschaete	42
6. 7.	1525	Lt d R Klein –13	Sopw 2-seater	Frezenberg	43
7. 7.	1105	Lt d R Krüger – 1	Sopw Triplane	W of Wervicq	44
7. 7.	1430	Vzfw Clausnitzer – 3	Nieuport	between Gheluvelt & Zillebeke	45
7. 7.	1807	Lt d R Klein – 14	Sopwith	between Houthem & Comines	46
7. 7.	1820	Lt d R Anders – 1	Sopw 2-seater	Hollebeke	47
11. 7.	1505	Lt d R Klein – 15	Balloon	W of Wytschaete	48
11. 7.	1507	Lt d R Klein – 16	Balloon	W of Wytschaete	49
11. 7.	1510	Vzfw Wüsthoff – 3	Balloon	W of Wytschaete	50
11. 7.	2145	Vzfw Patermann – 2	SPAD/Sopw [D.H.5]	Houthem	51
†11. 7.	1100	Vzfw Patermann	KiA	Gheluvelt	
12. 7.	2105	Vzfw Marquardt – 1	Sopwith	Zandvoorde	52
12. 7.	2120	Lt d R Hübner – 1	Sopw Triplane	Zuidschoote	53
*13. 7.	1130	Lt d R Klein	WiA		
*16. 7.	1735	Vzfw Clausnitzer (Alb D.V 1162/17)	FtL/PoW	SE Poperinghe (G 56)	
16. 7.	1815	Vzfw Wüsthoff – 4	Balloon	Kemmel	54
†17. 7.	1315	Lt d R Krüger	KiA	between Wervicq & Comines	
20. 7.	0900	Lt von Boenigk – 1	Sopwith (Nieuport 17)	NW of Tenbrielen	55
20. 7.	2120	Vzfw Wüsthoff – 5	Sopwith	between Becelaere & Gheluvelt	56
22. 7.	1040	Lt von Döring – 4 (contested by Lt Adam, Jasta 6)	SPAD S.VII	between Sangelaere & Mangelaere	57
22. 7.	2050	Lt von Döring – 5	Nieuport	Oosttaverne, over forward lines	58
27. 7.	2040	Vzfw Wüsthoff – */6	Sopwith	Dadizele	FtL
28. 7.	2100	Lt von Boenigk – 2	Sopw Camel	Moorslede	59
31. 7.	1250	Lt d R Hübner – 2	Bristol F.2B	S of Zillebeke	60
31. 7.	1445	Vzfw Wüsthoff – 6/7	F.E.2	Verbrandenmolen	61
4. 8.	2055	Lt. d R Hübner – 3	Caudron	Reninghe	62
5. 8.	1500	Lt.d.R Wüsthoff – 7/8	Nieuport 23	W of Ypres	63
5. 8.	1515	Lt von Boenigk – */3	Sopw Camel	W of Staden	

Date	Time	Pilot & Victory Number	Aircraft Type	Location	Status
*10. 8.	2000	Lt d R Rouselle	WiA/FtL	Artoishoek	
13. 8.	2000	Lt d R Hübner – 4/*	British 1-seater	NW of Ypres	64
†14. 8.	2035	Lt d R R. Hübner	KiA	Slypskappelle	
18. 8.	1205	Lt Schulze – 1/*	R.E.8	Boesinghe	65
23. 8.	0905	Oblt von Boenigk – 3	Sopw Triplane	Boesinghe, N of Ypres	66
3. 9.	0830	Lt d R Wüsthoff – 8/9	Sopw Camel	S of Tenbrielen	67
3. 9.	1210	Oblt von Döring – */6	R.E.8	NW of Houthem	68
3. 9.	1700	Lt d R Wüsthoff –9/10	R.E.8	E of Zillebeke	69
3. 9.	2000	Oblt von Boenigk – */4	Sopwith	Houthem	
3. 9.	2015	Oblt von Boenigk – 4/5	Sopwith	near Tenbrielen	70
4. 9.	0805	Lt d R Wüsthoff – 10/11	Nieuport 23	NW. of Polygon Wood	71
4. 9.	1045	Lt d R Wüsthoff – 11/12	Sopwith	Ypres	72
5. 9.	1000	Lt d R Wüsthoff – 12	Sopwith	N of Zillebeke Lake	73
9. 9	1905	Oblt von Boenigk – 5	Sopw Triplane	between Langemarck & Poelkappelle	74
11. 9.	1020	Lt d R Wüsthoff –16/13	Sopwith	between Langemarck & St-Julien	75
12. 9.	2000	Lt d R Wüsthoff – 13/14	Sopwith	between Deûlémont & Armentières	76
13. 9.	0830	Lt d R Wüsthoff – 14/15	Sopw Triplane	S of Wervicq	77
15. 9	1930	Lt d R Wüsthoff – */16	Sopwith	NW of Wervicq	78
16. 9.	1245	Oblt von Döring – 8/7	Sopw	W of Staden	79
16. 9.	1245	Lt d R Wüsthoff – 15/17	Sopwith	W of Staden	80
17. 9.	0840	Lt d R Hertz – */1	Nieuport	Houthulst Forest	81
20. 9.	1215	Lt d R Wüsthoff – 17/18	SPAD S.7	near America	82
20. 9.	1230	Oblt von Döring – */8	SPAD	S of Ypres	83
20. 9.	1430	Lt d R Wüsthoff – 18/19	SPAD	W of Langemarck	84
22. 9.	1410	Lt d R Wüsthoff – 19/20	Sopwith	Langemarck	85
23. 9.	1130	Oblt von Döring – 7/9	Sopwith	Langemarck	86
24. 9.	1650	Lt d R Wüsthoff – 20/21	Sopwith	Moorslede	87
26. 9.	1040	Lt d R Wüsthoff – 21/22	SPAD S.7	between Becelaere & Bellewarde Lake	88
26. 9.	1040	Lt Joschkowitz – */1	SPAD S.7	Becelaere	89
5.10.	0745	Lt d R Wilde – 1	Sopw Triplane	Dadizele	90
21.10.	1600	Oblt von Döring – 9	S.E.5	between Moorslede & Vierkavenhoek	91
27.10.	0930	Lt d R Wüsthoff – 22	Sopw Triplane	between Poelkappelle & Hooge	92
31.10.	1230	Lt d R Wüsthoff – 23	S.E.5	Bellewarde Lake	93
5.11.	1245	Lt d R Wüsthoff – 25/24	Sopw Camel	Poelkappelle	94
5.11.	1300	Lt d R Wüsthoff – 24/25	Sopwith	S of Staden	95
9.11.	1030	Lt d R Wüsthoff – 26	R.E.8	N of Bellewarde Lake	96
†30.11.	1135	Lt Schulze	KiC	Fontaine-Notre-Dame	97
5.12.	1235	Lt d R Koepsch – 1	Sopwith	Graincourt	98

1918

Date	Time	Pilot & Victory Number	Aircraft Type	Location	Status
*8. 3.		Lt Skauradzun (Pfalz D.III 4042/17)	WiA		

(10 March 1918: German time synchronised with Allied time)

Date	Time	Pilot & Victory Number	Aircraft Type	Location	Status
10. 3.		Lt d R Wüsthoff – 27	Sopw Camel	Souchez	99
12. 3.	1305	Lt d R Wüsthoff – */28	S.E.5	between La Bassée & Béthune	100
28. 3.	0930	Lt von Rautter – 1	Sopw Camel	Suzanne-sur-Somme	101
*28. 3.		Lt von der Osten (Alb D.V 4566/17)	WiA		
1. 4.	0800	Lt d R Siempelkamp – 1	Sopw Camel	SE of Fouilloy	102
3. 4.	1005	Lt von Rautter – 2	Arm-Whit F.K.8	1 km E of Blangy-Tronville	103
12. 4.	1400	Lt Hübner – 1	SPAD	Bayonvillers	104

Date	Time	Pilot & Victory Number	Aircraft Type	Location	Status
12. 4.	1400	Lt von Rautter – 3	French SPAD	Bayonvillers	105
(16 April 1918: German time one hour ahead of Allied time)					
23. 4.	0655	Lt d R Koepsch – 2	S.E.5	N of Sailly-Laurette	106
3. 5.	1100	Lt Hübner – 2	Arm-Whit F.K.8	between Buire & Morlancourt	107
3. 5.	1750	Lt von Rautter – 4	Bréguet	Chuignes	108
3. 5.	2050	Lt von Winterfeld – 1	Arm-Whit F.K.8	S of Blangy-Tronville	109
6. 5.	0815	Lt von Rautter – 5	R.E.8	S. of Méricourt	110
9. 5.	1315	Lt von Rautter – 6	D.H.9	Wiencourt	111
10. 5.	1640	Lt von Rautter – 7	Bristol F.2B	Chuignes	112
10. 5.	2025	Lt von Winterfeld – 2	Sopw Camel	between the lines, N of Le Hamel	113 / 113
10. 5.	2030	Lt von Rautter – 8	D.H.9	Rosières	114
15. 5.	1115	Lt von Gluczewski – */1	Bréguet	N of Harbonnières	115
15. 5.	1210	Sgt Schmutzler – 1	Sopw Camel	SW of Marcelcave	116
15. 5.	1215	Lt von Rautter – 9	Sopw Camel	S of Aubercourt	117
15. 5.	1805	Lt von Rautter – 10	Bréguet	N of Harbonnières	118
*16. 5.	1615	Lt Hübner (Fok Dr.I 546/17)	FtL/PoW	Corbie (G/5th Bde/8)	
†16. 5.	2000	Sgt Schmutzler	KiA	Rosières	119
17. 5.	1230	Lt d R Drekmann – 2	SPAD	Framerville	120
17. 5.	1705	Lt von Rautter – 12/11	S.E.5	S. of Foucaucourt	121
18. 5.	1240	Lt von Rautter – 13/12	D.H.9	Aubercourt	122
20. 5.	1125	Lt von Rautter – 11/13	Bristol F.2B	Lamotte-Warfusée	123
27. 5.	1815	Lt von Rautter – 14	Bréguet	Pont-Arcy	124
31. 5.	1255	Lt von Rautter – 15	Bréguet	SW of Soissons	125
†31. 5.		Lt von Rautter	KiA	Soissons	126
31. 5.	1300	Lt d R Udet – */24	Bréguet	SW of Soissons	127
2. 6.	1155	Lt d R Udet – 24/25	Bréguet	NW of Neuilly	128
2. 6.	1820	Lt d R Maushake –*	Bréguet	Montigny-l'Allier	FtL
4. 6.	1845	Lt d R Drekmann – 3	SPAD	Longpont	129
5. 6.	1200	Lt d R Udet – 25/26	French SPAD	S of Buzancy	130
6. 6.	1140	Lt d R Udet – 27	SPAD	S of Faverolles	131
7. 6.	0700	Lt d R Udet – 28 (1900 in his book)	SPAD	E of Villers-Cotterêts	132
13. 6.	0545	Lt d R Udet – 29 (1745 in his book)	SPAD	NE of Faverolles	133
13. 6.	0545	Lt d R Drekmann – 4 (1745 in Udet's book)	SPAD	NE of Noroy	134
14. 6.	0800	Lt d R Udet – 30 (2000 in his book)	SPAD	N of St-Pierre-Aigle	135
23. 6.	1210	Lt d R Udet – 31	Bréguet	La-Ferté-Milon	136
23. 6.	2015	Lt d R Udet – 32	Bréguet	Crouy	137
24. 6.	1000	Lt d R Udet – 33	Bréguet	SE of Montigny	138
25. 6.	1845	Lt d R Udet – 34	SPAD	woods NE of Longpont	139
25. 6.	1845	Lt d R Udet – 35	SPAD	Chavigny Ferme	140
27. 6.	2000	Lt d R Drekmann – 5	Balloon	Villers-Cotterêts	141
28. 6.	0945	Lt d R Drekmann – 6	SPAD	Puiseux	142
28. 6.	0945	Lt d R Maushake – 1/2	SPAD	E of Vierzy	143
28. 6.	0950	Lt d R Meyer – */2	SPAD	Villers-Cotterêts	144
*29. 6.	0740	Lt d R Udet (Fok D.VII 4253/18)	SD/P	Cutry	
29. 6.		Lt d R Udet – 39	SPAD		145
30. 6	2000	Lt d R Udet – */36	SPAD	Faverolles	146
1. 7.	1045	Lt d R Udet – 40/37 (1145 in his book)	Bréguet	between Pierrefonds & Mortefontaine	147
1. 7.	2055	Lt d R Udet – 36/38	French SPAD	E of Faverolles	148
2. 7.	0815	Lt d R Udet – 37/39	Nieuport	between Bézu & St-Germain	149

Date	Time	Pilot & Victory Number	Aircraft Type	Location	Status
3. 7.	0820	Lt d R Drekmann – 7	Bréguet	Nouvron	150
3. 7.	0825	Lt d R Drekmann – 8	SPAD	NW of Dompierre	151
3. 7.	0825	Lt d R Udet – 38/40	French SPAD	E of Laversine	152
15. 7.	1640	Lt d R Meyer – 3	French SPAD	N of Fossoy	153
*16. 7.	1930	Lt.d.R Bender	SD/P		
		(Fok D.VII (OAW) 2063/18)			
17. 7.	1045	Lt d R Maushake – 2	Bréguet	Vincelles, N of	154
				Dormans	
17. 7.	1050	Lt d R Koepsch – 3	Bréguet	Comblizy	155
18. 7.	0925	Lt d R Maushake – 3	D.H.9	SW of Anthenay	156
18. 7.	0930	Lt d R Meyer – 4	Sopw Camel	Mareuil	157
19. 7.	1530	Lt d R Maushake – 4	French SPAD	Hartennes	158
20. 7.	0830	Lt d R Drekmann – 9	D.H.9	Morsain	159
		(2025 in Udet's book)			
22. 7.	2030	Lt d R Koepsch –4	D.H.9	S of Braisne	160
25. 7	1930	Lt d R Drekmann –10	French SPAD	Oulchy	161
30. 7.	1950	Lt d R Drekmann – 11	SPAD	N of Grand-Rozoy	162
		(1830 in Udet's book)			
†30. 7.	1835	Lt d R Drekmann	KiA	Grand-Rozoy	163
1. 8.	0930	Lt d R Jessen – 1	Nieuport	Cuiry-Housse	164
1. 8.	0930	Lt d R Koepsch – 5	US Nieuport 28	S of Braisne	165
1. 8.	0930	Lt d R Udet – 41	Nieuport	NE of Cramaille	166
1. 8.	1215	Lt d R Udet – 42	Bréguet	N of Muret-et-Crouttes	167
1. 8.	1930	Lt d R Udet – 43	SPAD	N of Beugneux	168
		(2030 in his book)			
4. 8.	2000	Lt d R Jessen – 2	SPAD	N of Vauxtin	169
4. 8.	2000	Lt d R Udet – 52/44	SPAD	S of Braisne	170
8. 8.	1730	Lt d R Udet – 45	S.E.5	Fontaine-lès-Cappy	171
8. 8.	1830	Lt d R Udet – 46	S.E.5	SE of Barleux	172
8. 8.	1830	Lt d R Udet – 44/47	Sopw Camel	SE of Foucaucourt	173
9. 8.	1620	Lt d R Maushake – *	D.H.9		
9. 8.	1625	Lt d R Udet – 47/48	Sopw Camel	S of Vauvillers	174
9. 8.	2120	Lt d R Udet – 48/49	Sopw Camel	SE of Herleville	175
*9. 8.		Lt d R Reinhardt	WiA	Tincourt	
10. 8.	1120	Lt d R Udet – 49/50	Sopw Camel	S of Maricourt	176
10. 8.	1550	Lt d R Maushake – 5/7	R.E.8	S of Vauvillers	177
10. 8.	1945	Lt d R Udet – 50/51	Sopw Camel	S of Fay	178
11. 8.	1000	Lt d R Udet – 51/52	D.H.12	Chaulnes	179
12. 8.	1130	Lt d R Udet – 53	S.E.5	Péronne	180
13. 8.	1945	Lt d R Koepsch – 6	Bréguet	Bilancourt	181
14. 8.	1900	Lt d R Udet – 54	Bristol F.2B	S of Vermandovillers	182
15. 8.	1715	Lt d R Udet – 55	Sopw Camel	Herleville	183
16. 8.	1040	Lt d R Udet – 56	SPAD	S of Foucaucourt	184
21. 8.	1040	Lt d R Udet – 57	S.E.5	S of Hébuterne	185
21. 8.	1920	Lt d R Udet –58	Sopw Dolphin	S of Courcelles	186
22. 8.	0840	Lt d R Udet – 59	Sopw Camel	N of Bray	187
22. 8.	1230	Lt d R Udet – 60	S.E.5	W of Maricourt	188
*24. 8.		Oblt Grosch	WiA	Guise	
31. 8.	1620	Lt d R Koepsch – 7	S.E.5	Combles	189
5. 9.	1900	Lt d R Koepsch – 8	S.E.5	Paillencourt	190
†5. 9.		Lt von Winterfeld	KiA	St-Amand	
		(Fok D.VII)		(G/3rd Bde/17)	
6. 9.	1045	Lt d R Maushake – 7	Sopw Camel	SE of Aubencheul	191
26. 9.	1615	Lt von Gluszewski – 2	D.H.4/D.H.9	SE of Kemnat	192
26. 9.	1710	Oblt Udet – 61	D.H.4/D.H.9	Monteningen	193
26. 9.	1715	Oblt Udet – 62	D.H.4/D.H.9	S of Metz	194
26. 9.	1715	Lt d R Kraut – 1	D.H.4/D.H.9	Buchingen	195
3.11.	1650	Lt d R Hildebrandt –1	SPAD		196
3.11.	1650	Lt d R Geppert – 1	SPAD		197

Date	Time	Pilot & Victory Number	Aircraft Type	Location	Status
3.11.	1650	Lt d R Reinhardt – 1	SPAD		198
4.11.	1450	Lt d R Koepsch – 9	D.H.9	SW of Montmédy	199
4.11.	1650	Lt d R Noltenius – 21	D.H.9	Carignan	200
5.11.	1035	Lt d R Bahlmann – 1	D.H.4		201

JASTA 6

Date	Time	Pilot & Vic. #	Aircraft Type	Location	Status
1916					
20.10.		Vzfw Kress – 3	Morane Parasol		1
22.10.		Lt Mallinckrodt – *	Nieuport		
26.10.		Lt Nauck – 1	Farman		2
28.10.		Lt Mallinckrodt – 1	Caudron	Villeselve	3
28.10.		Lt d R Deilmann –*	Caudron		
2.11.		Vzfw Kress – 4	Voisin		4
3.11.		Vzfw Kress – *	2-seater		
3.11.		Hptm Wulff – 2	2-seater		5
9.11.		Hptm Wulff – 3	Caudron		6
9.11.		Lt d R Zschunke –*	Caudron		FtL
†10.11.		Vzfw Kress	KiA	Chaulnes	
16.11.		Lt d R F. Loerzer – 1	Caudron	SE of Pressoire	7
†16.11.		Lt Wever	KiA	Pressoire Wood	
*26.11.		Lt d R Zschunke	WiA		
26.12.		Lt Mallinckrodt –*	Caudron		FtL
1917					
25. 1.		Vzfw Holler – 1	Nieuport 741(?)	W of Roye	8
11. 2.		Vzfw Holler – 2	RFC Caudron	Berny, SW of Péronne	9
15. 3.	1730	Lt d R Küppers – 1	'Vikkers'	between Péronne & Bouchavesne	10
16. 3.		Fwlt Schubert – 1	Balloon	S of Roye	11
25. 3.		Lt d R Deilmann – 3	Sopw 1½-Str 7763	Ponchaux	12
(25 March 1917: German time synchronised with Allied time)					
25. 3.		Vzfw Häusler – 1	Sopwith	Sablonière	13
†8. 4.		Lt Nauck (Alb D.III 2234/16)	KiA	Villevegne, near St-Quentin (G 21)	
(17 April 1917: German time one hour ahead of Allied time)					
1. 5.	0815	Lt d R Deilmann – *	Sopw 1-seater	W of St-Quentin	FtL
1. 5.	0815	Vzfw Ey – *	Sopwith	Francilly	
2. 5.	0830	Lt Bernert – 24	Nieuport	S of St-Quentin	14
2. 5.	1840	Lt Bernert – 26	Balloon	Hervilly	15
4. 5.	1845	Lt Bernert – *	Balloon	Nauroy	
7. 5.	1540	Lt Bernert – 25	B.E.[2e] [A.2801]	Pontruet, near St-Quentin	16
10. 5.	1500	Vzfw Krebs – 2	RFC 'lattice-tail'	Briastre, N of Le Cateau	17
11. 5.	0935	Vzfw Krebs – 1	Sopwith	S of Lesdain	18
11. 5.	2045	Lt d R Küppers – 2	Nieuport	NE of Hargicourt	19
†18. 5.		Vzfw Ey	KiC		
19. 5.	1720	Lt Bernert – *	Vikkers [F.E.2b]	Villers-Guislain	FtL
19. 5.	1720	Vzfw Holler – 1/3	Vikkers [F.E.2b]	Villers-Guislain	20
30. 5.	0810	Vzfw Holler – 4	Sopwith	Ponchause	21
6. 6.	1355	Vzfw Krebs – 3	RFC 'lattice-tail'	SE of Le Catelet	22
14. 6.	0830	Lt d R Küppers – 3	Sopwith	NW of Dadizele	23
14. 6.	0830	Vzfw Krebs – 4	Sopw Triplane	E of Ypres, W of Poezelhoek Castle	24
16. 6.	1900	Oblt Dostler – 9	Sopwith	Houthem	25
16. 6.	1905	Vzfw von Raffay – 2	F.E.	NE of Ypres	26
16. 6.	1906	Fwlt Schubert – *	Sopwith	Warneton	FtL
16. 6.	1910	Oblt Dostler – 10	F.E.	Korentje, W of Ypres	27

Date	Time	Pilot & Victory Number	Aircraft Type	Location	Status
17. 6.	0955	Lt d R Pollandt – 1	S.E.5	W of Lille	28
17. 6.	1002	Vzfw Krebs – 5	S.E.5	W of Lille	29
17. 6.	2120	Oblt Dostler – 11	F.E.	St-Eloi	30
20. 6.	1800	Oblt Dostler – 12	Balloon	Bailleul area	31
20. 6.	1800	Lt d R Reiher – 1	Balloon	Bailleul area	32
†24. 6.		Lt d R Reiher (Alb D.V)	KiA	Ypres (G 49)	
5. 7.	1820	Oblt Dostler – 13	Balloon	N of Ypres	33
7. 7.	1135	Vzfw Krebs – 6	R.E.8	near Zillebeke	34
7. 7.	1205	Oblt Dostler – 14	Sopw 2-seater	Deûlémont, S of Warneton	35
12. 7.	1145	Lt d R Deilmann – 4	Nieuport	Hollebeke	36
12. 7.	1150	Oblt Dostler – 15	Sopwith	between Houthem & Hollebeke	37
12. 7.	1845	Lt d L Adam – 4	Sopwith	NE of Dickebusch Lake	38
12. 7.	1940	Lt d R Küppers – 4	Sopwith	Wytschaete	39
12. 7.	2130	Oblt Dostler – 16	Sopwith	near Zillebeke	40
13. 7.	1120	Lt d R Deilmann – 5	Nieuport	Zandvoorde	41
13. 7.	1130	Lt d L Adam – 5	Nieuport	Velhoek, NE of Ypres	42
13. 7.	1130	Vzfw Krebs – 7	Sopwith	between Zonnebeke & Moorslede	43
13. 7.	1135	Vzfw Krebs – 8	Sopwith	between St-Julien & Zonnebeke	44
13. 7.	1135	Oblt Dostler – 17	Sopwith	S of Becelaere	45
13. 7.	1140	Oblt Dostler – 18	Nieuport	N of Zonnebeke	46
16. 7.†	1945	Vzfw Krebs (Alb D.V 2129/17)	KiA	NE of Zonnebeke	
16. 7.	2005	Lt d L Adam – 6	Sopwith	Zonnebeke	47
†13. 7.	1315	Lt Krüger	DoW	Comines	
17. 7.	2105	Lt Tüxen – 1	Sopw	E of Comines	48
		(contested by Lt Deilmann, Jasta 6 and Vfw Wüsthoff, Jasta 4)			
20. 7.	0740	Lt d L Adam – 7	'lattice-tail'	SW of Ypres	49
20. 7.	0840	Lt W. Stock – */1	R.E.8	Armentières	50
21. 7.	2025	Fwlt Schubert – 2	SPAD	W of Roubaix	51
		(contested by Lt Mohnike, Jasta 11)			
25. 7.	1820	Lt d L Adam – 10/8	SPAD	Nordhofwyk, N of Ypres	52
28. 7.	1150	Vzfw Küllmer – 1	Nieuport	S of Dadizeele, N of Terhand	53
28. 7.	1210	Lt d L Adam – 8/9	Sopw/Nieuport	between Terhand & Becelaere	54
28. 7.	1850	Oblt Dostler – 19	D.H.4	NE of Courtrai	55
28. 7.	1850	Lt d R Czermak – 1	DH	Meulebeke, SW of Thielt	56
28. 7.	1855	Lt d L Adam – 9/10	'lattice-tail'	Ostrosebeke	57
28. 7.	1855	Lt d R Tüxen – 2	DH	E of Ingelmunster	58
28. 7.	1900	Oblt Dostler – 20	DH	Ostrosebeke	59
28. 7.	1900	Lt W. Stock – 1/2	DH	Kruishoutem railway station of Deinze	60
31. 7.	1405	Oblt Dostler – 21	Nieuport	W of Bellewarde Lake	61
9. 8.	1855	Oblt Dostler – 22	Nieuport	between Poelkappelle & Houthulst Forest	62
10. 8.	1530	Lt W. Stock – 2/3	Sopwith	N of Dadizeele	63
12. 8.	1555	Oblt Dostler – 23	SPAD/Sopw	W of Gheluwe	64
12. 8.	2110	Lt d L Adam – 11	RFC biplane	Poperinghe area	65
14. 8.	1930	Lt d L Adam – 12	Sopw 2-seater	Houthulst Forest	66
14. 8.	1930	Oblt Dostler – 24	Sopwith	between St-Julien & Poelkappelle	67
14. 8.	1930	Lt d R Czermak – *	Sopwith	W of Langemarck	FtL

Date	Time	Pilot & Victory Number	Aircraft Type	Location	Status
17. 8.	0810	Oblt Dostler – 25	Martinsyde	N of Menin	68
17. 8.	1110	Lt d R Deilmann – */6	F.E.[2d]	Zonnebeke	69
18. 8.	2015	Oblt Dostler – 26	D.H.4	Roeselare	70
21. 8.	1208	Oblt Dostler – *	biplane	Zonnebeke, over	
		(Kofl 4. credits)		forward lines	
†21. 8.	1200	Oblt Dostler	KiA	St-Julien	
		(Alb D.Va)		(G 64)	
31. 8.	1950	Lt d L Adam – 13	Sopwith	NW of Zonnebeke	71
3. 9.	1950	Lt d L Adam – 14	Nieuport	Koelenberg	72
15. 9.	1900	Lt d L Adam – 17/15	Sopw 1-seater	N of Ypres	73
17. 9.	0720	Vzfw Bachmann – */1	Sopwith	S of Zillebeke Lake	
19. 9.	1000	Lt d L Adam – 18/16	R.E.8	W of Ypres	74
19. 9.	1005	Lt d L Adam – 15/17	Sopwith	Houthulst Forest	75
19. 9.	1005	Lt d R Galetschky – */1	Sopwith	Houthulst Forest	
20. 9.	0940	Lt d L Adam – 19/17	Sopwith	W of Bellewarde Lake	76
20. 9.	0950	Lt d L Adam – 16/18	Sopwith	near Becelaere	77
20. 9.	0950	Lt K. Stock – */1	Sopw Triplane	Becelaere area	
20. 9.	1400	Vzfw Bachmann – 1/2	Balloon	Kemmel	78
23. 9.	1045	Lt. d L Adam – 20/19	R.E.8	N of Ypres	79
26. 9.	0720	Lt K. Stock – 1/2	SPAD	Becelaere	80
*30. 9.		Vzfw Stumpf	IiC		
7.10.	0810	Lt d R Galetschky – 1/2	R.E.8	Ypres – Menin road	81
†21.10.	1120	Vzfw Bachmann	KiA	Ypres	
27.10.	1420	Vzfw Hemer – 1	R.E.8	N of Gheluvelt	82
6.11.	0845	Vzfw Stumpf – 1	Nieuport	Zonnebeke	83
6.11.	0850	Lt d L Adam – 21	Sopwith	W of Passchendaele	84
*11.11.	1400	Lt Tüxen	C/Ui		
		(Fok D.V 2642/16)		(aircraft destroyed)	
12.11.	1035	Vzfw Hemer – 2	R.E.8	N of Ypres	85
†15.11.	0920	Lt d L Adam	KiA	NW of Kortewilde	
		(Alb D.V 5222/17)			
23.11.	1500	Lt d R Küppers – 5	Sopwith	W of Cambrai	86
29.11.	0945	Fwlt Schubert – */3	S.E.5	Wambaix	FtL
30.11.	1545	Lt d R Janzen – 2	Sopwith	4 km SW of Marcoing	87
10.12.	1320	Lt d R Janzen – 3	Sopwith	SE of Gonnelieu	88

1918

Date	Time	Pilot & Victory Number	Aircraft Type	Location	Status
4. 1.	1220	Oblt Reinhard – 7	Bristol F.2B	500m S of Niergnies,	89
				S of Cambrai	
18. 1.	1030	Lt von Breiten-	Sopwith	Hargicourt area,	FtL
		Landenberg – */5		within British lines	
16. 2.	1345	Oblt Reinhard – 8	Bristol F.2B	Fayet, W of St-Quentin	90
9. 3.		Lt d R Janzen – *	Sopwith	W of Le Catelet	

(10 March 1918: German time synchronised with Allied time)

Date	Time	Pilot & Victory Number	Aircraft Type	Location	Status
10. 3.	1420	Vzfw Hemer – 3	Sopw Camel	Mont Bréhain	91
*10. 3.		Sgt Beschow	WiA		
13. 3.	1040	Vzfw Hemer – 4	S.E.5a	S of Cambrai	92
18. 3.	1105	Oblt Reinhard – 9	D.H.4/	St-Souplet	93
			Bristol F.2B		
18. 3.	1105	Lt d R Kirschstein – 1	Sopw Camel	Vaux-Andigny	94
27. 3.	0750	Vzfw Hemer – 5	Bristol F.2B	SE of Albert	95
27. 3.	0920	Lt d R Janzen – 4	R.E.8	Aveluy Wood	96
27. 3.	1140	Hptm Reinhard – 10	R.E.8	S of Morcourt	97
27. 3.	1520	Lt d R Kirschstein –2	Arm-Whit F.K.8	3km SW of Albert	98
			B.5773		
27. 3.	1525	Lt d R Kirschstein – 3	Sopw Camel	5km NE of Albert	99
27. 3.	1525	(Jasta 6 unidentified)	R.E.8	8.5km E of Albert	100
1. 4.	0800	Vzfw Hemer – 6	Bristol F.2B	Achiet-le-petit	101
1. 4.	1305	Hptm Reinhard – 11	S.E.5	Martinpuich	102

Date	Time	Pilot & Victory Number	Aircraft Type	Location	Status
2. 4.	1805	Lt d R P. Wenzel – 1	Bristol F.2B	NE of Bray	103
2. 4.	1820	Lt d R Kirschstein – 4	S.E.5a	2km W of Harbonnières	104
6. 4.	1525	Lt d R Kirschstein – 5	Sopw Camel	2km NE of Warfusée	105
6. 4.	1715	Vzfw Hemer – 7	S.E.5a	S of Demuin, Hill 102	106
7. 4.	1145	Lt d R Kirschstein – 6	Sopw Camel	S of Roman Road, intersection between Proyart & Harbonnières	107
12. 4.	1330	Hptm Reinhard – */12	SPAD	N of Roye	108
*12. 4.		Lt d R Wolff	WiA		
(16 April 1918: German time one hour ahead of Allied time)					
*19. 4.		Lt d R Wolff	WiA		
3. 5.	1220	Lt d R Bretschneider-Bodemer –1	SPAD or Bréguet	between Cayeux & Caix	109
3. 5.	1250	Lt d R Kirschstein – 7	French SPAD	W. Rosières	110
4. 5.	1750	Lt d R Bretschneider-Bodemer – 2	Bréguet	200m S of Champien	111
4. 5.	1955	Lt d R Janzen – 5	French SPAD	S of Etinehem	112
9. 5.	1230	Vzfw Hemer – 8	R.E.8	E of Cachy	113
10. 5.	1950	Lt.d R P. Wenzel – 2	Sopw Camel	SW of Caix	114
10. 5.	1950	Vzfw Hemer – 9	Sopw Camel	Cerisy	115
10. 5.	1950	Lt d R Kirschstein – 8	Sopw Camel	Chipilly	116
10. 5.	2000	Lt d R P. Wenzel – 3	D.H.9	between Vrely & Chaulnes	117
15. 5.	1030	Lt d R P. Wenzel – 4	D.H.4	Aveluy	118
15. 5.	1205	Lt d R Kirschstein – 9	Sopw Camel	E of Demuin	119
15. 5.	1250	Lt d R Janzen – 6	Bristol F.2B	N of le Hamel	120
15. 5.	1515	Lt d R Kirschstein – 10	Bristol F.2B	SE of Caix	121
15. 5.	1820	Lt d R Kirschstein – 11	Bristol F.2B	Orvillers	122
16. 5.	1440	Lt d R Kirschstein – 15/12	Bristol F.2B	Sailley-le-Sec	123
16. 5.	2110	Lt d R Kirschstein – 12/13	S.E.5a	Contalmaison	124
17. 5.	1110	Lt d R Kirschstein – 13/14	Bréguet	Cappy	125
17. 5.	1115	Lt d R Janzen – 8/7	Bréguet	E of Cachy	126
18. 5.	0700	Lt d R Kirschstein – 14/15	Bréguet	E of Caix	127
19. 5.	1940	Vzfw Hemer – 10	SPAD	Harbonnières	128
20. 5.	0930	Lt d R Janzen – 7/8	Sopw Camel (Dolphin?)	le Hamel	129
20. 5.	0930	Lt d R Bretschneider-Bodemer – 3	S.E.5a (Dolphin?)	Harbonnières	130
30. 5.	1030	Lt d R Janzen – 9	SPAD	Beuvardes	131
31. 5.	1435	Lt d R Kirschstein – */16	Bréguet	Grand-Rozoy	132
31. 5.	1940	Lt Skowronski – */1	Bréguet	Marizy-St-Mard	133
2. 6.	1720	Lt d R Janzen – 10	SPAD 2-seater	W of Ploisy	134
2. 6.	1735	Lt d R Kirschstein – 18/17	SPAD 2-seater	near Cagny	135
2. 6.	1900	Lt d R Kirschstein – 22/18	Bréguet	near Troësnes	136
*2. 6.		Lt Heidenreich (Fok D.VII)	FtL/PoW		
3. 6.	1250	Lt Skowronski – 2	SPAD	SE of Neuilly	137
3. 6.	1930	Lt d R Kirschstein –19	Bréguet	Fère-en-Tardenois	138
3. 6.	1930	Lt d R Bretschneider-Bodemer – 4	Bréguet	near Epaux-Bézu	139
3. 6.	1935	Lt d R Kirschstein – 23/20	Bréguet	near Epaux-Bézu	140
5. 6.	1135	Lt d R Kirschstein – 16/21	SPAD	near Villemont	141
5. 6.	1140	Lt d R Janzen – 11	SPAD	near Vierzy	142
5. 6.	1735	Lt d R Kirschstein – 20/22	Bréguet	near Ambleny	143
5. 6.	1735	Lt d R R. Wenzl – 3/4	Bréguet	near Soissons	144
5. 6.		Lt Skowronski – 3	Bréguet	Montigny-Lengrain	145
5. 6.	2025	Lt d R Kirschstein – 21/23	SPAD	Chezy-en-Orxois	146
5. 6.	2025	Lt d R Janzen – 12	French SPAD	La Ferté-Milon	147
7. 6.	0705	Lt d R Janzen – 13	SPAD	E of Villers-Cotterêts	148

Date	Time	Pilot & Victory Number	Aircraft Type	Location	Status
7. 6.	0710	Lt d R Kirschstein –24	SPAD	near Montgobert	149
13. 6.	0630	Lt d R Bretschneider-Bodemer – 5	SPAD	Château-Thierry	150
14. 6.	0900	Lt d R Kirschstein – 26/25	Balloon	Villers-Cotterêts	151
14. 6.	0915	Lt d R Kirschstein – 25/26	SPAD	Villers-Cotterêts	152
20. 6.	1910	Lt d R P. Wenzel – 5	Bréguet	N of La Ferté-Milon	153
24. 6.	0945	Lt d R Kirschstein – 27	Bréguet	Oulchy-le-Château	154
28. 6.	1230	Vzfw Hemer – 11	SPAD 2-seater	Silly-la-Poterie	155
3. 7.	0800	Vzfw Hemer – 12	SPAD	E of Courtieux	156
3. 7.	1910	Lt d R Nöldecke – 1	SPAD		157
15. 7.	1045	Lt d R P. Wenzel – 6	Balloon	Breuil Wood	158
16. 7.	0525	Lt d R Bretschneider-Bodemer – 6	SPAD 2-seater	Juvigny	159
16. 7.	0530	Vzfw Hemer – */13	Sopw Camel	S of Dormans	160
16. 7.	0535	Vzfw Hemer – */14	Sopw Camel	S of Dormans	161
†16. 7.		Lt d R Kirschstein & Lt Markgraf (Hann CL.IIIa)	KiC	Magneux, near Fismes	
17. 7.	1035	Lt d R P. Wenzel – */7	Bréguet	Chavigny	162
17. 7.	1035	Lt d R Matzdorf – */1	Bréguet		163
17. 7.	1040	Lt d R Rolff – */1	Bréguet		164
18. 7.	0915	Vzfw Hemer – 16/15	Bréguet		165
†18. 7.		Lt d R Bretschneider-Bodemer	KiA	Grand-Rozoy	
20. 7.	0835	Lt d R P. Wenzel – 7/8	Balloon	NW of Longpont	166
22. 7.	1620	Lt d R R. Wenzl – 4	SPAD		167
22. 7.	1620	Vzfw Hemer –13/16	SPAD		168
*22. 7.		Lt d R Nöldecke	WiA		
29. 7.	1210	Lt d R P. Wenzel – 9	Bréguet	Couvrelles	169
*30. 7.		Lt d R Raffay	I/A		
31. 7.	1840	Lt d R Rolff – 2	Nieuport		170
1. 8.	0910	Vzfw Hemer – 17	Nieuport	Fère-en-Tardenois	171
1. 8.	0915	Lt d R R. Wenzl – 5	Nieuport	Fère-en-Tardenois	172
1. 8.	0940	Vzfw Hemer – */18	Nieuport	Fère-en-Tardenois	173
*1. 8.		Lt d R P. Wenzel	WiA		
8. 8.	1900	Vzfw Hemer – 18/19	D.H.9	Nesle	174
8. 8.	1930	Uffz Reimers – 1		Réthencourt	
8. 8.	1940	Lt d R R. Wenzl – 6	D.H.9	Genermont	175
9. 8.	0800	Lt d R P. Wenzel – 10	D.H.9	Vauvillers	176
9. 8.	0800	Uffz Reimers – 2	D.H.9	Epénancourt	177
*9. 8.		Vzfw Hemer	WiA		
†11. 8.		Lt von der Wense	KiA	between Péronne & Herbécourt	
*11. 8.		Lt d R P. Wenzel	WiA		
16. 8.	1230	Lt d R Rolff – */3	Sopw Camel	Mesnil	178
*16. 8.		Vzfw Lechner	IiC		
19. 8.	0950	Lt d R Matzdorf – 2	Sopw Camel	E of Beauvais	179
†19. 8.	0950	Lt.d.R Rolff (Fok E.V)	KiC	Bernes	
*27. 8.		Lt d R Wolff	WiA/FtL	W of Nesle	
4. 9.	1100	Lt d R R. Wenzl – 7	Sopw Camel	S of Raillencourt	180
†4. 9.		Uffz Reimers	KiA	Ligny-St-Flochel	
5. 9.	1525	Lt d R R. Wenzl – 8	Balloon	Croisilles	181
5. 9.	1525	Lt Schliewen – 1	Balloon		182
†8. 9.		Gefr Blümener	KiA	Beaurevoir	
15. 9.	1235	Lt d R Neckel – 25	Bristol F.2B		183
18. 9.		Lt d R Neckel – 26	D.H.4	Conflans	184
6.10.	1115	Lt d R Noltenius –	Balloon	Puvenelle Wood	185
10.10.	1500	Lt d R Noltenius – 15	SPAD	Fontaine	186
23.10.	1615	Lt d R Neckel – 27	A.R.2		187

Date	Time	Pilot & Victory Number	Aircraft Type	Location	Status
29.10.	1100	Lt d R R. Wenzl – 9	SPAD	Sommerance	188
29.10.	1625	Lt Schiemann – 2	SPAD		189
29.10.	1630	Lt d R Rieth – 1	SPAD		190
†29.10.		Lt d R Fischer	KiA	Montfaucon	
30.10.	1645	Lt d R Neckel – 28	SPAD		191
31.10.	1250	Lt d R Neckel – 29	SPAD 2-seater		192
3.11.	1455	Lt.d.R R. Wenzl – 10	SPAD	Montfaucon	193
3.11.	1455	Lt d R R. Wenzl – 11	SPAD	Montfaucon	194
5.11.	1010	Lt d R R. Wenzl – 12	D.H.4		195
6.11.	1130	Lt d R Neckel – 30	SPAD	Woevre Forest	196

JASTA 10

Date	Time	Pilot & Victory Number	Aircraft Type	Location	Status
1916					
16.10.		Oblt Linck	F.E.2b	Vitry, SW of Douay	FtL
*16.10.		Gefr Beerendonk	WiA	Monchy-le-Preux,	
20.10.			B.E.12	E of Arras	1
†22.10.		Oblt Linck	KiA	Provin, near Lille	
*22.10.		Offstlvtr Viereck	WiA	Provin	
1917					
4. 1.	1515	Lt Mallinckrodt – 2	Sopw Pup	Neufchâtel, N of Reims	2
(25 March 1917: German time synchronised with Allied time)					
25. 3.		Vzfw Aue – 4	Nieuport 3418	Champ, near Verdun	3
28. 3.		Lt Loewenhardt –	Balloon	Récicourt, near Verdun	n/c
4. 4.		Lt Loewenhardt – 1	Balloon		4
(17 April 1917: German time one hour ahead of Allied time)					
2. 5.	1915	Vzfw Heldmann –		W of Souchez	n/c
*3. 5.	1600	Gefr Lemke (Alb D.II 473/16)	FtL/PoW	Abbeville (G 32)	
10. 5.		Vzfw Heldmann –	Sopw Triplane	Lens	FtL
23. 5.	2115	Vzfw Aue –	Sopw Triplane	Carvin	n/c
27. 5.	0730	Vzfw Aue –	Sopw Pup	Etaing	
27. 5.	0745	Uffz Oppel	Sopwith	Fampoux	
7. 6.	0720	Gefr Brettel – 1	SPAD	Rumbeke	5
7. 6.	0815	Offstlvtr Aue – 5	SPAD	Oucken	6
27. 6.	1610	Lt d R Dossenbach – 15	Balloon	Ypres	7
†3. 7.		Lt d R Dossenbach	KiA	Frezenberg	
22. 7.	1040	Vzfw Heldmann – 1	R.E.8	Deûlémont	8
24. 7.	2035	Oblt d R von Althaus – 9	Sopw Camel	SE of Moorslede	9
28. 7.	2115	Oblt Weigand – 1	Sopwith	Roulers	10
29. 7.	0755	Vzfw Heldmann – 2 (contested by Vfw Wüsthoff, Jasta 4)	Sopwith	between Hooge & Westhoek	11
10. 8.	1625	Lt d R Voss – 35	SPAD	SW of Klerken, S of Dixmuide	12
10. 8.	1625	Uffz Brettel – 2	SPAD	near Klerken	13
14. 8.	1015	Lt Loewenhardt – 2	R.E.8	Zillebeke Lake	14
14. 8.	1045	Oblt Weigand – 2	Sopwith	Nieuwkapelle SW of Dixmuide	15
15. 8.	1910	Lt d R Voss – 36	F.E.2d	between Zillebeke Lake & Ypres	16
*15. 8.	1920	Uffz Brettel	WiA	Moorslede	
16. 8.	2100	Lt d R Voss – 37	Sopwith	near St-Julien	17

Date	Time	Pilot & Victory Number	Aircraft Type	Location	Status
17. 8.	1015	Lt d R Ohlrau – 1	Sopwith	Becelaere	18
*17. 8.	1920	Uffz Brettel	WiA	Moorslede	
23. 8.	1010	Lt d R Voss – 38	SPAD	between Nordschoote & Nieuwkapelle, SW of Dixmuide	19
3. 9.	0952	Lt d R Voss – 39	Sopwith	Zandvoorde, N of Houthem	20
5. 9.	1550	Lt Loewenhardt – 4/3	Sopw Pup	St-Julien	21
5. 9.	1550	Lt d R Voss – 41/40	Sopw Pup	St-Julien	22
5. 9.	1630	Lt d R Voss – 40/41	Caudron	between Bixschoote & Langemarck	23
6. 9.	1635	Lt d R Voss – 42	F.E.2d	between St-Julien & Boezinge	24
9. 9.	2055	Lt Loewenhardt – 3/4	Balloon	near Elverdinge	25
10. 9.	1750	Lt d R Voss – 44/43	Sopw Camel	between Langemarck and Passchendaele	26
10. 9.	1755	Lt d R Voss – 45/44	Sopw Camel	between Langemarck and Passchendaele	27
10. 9.	1815	Lt d R Voss – 46/45	SPAD S.7	between Passchendaele & Westrosebeke	28
11. 9.	1020	Oblt Weigand – */3	SPAD	Bixschoote	29
11. 9.	1030	Lt d R Voss – 43/46	1-seater	Langemarck	30
11. 9.	1625	Lt d R Voss – 47	Sopw Camel	between Langemarck & St-Julien	31
*14. 9.	1725	Oblt Weigand	WiA		
*19. 9.	1000	Offstlvtr Aue	WiA/FtL	Roulers	
*20. 9.	1110	Lt Loewenhardt	WiA	Roulers	
21. 9.	1445	Lt d R Bellen – 1	Balloon	Elverdinge, NW of Ypres	32
21. 9.	1925	Lt Loewenhardt – 5	Balloon	between Ypres & Vlamertinghe	33
23. 9.	0930	Lt d R Voss – 48	D.H.4	S of Roulers, Ledeghem	34
†23. 9.	1900	Lt d R Voss (Fok F.I 103/17)	KiA	St-Julien (G 72)	
†25. 9.	1740	Oblt Weigand	KiA	Houthulst Forest	
†25. 9.	1742	Uffz Werkmeister	KiA	Houthulst Forest	
*26. 9.	1110	Lt Loewenhardt	WiA/FtL	Roulers	
†2. 10.	1030	Lt Römer	KiA	Westrosebeke	
*2. 10.		Lt d R Rüdenberg	FtL	Aarsele	
2.10.	1040	Lt d R Klein – 17	D.H.4	Meulebeke	35
*11.10.		Lt d R Bellen	WiA		
12.10.	1220	Lt d R Klein – 18	Sopw Camel	Lauwe	36
13.10.	0900	Lt d R Klein – 19	Sopw Pup	Praet Bosch	37
14.10	1830	Lt Loewenhardt – 6	Balloon	NW of Ypres	38
18.10.	0945	Lt Loewenhardt – 7	Bristol F.2B	near Ardoie Castle	39
18.10.	0955	Lt d R Klein – 22/20	Bristol F.2B	near Staden & Roulers	40
*20.10.	1310	Uffz Hardel	WiA/FtL	Potteribrug	
*6.11.	0830	Lt Loewenhardt	FtL	St-Eloi-Winkel	
*8.11.		Flgr Riensberg	IiC		
18.11.	0925	Vfw Wawzin – */1	SPAD	N of Ypres	41
* 25.11.	1020	Lt d R Klein	Ac	Iwuy	
29.11.	1000	Lt d R Klein – 20/21	Sopwith	near Crevecoeur, S of Cambrai	42

APPENDIX 1: DAILY VICTORY AND CASUALTY LISTS OF JG I UNITS

Date	Time	Pilot & Victory Number	Aircraft Type	Location	Status
29.11.	1000	Lt d R Heldmann – 3	Sopwith	near Crevecoeur	43
30.11.	1230	Lt d R Klein – 21/22	Balloon	S of Ribécourt, W of Cambrai	44
†30.11.	1510	Lt Demandt (Pfalz D.IIIa)	KiA	NE of Flesquières (G 93)	
30.11.	1545	Lt Loewenhardt – 8	Sopwith	between Moeuvres & Bourlon Wood	45
5.12.	1120	Vfw Barth – */1	Bristol F.2B	N of Cambrai	46
*27.12.		Vzfw Hecht (Pfalz D.III 1370/17)	FtL/PoW	(G 110)	
1918					
5. 1.	1605	Lt Loewenhardt – 9	Balloon	Attilly, W of St-Quentin	47
18. 1.	1023	Lt Loewenhardt – 10	Bristol F.2B	Le Catelet, le petit Priel	48
†18. 1.	1030	Flgr Riensberg (Pfalz D.III 4059/17)	KiA	Beaurevoir	
†30. 1.		Vzfw Barth (Alb D.V 4565/17)	KiA	Anneux	
2. 2.	1540	Lt d R Kühn – 3	S.E.5a FtL	Bouchain	49
*12. 2		Lt d R Bender	FtL	Brussels	
*19. 2.	1300	Lt d R Klein (Pfalz D.III 4283/17)	WiA		
8. 3.	1220	Lt d R Heldmann – 4	Bréguet	Fresnoy-le-Grand	50
8. 3.	1230	Lt d R Heldmann – 5/*	Bréguet		
(10 March 1918: German time synchronised with Allied time)					
12. 3.	1945	Lt Loewenhardt – 12/11	Balloon	W of La Bassée	51
12. 3.	1945	Lt d R Bohlein – 1	Balloon	W of La Bassée	52
15. 3.	1905	Lt Loewenhardt – 11/12	Balloon	Villers-Faucon	53
†16. 3.	1100	Lt Bohlein	KiA	Marcq	
18. 3.	1110	Lt Loewenhardt – 13	Bréguet	S of Le Cateau	54
21. 3.	1310	Lt Loewenhardt – 14	Balloon	Fins	55
21. 3.	1355	Lt d R Friedrichs – 1	Balloon	Ruyaulcourt	56
27. 3.	0750	Lt Loewenhardt – 15	D.H.4	W of Miraumont	57
27. 3.	1030	Lt d R Friedrichs – 2	S.E.5a	N of Pozières	58
28. 3.	1115	Lt d R Weiss – 11/13	Bristol F.2B	near Sailly	59
12. 4.	1225	Lt Loewenhardt – 18/16	Sopw Camel	NW of Péronne	60
(16 April 1918: German time one hour ahead of Allied time)					
*22. 4.		Offstlvtr Aue	FtL		
*22. 4.		Flgr Nitsche	FtL		
23. 4.	0830	Lt Loewenhardt – 16/17	Bristol F.2B	FtL W of Morval	61
2. 5.	1230	Lt Loewenhardt – 17/18	S.E.5a	N of Manancourt	62
3. 5.	1215	Offstlvtr Aue – 6	Bristol F.2B	Proyart	63
*3. 5.	1600	Gefr Lemke Alb D.II 473/16	FtL/PoW	Fampoux, E of Arras (G 32)	
3. 5.	1850	Lt d R Friedrichs – 3	D.H.9	Fontaine-lès-Cappy	64
4. 5.	1930	Lt d R Heldmann – 5	S.E.5a	Mametz	65
9. 5.	1950	Lt Loewenhardt – 20/19	Sopw Camel	le Hamel	66
10. 5.	0745	Lt Loewenhardt – 19/20	D.H.9	Chaulnes	67
15. 5.	0815	Lt d R Friedrichs – 4	Sopw Camel	NW of Albert	68
15. 5.	1325	Lt Loewenhardt – 21	D.H.9	Mametz	69
16. 5.	1545	Lt Loewenhardt – 22	SPAD	Maricourt	70
18. 5.	0730	Lt d R Friedrichs – 5	Balloon	Ransart	71
18. 5.	0745	Lt Loewenhardt – 23	Sopw Camel	Beaucourt	72

Date	Time	Pilot & Victory Number	Aircraft Type	Location	Status
20. 5.	0730	Lt Loewenhardt – 24	Balloon	Ransart, SW of Arras	73
28. 5.	1730	Lt d R Friedrichs – 6	Balloon	S of Chavigny	74
*31. 5.		Lt Rademacher	FtL/PoW		
		(Alb D.Va)		(G/2nd Bde/13)	
2. 6.	1745	Lt Loewenhardt – 25	SPAD	La Croix	75
3. 6.	1830	Lt Loewenhardt – 26	SPAD	Dammard	76
5. 6.	0745	Lt.d.R Grassmann – 1	Balloon	Château-Thierry	77
5. 6.	1120	Lt d R Friedrichs – 7	Balloon	N of Villers-Cotterêts	78
5. 6.	1845	Lt Loewenhardt – 27	SPAD	Château-Thierry	79
5. 6.	1845	Lt d R Heldmann – 6	SPAD	Château-Thierry	80
5. 6.	2010	Lt d R Friedrichs – 8	Balloon	N of Villers-Cotterêts	81
6. 6.	0725	Lt d R Friedrichs – 9	Balloon	S of Dormans	82
6. 6.	0750	Lt Otto – 1	Balloon	Villers-Cotterêts	83
*6. 6.	0750	Lt Otto	WiA	Villers-Cotterêts	
8. 6.	0710	Lt d R Friedrichs – 10	Balloon	Rosnay	84
9. 6.	1630	Lt d R Friedrichs – 13/11	Bréguet	W of Villers-Allerand	85
16. 6.	0645	Offstlvtr Aue – 7	Balloon	Villers-Cotterêts	86
16. 6.	0700	Lt d R Friedrichs – 11/12	Balloon	Vendresse	87
22. 6.	0845	Lt Loewenhardt – 28	Bréguet	Beauvardes	88
23. 6.	0945	Lt d R Heldmann – 7	SPAD	Epaux	89
23. 6.	0945	Sgt Schumacher – 1	SPAD	Fossoy	90
23. 6.	0945	Lt d R Friedrichs – 12/13	SPAD	W of Fossoy	91
25. 6.	2040	Lt d R Friedrichs – 14	Balloon	Roches Wood	92
26. 6.	2025	Sgt Schumacher – 2	Balloon	La Ferté-Milon	93
27. 6.	0900	Lt d R Friedrichs – 15	SPAD	La Ferté-Milon	94
27. 6.	0915	Lt Loewenhardt – 30/29	SPAD	Dommières	95
27. 6.	1300	Lt d R Friedrichs – 16	SPAD	Neuilly	96
28. 6.	0820	Lt Loewenhardt – 29/30	SPAD	Billy-sur-Aisne	97
28. 6.	0830	Lt d R Friedrichs – 17	SPAD	Longpont	98
28. 6.	1230	Lt Loewenhardt – 29/30	SPAD 2-seater	N of Dampleux	99
30. 6.	1040	Lt d R Friedrichs – 18	Balloon	Fleury	100
30. 6.	1105	Lt d R Grassmann – 2	Balloon	Château-Thierry	101
30. 6.	1550	Sgt Schumacher – 3	Balloon	Château-Thierry	102
30. 6.	1555	Lt d R Friedrichs – */19	SPAD	Château-Thierry	103
30. 6.	2000	Lt Loewenhardt – 34/32	SPAD	La Ferté-Milon	104
†30. 6.		Lt d R Feige	KiA	Noroy	
1. 7.	1030	Sgt Schumacher – 4	Balloon	Cuchery	105
2. 7.	0810	Lt Loewenhardt – 31/33	Nieuport 28	Bennes	106
2. 7.	0815	Lt Loewenhardt – 32/34	Nieuport 28	Courchamps	107
2. 7.	0820	Lt d R Friedrichs – 20	Nieuport 28	Etrépilly	108
8. 7.	1230	Lt d R Friedrichs – 21	Nieuport 28	S of Sarcy	109
14. 7.	0815	Lt Loewenhardt – 39/35	Bréguet	Verdilly	110
15. 7.	1307	Lt Loewenhardt – 36	Sopw Camel	N of Dormans	111
†15. 7.	2100	Lt d R Friedrichs	KiA	Arcy, NW of	
		(Fok D.VII 309/18)		Beugneux	
16. 7.	1355	Gefr Möller – 1	SPAD		112
16. 7.	1820	Lt Loewenhardt – 35/37	SPAD	Juvigny	113
18. 7.	0620	Lt Loewenhardt – 40/38	SPAD	Chouy	114
18. 7.	0629	Vzfw Schumacher – 5	SPAD	Chouy	115
18. 7.	0735	Lt d R Heldmann – 8	SPAD	Chaudun	116
†18. 7.		Gefr Möller	KiA	Chaudun	
18. 7.	1430	Lt Loewenhardt – 41/39	SPAD	Grisolles	117
19. 7.	1130	Lt Loewenhardt – 42/40	SPAD	Courchamps	118

Date	Time	Pilot & Victory Number	Aircraft Type	Location	Status
19. 7.	2050	Lt Loewenhardt – 43/41	SPAD	Verdilly	119
21. 7.	2015	Lt Loewenhardt – */42	Sopw Camel	Fère-en-Tardenois	120
22. 7.	2030	Lt Loewenhardt – 37/43	Sopw Camel	Longpont	121
*24. 7.		Vzfw Schumacher	WiA		
25. 7.	2050	Lt Loewenhardt – 44	SPAD	Villers-Hélon	122
28. 7.	1510	Lt Loewenhardt – 45	SPAD	Fère-en-Tardenois	123
28. 7.	1950	Lt Grassmann – 3	Sopw	Camel S of Saponay	124
29. 7.	1930	Lt Loewenhardt – 46	SPAD	Coincy	125
30. 7.	1510	Lt Loewenhardt – 47	Sopw Camel	Arcy	126
30. 7.	2010	Lt Loewenhardt – 48	Sopw Camel	Saponay	127
†1. 8.		Lt d R Lehmann	KiA	Fère-en-Tardenois	
*4. 8.		Uffz Strecker	IiC		
8. 8.	1245	Lt Loewenhardt – 49	Sopw Camel	Proyart	128
8. 8.	1750	Lt Loewenhardt – 50	Sopw Camel	E of Bray	129
8. 8.	1830	Lt Grassmann – 5/4	Bristol F.2B	Chaulnes	130
8. 8.	1850	Lt Loewenhardt – 51	Sopw Camel	Estrées	131
9. 8.	0725	Lt d R Heldmann – 9	Sopw Camel	Chuignolles	132
9. 8.	0740	Lt Loewenhardt – 52	Sopw Camel	Estrées	133
9. 8.	1855	Lt Loewenhardt – 53	Sopw Camel	S. of Cérisy	134
10. 8.	1215	Lt Loewenhardt – 54	S.E.5a	Chaulnes	135
†10. 8.	1215	Lt Loewenhardt	KiC	Chaulnes	
11. 8.	1855	Lt Grassmann – 4/5	Sopw Dolphin	Eclusier	136
11. 8.	1900	Lt d R Heldmann – 10	Sopw Dolphin	E of Frise	137
19. 8.	0842	Lt d R Laumann – */25	S.E.5a	Bapaume	138
19. 8.	0900	Lt d R Heldmann – 11	S.E.5a	Aveluy	139
19. 8.	0900	Offstlvtr Aue – 8	Sopw Camel	SW of Puisieux	140
*21. 8.		Uffz Klamt	WiA		
22. 8.	1245	Lt d R Laumann – 24/26	S.E.5a	Bécordel-Bécourt	141
22. 8.	1745	Lt d R Kohlbach – 3	S.E.5a	Cappy	142
22. 8.	1745	Lt d R Laumann – 24/26	S.E.5a	NW of Bray-sur-Somme	143
30. 8.	0955	Lt d R Laumann – 26/28	Sopw Camel	Estrées	144
30. 8.	0900	Offstlvtr Aue – 9	Sopw Camel	Estrées	145
*5. 9.		Uffz Doerflinger (Fok D.VII)	SD	front lines	
15. 9.	1255	Lt d R Kohlbach – 4	Sopw Camel	Cantaing	146
25. 9.	0950	Lt Grassmann – 6	Balloon	S of Pont-à-Mousson	147
4.10.	1130	Offstlvtr Aue – 10	Balloon	Montfaucon	148
*4. 10.		Lt Schibilsky	SD/PoW		
10.10.	1650	Lt d R Heldmann – 12	SPAD	Dannevoux	149
10.10.	1650	Lt Grassmann – 7	SPAD	Fontaines	150
10.10.	1650	Lt.d.R Kohlbach – 5	SPAD	Between Lion-dont-Dun & Fontaines	151
*10.10.		Lt d R Kohlbach	SD/PoW	Lion-dont-Dun	
*18.10.		Lt d R Böhren	WiA/PoW		
29.10.	1655	Lt Grassmann – 8	SPAD	Cierges	152
30.10.	1700	Lt d R Heldmann – 13	SPAD	S. of Damvillers	153
30.10.	1735	Lt Grassmann – 9	Sopw Camel	Brière Ferme	154
5.11.	1035	Lt d R Heldmann – 14	SPAD	Sivry	155
†5.11.		Lt d R Kirst	KiA	Loupoy	
6.11.	1130	Lt Grassmann – 10	SPAD	Sivry	156
6.11.	1130	Lt d R Heldmann – 15	SPAD	NE of Sivry	157

JASTA 11

Date 1917	Time	Pilot & Victory Number	Aircraft Type	Location	Status
23. 1.	1605	Lt M. Frhr von Richthofen – 17	F.E.8	SW of Lens	1
24. 1.	1215	Lt M. Frhr von Richthofen – 18	F.E.2b	W of Vimy	2
29. 1.		Lt Simon	WiA		
1. 2.	1600	Lt M. Frhr von Richthofen – 19	B.E.2d 6742	SW of Thélus	3
5. 2.	1700	Vzfw Festner – 1	B.E.2	NE of Arras, near la Neuville	4
5. 2.		Vzfw Baierlein	B.E.2	N of Arras	n/c
14. 2.	1300	Lt M. Frhr von Richthofen – 20	B.E.2d 6231	Lens–Hulluch Road, E of Loos	5
14. 2.	1700	Lt M. Frhr von Richthofen – 21	B.E.2c	Mazingarbe (over British lines)	6
16. 2.	1700	Vzfw Festner – 2	F.E.8	between Liévin & Grenay	7
16. 2.	1200	Lt C. Allmenröder –1	B.E.2c 4179	Roeux, E. of Arras	8
4. 3.	1200	Lt Schaefer – 2	Sopw 1½-Strutter 4594	forward trenches, SW of Haisnes	9
4. 3.	1250	Lt M. Frhr von Richthofen – 22	B.E.2d 5785	N of Loos	10
4. 3.	1620	Lt M. Frhr von Richthofen – 23	Sopw 1½-Str A1108	Acheville	11
6. 3.	1145	Lt Schaefer – 3	Sopw 1½-Str	Lens	12
6. 3.	1145	Lt Schaefer – 4	Sopw 1½-Str	Lens	13
*6. 3.	1200	Lt E. Lübbert	WiC	Lens	
6. 3.	1230	Lt K. Wolff – 1	B.E.2d 5856	Givenchy	14
6. 3.	1700	Lt M. Frhr von Richthofen – 24	B.E.2e	Souchez	15
6. 3.	1720	Lt Schaefer – */5	Sopw 1½-Str	Lens	16
6. 3.	1720	Lt Schaefer – */6	Sopw 1½-Str	Lens	17
9. 3.	1020	Lt Schaefer – 5	F.E.8 6397 40 Sqn, RFC	between Meurchin & Faschoda	18
9. 3.	1020	Lt Schaefer – 6	F.E.8 4874 40 Sqn, RFC	between Meurchin & Pont-à-Vendin	19
9. 3.	1020	Lt K. Wolff – 2	F.E.8 6456 40 Sqn, RFC	between Meurchin & Annay	20
9. 3.	1020	Lt C. Allmenröder – 2	F.E.8 40 Sqdn, RFC	Meurchin, W of Hulluch	21
9. 3.	1200	Lt M. Frhr von Richthofen – 25	D.H.2 A2571	between Roclincourt & Bailleul[-Sir-Berthoult]	22
11. 3.	1120	Lt Schaefer – 7	B.E.2c	Loos	23
11. 3.	1145	Lt Krefft – 1	F.E.2b	W of Souchez, between Givenchy [-en-Grohelle] & Vimy	24
11. 3.	1200	Lt M. Frhr von Richthofen – 26	B.E.2d A2571	Vimy	25
17. 3.	1145	Oblt M. Frhr von Richthofen – 27	F.E.2b A5439	between Bailleul & Oppy	26
17. 3.	1145	Lt C. Allmenröder – 3	Sopw 1½-Str A1111	between Athies & Oppy, Point du Jour	27
17. 3.	1145	Lt K. Wolff – 3	Sopw 1½-Str	Bailleul-Sir-Berthoult	28
17. 3.	1700	Oblt M. Frhr von Richthofen – 28	B.E.2c	Souchez, W of Vimy	29
21. 3.	1530	Lt C. Allmenröder – 4	B.E.2	Loos	30
21. 3.	1725	Oblt M. Frhr von Richthofen – 29	B.E.2f	N of Neuville-Vitasse	31
24. 3.	1055	Lt Schaefer – 8	Sopw 1½-Str	Anzin, N of Arras	32
24. 3.	1155	Oblt M. Frhr von Richthofen – 30	SPAD S.7 A6706	between Vimy & Givenchy-en-Gohelle	33
(25 March 1917: German time synchronised with Allied time)					
25. 3.	1155	Oblt M. Frhr von Richthofen – 31	Nieuport	Tilloy	34

Date	Time	Pilot & Victory Number	Aircraft Type	Location	Status
28. 3.	1715	Lt L. Frhr von Richthofen – 1	F.E.2b	S of Lens	35
30. 3.	1145	Lt K. Wolff – 4	Nieuport	between Gavrelle & Fresnoy, NW of Arras	36
30. 3.	1415	Lt C. Allmenröder – 5	Nieuport	between Fresnoy & Bailleul (-Sir-Berthoult)	37
†30. 3.	1415	Lt E. Lübbert	KiA	Bailleul (-Sir-Berthoult)	
31. 3.	0745	Lt K. Wolff – 5	F.E.2b	Gavrelle	38
2. 4.	0835	Oblt M. Frhr von Richthofen – 32	B.E.2d 5841	Farbus, NE of Arras	39
2. 4.	0930	Lt C. Allmenröder – 5/6	B.E.2d 7061	Angres, SW of Lens	40
2. 4.	1000	Vzfw Festner – 3	F.E.2d	Auby, N of Douai	41
2. 4.	1000	Lt Krefft – 2	F.E.2d A5151	Oignies, N of Douai	42
2. 4.	1120	Oblt M. Frhr von Richthofen – 33	Sopw 1½-Str A2401	Givenchy (-en-Gohelle)	43
3. 4.	1615	Oblt M. Frhr von Richthofen – 34	F.E.2d A6382	between Lens & Liéven	44
3. 4.	1620	Lt Schaefer – 9	F.E.2d A6371	Avion, S of Lens	45
3. 4.	1717	Vzfw Festner – */6 (Kofl 6. records)	F.E.2	Méricourt	n/c
3. 4.	1720	Vzfw Festner – */4 (Kofl 6. records)	F.E.2	Hendecourt	n/c
5. 4.	1100	Lt Simon – 1	Bristol F.2A A3320	between Monchecourt and Auberchicourt	46
5. 4.	1100	Oblt M. Frhr von Richthofen – 35	Bristol F.2A A3343	Cuincy	47
5. 4.	1100	Oblt M. Frhr von Richthofen – 36	Bristol F.2A A3340	Lewarde, SE of Douai	48
5. 4.	1100	Vzfw Festner – 4/5	Bristol F.2A	Méricourt	49
5. 4.	1830	Vzfw Festner – 5/7	Nieuport/F.E.2	SW of Bailleul (-Sir-Berhoult) & Roclincourt	50
6. 4.	1015	Lt K. Wolff – 6	R.E.8 A3421	Bois Bernard	51
6. 4.	1018	Lt Schaefer – 10	B.E.2	Givenchy-en-Gohelle	52
6. 4.	1037	Lt Schaefer-11	Sopwith	Souchez, W of Vimy	53
7. 4.	1745	Lt K. Wolff – 7	Nieuport	Mercatel	54
7. 4.	1745	Rittm M. Frhr von Richthofen – 37	Nieuport	Mercatel	55
7. 4.	1745	Lt Schaefer – 12	Nieuport	Mercatel	56
7. 4.	1910	Vzfw Festner – 6/7	Sopwith	between Mont St-Eloi & Maroeuil	57
8. 4.	0930	Vzfw Festner – 7/8	Nieuport (?) 2865	E of Vimy	58
8. 4.	1140	Rittm M. Frhr von Richthofen – 38	Sopw 1½-Str	Farbus	59
8. 4.	1445	Lt Schaefer – 13	D.H.4 A2140	Epinoy	60
8. 4.	1445	Lt K. Wolff – 8	D.H.4 A2141	Blécourt	61
8. 4.	1640	Rittm M. Frhr von Richthofen – 39	B.E.2e A2815	Vimy	62
9. 4.	1910	Lt Schaefer – 14	B.E.2d 5742	Aix-Noulette	63
11. 4.	0905	Vzfw Festner – 8/9	B.E.2d	N of Fampoux	64
11. 4.	0910	Lt Schaefer – 15	B.E.2d	forward lines, near Fampoux	65
11. 4.	0910	Lt K. Wolff – 9	Bristol F.2A A3338	Mouville Ferme	66
11. 4.	0910	Lt L. Frhr von Richthofen – 2	Bristol F.2A A3323	Mouville Ferme, S of Arras	67
11. 4.	0925	Rittm M. Frhr von Richthofen – 40	B.E.2c	Willerval	68
11. 4.	1250	Lt Schaefer – 16	Sopw 2-seater	E of Arras cemetery	69
11. 4.	1250	Lt L. Frhr von Richthofen – 3	Sopw 2-seater	NE of Fampoux	70
13. 4.	0851	Vzfw Festner – 9	R.E.8 A3199	between Etaing & Dury	71
13. 4.	0855	Lt L. Frhr von Richthofen – 4	R.E.8	Vitry	72
13. 4.	0855	Lt L. Frhr von Richthofen – 5	R.E.8	E of Roeux & Pelves	73

APPENDIX 1: DAILY VICTORY AND CASUALTY LISTS OF JG I UNITS

Date	Time	Pilot & Victory Number	Aircraft Type	Location	Status
13. 4.	0856	Rittm M. Frhr von Richthofen – 41	R.E.8	between Vitry & Brebières	74
13. 4.	0856	Lt K. Wolff – 10	B.E.2 '9625'	N of Vitry-en-Artois	75
13. 4.	1235	Lt K. Wolff – 11	F.E.2d	S of Bailleul	76
13. 4.	1245	Rittm M. Frhr von Richthofen – 42	F.E.2b	W of Monchy, near Feuchy	77
13. 4.	1630	Lt K. Wolff – 12	Nieuport	S of Monchy-le-Preux	78
13. 4.	1630	Lt Schaefer – */17	Nieuport	Monchy	n/c
13. 4.	1640	Lt Schaefer – 17/18	Nieuport	Le Point-du-Jour	79
13. 4.	1630	Lt K. Wolff – 12	Nieuport	S of Monchy-le-Preux	80
13. 4.	1852	Lt K. Wolff – 13	Martinsyde	Rouvroy	81
13. 4.	1930	Lt Schaefer – */19	B.E.2	Harnes	82
13. 4.	1930	Vzfw Festner – 10	F.E.2b A784	E of Harnes	83
13. 4.	1930	Rittm M. Frhr von Richthofen – 43	F.E.2b 4997	Noyelle-Godault, near Hénin-Liétard	84
14. 4.	0915	Rittm M. Frhr von Richthofen– 44	Nieuport A6796	S of Bois Bernard, near Fresnoy	85
14. 4.	0920	Lt K. Wolff – 14	Nieuport B1511	SE of Drocourt	86
14. 4.	0920	Lt L. Frhr von Richthofen – 6	Nieuport A6772	E of Fourquières	87
14..4.	0923	Vzfw Festner – 11	Nieuport	Gavrelles	88
14. 4.	1705	Lt Schaefer – 18	F.E.2b	Woods 3 km S of château between Liéven & Eleu	89
14. 4.	1720	Lt Schaefer – 19	R.E.8	La Coulette, W of Avion	90
14. 4.	1823	Lt L. Frhr von Richthofen – 7	Sopwith	between Vimy & Farbus	91
14. 4.	1829	Lt K. Wolff – 15	SPAD	Bailleul	92
16. 4.	1030	Lt L. Frhr von Richthofen – 8	Nieuport	between Roeux & Pelves	93
16. 4.	1030	Lt K. Wolff – 16	Nieuport	NE of Roeux between Fampoux & Biache	94
16. 4.	1030	Vzfw Festner – 12	Nieuport	between Fampoux & Biache	95
16. 4.	1730	Rittm M. Frhr von Richthofen – 45	B.E.2c	between Gavrelle & Bailleul	96
(17 April 1917: German time one hour ahead of Allied time)					
21. 4.	1725	Lt Schaefer – 20	Nieuport	E of Fresnes	97
21. 4.	1730	Lt L. Frhr von Richthofen – 9	B.E.2g	NW of Arleux, near Farbus	98
21. 4.	1730	Lt K. Wolff – 17	B.E.2g	NW of Arleux, near Willerval	99
21. 4.	1745	Lt K. Wolff – 18	Nieuport	E of Fresnes	100
21. 4.	1745	Lt Schaefer – */21	Sopw 2-seater	E of Fresnes	101
22. 4.	1710	Rittm M. Frhr von Richthofen – 46	F.E.2b	Cagnicourt	102
22. 4.	1710	Lt K. Wolff – 19	F.E.2b	Hendecourt	103
22. 4.	2005	Lt K. Wolff – 20	Morane Parasol	Havrincourt	104
22. 4.	2020	Lt Schaefer – 21/22	Austin biplane	NW of the fork, Monchy–Tilloy, Monchy–Feuchy	105
23. 4.	1213	Rittm M. Frhr von Richthofen – 47	B.E.2f	between Avion & Méricourt, E of Vimy	106
23. 4.	1215	Lt L. Frhr von Richthofen – 10	B.E.2g	Vimy	107
24. 4.	0850	Lt Krefft – */* (Kofl 6. records)	E.A.	Arras	n/c
†25. 4.	0710	Vzfw Festner (Alb D.III)	KiA	Gavrelle (G 26)	
25. 4.	1030	Lt C. Allmenröder – 7	Austin/B.E.2	Guémappe	108
25. 4.	1045	Lt Schaefer – 22/23	F.E.2b	NW of Bailleul	109
25. 4.	2010	Lt Schaefer – 23/24	Bristol F.2A	Roeux railway station	110
26. 4.	1635	Lt K. Wolff – 21	B.E.2g	E of Gavrelle	111
26. 4.	1845	Lt L. Frhr	B.E.2g	between Vimy	112

Date	Time	Pilot & Victory Number	Aircraft Type	Location	Status
		von Richthofen – 11		& Farbus	
26. 4.	1848	Lt C. Allmenröder – 8	B.E.2g	Vimy Ridge	113
27. 4.	2015	Lt L. Frhr	F.E.2b	Fresnes	114
		von Richthofen – 12			
27. 4.	2020	Lt K. Wolff – 22	F.E.2b	S of Gavrelle	115
27. 4.	2025	Lt C. Allmenröder – 9	B.E.2c	between Athies	116
				& Fampoux	
28. 4.	0930	Rittm M. Frhr	B.E.2e	E of Pelves	117
		von Richthofen – 48			
28. 4.	1120	Lt K. Wolff – 23	B.E.2f	between Oppy	118
				& Gavrelle	
28. 4.	1745	Lt K. Wolff – 24	B.E.2g	W of Gavrelle	119
29. 4.	1215	Rittm M. Frhr	SPAD S.7	Lécluse	120
		von Richthofen – 49			
29. 4.	1215	Lt K. Wolff – 25	SPAD S.7	between Izel & Sailly	121
29. 4.	1215	Lt L. Frhr	SPAD S.7	between Izel & Sailly	122
		von Richthofen – 13			
29. 4.	1655	Rittm M. Frhr	F.E.2b	SW of Inchy	123
		von Richthofen – 50			
29. 4.	1700	Lt K. Wolff – 26	F.E.2b	S of Pronville	124
29. 4.	1925	Rittm M. Frhr	B.E.2e	Roeux	125
		von Richthofen – 51			
29. 4.	1945	Rittm M. Frhr	Sopw Triplane	near Lens, between	126
		von Richthofen – 52		Billy-Montigny &	
				Saullaumines	
29. 4.	1950	Lt L. Frhr	B.E.2e	between Monchy	127
		von Richthofen – 14		& Pelves	
30. 4.	0715	Lt L. Frhr	B.E.2g	near Méricourt,	128
		von Richthofen – 15		between Vimy & Willerval	
30. 4.	0750	Lt L. Frhr	F.E.2d	Izel	129
		von Richthofen – 16			
30. 4.	1735	Lt Wolff – */27	B.E.2e	Fresnes	130
1. 5.	1050	Lt Wolff – 28	Sopw Triplane	Phalempin, S of Seclin	131
1. 5.	1855	Lt Wolff – 27/29	F.E.2b	Fresnoy,	132
				S of Bois Bernard	
1. 5.	1900	Lt L. Frhr	F.E.2d	Gavrelle,	133
		von Richthofen – 19/17		W of Acheville	
6. 5.	1050	Lt L. Frhr	Bristol	E of Givenchy	134
		von Richthofen – 20/18			
7. 5.	1200	Lt C. Allmenröder – 10	B.E.2c	Fresnoy	135
7. 5.	1830	Lt L. Frhr	Nieuport	Gavrelle	136
		von Richthofen – 21/19			
7. 5.	2030	Lt L. Frhr	'Triplane'	near Annoeullin	137
		von Richthofen – 17/20	(S.E.5a)		
7. 5.		Lt d R Maashoff – 1	Bristol	near Fresnes	138
*7. 5.		Lt Plüschow	WiA	E of Gouy-sous-Bellonne	
9. 5.	1830	Lt L. Frhr	Bristol F.2B	Roeux–Gavrelle road	139
		von Richthofen – 22/21			
10. 5.	0740	Lt C. Allmenröder – 11	Sopw Pup	Vitry	140
10. 5.	0750	Lt L. Frhr	Sopw Pup	between Sailly	141
		von Richthofen – 18/22		& Vitry	
11. 5.	1225	Lt.d.R Maashoff – 2	B.E.2	Willerval	142
11. 5.	1710	Lt L. Frhr	Bristol F.2B	Izel	143
		von Richthofen – 23			
11. 5.	1715	Lt W. Allmenröder – 2	Bristol F.2B	near Beaumont,	144
				N of Oppy	
13. 5.	1135	Lt L. Frhr	B.E.2	Arleux	145
		von Richthofen – 24			
*13. 5.		Lt. L. Frhr von	WiA	Arleux	
		Richthofen			
13. 5.	1145	Lt C. Allmenröder	R.E.8	near Arleux	146
		– 13/12			
13. 5.	2115	Lt C. Allmenröder	Sopwith	Ostricourt	147
		– 12/13			
13. 5.	2120	Lt d R Hintsch – 2	Nieuport	Fresnes	148
14. 5.	1130	Lt C. Allmenröder – 14	B.E.2	Guémappe	149

Date	Time	Pilot & Victory Number	Aircraft Type	Location	Status
18. 5.	2005	Lt C. Allmenröder - 15	B.E.2	Fontaine, S of Monchy	150
19. 5.	0910	Lt C. Allmenröder – 16	Sopwith	Béthune, Fosse	151
23. 5.	2115	Lt d R Hintsch – 3 (contested by Vfw Aue, Jasta 10)	Sopw Triplane	Carvin, SW of Faschoda	152
24. 5.	0850	Lt C. Allmenröder – 17	Sopwith	Boiry-Notre-Dame	153
24. 5.	0902	Lt C. Allmenröder – 18	Sopw Triplane	Izel-Ferme, Flers, N of Douai	154
24. 5.	0915	Lt d R Maashoff – 3 (contested by Ltn Frhr von Beaulieu, Jasta 7)	Sopw Triplane	between Izel & Flers	155
*24. 5.		Lt W. Allmenröder	WiA	Lens, N of Fouquières	
†25. 5.		Lt d R Hintsch	KiA	Villers-lès-Cagnicourt	
25. 5.	1035	Lt C. Allmenröder – 19	Nieuport	Rémy, Bois-du-Vert	156
25. 5.	2045	Lt C. Allmenröder – 20	Bristol F.2B	Monchy	157
28. 5.	0830	Lt C. Allmenröder – 21	Sopw Pup	between Feuchy & Tilloy	158
29. 5.	1750	Lt C. Allmenröder – 22	R.E.8	Oppy, N of Gavrelle	159
1. 6.	1158	Lt Brauneck – 7	R.E.8	Méricourt, near Avion	160
3. 6.	0730	Lt C. Allmenröder – 23	Nieuport	Monchy	161
4. 6.	1925	Lt C. Allmenröder – 24	R.E.8	between Croisilles & Cagnicourt, SE of Arras	162
*4. 6.	1920	Lt Simon (Alb D.III 2015/16)	FtL/PoW	between Cagnicourt & Arras (G 42)	
4. 6.	2215	Lt C. Allmenröder – 25	R.E.8	Monchy, SE of Arras	163
5. 6.	1120	Lt C. Allmenröder – 26	Sopw 1½-Str	Terhand, at Wytschaete bend	164
5. 6.	1120	Lt Brauneck – 8	Sopw 1½-Str	Terhand, at Wytschaete bend	165
5. 6.	1120	Lt Niederhoff – 5	Sopw 1½-Str	Terhand, at Wytschaete bend,	166
18. 6.	0950	Lt C. Allmenröder – 26	Nieuport	Verlorenhoek	167
18. 6.	1315	Rittm M. Frhr von Richthofen – 53	R.E.8	N of Ypres	
†18. 6.	1245	Lt Bordfeld	KiA	Zandvoorde	
23. 6.	2115	Rittm M. Frhr von Richthofen – 54	SPAD	Dickebusch, N of Ypres	
24. 6.	0920	Lt C. Allmenröder – 28	Sopw Triplane	Polygon Wood	168
24. 6.	0920	Lt Groos – 2	Sopw Triplane	between Keibergmolen & Lichtensteinlager	169
24. 6.	0930	Rittm M. Frhr von Richthofen – 55	D.H.4	Becelaere	
25. 6.	1735	Rittm M. Frhr von Richthofen – 56	R.E.8	Trenches near Le Bizet	
25. 6.	0846	Lt C. Allmenröder – 29	Sopw Triplane	W of Quesnoy	170
26. 6.	2200	Lt C. Allmenröder – 30	Nieuport	near Ypres	171
†27. 6.	0945	Lt C. Allmenröder	KiA	Zillebeke	
2. 7.	1020	Rittm M. Frhr von Richthofen – 57	R.E.8	Deûlémont	
2. 7.	1025	Lt Groos – 3	R.E.8	near Messines	172
*6. 7.	1130	Rittm M. Frhr von Richthofen	WiA	Wervicq	
6. 7.	2120	Lt K. Wolff – 32	R.E.8	Zillebeke, SW of Ypres	173
7. 7.	1100	Lt K. Wolff – 33	Sopw Triplane	Comines	174
7. 7.	1110	Lt d R Niederhoff – 4 (contested by Oblt von Doering, Jasta 4)	Sopw Triplane	Bousbecque	175
7. 7.	1810	Vzfw Lautenschlager – 1 (contested by Vzfw Clausnitzer, Jasta 4)	Sopw 1½-Str	between Houthem & Wytschaete	176
*11. 7.	1020	Lt K. Wolff	WiA		
11. 7.	2115	Lt Mohnike – 3	Sopw Triplane	Comines	177
17. 7.	1110	Lt d R Niederhoff – 5 (contested by Uffz Brettel, Jasta 10)	Nieuport	Nordschoote	178
*17. 7.	2055	Lt d R Meyer	WiA	Ypres	
20. 7.	2110	Lt d R Niederhoff – 6 (contested by Vzfw Küllmer, Jasta 6)	Sopw	Zonnebeke	179
22. 7.	1125	Lt Brauneck – 9	Sopw Triplane	E of Kortewilde	180
22. 7.	1130	Lt d R Niederhoff – 7	Sopw 1½-Str	SW of Zonnebeke	181

Date	Time	Pilot & Victory Number	Aircraft Type	Location	Status
22. 7.	1130	Oblt Reinhard – 1	Sopw 1½-Str	Warneton	182
		(contested by Lt Deilmann, Jasta 6 and Vfw Küllmer, Jasta 6)			
†26. 7.	2045	Lt Brauneck	KiA	S of Zonnebeke	
27. 7.	2040	Lt von Schoenebeck – 1	Sopw Triplane	Beitem	183
†28. 7.	1200	Lt d R Niederhoff	KiA	Becelaere, W of Terhand	
28. 7.	1720	Lt Bockelmann – */2	Caudron	Merckem	184
28. 7.	2100	Lt Mohnike – 4	B.E.2	between Becelaere & Moorslede	185
31. 7.	1300	Lt Meyer – 1	R.E.8	Deimlingseck	186
27. 7.	1310	Lt von Schoenebeck – 2	R.E.8	Frezenberg	187
12. 8.	0850	Lt Stapenhorst – 1	Sopwith	NW of Bixschoote	188
13. 8.	0920	Lt Bockelmann – 2/3	Pusher biplane	Schellebeke, E of Ghent	189
13. 8.	1045	Oblt Reinhard – 2	Sopw 1½-Str	Grotenmolen, N of Polygon Wood	190
*14. 8.	0920	Lt H. J. Wolff	WiA	Zillebeke Lake	
14. 8.	1040	Oblt Reinhard – 3	R.E.8	Boesinghe	191
14. 8.	1045	Oblt Reinhard – 4	SPAD	2 km N of Boesinghe	192
14. 8.	1735	Lt d R F. Müller – 1	Sopwith	N of Bixschoote	193
14. 8.	1840	Lt K. Meyer – */2	Sopwith	Wytschaete	194
16. 8.	0755	Rittm M. Frhr von Richthofen – 58	Nieuport 23	SW of Houthulst Forest	
16. 8.	1120	Lt Groos – 4	Sopw Triplane	Hollebeke, near Zillebeke Lake	195
16. 8.	1220	Lt Mohnike – 5	Martinsyde 1-seater	N of Linselles	196
17. 8.	0725	Lt Groos – 5	S.E.5a	W of Passchendaele	197
17. 8.	2055	Lt von der Osten – 1	Bristol F.2B	Staden	198
17. 8.	0750	Lt Groos – 6	Sopwith	S of Poelkappelle, near Houthulst Wood	199
25. 8.	2055	Lt von der Osten – 2	Sopw Triplane	between Passchen-daele & Langemarck	200
26. 8.	0730	Rittm M. Frhr von Richthofen – 59	SPAD S.7	between Poelkappelle & Langemarck	
		(victory credited to JG I's overall score)			
26. 8.	1045	Oblt Reinhard – 6/5	R.E.8	near Bixschoote	201
1. 9.	0750	Rittm M. Frhr von Richthofen – 60	R.E.8	Zonnebeke	
1. 9.	0815	Oblt Reinhard – */6	Sopw Camel	Zonnebeke	202
3. 9.	0735	Rittm M. Frhr von Richthofen – 61	Sopw Pup	S of Bousbecque	
3. 9.	0730	Lt Mohnike – 6	Sopw Pup	S of Tenbrielen, near Wervicq	203
3. 9.	1000	Lt von Schoenebeck – 3	Sopw Triplane	E of Hollebeke	204
3. 9.	1018	Lt Stapenhorst – 2	Sopw Triplane	between Hollebeke & Wytschaete	205
*3. 9.	1430	Lt Bockelmann	WiA	Bousbecque	
4. 9.	0840	Lt Mohnike – 7	Sopw Camel	Becelaere	206
4. 9.	0840	Lt Stapenhorst – 3/*	Sopw Camel	S of Becelaere	207
*4. 9.	0915	Oblt Reinhard	WiA	N of Houthulst Forest	
9. 9.	1250	Lt Stapenhorst – 4	SPAD	between Zonnebeke & Frezenberg	208
*14. 9.	0940	Lt Groos	WiA	near Ypres	
15. 9.	1245	Lt von der Osten – 3	Sopwith	Frezenberg	209
†15. 9.	1730	Oblt K. Wolff (Fok F.I 102/17)	KiA	Nachtigal, N of Wervicq	
*20. 9.		Lt Just	FtL	Becelaere	
9.10.	1430	Lt d R F. Müller – 2	Nieuport	Gheluwelt	210
*20.10.	1200	Lt Gerstenberg	WiA	Vossemolen	
†27.10.	0830	Lt d R F. Müller (Fok D.V)	KiC	Courtrai	
†29.10.	1045	Vzfw Lautenschlager (Fok Dr.I 113/17)	KiA	N of Houthulst Wood	
*30.10.	0950	Rittm M. Frhr von Richthofen (Fok Dr.I 114/17)	FtL	Zilverberg	

Date	Time	Pilot & Victory Number	Aircraft Type	Location	Status
*30.10.	0950	Lt L. Frhr von Richthofen (Fok Dr.I)	FtL	Zilverberg	
†31.10.	1520	Lt.d.R Pastor (Fok Dr.I 121/17)	KiA	Moorsele	
9.11.	1030	Lt L. Frhr von Richthofen – 25	Bristol F.2B	NW of Zonnebeke	211
23.11.	1400	Rittm M. Frhr von Richthofen – 62	D.H.5	SE of Bourlon Wood	
23.11.	1400	Lt L. Frhr von Richthofen – 26	Bristol F.2B	2 km W of Séranvillers	212
*23.11.		Lt H. J. Wolff	IiC	Avesnes-le-Sec	
*23.11.		Lt von Schoenebeck	FtL	Epinoy	
30.11.	1345	Lt von der Osten – 4	D.H.5	S of Bourlon Wood	213
30.11.	1430	Rittm M. Frhr von Richthofen – 63	S.E.5a	Moeuvres	
30.11.	1445	Lt Gussmann – 2	D.H.5	between Bourlon Wood & Moeuvres	214
*4.12		Lt Gussmann (Alb D.V 4628/17)	Ac	Avesnes-le-Sec	
*4.12		Lt von Linsingen (Alb D.V 2161/17)	Ac	Avesnes-le-Sec	
* 4.12		Lt Schweinitz (Alb D.V 5313/17)	Ac	Avesnes-le-Sec	
12.12.	1320	Lt d R Just – 1	Balloon	Ruyaulcourt	215
15.12.	1025	Lt von der Osten – 5	S.E.5a	Havrincourt	216
†27.12.	1435	Lt von Schweinitz (Alb D.V 5313/17)	Ac/DoW	Avesnes-le-Sec	
1918					
13. 1.	1637	Lt Steinhäuser – 2	Balloon	Heudecourt, W of Le Catelet	217
*13. 1.		Lt Stapenhorst (Fok Dr.I 144/17)	FtL/PoW	(G 125)	
*24. 1.	1535	Lt von Linsingen (Pfalz D.III 4223/17)	IiC	Along road Cambrai to Iwuy	
2. 2.	1720	Lt Steinhäuser – 3/*	R.E.8	Havrincourt Wood	218
*3. 2.		Lt H. J. Wolff (Fok Dr.I 155/17)	FtL	Villers-Outreaux	
*17. 2.	1230	Lt F-W. Lübbert	WiA	Rumilly	
*1. 3.		Lt Mohnike (Fok Dr.I 155/17)	WiA		
*1. 3.		Lt Just (Fok Dr.I 110/17)	WiA		
†6. 3.	1040	Lt d R Bahr (Fok Dr.I 106/17)	KiA	between Nauroy & Etricourt	
(10 March 1918: German time synchronised with Allied time)					
11. 3.	1310	Lt L. Frhr von Richthofen – 27	Bristol F.2B	NE of Fresnoy-le-Petit	219
11. 3.	1310	Vzfw Scholz – 3/2	S.E.5a	Holnon Wood	220
12. 3.	1100	Lt L. Frhr von Richthofen – 28	Bristol F.2B	Menetz	221
12. 3.	1100	Lt L. Frhr von Richthofen – 29	Bristol F.2B	Cléry	222
12. 3.	1100	Lt Steinhäuser	Bristol F.2B	Beauvais	223
12. 3.	1115	Rittm M. Frhr von Richthofen – 64	Bristol F.2B	Nauroy	
*13. 3.	1030	Lt L. Frhr von Richthofen (Fokker Dr.I 454/17)	FtL/IiC	Avoingt	
13. 3.	1035	Rittm M. Frhr von Richthofen – 65	Sopw Camel	between Gonnelieu & Banteux	
13. 3.	1040	Vzfw Scholz – 2/3	Sopw Camel	between Vaucelles & Les rues des vignès	224
*17. 3.		Lt Steinhäuser	WiA/FtL	Briastre	
18. 3.	1100	Lt d R Gussmann-3	Bristol F.2B	Joncourt	225
18. 3.	1115	Rittm M. Frhr von Richthofen – 66	Sopw Camel	road between Molain & Vaux-Andigny	
18. 3.	1115	Lt H. J. Wolff – 6/1	S.E.5a	Escaufort	226

Date	Time	Pilot & Victory Number	Aircraft Type	Location	Status
18. 3.	1120	Vzfw Scholz – 4	Sopw Camel	La Vallée Mulâtre	227
18. 3.	1122	Vzfw Scholz – */5	Sopw Camel	Honnechy	228
*24. 3.	0930	Lt Keseling	FtL/PoW		
		(Fok Dr.I 147/17)		(G 158)	
24. 3.	1445	Rittm M. Frhr	S.E.5a	Combles	
		von Richthofen – 68/67			
25. 3.	1555	Rittm M. Frhr	Sopw. Camel	Contalmaison	
		von Richthofen – 67/68			
26. 3.	1645	Rittm M. Frhr	Sopw Dolphin	S of Contalmaison	
		von Richthofen – 69			
26. 3.	1700	Rittm M. Frhr	R.E.8	NE of Albert	
		von Richthofen – 70			
26. 3.	1700	Lt d R Gussmann – 4	Sopw Camel	N of Albert	229
27. 3.	0900	Rittm M. Frhr	Sopw Camel	Aveluy/Ancre,	
		von Richthofen – 71		1 km NE of Aveluy	
27. 3.	1150	Lt d R Udet – 22	R.E.8	S of Albert	230
27. 3.	1205	Vfw Scholz – 5/6	Bristol F.2B	1 km S of Albert	231
27. 3.	1630	Rittm M. Frhr	Bristol F.2B	Faucaucourt	
		von Richthofen – 72			
27. 3.	1635	Rittm M. Frhr	Bristol F.2B	NE of Chuignolles	
		von Richthofen – 73			
28. 3.	1150	Lt d R Udet – 21/23	Sopw Camel	between Thiepval	232
				& Courcelette	
28. 3.	1230	Rittm M. Frhr	Arm-Whit F.K.8	small forest	
		von Richthofen – 74		E of Méricourt	
1. 4.	0900	Lt H. J. Wolff – 1/2	D.H.4	Grévillers	233
1. 4.	1700	Lt H. J. Wolff – 2/3	S.E.5a	forest NE	234
				of Moreuil	
2. 4.	1235	Rittm M. Frhr	R.E.8	over Hill 106	
		von Richthofen – 75		NE of Moreuil	
2. 4.	1650	Lt H. J. Wolff – 3/4	Bristol F.2B	along Roman Road	235
				between Morcourt	
				& Harbonnières	
2. 4.	1700	Lt d R Weiss-12/14	Bristol F.2B	along Roman Road	236
				between Morcourt	
				& Harbonnières	
6. 4.	1415	Lt d R Udet – 23	Sopw Camel	forest S of Hamel	237
6. 4.	1500	Lt H. J. Wolff – 5	Bristol F.2B	NE of Vauvillers	238
6. 4.	1545	Rittm M. Frhr	Sopw Camel	NE of Villers-Brettoneux	
		von Richthofen – 76			
6. 4.	1555	Lt H. J. Wolff – 6	Sopw Camel	E of Lamotte	239
6. 4.	1600	Lt d R Weiss –13/15	Sopw Camel	S edge of Marcelcave	240
6. 4.	1605	Vzfw Scholz – 6/7	Sopw Camel	Cerisy	241
6. 4.	1610	Lt Just – 2	Sopw Camel	Méricourt	242
6. 4.	1750	Lt d R Weiss – 14/16	Sopw Camel	crossroads 3 km	243
				NE of Sailly-le-Sec	
7. 4.	1130	Rittm M. Frhr	S.E.5a	Hangard	
		von Richthofen – 77			
7. 4.	1150	Lt H. J. Wolff – */7	S.E.5a (FtL)	N of Dommartin	244
7. 4.	1205	Rittm M. Frhr	Sopw Camel	over Hill 104,	
		von Richthofen – 78		N of Villers-Brettoneux	
*7. 4.		Lt Gussmann	WiA		
†12. 4.	1510	Uffz Eiserbeck	KiA	hill S of Méault	
(16 April 1918: German time one hour ahead of Allied time)					
20. 4.	1840	Lt d R Weiss – 15/17	Sopw Camel	S of Bois de Hamel	245
20. 4.	1840	Rittm M. Frhr	Sopw Camel	S. of Bois de Hamel	
		von Richthofen – 79			
20. 4.	1843	Rittm M. Frhr	Sopw Camel	Villers-Brettoneux	
		von Richthofen – 80			
21. 4.	1150	Lt H. J. Wolff – 7/8	Sopw Camel	S of Hamelet	246
†21. 4.	1155	Rittm M. Frhr	KiA	Vaux-sur-Somme	
		von Richthofen			
		(Fok Dr.I 425/17)		(G/5th Bde/2)	
22. 4.	1158	Lt d R Weiss – 16/18	Sopw Camel	forest N of Moreuil	247
†2. 5.	1300	Lt d R Weiss	KiA	S of Etinehem, near	
		(Fok Dr.I 545/17)		Méricourt	

Date	Time	Pilot & Victory Number	Aircraft Type	Location	Status
†2. 5.	1750	Vfw [Lt d R] Scholz (Fok Dr.I 591/17)	KiC	Cappy	
*3. 5.		Lt d R Just	WiA	Proyart	
9. 5.	2000	Hptm Reinhard – 13/14	Sopw Camel	W of Morlancourt	
10. 5.		Oblt E. von Wedel – 1	Sopw Camel	Cérisy	248
10. 5.		Lt Steinhäuser – 5	Sopw Camel	N of Cérisy	249
10. 5.		Lt H. J. Wolff – 9	Sopw Camel	S of Sailly-Laurette	250
15. 5.	1510	Lt H. J. Wolff – 10	Bristol F.2B	W of Guillaucourt	251
15. 5.	1515	Oblt E. von Wedel –2	Bristol F.2B	SE of Guillaucourt	252
†16. 5.	0820	Lt H. J. Wolff	KiA	N of Lamotte Ferme	
19. 5.	1130	Lt Steinhäuser – 7/6	Bristol F.2B	Hamel	253
19. 5.	2000	Oblt E. von Wedel –3	SPAD	E of Harbonnières	254
19. 5.	2010	Lt Steinhäuser – 6/7	D.H.9	Villers-Brettoneux	255
19. 5.	2010	Vzfw Gabriel – 2	D.H.9	NE of Marcelcave	256
31. 5.	1945	Hptm Reinhard – */14	SPAD	Bonneuil	
31. 5.	2040	Oblt E. von Wedel – */3	SPAD	Bois de Burbillon	257
1. 6.	1710	Vfw Gabriel – 3	French SPAD	Fleury	258
2. 6.	1745	Lt Steinhäuser – 8	SPAD 2-seater	S of Troësnes	259
2. 6.	1745	Hptm Reinhard – 16/15	SPAD 2-seater	S of Bonnes	
2. 6.	2030	Hptm Reinhard – 17/16	SPAD 2-seater	La Ferté-Milon	
2. 6.	2100	Hptm Reinhard – 18/17	SPAD 2-seater	Buisson de Borny Wood	
4. 6.	1725	Hptm Reinhard –14/18	SPAD 2-seater	Dammard	
4. 6.	1725	Lt W. Frhr von Richthofen – 1	SPAD 2-seater	W of Dammard	260
4. 6.	2040	Oblt E. von Wedel – 5	SPAD 2-seater	Faverolles	261
9. 6.	0900	Lt Steinhäuser – 9	SPAD	Cravencon	262
9. 6.	0900	Oblt E. von Wedel – 6	SPAD	Longpont	263
9. 6.	0900	Hptm Reinhard – 19	SPAD	Dommiers	
9. 6.	1220	Lt W. Frhr von Richthofen – 2	SPAD	Tartiers	264
9. 6.	1220	Lt Steinhäuser – 10	SPAD	St-Bandry	265
10. 6.	1635	Vzfw Gabriel – 4	Balloon		266
12. 6.		Hptm Reinhard – 20	SPAD 2-seater		
13. 6.	1605	Vzfw Gabriel – 5	SPAD		267
16. 6.	1000	Vzfw Gabriel – 6	Balloon		268
†26. 6.	0800	Lt Steinhäuser	KiA	Neuilly	
28. 6.	0900	Lt Mohnicke – 8	SPAD		269
28. 6.	0905	Lt Mohnicke – 9	SPAD		270
30. 6.		Vzfw Gabriel – 7/*	Sopw Dolphin		271
†30. 6.	2000	Lt Hofmann	KiA	Passy	
†3. 7.		Hptm Reinhard	KiC	Berlin Adlershof	
18. 7.	0815	Oblt Göring – 22	SPAD	wooded ravine near St-Bandry	
18. 7.	0830	Oblt E. von Wedel – 8/7	SPAD		272
18. 7.	0950	Vzfw Gabriel – 8	SPAD		273
18. 7.	1000	Vzfw Gabriel – 9	SPAD		274
18. 7.	1022	Vzfw Gabriel – 10	Bréguet		275
18. 7.	1530	Vzfw Gabriel – 11	SPAD		276
21. 7.	2015	Oblt E. von Wedel – 7/8	Sopw Camel		277
21. 7.	2015	Lt W. Frhr von Richthofen – 3	Sopw Camel		278
25. 7.	0750	Lt L. Frhr von Richthofen – 30	Sopw Camel	Fismes	279
†25. 7.	1945	Lt Graf von Hohenau	WiA/DoW (26.7.18)		
25. 7.	2030	Lt d R Just– 3	SPAD 2-seater		280
*25. 7.		Lt von Dorrien	WiA		
29. 7.	1215	Oblt E. von Wedel – 9	Bréguet		281
1. 8.	1305	Lt Groos – 7	SPAD		282
1. 8.	1310	Lt L. Frhr von Richthofen – 31	SPAD		283
1. 8.	2025	Lt L. Frhr von Richthofen – 32	SPAD		284
8. 8.	1730	Lt L. Frhr von Richthofen – 34/33	Sopw Camel	W of Péronne	285
8. 8.	1745	Lt L. Frhr von Richthofen – 33/34	S.E.5a		286

Date	Time	Pilot & Victory Number	Aircraft Type	Location	Status
8. 8.	1850	Lt L. Frhr von Richthofen – 35	S.E.5a	Estrées	287
9. 8.	0730	Lt L. Frhr von Richthofen – 37/36	D.H.9	Villers-Carbonnel	288
9. 8.	0735	Lt d R Just – 4	Sopw Camel		289
9. 8.	1840	Lt L. Frhr von Richthofen – 38/37	D.H.9	Foucaucourt	290
10. 8.	1215	Lt d R von Köckeritz – 1	S.E.5a		291
*10. 8.	1215	Lt Wenz	P/OK	Chaulnes	
11. 8.	0930	Lt L. Frhr von Richthofen – 36/38	D.H.9		292
†11. 8.		Lt d R Festler	KiA	La Chapelle	
12. 8.	0930	Lt W. Frhr von Richthofen – 4/5	Sopw Camel	E of Péronne	293
12. 8.	0935	Lt d R Just – 5	Sopw Camel	E of Péronne	294
12. 8.	0935	Lt L. Frhr von Richthofen – 39	Sopw Dolphin	NW of Péronne	295
12. 8.	0950	Lt L. Frhr von Richthofen – 40	Sopw Camel	NW of Misery	296
*13. 8.		Lt L. Frhr von Richthofen	WiA		
*23. 8.		Lt Frhr von Barnekow		WiA	
31. 8.	1945	Oblt E. von Wedel – 10	Sopw Dolphin	SW of Péronne	297
31. 8.	1945	Lt d R Schulte-Frohlinde – 1	Sopw Camel		298
31. 8.	1945	Lt d R von Köckeritz – 2	RFC biplane		299
2. 9.	0955	Oblt E. von Wedel – 11	'armoured aircraft'	Frémicourt	300
4. 9.	1715	Lt d R Just – 6	Balloon	Barastre	301
6. 9.	0945	Lt W. Frhr von Richthofen – 5	Sopw Dolphin	E of St-Quentin	302
7. 9.	1300	Lt d R Schulte-Frohlinde – 2	S.E.5a		303
7. 9.	1940	Lt W. Frhr von Richthofen – 6	S.E.5a	W of Le Catelet	304
7. 9.	1945	Lt W. Frhr von Richthofen – 7	S.E.5a	W of Le Catelet	305
7. 9.	1945	Oblt E. von Wedel – 12	S.E.5a	Le Catelet	306
19. 9.	1600	Lt d R Schulte-Frohlinde – 3	Bristol F.2B	Belle-Eglise	307
16.10.	1200	Vzfw Niemz – 3	SPAD	near Aire River	308
23.10.	1255	Lt d R Noltenius – 16	Balloon	Chatel-Chéhéry	309
23.10.	1605	Lt d R Noltenius – 17	SPAD	Aire River	310
23.10.	1735	Lt d R Noltenius – 18	Balloon	Baulny	311
28.10.	1700	Lt d R Noltenius – 19	Balloon	Eclisfontaine	312
3.11.	1515	Lt d R Noltenius – 20	D.H.9	Barricourt	313
3.11.	1550	Lt d R von Köckeritz – 3	SPAD		314
3.11.	1605	Lt d R Gussmann – 5	A.R.		315
4.11.	1645	Vzfw Niemz – 4	D.H.9		316
4.11.	1600	Lt d R Schulte-Frohlinde-4	D.H.9		317
5.11.	1030	Lt W. Frhr von Richthofen – 8	D.H.9	S of Montmédy	318
5.11.	1035	Oblt E. von Wedel – 13	SPAD		319

Jagdgeschwader and Jagdstaffel Organisation Charts

The institution of single-seat fighter units during the First World War has been much discussed by researchers who have had to work with imperfect records. With the emergence of the German Ministry's organisational manual (*Teil 10 Abschnitte B, Fliegerformation*, Berlin, 1918) fighter unit development has become much clearer. The following material is from that source and should settle any future questions about the derivation of JG I and other fighter units noted in this book.

Unit	Establishment Date	Place	Conforming to Orders of	Date of Mobilization	Additional Information
JG 1	23.6.17	Front	Generalstab Ic 58341/ Kriegsministerium Nr. 709.10.17.A.7.L. of 23.6.17	23.6.17	comprising Jastas 4, 6, 10, 11
JG 2	2.2.18	Front	Kriegsministerium Nr. 4524.18.A.7.L. of 16.3.18	2.2.18	Jastas 12, 13, 15, 19
JG 3	2.2.18	Front	Ditto	2.2.18	Jastas 2, 26, 27, 36
JG 4b	10.10.18	Front	Bayerisches Kriegsministerium	10.10.18	Jastas 23b, 32b, 34b, 35b
Jasta 1	22.8.16	Kofl 1	Chef des Feld-flugwesens West Nr. 22429 FL.	22.8.16	
Jasta 1 Heeresgruppe F	1.1.18	Front	KM Nr. 335.18. A.7.L.IV.C. of 18.1.18	25.1.18	former Jasta 55
Jasta 2	10.8.16	FEA 7	Chef des Feldfl.W. Nr. 22429 Fl.	10.8.16	changed to Jasta Boelcke 17.12.16
Jasta 3	10.8.16	FEA 5	Ditto	1.9.16	
Jasta 4	25.8.16	FEA 9	KM Nr. 929.16. g.A.7.L. of 31.8.16	25.8.16	
Jasta 5	21.1.16	Kdo. KG 1	Feldflugchef Nr. 10083.Fl. of 15.1.16	21.1.16	changed to Jasta 5 KM Nr. 929.16. a.7.L. of 10.8.16
Jasta 6	25.8.16	Front	KM 929.16. g.A.7.L., 31.8.16 of 31.8.16 /AOK 5 Ia.2394 of 25.8.16	25.8.16	former Fokkerstaffel Sivry
Jasta 7	23.8.16	Front	Ditto	21.9.16	
Jasta 8	10.9.16	FEA 10	Chef des Feldfl.W. Nr. 24281.Fl. of 10.9.16	10.9.16	
Jasta 9	1.6.16	AOK 3	KM Nr. 269.10.16. A.7.L. of 1.6.16; changed on 28.9.16	5.10.16	former Armeestaffel AOK 3
Jasta 10	28.9.16	Kofl 6	KM Nr. 269.10.16. A.7.L. of 28.9.16	6.10.16	previously KEK 3
Jasta 11	28.9.16	Kofl 6	Ditto	11.10.16	
Jasta 12	28.9.16	Kofl 6	Ditto	28.9.16	former Fokkerstaffel West AOK 7
Jasta 13	28.9.16	Kofl C	Ditto	15.10.16	

Unit	Establishment Date	Place	Conforming to Orders of	Date of Mobilization	Additional Information
Jasta 14	28.9.16	A Abt C	KM Nr. 269.10.16. A.7.L. of 28.9.16 / Chef des Feldfl.W. Nr. 25367.Fl.	28.9.16	former Fokkerstaffel Falkenhausen
Jasta 15	28.9.16	A Abt B	KM Nr. 269.10.16. A.7.L.	10.10.16	former KEK Habsheim
Jasta 16b	10.16	A Abt B	Kogenluft Nr. 26441 of 28.10.16; changed on 1.11.16 and Bayer. KM Nr. 111847.A. of 17.7.17	10.16	former KEK Ensisheim
Jasta 17	23.10.16	Kofl 6	Kogenluft Nr. 26665.Fl. of 23.10.16	11.11.16	
Jasta 18	30.10.16	FEA 12	Kogenluft Nr. 54427 of 30.10.16	30.10.16	
Jasta 19	25.10.16	AFP 1	Kogenluft Nr. 26806 of 25.10.16	25.10.16	
Jasta 20	25.10.16	AFP 2	Ditto	25.10.16	
Jasta 21s	25.10.16	AFP 3	KM Nr. 1145.16. g.A.7.L. of 29.11.16	6.12.16	Saxon unit from 24.11.17 per KM Nr. 864.11.17. A.7.L.
Jasta 22s	16.11.16	Stofl 7	Ditto	1.12.16	Saxon unit per order noted above
Jasta 23b	25.10.16	A Abt Strantz	KM Nr. 1145.16. g.A.7.L. of 29.11.16/B.KM Nr. 111847.A. of 17.7.17	31.12.16	changed to Bavarian unit
Jasta 24s	25.10.16	Kofl A	KM Nr. 1145.16. of 29.11.16	25.10.16	Saxon unit from 24.11.17 per g. A.7.L. KM Nr. 864.11.17. A.7.L.
Jasta 25	28.11.16	Kofl 11	KM Nr. 1145.16 g.A.7.L. of 28.11.16	1.12.16	
Jasta 26	14.12.16	Kofl 9	Ditto	18.1.17	
Jasta 27	5.2.17	Kofl 9	Ditto	5.2.17	
Jasta 28w	14.12.16	Kofl 10	Ditto	21.1.17	
Jasta 29	28.12.16	FEA 5	Ditto	12.2.17	
Jasta 30	14.12.16	FEA 11	Ditto	21.1.17	
Jasta 31	14.12.16	FEA 11	Ditto	5.2.17	
Jasta 32b	14.12.16	FEA 9	KM Nr. 1425.16 g.A.7.L. of 14.12.16 B.Km.Nr. 111847.A. of 17.7.17	22.2.17	changed to Bavarian unit
Jasta 33	14.12.16	FEA 3	KM Nr. 1425.16 g.A.7.L. of 14.12.16	1.3.17	
Jasta 34b	20.2.17	FEA 1	B.KM Nr.11187.A. of 17.7.17	20.2.17	
Jasta 35b	14.12.16	FEA 6	Ditto	1.3.17	
Jasta 36	11.1.17	FEA 11	Ditto	21.2.17	belongs to JG 3
Jasta 37	10.1.17	FEA 8	Ditto	10.1.17	
Jasta 38	30.6.17	AOK Scholtz	KM Nr. 1263.6.17. A.7.L.	30.6.17	
Jasta 39	30.6.17	FEA 5	Ditto	10.8.17	

Unit	Establishment Date	Place	Conforming to Orders of	Date of Mobilization	Additional Information
Jasta 40s	30.6.17	FEA 6	Ditto	15.8.17	Saxon unit from 24.11.17 per KM Nr. 864.11.17. A.7.L.
Jasta 41	18.6.17	FEA 4	KM Nr. 744.17 g.A.7.L. of 18.6.17	5.8.17	
Jasta 42	6.12.17	FEA 3	Ditto		18.12.17
Jasta 43	6.12.17	FEA 4	Ditto	18.12.17	
Jasta 44s	11.12.17	FEA 6	Ditto	23.12.17	
Jasta 45	11.12.17	FEA 1	Ditto	23.12.17	
Jasta 46	11.12.17	FEA 8	Ditto	25.12.17	
Jasta 47w	16.12.17	FEA 10	Ditto	26.12.17	
Jasta 48	16.12.17	FEA 11	Ditto	1.1.18	
Jasta 49	23.12.17	FEA 12	Ditto	9.1.18	
Jasta 50	23.12.17	FEA 13	Ditto	5.1.18	
Jasta 51	27.12.17	FEA 14	Ditto	9.1.18	
Jasta 52	27.12.17	FEA 7	Ditto	9.1.18	
Jasta 53	27.12.17	FEA 9	Ditto	7.1.18	
Jasta 54s	1.1.18	FEA 6	Ditto	15.1.18	
Jasta 55	1.1.18	FEA 2	Ditto	25.1.18	later Jasta 1 of Heeresgruppe F
Jasta 55		Idflieg	KM Nr. 21370.18. g.A.7.L.IV.C. of 29.10.18		was to have been established 1.4.19
Jasta 56	1.1.18	Geschw.-Schule Paderborn.	KM Nr. 1744.17 g.A.7.L.	12.1.18	
Jasta 57	6.1.18	Beob.-Schule Königsberg	Ditto	19.1.18	
Jasta 58	6.1.18	Beob.-Schule Thorn	KM Nr. 744.17 g.A.7.L.	20.1.18	
Jasta 59	6.1.18	Beob.-Schule Schwerin	Ditto	21.1.18	
Jasta 60	11.1.18	Beob.-Schule Jüterbog	Ditto	24.1.18	
Jasta 61	11.1.18	Beob.-Schule Cologne	Ditto	23.1.18	
Jasta 62	16.1.18	Beob.-Schule West	Ditto	25.1.18	
Jasta 63	16.1.18	Beob.-Schule Warsaw	Ditto	26.1.18	
Jasta 64w	23.1.18	FEA 10	Ditto	4.2.18	
Jasta 65	23.1.18	FEA 7	Ditto	4.2.18	
Jasta 66	27.1.18	FEA 5	Ditto	5.2.18	
Jasta 67	27.1.18	FEA 9	Ditto	5.2.18	
Jasta 68	1.2.18	FEA 3	Ditto	10.2.18	
Jasta 69	1.2.18	FEA 4	Ditto	10.2.18	
Jasta 70	6.2.18	FEA 11	Ditto	18.2.18	
Jasta 71	6.2.18	FEA 13	Ditto	17.2.18	
Jasta 72s	11.2.18	FEA 6	Ditto	20.2.18	

Unit	Establishment Date	Place	Conforming to Orders of	Date of Mobilization	Additional Information
Jasta 73	11.2.18	FEA 14	Ditto	20.2.18	
Jasta 74	16.2.18	FEA 1	Ditto	25.2.18	
Jasta 75	16.2.18	FEA 2	Ditto	25.2.18	
Jasta 76b	14.12.16	b.FEA 1	KM Nr. 744.17 g.A.7.L./ B.KM Nr. 144592 of 7.9.17	15.10.17	
Jasta 77b	25.11.17	b.FEA 1	Ditto	25.11.17	
Jasta 78b	15.11.17	b.FEA 1	Ditto	15.11.17	
Jasta 79b	28.1.18	b.FEA 1	Ditto	28.1.18	
Jasta 80b	15.2.18	b.FEA 2	Ditto	16.2.18	
Jasta 81	15.6.17	Ob.Ost	Ob.Ost Nr. 4685. Ib.17, 4578. Ib.17 and KM Nr. 453. 9.17.A.7.L. of 24.9.17	15.6.17	changed from Jagdflieger Ob.Ost on 1.10.17
Jasta 82	November 1918		KM Nr. 21370.18 A.7.L.IV.C. of 29.10.18	Since formation	former Kest 2
Jasta 83	November 1918		Ditto	Ditto	former Kest 3
Jasta 84w	November 1918		Ditto	Ditto	former Kest 4a and 4b (Württ.)
Jasta 85	November 1918		Ditto	Ditto	former Kest 5
Jasta 86	November 1918		Ditto	Ditto	former Kest 6
Jasta 87	November 1918		Ditto	Ditto	former Kest 7
Jasta 88	November 1918		Ditto	Ditto	former Kest 8
Jasta 89	November 1918		Ditto	Ditto	former Kest 9
Jasta 90	November 1918		Ditto	Ditto	former Kest 1a and 1b

Bibliography

Books

Albedyll, K., von, *Gedenkblätter der Königen-Kürassiere mit Nachträgen und Fortsetzung der Personalien aus der Regiments – Geschichte bis 1919*. Pasewalk, 1919

Bartlett, C., *Bomber Pilot 1916–1918*. London, 1974

Bishop, W., *Winged Warfare*. London, 1918

Bodenschatz, K., *Jagd in Flanderns Himmel – Aus den sechzehn Kampfmonaten des Jagdgeschwaders Freiherr von Richthofen*. Munich, 1935

Böhme, E. (ed. J. Werner), *Briefe eines deutschen Kampffliegers an ein junges Mädchen*. Leipzig, 1930

Boelcke, O., *Hauptmann Boelckes Feldberichte*. Gotha, 1916

Bowyer, C., *Albert Ball, V.C.* Wrexham, 2nd edn, 1994

– *For Valour – the Air V.C.s*. London, 1978

– *The Flying Elephants – A History of No. 27 Squadron*. London, 1972

Bruce, J., *British Aeroplanes 1914–1918*. London, 1969

Carisella, P. and Ryan J., *Who Killed the Red Baron?* Wakefield, Mass., 1969

Cole, C. (ed.), *Royal Air Force 1918*. London, 1968

Collishaw, R., *Air Command – A Fighter Pilot's Story*. London, 1973

Cuneo, J., *Winged Mars*, vol. II, *The Air Weapon 1914–1916*. Harrisburg, 1947

Cutlack, F., *The Official History of Australia in the War of 1914–1918*. vol. VIII, 1933, p. 251

Dickhuth-Harrach, G. von (ed.), *Im Felde unbesiegt*, vol. I, Munich, 1921

Dollfus, C. and Bouché, H., *Histoire de l'Aéronautique*. Paris, 1932

Eberhardt, W. von (ed.), *Unsere Luftstreitkräfte 1914–1918*. Berlin, 1930

Esposito, V. (ed.), *A Concise History of World War I*. New York, 1965

Franks, N. and Bailey, F., *Over the Front*. London, 1992

Franks, N., Bailey, F. and Guest, R., *Above the Lines*. London, 1993

Franks, N., Giblin, H. and McCrery, N., *Under the Guns of the Red Baron*. London. 1995

Franks, N., Bailey, F. and Duiven, R., *The Jasta Pilots*. London, 1996

Gibbons, F., *The Red Knight of Germany*. New York, 1927

Goodspeed, D., *Ludendorff – The Genius of World War I*. Boston, 1966

Haehnelt. W. (ed.), *Ehrenliste der im Flugdienst während des Weltkrieges gefallenen Offiziere der deutschen Fliegerverbände*. Berlin, 1920

Hall, J., and Nordhoff, C. (eds.), *The Lafayette Flying Corps*, vol. I, Boston, 1920

Hamilton, E., *Mythology*. Boston, 1965

Hartney, H., *Up And At 'Em*. Harrisburg, 1940

Harvey, W., *'Pi' in the Sky – A History of No. 22 Squadron RFC & RAF in the War of 1914–1918*. Leicester, 1971

Haythornthwaite, P., *The World War One Source Book*. London, 1994

Henshaw, T., *The Sky Their Battlefield*. London, 1995

Hildebrand, K., *Die Generale der deutschen Luftwaffe*, Osnabrück, vol. I, 1990; vol. II, 1991; vol. III, 1992

Hobson, C., *Airmen Died in the Great War 1914–1918*. London, 1995

Hoeppner, E., von. *Deutschlands Krieg in der Luft*. Leipzig, 1921

Immelmann, F., *Immelmann 'Der Adler von Lille'*. Leipzig, 1934

Ishoven, A. van (ed. C. Bowyer), *The Fall of an Eagle – The Life of Fighter Ace Ernst Udet*. London, 1979

Italiaander, R., *Manfred Freiherr von Richthofen – Der beste Jagdflieger des grossen Krieges*. Berlin, 1938

Jones, H. A., *The War in the Air*. Oxford, vol. II, 1928; vol. III, 1931; vol. IV, 1934

Kempe, R., *Immelmann und andere sächsische Fliegerhelden*. Dresden, 1939

Kilduff, P., *Germany's First Air Force 1914–1918*. London, 1991; 1996

– *Richthofen – Beyond the Legend of the Red Baron*, London and New York, 1993

Lamberton, W., *Fighter Aircraft of the 1914–1918 War*. Letchworth, 1960

Liddell Hart, B., *The Real War 1914–1918*. Boston, 1964

Macmillan, N., *Into the Blue*. London, 1929

Mann, T. (trans. H. Lowe-Porter), *Essays of Three Decades*. New York, 1971

Möller, H., *Kampf und Sieg eines Jagdgeschwaders*. Berlin, 1939

Moncure, J., *Forging the King's Sword – Military Education Between Tradition and Modernization: The Case of the Royal Prussian Cadet Corps, 1871–1918*. New York, 1993

Morris, A., *Bloody April*. London, 1967

Neumann, G. (ed.), *Die deutschen Luftstreitkräfte im Weltkriege*. Berlin, 1920

– *In der Luft unbesiegt*. Munich, 1923

Nietzsche, F., *The Philosophy of Nietzsche*. (trans. T. Common and C. Fadiman). New York, 1961

Nowarra, H., *Eisernes Kreuz und Balkenkreuz*. Mainz, 1968

O'Connor, N., *Aviation Awards of Imperial Germany in World War I and the Men who Earned Them*. Princeton, vol. I, *Kingdom of Bavaria*, 1988; vol. II, *Kingdom of Prussia*, 1990; vol. III, *Kingdom of Saxony*, 1993; vol. IV, *Kingdom of Württemberg*, 1995

Perthes, J., *Ehrentafel der Kriegsopfer des reichsdeutschen Adels 1914– 1919*. Gotha, 1921

Revell, A., *High in the Empty Blue – The History of 56 Squadron, RFC/RAF 1916–1920*. Mountain View, Cal., 1995

Richthofen, K. von., *Mein Kriegstagebuch*. Berlin, 1937

Richthofen, M. von., *Ein Heldenleben*. Berlin, 1920

– *Der rote Kampfflieger*. Berlin, 1933; English trans. P. Kilduff, *The Red Baron*. New York, 1969

Rickenbacker, E., *Fighting the Flying Circus*. New York, repr. 1967

Ritter, H., *Der Luftkrieg*. Berlin, 1926

Robertson, B., *Air Aces of the 1914–1918 War*. Letchworth, 1959

– *British Military Aircraft Serials 1911–1971*. London, 1971

Schäfer, K., *Vom Jäger zum Flieger*. Berlin, 1918

Schweckendiek, O., *Der Kampfflieger Lothar Freiherr von Richthofen*. Hamburg, 1938.

Shores, C., Franks, N. and Guest, R. *Above the Trenches*. London, 1990

Showalter, E., *Bad Kreuznach als Sitz des grossen Hauptquartiers im ersten Weltkrieg*. Bad Kreuznach, 1981

Supf, P., *Das Buch der deutschen Fluggeschichte*, Stuttgart, vol. I, 1956; vol. II, 1958

Taylor, G., *Sopwith Scout 7309*. London, 1968

Theilhaber, F., *Jüdische Flieger im Weltkrieg*. Berlin, 1924

Udet, E., *Mein Fliegerleben*. Berlin, 1935

Uebe, F., *Ehrenmal des preussischen Offizierkorps*. Berlin, 1939

Vanoverbeke, L., *Moorsele – één dorp, twee vliegvelden*. Kortrijk, 1993

'Vigilant' (C. Sykes)., *German War Birds*. London, 1931

– *Richthofen – The Red Knight of the Air*. London, n.d.

Welkoborsky, N., *Vom Fliegen, Siegen und Sterben einer Feldflieger-Abteilung*. Berlin, 1939

Wenzl, R., *Richthofen-Flieger*. Freiburg im Breisgau, *c.*1930

Wilhelm II, The Kaiser. *My Memoirs: 1878–1918*. London, 1922

Wise, S., *Canadian Airmen and the First World War*. Toronto, 1980

Woodman, H., *Early Aircraft Armament – The Aeroplane and the Gun up to 1918*. London, 1989

Zeidelack, M. (ed.), *Bayerische Flieger im Weltkrieg*. Munich, 1919

Zuerl, W., *Pour le Mérite-Flieger*. Munich, 1938

British Air Ministry, *Handbook of the German Army in War. April, 1918*. London, repr. 1996

– *Handbook of German Military and Naval Aviation (War)*. London, repr. 1995

Deutscher Offizierbund, (eds.), *Ehrenrangliste des ehemaligen deutschen Heeres*, vols. I and II, Osnabrück, repr. 1987

General Staff, *Handbook of the German Army in War, April 1918*. London, repr. 1996

Wolff'schen Telegr.-Bureaus, *Amtliche Kriegsdepeschen nach Berichten des*. vols. 1 and 3, Berlin, n.d.

Stammliste der Offiziere des 6. Badischen Infanterie Regiments 'Kaiser Friedrich III'., Nr. 114, Konstanz, 1904

Documents

AOK 1. Armee Berichte, in the field, 1916

AOK 5. Armee Berichte, 1916

AOK 6. Armee Berichte, 1916

État Nominatif des militaires du Personnel Navigant de l'Aéronautique, tués, blessés ou disparus aux Armées durant le mois d'Octobre 1916. In the field, 1916, 1917, 1918

GHQ American Expeditionary Force, *Summary of Air Information*, 1918

Kommandeur der Flieger der 2. Armee Wochenberichte, 1918

Kommandeur der Flieger der 4. Armee Wochenberichte, 1917

Kommandeur der Flieger der 7. Armee Fliegertagesmeldungen, 1918

Kommandeur der Flieger der 18. Armee Wochenberichte, 1918

Stabsoffizier der Flieger der 1. Armee Wochenberichte, 1916

Stabsoffizier/Kommandeur der Flieger der 6. Armee Wochenberichte, 1916, 1917

Kogenluft, *Nachrichtenblatt der Luftstreitkräfte*. Berlin, vol. 1, 1917; vol. 2, 1918

Kriegsministerium (organizational manual), *Teil 10 Abschnitt B, Flieger-Formationen*. Berlin, 1918.

Richthofen combat reports (trans.), Public Record Office, London, n.d. (PRO File Air 1/686/21/13/2250 XC15183)

ROYAL FLYING CORPS/ROYAL AIR FORCE:

Communiqués from the field, 1918 (PRO Air 1/2097/207/14/1)

No. 1 Squadron combat reports, 1917, 1918 (PRO Air 1/1216/204/5/2634/1 Sqn)

No. 2 Squadron combat reports, 1918, (PRO Air 1/1216/204/5/2634/2 Sqn)

No. 3 Squadron combat reports, 1918 (PRO Air 1/1216/204/5/2634/3 Sqn)

No. 11 Squadron combat reports, 1917, 1918 (PRO Air 1/1219/204/5/2634/11 Sqn)

No. 16 Squadron combat reports, 1918 (PRO Air 1/1219/204/5/2634/16 Sqn)

No. 19 Squadron combat reports, 1916, 1917, 1918 (PRO Air 1/1220/204/5/2634/19 Sqn)

No. 20 Squadron combat reports, 1917 (PRO Air 1/1220/204/5/2634/20 Sqn)

No. 22 Squadron combat reports, 1918 (PRO Air 1/1220/204/5/2634/22 Sqn)

No. 24 Squadron combat reports, 1918 (PRO Air 1/1220/204/5/2634/24 Sqn)

No. 29 Squadron combat reports, 1917 (PRO Air 1/1221/204/5/2634/29 Sqn)

No. 32 Squadron record book, 1917 (PRO Air 1/1493/204/38/3)

No. 45 Squadron record book, 1917 (PRO Air 1/1787/204/151/5)

No. 54 Squadron combat reports, 1917, 1918 (PRO Air 1/1223/204/5/2634/54 Sqn)

No. 54 Squadron record book, 1917 (PRO Air 1/1567/204/80/53)

No. 56 Squadron combat reports, 1917 (PRO Air 1/1912/204/229/21)

No. 70 Squadron combat reports, 1917 (PRO Air 1/1226/204/5/2634/70 Sqn)

No. 73 Squadron combat reports, 1918 (PRO Air 1/1226/204/5/2634/73 Sqn)

No. 84 Squadron combat reports, 1918 (PRO Air 1/1227/204/5/2634/84 Sqn)

No. 201 Squadron record book, 1918 (PRO Air 1/1502/204/40/11)

No. 209 Squadron combat reports, 1918 (PRO Air 1/2222/209/40/17)

No. 209 Squadron record book, 1918 (PRO Air 1/1858/204/214/6)

Periodical Summary of Aeronautical Information, 1917

Summary of Air Intelligence, 1918

War Diary, in the field, 1916, 1917, 1918 (PRO Air 1/1184 -1188/204/5/2595)

Western Front Casualty List, in the field, 1916, 1917, 1918 (PRO Air I/967/204/5/1097–969/204/5/1102)

Royal Naval Air Service:

No. 1 Squadron combat reports, 1917 (PRO Air 1/1216/204/5/2634/1 Naval Sqn)

No. 3 Squadron combat reports, 1917 (PRO Air 1/1216/204/5/2634/3 Naval Sqn)

No. 10 Squadron combat reports, 1917 (PRO Air 1/1219/204/5/2634/10 Naval Sqn)

US Air Service:

Air Service Bulletin, 1918 (RG 120 – Records of the American Expeditionary Forces, 1917–1923), Washington, 1959

Gorrell's History of the Air Service, Individual Combat Reports of Americans Serving with the RAF, vol. B-13 (RG 120 – Records of the American Expeditionary Forces, 1917–1923), Washington, 1959

Articles, Monographs and Periodicals

'A History of the 28th Aero Squadron' in Cross & Cockade Journal, 1971

Adam, R. 'Episodes' in Cross & Cockade Journal, 1972

Bailey, F., Bock, G., Browne, P., and Chamberlain, P. 'An Analysis of German

Balloon Claims on the Western Front During 1918' in *Cross & Cockade Journal*, 1983

Bailey, F., and Franks, N. '66 Squadron in France and Italy' in *Cross & Cockade (Great Britain) Journal*, 1975

Bruce, J. 'Fokker Dr.I' in *Aircraft Profile 55*, 1965

– 'Fokker Monoplanes' in *Aircraft Profile 38*, 1965

– 'Fokker D.VII' in *Aircraft Profile 67*, 1966

– 'Morane Saulnier Type L' in *Windsock Datafile 16*, 1989

– Chamberlain, P., and Bailey, F., 'An Analysis of German Balloon Claims on the Western Front During 1917' in *Cross & Cockade Journal*, 1975

– 'History of Escadrille Spa 93' in *Cross & Cockade (Great Britain) Journal*, 1978

Duiven, R., 'German *Jagdstaffel* and *Jagdgeschwader* Commanding Officers, 1916–1918' in *Over the Front*, 1988

Evans, W., 'Manfred Freiherr von Richthofen Victory List' in *Over the Front*, 1992

Ferko, A. E., 'The Origin of the First Jagdstaffeln, in *Cross & Cockade Journal*, 1965

– 'Jagdflieger Friedrich Noltenius, 1894–1936' in *Cross & Cockade Journal*, 1966

– 'Guynemer's Last Patrol' in *Cross & Cockade Journal*, 1974

– '*Fliegertruppe 1914–1918*', Salem, Ohio, 1980

– '*Richthofen*', Berkhamsted, 1995

Franks, N,. 'Max Immelmann's Victories' in *Cross & Cockade (Great Britain) Journal*, 1980

Gray, P., 'Albatros D.I – D.III' in *Aircraft Profile 127*, 1966

– 'Pfalz D.III' in *Aircraft Profile 43*, 1965

Grosz, P., 'The Agile and Aggressive Albatros' in *Air Enthusiast No. 1*, 1976

– 'Fokker D,VII' in *Windsock Datafile 9*, 1989

Grosz, P., and Ferko, A. E., 'The Fokker Dr.I – A Reappraisal' in *Air Enthusiast No. 8*, 1978

Hitchins, F., 'Enemy Aircraft in German Hands, June 1916– September 1918' in *Cross & Cockade Journal*, 1969

Joly, P., (trans. S. A. Williams), 'Victory List of Capitaine Georges Guynemer' in *Cross & Cockade Journal*, 1971

Kilduff, P., 'The History of Groupes de Bombardement 4 and 9' in *Cross & Cockade Journal*, 1974

– 'Honor Roll of the Fallen Fliers of Baden' in *Over the Front*, 1989

McGuire, R. (ed.), 'Documents Relating to Richthofen's Last Battle' in *Over the Front*, 1987

Miller, T., and Puglisi, W., 'Jasta B' in *Cross & Cockade Journal*, 1968

Nowarra, H., 'Reminiscences of Jasta 11' in *Cross & Cockade Journal*, 1960

O'Dwyer, W., 'Post-Mortem: Richthofen' in *Cross & Cockade Journal*, 1969

Osten, H-G. von der (ed. L. Zacharias), 'Memoirs of World War I with Jagdstaffeln 11 and 4' in *Cross & Cockade Journal*, 1974

Parks, J., 'No Greater Love: The Story of Lt. Wilbur W. White', in *Over the Front*, 1986

Puglisi, W., 'The 27th Aero Squadron's Black Day' in *Cross & Cockade Journal*, 1962

– 'German Aircraft Down in British Lines', Parts 1 and 2 in *Cross & Cockade Journal*, 1969

Revell, A., 'Aftermath' in *Cross & Cockade (Great Britain) Journal*, 1975

Rogers, L., 'RFC and RAF Casualties, 1917–1918' in *Cross & Cockade (Great Britain) Journal*, 1975, 1977

Schmeelke, M., 'Leutnant der Reserve Otto Brauneck' in *Cross & Cockade Journal*, 1983

– 'Leutnant der Reserve Otto Brauneck', Part II in *Over the Front*, 1986

Schnitzler, E., '*Carl Allmenröder der Bergische Kampfflieger*, Wald, 1927

Terry, G., 'The Development of Dornier Landplanes 1914–1918', in *Cross & Cockade (Great Britain) Journal*, 1981

Vann, R., and Waugh, C., 'Overseas and United Kingdom Presentation Aircraft 1914–1918' in *Cross & Cockade (Great Britain) Journal*, 1983

VanWyngarden, G., *Von Richthofen's Flying Circus – Colours and Markings of Jagdgeschwader Nr. 1*. Berkhamsted, 1995

Waugh, C., 'A Short History of 70 Squadron, RFC/RAF 1916–1919' in *Cross & Cockade Journal*, 1979

– 'A Longer History of No. 21 Squadron' in *Cross & Cockade Journal*, 1983

Whitford, R., 'Fundamentals of Fighter Design' in *Air International*, Stamford, 1996

Zickerick, W., 'Verlustliste der deutschen Luftstreitkräfte im Weltkriege' in *Unsere Luftstreitkräfte 1914–1918*, Berlin, 1930

Other sources

Adam, R., Correspondence and PoW Diary

Bock, G., *Kofl* and *Armee* Notes

Bufe, O., *Kriegsranglisten-Auszug* and *Personal-Bogen*, 1919

Falkenhayn, F. von, Correspondence

Krefft, K., *Personal-Bogen*, 1919

Prestien, F., Correspondence

Reinhard, W., *Personal-Bogen*, 1918

Schmutzler, C., Correspondence and Family Chronicle

Winterfeld, E. von, Correspondence and Family Chronicle.

Index

Telegraphen-Bataillon Nr 2, 35
Telegraphen-Bataillon Nr 3, 34
Ulanen-Regiment Nr 1, 126, 145
Ulanen-Regiment Nr 2, 241
Ulanen-Regiment Nr 7, 106, 181
Ulanen-Regiment Nr 15, 201
Ulanen-Regiment Nr 17, 217

II. PERSONNEL